Dear Amanda,

You are truly
the best!

Linda Jey

Open Banking

Open Banking

Edited by

LINDA JENG

OXFORD
UNIVERSITY PRESS

OXFORD
UNIVERSITY PRESS

Oxford University Press is a department of the University of Oxford. It furthers the University's objective of excellence in research, scholarship, and education by publishing worldwide. Oxford is a registered trade mark of Oxford University Press in the UK and certain other countries.

Published in the United States of America by Oxford University Press
198 Madison Avenue, New York, NY 10016, United States of America.

© Oxford University Press 2022

Library of Congress Cataloging-in-Publication Data
Names: Jeng, Linda, editor.
Title: Open banking / Linda Jeng.
Description: New York, NY : Oxford University Press, [2022] |
Includes bibliographical references and index.
Identifiers: LCCN 2021023459 (print) | LCCN 2021023460 (ebook) |
ISBN 9780197582879 (hardback) | ISBN 9780197582893 (epub) | ISBN 9780197582886 (updf) |
ISBN 9780197582909 (online)
Subjects: LCSH: Banks and banking—Security measures. | Confidential communications—Banking. |
Financial services industry—Security measures.
Classification: LCC HG1616.S37 O64 2022 (print) | LCC HG1616.S37 (ebook) | DDC 332.1028/9—dc23
LC record available at https://lccn.loc.gov/2021023459
LC ebook record available at https://lccn.loc.gov/2021023460

DOI: 10.1093/oso/9780197582879.001.0001

1 3 5 7 9 8 6 4 2

Printed by Integrated Books International, United States of America

Note to Readers
This publication is designed to provide accurate and authoritative information in regard to the subject matter covered. It is based upon sources believed to be accurate and reliable and is intended to be current as of the time it was written. It is sold with the understanding that the publisher is not engaged in rendering legal, accounting, or other professional services. If legal advice or other expert assistance is required, the services of a competent professional person should be sought. Also, to confirm that the information has not been affected or changed by recent developments, traditional legal research techniques should be used, including checking primary sources where appropriate.

(Based on the Declaration of Principles jointly adopted by a Committee of the American Bar Association and a Committee of Publishers and Associations.)

You may order this or any other Oxford University Press publication
by visiting the Oxford University Press website at www.oup.com.

To Conor
for banking on me

Contents

Contents

Foreword

The idea that "this time is different" has become so hackneyed that, perhaps understandably, academics and policymakers alike scoff at the latest innovations as but a mere repetition of earlier advances, but in other guises. But what readers will quickly discover in this extraordinary collection of articles is that not only is banking changing but also, more fundamentally, the very business of banking.

Linda Jeng—an expert in her own right with experience straddling central banking, the academy, capital markets, and technology—has assembled a world-class group of thought leaders to collectively launch the first systematic study of open banking. From Andres Wolberg-Stok to Zee Kin Yeong, the authors who have contributed their insight come from either the front lines of industry or the cutting edge of thought leadership. And in coordinating their perspectives across specialties and industry domains, the book lifts the proverbial hood for readers, allowing them a look at one of the first scholarly explorations of one of the most transformational developments in finance, and financial regulation, in a generation.

If data is the new gold, "open data" determines how it is mined, stored, and shared. It touches upon antitrust, the privacy of consumer data, cybersecurity, and how insights from data are unlocked. When in the wrong hands, open data risks abuse, manipulative practices, and even, potentially, discriminatory lending and exploitation. When used responsibly, opportunities for fairer credit scoring, new risk analytics, and stronger safeguards and integrity are possible. The stakes for consumers and the industry cannot be overstated.

This book will prove to be not only the first of its kind, but also one of the best. Its origins are academic—and birthed of rigorous inquiry with contributions from professors at Howard University, Hong Kong University, University of Luxembourg, and University of New South Wales (UNSW) Sydney. All the while, it showcases the latest insights from experts at Citi, the International Monetary Fund, the Federal Reserve Bank of San Francisco, Kabbage, Finicity, and the Union Bank of the Philippines—and many more—to bring a real-world, grounded insight to theory. It is a project that I have been extremely proud to watch develop and unfold as a community of thought leaders evolves and grows as the challenges and opportunities of fintech more generally become apparent. And it is work that I am delighted to learn from with others as I grapple with what really is "new" as novel technologies go mainstream.

Chris Brummer,
Professor and Faculty Director,
Institute of International Economic Law,
Georgetown University Law Center
Washington, DC
March 2021

List of Contributors

Douglas W. Arner, Kerry Holdings Professor in Law, RGC Senior Fellow in Digital Finance and Sustainable Development, and Associate Director, HKU-Standard Chartered Foundation FinTech Academy, University of Hong Kong

Kaitlin Asrow, Fintech Policy Advisor, Federal Reserve Bank of San Francisco

Steven Boms, Founder and President at Allon Advocacy, LLC and Executive Director, Financial Data and Technology Association of North America

Ghela Boskovich, Region Director and Head of Europe at Financial Data and Technology Association

Matthew Adam Bruckner, Associate Professor, Howard University School of Law

Ross P. Buckley, Australian Research Council Laureate Fellow; KPMG Law and King & Wood Mallesons Chair of Disruptive Innovation; and Scientia Professor, University of New South Wales Sydney

Don Cardinal, Managing Director, Financial Data Exchange

Brad Carr, Managing Director, Digital Finance at Institute of International Finance

Yan Carrière-Swallow, Senior Economist, Strategy, Policy and Review Department, International Monetary Fund

Nic Carter, Partner, Castle Island Ventures

Vikram Haksar, Assistant Director, Monetary and Capital Markets Department, International Monetary Fund

David Roi Hardoon, Senior Advisor, Union Bank of the Philippines & Managing Director, Aboitiz Data Innovation

Linda Jeng, Visiting Scholar on Financial Technology, Institute for International Economic Law, Georgetown University Law Center and Global Head of Policy, Transparent Financial Systems

Greg Kidd, Co-founder & CEO, GlobaliD

Jamie Leach, Region Director, Financial Data and Technology Association, Australia & New Zealand

Gavin Littlejohn, Chairman, Financial Data and Technology Association Global

Julie McKay, Former Region Director, Financial Data and Technology Association, Australia & New Zealand

Manasa Patnam, Economist, European Department, International Monetary Fund

Richard Prior, CEO, Financial Data and Technology Association

Sam Taussig, former Global Head of Policy and Special Product Development, Kabbage

Nick Thomas, Co-founder @ Finicity, Financial Data Exchange, Trust over IP Foundation, & the Bluetooth SIG

Andres Wolberg-Stok, Head of Strategy, Office of the CTO, Citi

Zee Kin Yeong, Deputy Commissioner, Personal Data Protection Commission (PDPC) of Singapore

Dirk A. Zetzsche, Professor of Law, ADA Chair in Financial Law (Inclusive Finance), Faculty of Law, Economics and Finance, University of Luxembourg, and Director, Centre for Business and Corporate Law, Heinrich-Heine-University, Düsseldorf, Germany

Inception to Open Banking

Linda Jeng[*,**]

1. Introduction

We are in the midst of a silent revolution. Our finances, our purchasing history, and our investments have been digitized and stored on machines since the computer was first used by banks in the 1950s and when large computing machines became accessible as tablet computers in the 1980s. Then the internet allowed people and companies to connect and transfer data over the net. With the rise of cloud computing, the cost of storing data has dropped immensely—so much so that it is now feasible for companies to store customer data in perpetuity. All this digital evolution has led us to a tipping point toward decentralized finance (DeFi) and the unbundling and platformization of financial services. This phenomenon has only accelerated with the advent of COVID-19 and the increased reliance on digital banking.

With additional computing power that is mobile and the size of our palms, we are continually connected to the internet via our smartphones and tablets. Our actions—browsing history, social media posts, transactional purchases, and information that make up our identities—are digitized and stored somewhere by some organization. Data[1] we personally generate, which I call personal data, has great commercial value now that it is inexpensive enough to store, aggregate, and analyze large amounts of data. Big Data provides insights about what we want to buy and who we want to vote for. Big Data also allows companies to efficiently target and advertise at scale to specific population groups. Financial technology firms (fintechs) can develop innovative services and products using insights gained from Big Data. This revolution in data-sharing—giving customers access to new services and products offered outside of traditional organizations—is best represented by a movement in financial services called "open banking."

There is no official definition for "open banking," and since the concept was introduced, "open banking" has quickly grown into "open finance." But at its core, "open banking" is the sharing of customer data by banks with other parties with the

[*] Linda Jeng is the Visiting Scholar on Financial Technology at Georgetown University Law Center's Institute of International Economic Law. She is also the Global Head of Policy at Transparent Financial Systems, Inc. Prior to these roles, she was with the Board of Governors of the Federal Reserve System, the Financial Stability Board, and the US Treasury Department.

[**] I wish to thank Chris Brummer for encouraging me to put together one of the first—if not the first—academic books on open banking. I also wish to thank Michael Barr for encouraging me to embark on this journey to be a senior fellow. Most importantly, I wish to thank my partner, Conor Healy, for his endless support and faith in me and to my daughter Isabel for reminding me to step away from my desk at the end of the day and to be present.

[1] I use the term "data" as a singular noun for the purposes of this introduction.

permission of customers.[2] This sharing of customer data must be triggered first by the customer's request to his or her bank to share his or her personal financial data with a specified third-party. The bank in turn shares the customer's data with the third-party, which is usually a fintech, or the bank allows the third-party to access the data held by the bank.

When banks are mandated to share data by the government or regulators, open banking is often referred to as capitalized "Open Banking." In this book, we use the broader definition from the Basel Committee on Banking Supervision's report on open banking and application programming interfaces (Basel Committee report),[3] which was authored by a working group that I led while I was with the Federal Reserve. The Basel Committee report defined "open banking" as

> the sharing and leveraging of customer-permissioned data by banks with third party developers and firms to build applications and services, such as those that provide real-time payments, greater financial transparency options for account holders, and marketing and cross-selling opportunities. Individual jurisdictions may define open banking differently.[4]

This seemingly simple act of sharing personal financial data triggers a variety of legal, ethical, and economic questions. It certainly did for banking regulators around the world, who sought to catch up on the topic after their counterparts in competition and antitrust mandated data-sharing in a number of jurisdictions, namely, the European Union, the United Kingdom, and Australia, in an attempt to improve competition in the banking sector.

The Basel Committee had to learn about data security issues around screen-scraping and data aggregators, which stored bank customers' login credentials and monetized customer data beyond the customer's initial use case. There was general agreement among regulators that sharing data via application programming interfaces (APIs) would be more secure than screen-scraping, but API banking does not address more fundamental questions of how API-based open banking would affect the business models of banks and the financial system.

Many other issues raised by open banking, especially data privacy, fall outside the traditional purview of bank regulators and even competition authorities. Issues of data privacy and security grew exponentially as customers increasingly interact directly with nonbanks via their mobile devices. These data privacy issues infiltrate all business sectors that use customer-generated data, including social media, technology, health, telecommunications, entertainment, and so forth. However, what is particular about open banking is that personal financial data is highly sensitive, perhaps second to personal health information. How much money we have in the bank account, how much money we owe, what our investments are, and how much money we make are all considered private and only up to us as individual customers to disclose. Our bank

---

[2] See Basel Committee on Banking Supervision, "Report on Open Banking and Application Programming Interfaces" (Nov. 2019). https://www.bis.org/bcbs/publ/d486.pdf.
[3] *Id.*
[4] *Id.* at p. 19 of the Glossary.

account login username and password (login credentials) are considered highly sensitive because a third-party could gain access to our bank account information and move money.

How much we spend, on what and on whom and at what time—these granular pieces of transactional data are very sensitive and also commercially very valuable. Do we as individuals own these pieces of our personal data? Or is the bank that spends money maintaining its customers' data the real data owner? If we do not own our data, can we at least control what personal data is shared, with whom, and how the data is used? Is it necessary to have informed consent in open data activities? And what counts as informed consent? When customers give fintechs permission to collect their private financial data held at banks, do customers fully understand that they are handing over the keys to their banking kingdom when they click "Continue" after downloading the smartphone app, handing their bank account login credentials to fourth-party data aggregators? Do customers know that they have consented to data aggregators signing on to their bank accounts multiple times a day and night to harvest their personal data? I argue that the current consent process does not provide for informed consent.[5] Among all the participants in an open banking ecosystem, the consumer suffers the most from data asymmetry.

In the end, what data protections should consumers have in an open data world in which personal data is regularly shared? What data rights should consumers be able to actively exercise? Should the data rights be based in the natural person or in the legal person, which could include a company or organization? Many jurisdictions around the world have tackled these issues by introducing data privacy regimes, such as the European Union's General Data Protection Regulation,[6] Australia's Consumer Data Rights framework,[7] Brazil's General Data Protection Law,[8] Mexico's Protection of Personal Data in Possession of Obligated Subjects,[9] and California's Consumer Privacy Act.[10]

However, the strength and resilience of an open data ecosystem can only be as strong as the data rights and protections that govern open data-sharing. In other words, road safety relies on commonly understood "rules of the road." This book explores not only where these roads might lead but also what traffic rules could be suitable.

Not every country must adopt the same set of data rights and protections. In some countries, the driving lane is on the left. In others, it is on the right. Each country has its own set of cultural values and beliefs. But in order to balance commercial interests

---

[5] Several pending lawsuits against Plaid, Inc. have been consolidated into one: In Re Plaid Inc. Privacy Litigation (Master Docket No. 4:20-cv-03056-DMR) (Aug. 17, 2020).

[6] European Parliament and Council of European Union (2016) *Regulation (EU) 2016/679*. Available at: https://eur-lex.europa.eu/legal-content/EN/TXT/HTML/?uri=CELEX:32016R0679&from=EN (accessed Dec. 2019).

[7] *Treasury Laws Amendment (Consumer Data Right) Bill 2019* (Cth). https://www.aph.gov.au/Parliamentary_Business/Bills_Legislation/Bills_Search_Results/Result?bId=r6281.

[8] Brazilian General Data Protection Law (LGPD), Federal Law No. 13,709/2018, which was published on August 15, 2018.

[9] The General Law for the Protection of Personal Data in Possession of Obligated Subjects (*Ley General de Protección de Datos Personales en Posesión de Sujetos Obligados*), which entered into force on January 27, 2017.

[10] California Consumer Privacy Rights Act of 2018 (CCPA). http://leginfo.legislature.ca.gov/faces/codes_displayText.xhtml?division=3.&part=4.&lawCode=CIV&title=1.81.5.

against private ones in open banking (or open data, for that matter), there must be a common set of data protections and rights that meets consumers' expectations.

The right to take your data with you would give consumers greater market power and help unstick deposits. Consumers also can exchange their data for value, perhaps even one day "bank their data"—however that might work. These outcomes will depend on how the right to data portability is designed. Some argue that Section 1033 of the Dodd-Frank Act provides this right in the United States, but Section 1033 only mentions that customers have the right to access their data and does not mention the right to transfer their data to a third-party.

No other data right than the right to data portability better demonstrates the need to match the needs of legal rights with technological capabilities. One's ability to take data with one is not possible without interoperability. APIs should help in this respect. However, open API standards are not currently converging into one global standard and are instead emerging as regional standards appear in the United States, the European Union (even different standards are emerging in Germany, France, and other EU member states), the United Kingdom, Japan, Singapore, India, Australia, and so forth. These different regional standards will lead to market fragmentation, unless there is interoperability between API standards and among all banks, fintechs, and companies outside the financial sector.

Open banking also raises the question of who is responsible for making the customer whole in the event of a fraudulent or erroneous transaction. Since Congress passed the Electronic Fund Transfer Act in 1978 and limited customer liability in online banking and bank debit card use, the retail payments sector has grown to include nonbank fintechs, such as peer-to-peer payment service providers like PayPal and Venmo. If a bad transaction took place on a fintech platform, customers often looked to their banks for restitution. The Consumer Financial Protection Bureau (CFPB) tried to address this gap in the implementing regulation (Regulation E) through its 2018 amendments to the Prepaid Card Rule,[11] treating customer's digital wallets at peer-to-peer (P2P) payment service providers as prepaid accounts.[12] The Prepaid Card Rule, which went into effect April 1, 2019, extended Regulation E's basic fraud protections for debit cards to prepaid cards and mobile prepaid accounts. However, customers who send an erroneous transaction from a prepaid account do not benefit from the error resolution procedures afforded to bank account customers. These erroneous transactions sent over service apps can occur all too easily with the tap of the wrong number or letter when inputting the recipient's identifying email address or phone number or when inputting the dollar amount to be transferred.

Data possesses vastly different economic features from those of traditional goods. Most goods can be consumed by only one person at a time, and once consumed, it cannot be consumed again. These goods are called *rival* goods. Data, in contrast, is a *nonrival* good. It can be used simultaneously by multiple parties and can be used over

---

[11] CFPB, Rules Concerning Prepaid Accounts Under the Electronic Fund Transfer Act (Regulation E) and the Truth in Lending Act (Regulation Z) (Feb. 13, 2018). Available at: https://www.consumerfinance.gov/rules-policy/final-rules/rules-concerning-prepaid-accounts-under-electronic-fund-transfer-act-regulation-e-and-truth-lending-act-regulation-z/.

[12] Venmo challenged CFPB's prepaid card rule. See *PayPal, Inc. v. Consumer Financial Protection Bureau* (filed DC Federal District Court Dec. 2019). CFPB moved for summary judgment in July 2020.

and over again. Data can be both excludable and nonexcludable. Even more revolu-
tionary is that data can be transformed by combining different sets of data to create a
set of recombinant data that possesses new and perhaps much greater economic value.
So the popular saying that "data is the new oil" is not accurate, at least not economically.
But the saying is accurate in that data is now what powers or will power economies
around the world.

The combination of inexpensive data storage and fast computing power is driving
artificial intelligence and machine learning (AI/ML) technologies. It is now possible to
quickly pull data from your bank account, credit card account, property holdings, social media, purchasing behavior, browsing history, and demographics—essentially, Big
Data—to assemble population profiles for the purposes of predicting likely future individual as well as population behavior, which can be used for credit underwriting, marketing profiling, and the development of new products and services. Fintech lenders
are leading the charge in increasing consumer access to credit, especially traditionally
underserved consumers, and for speeding up the loan approval process. However, the
AI/ML algorithms used by fintechs can also lead to unintended consequences, including reinforcing or even exacerbating biases. These biases can discriminate on the
basis of personal traits protected under law—race, marital status, nationality, gender,
age, or religion.

US consumer protections laws and regulations, some of which were updated by the
Dodd-Frank Act, had not envisaged the commercial use of Big Data. How should AI/
ML models be regulated? Can AI/ML models even be regulated? In the healthcare space,
the US Food and Drug Administration proposed in an April 2019 discussion paper that
AI/ML-based software, such as medical devices, may need pre-market reviews.[13] Can
US financial regulators feasibly request pre-market reviews of all the AI/ML models
used by banks and fintechs? Regulatory guidance could be given on guardrails around
AI model management that help to protect consumers as well as protect the safety and
soundness of banks.

In addition, we are now seeing growing popularity in AI-powered robo-advisers,
fraud detection, and faster credit underwriting. Through this democratization of financial services, the average consumer now has access to services previously only
afforded by the wealthy. However, democratization of financial services also introduces
new kinds of systemic risk. If many Americans are invested in the same products because robo-advisers give similar advice to similar groups of people, risk can quickly and
quietly build up in certain kinds of investment products and in certain sections of the
financial system.

A topic that this book touches upon is that of the need to revisit our competition and
antitrust policies given the newfound economic value of Big Data. The vastly different
economic features and values of data will necessitate the government to rethink how it
should assess competition when companies merge their data assets. Recent acquisitions
of Finicity by Mastercard and of Kabbage by American Express (and attempted acquisition of Plaid by Visa[14]) are examples of incumbent companies purchasing fintechs that

---

[13] U.S. Food & Drug Administration, *Proposed Regulatory Framework for Modifications to Artificial
Intelligence/Machine Learning 9AI/ML)-Based Software as a Medical Device (SaMD)* (Apr. 2019). https://
www.fda.gov/media/122535/download.

[14] https://www.justice.gov/opa/pr/visa-and-plaid-abandon-merger-after-antitrust-division-s-suit-block.

collect complementary and valuable data. These firms may operate in different business sectors, but they collect data on groups of individuals with significant overlap. However, data consolidation by combining data sets of two merging companies currently passes muster as long as the merging companies operate in different markets or the resulting market concentration is acceptable.

US antitrust laws were passed in 1890 and 1914[15] to promote competition. Current methodology for assessing mergers and acquisitions rely primarily on the Herfindahl-Hirschman Index (HHI), which is a straightforward metric of market concentration. However, HHI is not well suited for analyzing the effects of data consolidation on market power and consumers. As the US Department of Justice's lawsuit[16] against Visa's acquisition of Plaid shows, the Justice Department had focused its complaint on the US debit business, which Visa dominates. Its complaint did not and most likely could not examine the potential consequences of combining Visa's vast, granular transactional credit/debit card data with Plaid's rich, bank account data. It is hard to forecast what all the possible market outcomes could be from merging Big Data sets, but the old adage "knowledge is power" rings true for today's companies, whether they be new entrants or incumbents.

Fintechs depend on customer data to operate. Without customer data, they cannot provide the services and products for which they are obligated to provide under contract. They also cannot mine and package customer data to be consumed by others, who in turn rely on that data to conduct their activities. In 2008, we saw a liquidity crisis spread like wildfire through the global financial system. One day when our economies become true open data economies—we may have another kind of liquidity crisis—a shortage of data. For example, an integral firm in the customer data pipeline is disrupted. A disruption could happen when customers decide for any number of reasons to block a firm from accessing their personal data (this assumes there are substitutes in the ecosystem for the customer), or the firm suffered a cybersecurity incident. Upon disruption in the data feed pipeline, the firm could suffer a sudden data liquidity crunch, sending ripples to downstream consumers of data in the financial system.

"Open banking" will quickly become "open finance" and ultimately will grow over time into "open data," encompassing most sectors of the economy. The European Commission is already anticipating a convergence of "open finance" and cryptoassets in their September 2020 proposal to regulate cryptoassets.[17] The emergence of this new kind of data-driven economy raises new complexities stemming from both new and legacy laws and regulations, the changing role of the consumer demanding new financial services and products, and the practice of leveraging consumer-produced data to innovate new financial services and products—leading to structural gaps in consumer and data protection.

[15] Sherman Act of 1890 and the Clayton Act of 1914.

[16] Complaint, USA v. Visa Inc. and Plaid Inc. (N.D. Ca. (Nov. 5, 2020) (Case 3:20-cv-07810). Available at: https://www.justice.gov/opa/press-release/file/1334726/download.

[17] European Commission, Proposal for a "Regulation of the European Parliament and of the Council on Markets in Crypto-assets," and amending Directive (EU 2019/1937)(2020/0265 (COD)) (MiCA).

2. An Overview of This Volume

This book identifies and explores key themes and issues in open banking and open data for lawmakers, policymakers, and academics. Although US banks and market participants have been sharing customer-permissioned data for the past twenty years, and there have been recent but limited policy discussions, such as the Obama administration's failed Consumer Data Privacy Bill[18] and the Consumer Financial Protection Bureau's Data Aggregation Principles[19] and potential data-sharing rule,[20] "open banking" is still a little-known concept among consumers and policymakers in the United States. Against this backdrop, this collection of chapters, written by some of the world's leading experts, seek to identify and investigate an interdisciplinary set of legal, regulatory, and economic issues raised by "open banking."

This interdisciplinary project is tied to the DC Fintech Week Conference hosted by Georgetown University Law Center October 21–24, 2019, and the Data Symposium co-hosted by the Federal Reserve Bank of San Francisco and FinRegLab November 4 and 5, 2019. These two conferences—which gathered some of the world's leading legal experts, economists, tech developers, and regulators—identified and analyzed key issues arising from open banking and the sharing of personal customer data across global market, economic, and legal ecosystems. As such, this volume represents perspectives from across the regulatory ecosystem, and includes technologists and scholars and practitioners in banking law, digital privacy, and central banking. Together the experts writing here will present the first comprehensive overview of the silent revolution of open banking—allowing both specialists and the general reader to understand not only what is happening now but also the potentially enormous implications of current policy and industry decisions for the future development of our global economy.

This book begins with a description of how the traditional banking and payments ecosystem transformed with the entry of financial data aggregators and fintech service apps. In the first chapter, "Open Banking Ecosystem and Infrastructure: Banking on Openness," Andres Wolberg-Stok, Global Head of Strategy, Office of the CTO, at Citi, provides a historical overview beginning in the 1980s. Wolberg-Stok explores the flow of customer-permissioned data between financial institutions, data aggregators, and fintechs and just how today's data revolution is impacting the traditional business of banking, including some of the costs and benefits for consumers, monetary policy, and financial stability.

In Chapter 2, "Defining Data Rights and the Role of the Individual," Kaitlin Asrow, Senior Fintech Policy Advisor at the Federal Reserve Bank of San Francisco, interrogates the core principle of "data privacy" and an evolution to "data protection" and ultimately to "data rights." Data privacy, once just a term to describe keeping personal data private, has grown to encompass bigger concepts, such as "data protection" under the European

---

[18] https://obamawhitehouse.archives.gov/sites/default/files/privacy-final.pdf.

[19] CFPB, *Consumer Protection Principles: Consumer Authorized Financial Data Sharing and Aggregation* (Oct. 18, 2017). https://files.consumerfinance.gov/f/documents/cfpb_consumer-protection-principles_data-aggregation.pdf.

[20] CFPB, *Advance Notice of Proposed Rulemaking on Consumer Access to Financial Records* (Oct. 22, 2020). https://files.consumerfinance.gov/f/documents/cfpb_section-1033-dodd-frank_advance-notice-proposed-rulemaking_2020-10.pdf.

Union's General Data Protection Regulation (GDPR) and "data empowerment" in India under its Data Empowerment and Protection Architecture. In this piece, Asrow argues that a baseline of consumer "data protection" and "data rights" can help to effectively manage a data-based economy, including structures such as Open Banking. She analyzes the challenges of current US data regimes under the Gramm-Leach-Bliley Act, the Fair Credit Reporting Act, Section 1033 of the Dodd-Frank Act, and the California Data Privacy Act, and proposes a path toward modernizing our data governance frameworks with a particular focus on the role of the consumer.

Chapter 3, "Customer Protection and the Liability Conundrum in an Open Finance Ecosystem," examines what is arguably the most difficult challenge in open banking. Authored by Steven Boms, Executive Director of the Financial Data and Technology Association's North American Chapter and President of Allon Advocacy, and Sam Taussig, former Global Head of Policy at Kabbage, this chapter explores why this issue is particularly challenging in various jurisdictions, such as the United Kingdom, continental Europe, and the United States. Boms and Taussig describe current gaps in the US customer liability framework under Regulation E of the Electronic Fund Transfers Act and suggest shared liability and traceability-based policy options for modernizing the regulatory environment.

In Chapter 4, "Artificial Intelligence and Machine Learning: The Opportunities and Challenges of Using Big Data," Matthew Adam Bruckner, Associate Professor of Law, Howard University School of Law, explores the potential offered by Big Data, artificial intelligence, and machine learning in financial services. Using data from fintech lenders such as Lending Club and Upstart, several recent studies suggest that fintech lenders' use of nontraditional ("alternative") data presents significant opportunities to greatly improve financial inclusion. For example, the CFPB's analysis of Upstart's lending data found that "the tested model approves 27% more applicants than the traditional model, and yields 16% lower average APRs for approved loans." But a recent report from the Student Borrower Protection Center warned that fintech lenders' use of educational data points may penalize Black and Hispanic borrowers for attending a community college, a historically Black college or university, or a Hispanic-serving institution. Bruckner explains the current regulatory environment, including how certain fair lending rules can foster innovation in credit underwriting and where the use of nontraditional data can violate these legal and regulatory protections. He also outlines key trade-offs regulators need to consider and the limits of building fair AI/ML-based credit algorithms and underwriting models.

In Chapter 5, "Data Access Technology Standards: A History of Open Banking Data Access," Don Cardinal, Managing Director of the Financial Data Exchange (FDX), and Nick Thomas, Co-Founder of Finicity (a Mastercard company) and FDX, present a definitive history of consumer-permissioned financial data access, how technology standards have evolved globally over the last twenty years, the current state of data access standards efforts, and a survey of data-sharing standards developing across the globe. The authors begin with a history of OFX and consumer-permissioned data access via Data Aggregation, including screen-scraping, mobile and web "backend" APIs, custom APIs, and various formatted data standards. They follow with a history of modern standards development efforts to move away from credential-based to token-based data access methods using OAuth and standardized APIs. Cardinal and

Thomas describe the development of regional and global industry-led standards in the Americas, Europe, and Asia, and outline some of the challenges to adopting a universal technology standard.

Chapter 6, "Taking Your Data with You: Singapore's Approach to Data Portability," authored by Zee Kin Yeong, Deputy Commissioner of Singapore's Personal Data Protection Commission, and David Roi Hardoon, Senior Advisor of the Union Bank of the Philippines, provides an overview of Singapore's recently announced regulatory regime on data portability. Many authorities view open banking as a means to increase competition among and with banks and to decrease stickiness of bank deposits. However, bank deposits will remain sticky if customers cannot easily port their personal account information to other financial institutions. Yeong and Hardoon expound on the challenges and opportunities offered by data portability and offer lessons learned to date.

Chapter 7, "Open Banking and the Economics of Data," by Yan Carrière-Swallow and Vikram Haksar, both of the International Monetary Fund, provides an economic framework for thinking about the value of individual data and the game-changing implications of data's unique economic features for the broader economy. The authors explain how data is poorly characterized by the common analogy of being the "new oil" and is, in fact, more versatile. Due to its nonrival economic characteristic, data can be reused, consumed by multiple parties, transferred across networks, and combined with other data to create new products and services. This piece explores the economics of how data is produced, consumed, and monetized and the implications of data proliferation for the provision of financial services, and discusses key economic questions surrounding open banking as a consumer-centric data policy framework for the financial sector.

The book then switches gears and begins a few regional surveys starting with Chapter 8. "Open Banking, Open Data, and Open Finance: Lessons from the European Union." Authored by Douglas W. Arner, Kerry Holdings Professor in Law, Hong Kong University; Ross P. Buckley, KPMG Law – KWM Professor of Disruptive Innovation, UNSW Sydney: and Dirk Zetzsche, ADA Chair, Faculté de Droit, d'Économie et de Finance, University of Luxembourg, this chapter explores how Europe's path to 'open finance' and 'open data' rests upon the apparently unrelated pillars of: (1) open banking regulation; (2) strict data protection rules; (3) extensive post-Global Financial Crisis reporting requirements; and (4) a pan-European legislative framework for digital identification. It analyses how these regimes interact and distils some lessons for other societies facing choices as to the role of data in their future.

In Chapter 9, "United Kingdom: The Butterfly Effect," Gavin Littlejohn, Ghela Boskovich, and Richard Prior of the Financial Data and Technology Association chart the origins of the United Kingdom's Open Banking regime beginning with the European Union's plans to revise its Payment Services Directive almost a decade ago. The United Kingdom's Competition and Markets Authority seized the opportunity to enhance the EU approach, and the UK approach has since served as an example for a number of other countries. The authors tell a detailed story of the UK Open Banking journey, including the establishment of the Open Banking Implementation Entity, which is responsible for coordinating the delivery of Open Banking in the UK market. The United Kingdom developed its own standards-based approach, rather than follow the European Union's specification-oriented approach. The authors describe these divergent paths and detail how the market has been developing since the United Kingdom's implementation, sharing lessons learned and examining expected future trends.

In Chapter 10, "The Australian Consumer Data Right: The Promise of Open Data," Jamie Leach and Julie McKay, Region Director and former Region Director, respectively, of the Financial Data and Technology Association, Australia & New Zealand , explore how the Australian Open Banking regime is expected to develop within the broader framework of the Consumer Data Right. Unlike several other open banking countries, Australia is pursuing a read-only way of sharing data that does not allow for payment execution unlike in the European Union, but is pursuing an economy-wide approach to data-sharing, beginning with the banking sector, then rolling out to the energy and telecom sectors, prior to possible further extensions. Leach and McKay explain how Australia through its Consumer Data Right intends to ultimately build a national open data economy. The authors explore the origin of open data in Australia and its serious consideration of requiring data reciprocity. They map the process for finalizing details of the open data framework. They also describe how industry is changing in anticipation, including the voluntary uptake of open banking APIs, for instance, in the accounting and bookkeeping sectors. They describe some of the key implementation challenges, including international coordination and also touch on potential opportunities for the Australian economy.

Chapter 11 continues the regional survey with "India's Approach to Open Banking: Some Implications for Financial Inclusion," by Yan Carrière-Swallow, Vikram Haksar, and Manasa Patnam, all of the International Monetary Fund. The authors examine how the development of the digital infrastructure known as the "India Stack"—including an interoperable payments system, a universal digital ID, and other features—is delivering on the government's objective to expand the provision of financial services. While each individual component of the India Stack is important, the authors argue that its key overarching feature is a foundational approach of providing extensive public infrastructures and standards that generates important synergies across the layers of the Stack. Until recently, a large share of India's population lacked access to formal banking services and was largely reliant on cash for financial transactions. The expansion of mobile-based financial services that enable simple and convenient ways to save and conduct financial transactions has provided a novel alternative for expanding the financial net. The Stack's improved digital infrastructures have already allowed for a rapid increase in the use of digital payments and the entry of a range of competitors including fintech and BigTech firms.

Chapter 12, "Digital Identity: Exploring a Consumer-Centric Identity for Open Banking," authored by Greg Kidd, Founder & CEO of GlobaliD, with an exploration of open banking and digital identity. Customer verification is one of the major challenges in open banking. Kidd explores the concept of digital identity, beginning with the history of identity verification and the different kinds of attestations used today. Then the author describes digital IDs and what problems they can solve. Today, some countries have responded to the need to easily authenticate people in a digital economy by implementing centralized public IDs, such as India's Aadhaar, Estonia's e-ID, and Singapore's Singpass. In fact, India's Aadhaar is the world's largest single biometric identity system. Other countries have private models, including Canada's Verified.Me,

Sweden's BankID, and Freja eID+. These private models tend to be more decentralized and can use different kinds of attestation to verify someone's identity. Using the notion that the individual controls his or her data, Kidd then proposes design principles for self-sovereign digital identities that can be controlled by the individual and examines market challenges for making this a reality.

Chapter 13, "Decentralized Finance: The Future of Crypto and Open Finance?," by Nic Carter, Partner at Castle Island Ventures, examines DeFi and how both cryptoassets and open banking are manifestations of the same DeFi movement. He identifies and dissects common features and objectives shared by both crypto-finance and open banking. More intriguing, the author predicts that both phenomena will converge and explores the unknown potential of decentralized financing fully powered by blockchain technology and what such an open finance future could look like.

Brad Carr, Managing Director of Digital Finance at the Institute of International Finance, concludes the book with a futurist exploration of open banking in *From Open Banking to Open Data and Beyond: Competition and the Future of Banking*. He argues that the development of open banking to "open data" will have a transformative impact on business models of not only banks but all incumbent firms. He explores the opportunities and challenges of data proliferation and what "open data" sharing could look like. He argues that data asymmetry can hurt competition and how open data flows will impact entire business sectors and perhaps favor BigTechs. Carr explores how data asymmetries can harm competition and the potential efficiencies and inefficiencies of reciprocal data-sharing in which tech companies share their data with banks. Perhaps, banks, which are becoming tech companies in their own right, could become BigTechs, and BigTechs will either become banks or partner with banks. Finally, the author explores how platformization of financial services will change the entire landscape of finance, including our very identity.

Open Banking Ecosystem and Infrastructure: Banking on Openness

*Andres Wolberg-Stok**

1. Introduction: The Dematerialization of Banking on Its Way to Ubiquity

As you will find out over the course of the chapters that follow, "open banking" means different things to different people, in different places, at different times. Chances are you are also bringing to your role as a reader your own implicit assumptions for or against one of those meanings of open banking, or perhaps a set of explicit views shaped by your personal or professional experiences.

Here is an overarching perspective to help you keep an open mind. Beyond any specific definitions, think of open banking as a component—not the only one, nor the last—on a decades-long journey toward not just the digitalization but the actual dematerialization of cash and financial services, and toward their increasingly seeping infiltration into ever-deeper layers of consumers' lives, both in real life and in the digital sphere (if there is still a distinction).

This dematerialization is born of shifts from the tangible to the intangible, from the macro physical to the electronic, from in-person to virtual modes, from old, coarsely nodal distribution networks to new ones of infinitely fine-grained ubiquity, and from closed, protective systems to open, collaborative ones. These more recent architectures have spawned an entirely new ecosystem: the ecosystem of open banking.

Powering this paradigm shift are the constant progression of technology-powered advances in search of increased convenience for users, increased efficiencies, lower costs, and, increasingly, a generational competition between established financial services players and ambitious newcomers set on disruption.

In years to come, this dematerialization of finance will only accelerate as memories of the pandemic of 2020 make physical cash increasingly inconvenient, unappealing, and scary to handle, as advanced modes of remote interaction become the default choice for most people.

---

* Andres Wolberg-Stok is the Head of Strategy for the Office of the CTO at Citi.

Andres Wolberg-Stok, *Open Banking Ecosystem and Infrastructure: Banking on Openness* In: *Open Banking*. Edited by: Linda Jeng, Oxford University Press. © Oxford University Press 2022. DOI: 10.1093/oso/9780197582879.003.0002

2. Through a Consumer's Eyes: "Ever Closer" Client Touch Points

Seen through the eyes of people who are bank customers (a growing majority of the population) this progression could be described as an ever-closer relationship—one in which both the physical and the perceptual distance between clients and their accounts have kept shrinking decade after decade and year after year, becoming virtually nil. Conversely, the convenience and clients' degree of real-time control over their accounts have grown. In terms of major touch points for clients, this sequence stretches from automated teller machines (ATMs), via early home banking (before web browsers) and then online banking from your home or office, to mobile banking in your pocket, to wearable banking on your wrist, to "banking inside" functionality that morphs into seamless, dematerialized non-bank-branded experiences and interactions implanted within nonbank domains (for instance, seeing your available bank reward points as a payment option at the moment of checkout on a major online retailer's website).

Think back to half a century ago. The 1969 moon landing made civilization appear more advanced than it would have seemed if you had to interact with your bank in those days. In most cases, the only way to manage your accounts—beyond mailing checks for deposit, receiving printed periodic statements at home, or balancing your checkbook—would have been to go into your bank branch for an in-person interaction. You might have been able to call your branch manager on the phone, but otherwise, for the average bank customer, that was probably it. Granting access to your account data to anyone else would have involved giving them a certified power of attorney.

Things began to change when banks in countries like Sweden, the United Kingdom, and the United States started deploying rudimentary cash dispensers, the forebears of today's ATMs. The technology spread around the world. Even if those early ATMs were limited in their functionality, in essence, this constituted—to paraphrase first man on the moon Neil Armstrong—one small step for banks, but one giant leap for banking.

For the first time, you no longer needed to enter the bank branch physically to withdraw money or to get up-to-the-moment information on your balances. The bank was effectively coming out of its building to meet you on the street, or at least in its lobby.

If ATMs represented a small step away from the bank branch, the next phase would bring the bank much closer to clients with early attempts at "home banking" in the 1970s and scaled-up efforts in the 1980s. Since the internet had yet to be born, at first these services required customers to connect to bank systems via dial-up telephone landlines, using modems and dedicated software (distributed to clients on physical discs), which allowed for basic functions such as checking balances and paying bills. Over time, as ownership of personal computers grew and dial-up speeds began to improve, the popularity of these services would rise in parallel with the growth of online services in every other domain. So would early forms of open banking in which consumers were able to direct bookkeeping software to access their bank account information, turning those services effectively into some of the first "fintech" undertakings.

Driven by the popularity of the internet, increasingly broad ownership, and availability of computers at home and improving access speeds, online banking gained real scale in the late 1990s and early 2000s, with a major shift from prepackaged software distributed on magnetic floppy discs to access via browsers. Browser-based online banking allowed banks to improve and update the user experience continually from their end, without requiring customers to do anything on their side. Banks now found themselves in a commercial race with each other to provide ever more versatile, better designed, and easier-to-use services.

The advent of mobile banking took bank/customer proximity one big step further by decoupling the ability to access accounts from access to a computer, and by allowing on-the-go access from anywhere as long as data connectivity was available. Even in their own home, freed from the need to walk over to their desktop computer or wake up their laptop, consumers were beginning to indulge in what we started to call "couch banking" (in 2007, Citi became the first major US bank to offer a downloadable, carrier-independent mobile-banking application).

Simultaneous offerings of "text banking" for account-balance information—cell phone-based call-and-reply services over Short Message Service (SMS)—were quickly sidelined by the advent of the iPhone and its emulators, which made downloadable applications not only commonplace but, crucially, much easier to load onto one's phone and much more powerful, fast, and feature-rich. Banks once again stepped up their competition to evolve increasingly versatile apps with more and more features and better designs. The bank was now right in your pocket or in your hand.

In April 2015, banking leaped from the pocket to the wrist when the Apple Watch hit the market (Citi became the world's first bank with an app for the Apple Watch, having worked with Apple behind the scenes under strict secrecy as engineers at their Cupertino laboratories readied the wristwatch for launch).

Banking on your wrist seemed like the *ne plus ultra*, the end of history in bank/client intimacy, short of some dystopian science-fiction vision of subcutaneous banking implants: How could your bank get any closer to you than that? In reality, it was no such thing. It was merely the beginning of the end for the obligation for customers to come to a bank-branded touchpoint in order to manage their accounts. Things were about to get a lot more interesting.

A few months earlier, a seemingly less spectacular event—but an important milestone in open banking—was the start of a substitution of physical devices by virtual avatars, coupled with the emergence at significant scale of banking and payment functions on platforms not owned or branded by the banks. Plastic credit cards began to get virtualized as digital representations of themselves within mobile wallets from the likes of Apple, Samsung, and Google. Amazon and other e-commerce platforms also started offering bank rewards points as a payment method at checkout, with real-time point balances available to customers on the checkout screen itself rather than solely on their bank's website or mobile application. Apple Pay, then others, brought contactless payments to the point of sale, starting to make plastic cards redundant.

The dematerialization of banking had arrived, and with it, a growing ecosystem of interwoven functional and data relationships between consumers, their banks, and third-party applications offering additional (or substitute) features and services.

3. The Emergence of Nonbank Fintech and Data-Sharing

In parallel with this "ever closer" evolution of banks' touchpoints for client relationships, data exchanges between banks and a new breed of companies began to chip away at the ironclad fortifications around banks' data stores as far back as the early 1990s. Early examples were the multiple forms of bookkeeping and tax-filing software that originally depended on users to download their bank data to a spreadsheet. Eventually they began connecting directly to users' bank accounts—with their permission and using their bank credentials—to import the account data necessary to deliver on their function.

The dawn of online banking revealed a seemingly endless spectrum of possibilities for newcomers in this nascent fintech industry. Banks often like to underscore that they are the original fintechs: they have been adopting new technology and leveraging it for their work from the beginning, not just for accounting and record-keeping, or to combat fraud, but also to create better experiences using customer data. But the first major wave of startups backed by Silicon Valley venture capital could be identified in the late 1990s, as part of what we can now see in hindsight as the dotcom bubble.

In 1999, one of those startups was an international personal-finance undertaking called Latinstocks.com, with headquarters in Buenos Aires and offices in Sao Paulo, in Mexico City, and on Wall Street. From its early days, Latinstocks had set out to become a multibank distribution platform for a broad range of financial products, with consumer engagement driven by editorial content, and market news produced by an in-house team. The Exxel Group, Latin America's mightiest private equity fund at the time, had taken a controlling interest and recruited a team of executives with international experience to build Latinstocks into a pan-American powerhouse. (The Exxel Group hired me as Latinstocks' editor-in-chief.)

Latinstocks' relationship with banks in the markets in which it operated was complicated. On one hand, the startup aimed to help banks distribute their products—for a cut—and, therefore, it needed to be on good terms with them and to be able to share data in both directions. It also understood that most banks were having a hard time building modern client-facing online experiences on top of their aging infrastructures and batch processes. The startup offered to serve as a front end for them, pulling data from their systems to build a user interface of account information and services for their clients. At the same time, however, it publicly taunted incumbent banks with pledges to democratize financial services, to turn banks into dinosaurs, and to relegate them to the scrapheap of financial services history. It was an early case of the *coopetition*—the portmanteau of cooperation and competition—that still characterized much of the open banking ecosystem in the early 2020s.

Banks themselves also saw potential in these newcomers. For example, Citi had been considering taking a stake in Latinstocks, where I headed all content creation at the time, to help build up the bank's budding online presence in Latin America. The Exxel Group pulled the plug on the startup, however, after a failed private placement as the dotcom bubble began to burst in 2000. Latinstocks ceased to operate (and as a direct result of both the earlier negotiation and of the startup's collapse, I joined Citi). Earlier that same year, Spain's Banco Santander had bought out equity stakes held by Chase Capital, JP Morgan & Co, and Goldman Sachs and paid $529 million for a 75 percent stake in Patagon.com, a larger Latinstocks rival that had become Latin America's largest financial website. BBVA, the other Spanish banking giant, had earlier merged its own online banking unit with UK internet bank First-E.

Fintech, reborn from its dotcom ashes a few years later as account-aggregation services, began to gain traction in the United States. In the beginning, companies such as Yodlee, Intuit, and Mint provided a form of personal financial management by offering a single place for consumers to monitor their bank, credit card, loan, and brokerage accounts in an aggregated view across multiple financial institutions.

For the most part, these offerings were "read-only," meaning that while the aggregation services were able to extract their users' data from the users' banks, they did not provide transactional capabilities. If a user, having looked at her account balances on one of these aggregation services, decided that she wanted to transfer funds from one of her bank accounts to another, she would have to log in to one of the banks' websites or mobile apps in order to initiate that transfer. The same applied to paying bills or any other type of interaction that required not only "read" but also "write" capability: the ability to initiate a transaction.

Over time, data aggregators shifted from harvesting consumers' bank data solely for their own services to selling data-access services to the growing numbers of smartphone apps that set out to "unbundle" financial services by offering specific slivers of functionality that threatened to displace or disintermediate conventional banks.

To provide any sort of value to its users, fintech apps, almost by definition, must have access to the user's financial account data. Without it, an app would not know anything about the user and would not be able to offer anything more than generic guidance or advice—unless it required the user to input such data herself, which would be inconvenient and a major barrier to adoption and usage of the app.

As apps and the entrepreneurs behind them took aim at various bank services, the consulting firm CB Insights created a widely replicated map of this scenario, showing how numerous startups were attacking every element of a bank's offering (see Figure 1.1).

4. Accessing Data through the Back Door: "Screen-Scraping"

For years, banks had been making it possible for their customers to download account data in large batches, in spreadsheet form, or as comma-separated values data sets. What fintech apps needed now, however, was very different: they could not afford to depend on their users performing the data-fetching task on their behalf. They needed the data every day, if not more often. How to get it?

This need to access data with customers' permission was the foundation for a technique widely referred to as "screen-scraping." At its simplest, screen-scraping involves asking bank customers to hand over their user ID and password for their bank's website or app, and then utilizing these credentials to sign on to the bank, impersonating the user. All the account data and other information the user would be able to see on the bank's website can then be copy-pasted out by automated scripts, or "bots," parsed, and stored.

Figure 1.1 An often-shared depiction by research firm CB Insights (circa 2016) of how fintech startups focusing on narrow slivers of the financial services spectrum set out to pick at (or "unbundle") the tightly packaged offerings of a traditional bank—in this case, HSBC. https://cbi-blog.s3.amazonaws.com/blog/wp-content/uploads/2015/04/unbundling-of-europ ean-bank-v2.png.

Leaving aside the fact that banks themselves have used this type of data aggregation on behalf of their customers, the first and most obvious problem with screen-scraping is that asking bank customers to hand over to a third-party the keys to their banking relationship—like any other password—is a terrible security practice. Without external oversight or regulation, you would have no way to figure out whether appropriate security measures were in place for the way in which others store your bank user ID and password. If the user IDs and passwords became compromised, criminals would find themselves in possession of a significant part of what they would need in order to steal money from those accounts. During a "Fintech Summit" organized by the White House in 2016, a former official with the US Consumer Financial Protection Bureau (CFPB) described this threat as the equivalent of "an asteroid headed for planet Fintech," given the massive extinction of consumer trust it might spark if it materialized. Furthermore, changing passwords regularly is a good practice—but you would be discouraged from doing so if you knew that to update your bank password would also automatically break data access for your favorite fintech apps. Having shared your bank keys with third-parties would make you less inclined to change your password regularly, and therefore less secure, with your money consequently at greater risk. If, in addition, that third-party decides to make it easier for other apps to access your accounts by storing your secret answers to the bank's security questions, as has happened, then it goes without saying that your accounts are even further at risk. At least one US bank—not Citi—was able to trace fraud losses directly back to this practice of a third-party recording and storing consumers' answers to shared secret questions. In 2020, leading US data aggregator Plaid—which claimed to have access to the accounts of one in four Americans—became the target of a class-action lawsuit[1] charging that it "deceptively obtains bank account credentials from app users," that it "sells and otherwise exploits unlawfully-obtained private data," and that Plaid and its fintech clients "conceal Plaid's conduct from consumers." Also in 2020, US lawmakers called on the Federal Trade Commission to investigate whether fellow major aggregator Yodlee and its parent company, Envestnet, were breaking the law by selling "sensitive financial transaction data from tens of millions of Americans." They warned: "Consumers generally have no idea of the risks to their privacy that Envestnet is imposing on them."[2]

A second problem with screen-scraping relates to the frequency, duration, and breadth of data access. You may have found a fintech app you liked, and you may have intended for it to be able to access, say, your credit card data, once a week, until you told it to stop. Once you have handed over the keys to your bank account, though, you have given up control. A third-party equipped with those keys can come in and harvest not only that credit card information but also everything about your checking account, your certificates of deposit, your savings account, your brokerage account, and even your personal contact information to the extent that it is visible on your bank's website. You will never know what happens to all the data: Is it being taken? Is it being stored? Is it being used solely for what you wanted, or is it being aggregated with data from other people and resold (anonymized or not)? You may have assumed that your data would be accessed only once, for authentication purposes, when you connected a bank account to a payments app. Or you may have thought your data would be accessed regularly, but only once a week—and in reality, someone is coming in perhaps every night and signing on to your bank accounts with your credentials. Maybe you decide eventually that you no longer want to use that fintech app, for whatever reason. Will it stop harvesting your data? The only way to make sure would be to change your bank password, and thus break not only that app's ability to access but also that of every other fintech app you might also have connected to your accounts.

A third problem has to do with the invisibility of the entities that are coming to harvest the data. Bank website designs vary widely across the industry, and they are not static as they keep evolving. As the layout of a web page that displays account activity changes, the way data is arranged on that page can change as well. Values, dates, or descriptions can suddenly be displayed in, say, a different column from where they

---

[1] *Cottle et al. v. Plaid, Inc.* (4:20-cv-03056) District Court, N.D. California (2020). https://www.classaction.org/media/cottle-et-al-v-plaid-inc.pdf.

[2] Senators Ron Wyden and Sherrod Brown and Congresswoman Anna Eshoo, Letter to the Chairman of the Federal Trade Commission Joseph J. Simons (Jan. 17, 2020). https://www.wyden.senate.gov/imo/media/doc/011720%20Wyden%20Brown%20Eshoo%20Envestnet%20Yodlee%20Letter%20to%20FTC.pdf?mod=article_inline.

were just days earlier. And yet, for screen-scraped data to be accurate, the scripts that copy-paste the information out of a bank's website need to know exactly what they are "reading" and where. If a layout change breaks their ability to tell what they are harvesting, the resulting data can become gibberish and thus no longer accurate, leading to bad outcomes for the third-party's app users.

With thousands of banks to access, designing the right sign-on and copy-paste scripts for each bank is a task well beyond the reach of any single fintech app. This is where the data aggregators come back into the picture as a digital platform for open banking. At scale, they have been economically viable by continually scanning bank websites for design changes and updating their scripts accurate data harvests. Data aggregators can then charge fintech apps a fee for access to the consumer's data, and also anonymize and bundle data from many people at scale into attractive, valuable products for hedge fund managers and others who stand to gain from tracking real-time trends in people's spending. There is just one catch: as a consumer, you think you are giving your bank user ID and password to a specific fintech app whose services you think you will find useful. You would not realize, most likely, that in fact you are giving your keys to someone else: a data aggregator whose mere existence is probably not visible to you, whose data practices you do not understand or ignore, and whose security arrangements to keep your keys safe are undisclosed.

A fourth problem with screen-scraping, from a cyber-protection perspective, stems from the fact that at its core, it often does not look that different from a bad actor trying to sign on with someone else's stolen bank credentials. As a result, over time, and deferring to their customers' intent to share their data with a third-party, banks have had to start "white-listing" known data aggregators, to prevent their sophisticated defense systems from blocking aggregators' access. However, when banks instruct their systems not to block aggregators' access, they could be seen to be actively abetting the screen-scraping activities, even when they have no contractual protection in place and are not able to certify the safety and soundness of the arrangement or of the data aggregators' downstream data uses and practices. This creates potential regulatory exposure for banks, as highlighted in the United States by the Office of the Comptroller of the Currency in official guidance to banks.[3] This issue of liability is discussed in greater detail by Steven Boms and Sam Taussig in Chapter 3.

5. Come in through the Front Door, Won't You?

As tens of billions of dollars in venture capital flowed into fintech undertakings year after year, many banks began to understand that customers would probably be interested in supplementing their bank's services with those of some of the scores of new apps that were being offered. No bank, no matter its domestic size or global reach, could ever aspire to single-handedly outperform fintechs' collective capacity for innovating in new approaches and experiences, or to have the risk appetite to invest comparably large

---

[3] OCC Bulletin 2020-10, Third-Party Relationships: Frequently Asked Questions to Supplement OCC Bulletin 2013-29 (Mar. 5, 2020). https://www.occ.gov/news-issuances/bulletins/2020/bulletin-2020-10.html (see FAQ #4).

amounts of capital in projects with highly uncertain outcomes. This difficulty led to a paradigm shift. From walled gardens where banks were somewhat resistant to outflows of data in their control—even if at their customers' direction—many banks began to understand that attempting to keep their customers' data locked away from others would not be a smart or sustainable long-term strategy.

As the confrontational, competitive dynamic peaked between fintechs and financial service incumbents, we coined an ugly neologism, but one that continues to offer a promising model of interaction—"fintegration."[4] We defined it at the time (2015) as a critical new skill banks needed to develop: the ability to integrate the best that the vibrant fintech ecosystem had to offer, for the benefit of bank customers and shareholders alike. The key: banks would need to learn to redesign themselves from impregnable data fortresses into open-by-design platforms better suited for plugging in new value from the outside and allowing a quick evolution of best practices.

An obvious place to start was screen-scraping. Instead of that back door, with all its risks, a more modern approach would be for banks to start offering a properly monitored front door: a set of application programming interfaces (APIs), which are protocols that will be discussed in more detail by Don Cardinal and Nick Thomas in Chapter 5. These APIs would be officially sanctioned entry points where third-party apps or data aggregators could come knocking with the bank customer's consent and access the necessary data using a predefined call-and-response format. Compared to screen-scraping, APIs offered banks full control over who was coming to fetch what data, on behalf of which customer, when, and how often. If properly implemented, these APIs would also make it unnecessary for consumers to have to share their bank user IDs and passwords with anyone else, ever again.

In some parts of the world, governments decided to bolster the potential of the fintech ecosystem and encourage competition in financial services by making it mandatory for banks to begin offering APIs for consumer-directed data access.

As explored in Chapter 8, the European Union's Second Payment Services Directive (PSD2) of 2015 is among the best known of these efforts. Just a decade after adopting the original Payment Services Directive, the EU realized that technological progress had rendered its original legislation obsolete. The revised version would make it mandatory for banks to enable authorized third-party payment service providers not only to access their customers' data but also to set transactions in motion from outside the bank's systems. In parallel, the EU's General Data Protection Regulation (GDPR), which came into force in 2018, gave consumers broad rights to control what information companies across all domains store about them, and to access that information. Many other jurisdictions around the world, from Hong Kong and Australia to Mexico and Brazil, have since followed suit with some form of open banking, mandating either payment connections or only data access, along with data privacy initiatives in the same vein as the GDPR.

The Basel Committee on Banking Supervision (BCBS) produced in late 2019 the most comprehensive global overview to date of this growing trend toward open banking and toward encouraging or forcing banks to begin opening APIs for data

---

4 See p. 3, The Economist Intelligence Unit, "The Disruption of Banking" (2015). https://eiuperspectives.economist.com/sites/default/files/EIU-The%20disruption%20of%20banking_PDF_1.pdf.

access by consumer-authorized third-parties.[5] Some of its key findings were that traditional banking is evolving into open banking, that greater regulatory coordination is needed, and that "(o)pen banking brings potential benefits but also risks and challenges to customers, banks and the banking system."

In the United States, the government largely remained agnostic, supporting instead a market-driven approach in which it expected banks and fintechs to come to a working arrangement among themselves. The CFPB, an agency created after the 2008–2009 crisis, published in 2017 a set of nine nonbinding principles to govern consumer-directed data access.[6] It addressed the fundamental issues surrounding screen-scraping, including data scope and usability, the need to stop forcing consumers to hand over the digital keys to their bank accounts, and informed consent, among others. The CFPB did not choose to make use of its legal powers (Dodd-Frank Act § 1033) to force banks to share customer-permissioned data.

The following year, the US Treasury Department made the market-driven approach explicit. In a landmark 2018 report on regulatory modernization in financial services,[7] it affirmed consumers' right to grant third-parties the power to access their bank accounts, but stated:

> Treasury sees a need to remove legal and regulatory uncertainties currently holding back financial services companies and data aggregators from establishing data sharing agreements that effectively move firms away from screen-scraping to more secure and efficient methods of data access.
>
> Treasury believes that the U.S. market would be best served by a solution developed by the private sector, with appropriate involvement of federal and state financial regulators. A potential solution should address data sharing, security, and liability.

The US Treasury also signaled, however, that the government might resort to other approaches if the industry could not organize open banking on its own. Banks saw the writing on the wall and set to work.

Just months after the publication of the Treasury report, the industry's Financial Services Information Sharing and Analysis Center (FS-ISAC), whose mission is to ensure resilience and continuity of the global financial services infrastructure, spawned a new organization as a subsidiary in the United States: the Financial Data Exchange (FDX). While principally US-focused, FDX describes itself as having "an international membership that includes financial institutions, financial data aggregators, fintechs, payment networks, consumer groups, financial industry groups and utilities and other permissioned parties in the user permissioned financial data ecosystem", (see Figure 1.2).

---

[5] BIS Report on Open Banking and Application Programming Interfaces (Nov. 2019). https://www.bis.org/bcbs/publ/d486.pdf. (N.B. The curating editor of this book, Linda Jeng, chaired the BCBS working group that produced this report.)

[6] Consumer Financial Protection Bureau, "Consumer Protection Principles: Consumer-Authorized Financial Data Sharing and Aggregation" (Oct. 18, 2017). https://files.consumerfinance.gov/f/documents/cfpb_consumer-protection-principles_data-aggregation.pdf.

[7] See p. 198, U.S. Department of Treasury, "A Financial System That Creates Economic Opportunities: Nonbank Financials, Fintech, and Innovation" (July 2018). https://home.treasury.gov/sites/default/files/2018-08/A-Financial-System-that-Creates-Economic-Opportunities---Nonbank-Financials-Fintech-and-Innovation_0.pdf.

Conceptual Flow

End users permission data providers to share their financial account information with data recipients as shown below.

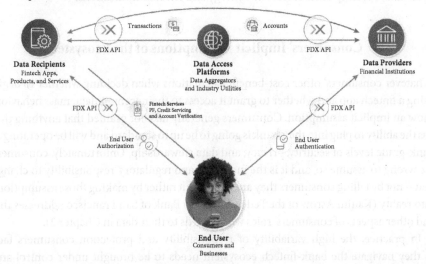

Figure 1.2 The Financial Data Exchange (FDX) view of the ecosystem around consumer-directed data-sharing (reproduced by permission of FDX).

FDX set about modernizing an earlier FS-ISAC standard, the so-called Durable Data API, into a proposed set of APIs technical standards for use by the entire ecosystem. Underlying the standards are what FDX terms the five core principles of user-permissioned data-sharing: Control, Access, Transparency, Traceability, and Security.

Separately, The Clearing House (TCH)—an association of two dozen of the largest US banks—created Connected Banking, a program designed to facilitate one-stop access to bank data through the use of common APIs and security standards, with a streamlined way for fintech companies to undergo due diligence and gain access on a standard contract that would avoid traditionally time-consuming individual negotiations with each bank.[8] In 2020, the TCH and eleven of its member banks acquired a platform designed as a bridge between financial institutions and data recipients, such as fintechs/data aggregators, and available to the entire financial services industry.[9] (Don Cardinal and Nick Thomas discuss approaches to data access standards in Chapter 5.)

The industry-led approach in the United States stands in contrast to government-driven approaches in other jurisdictions. India's choice, as Yan Carrière-Swallow, Vikram Haksar, and Manasa Patnam of the International Monetary Fund explain in Chapter 11, has been to take a more ambitious approach based on providing extensive public infrastructures and standards to operationalize user-authorized data portability across the economy based on a universal digital identity. Australia, on the other hand,

---

[8] https://www.theclearinghouse.org/connected-banking.
[9] The Clearing House, Press Release: "Financial Industry to Give Consumers More Control Over Their Data" (Feb. 20, 2020). https://www.theclearinghouse.org/payment-systems/articles/2020/02/02-20-2020-financial-industry-give-consumers-more-control-over-their-data.

has decreed a singular Consumer Data Right, which, as Jamie Leach and Julie McKay describe in Chapter 10, begins with open banking but is explicitly intended to grow into open data, covering other sectors like energy and telecommunications.

6. Consumers' Implicit Assumptions of the Ecosystem

Whatever consumers' other cost-benefit calculations when deciding whether to begin using a fintech app and whether to grant it access to their account data, mass behaviors show an implicit assumption. Consumers generally take for granted that anything that has the ability to plug into their bank is going to be up to standard and will be operating at bank-grade levels of security, privacy, and data stewardship. Unfortunately, consumers are wrong to assume so, and it is the industry's and regulators' responsibility to change that—not by telling consumers they are wrong, but rather by making those assumptions into reality (Kaitlin Asrow of the Federal Reserve Bank of San Francisco addresses this and other aspects of consumers' roles with regards to their data in Chapter 2).

In practice, the high variability of responsibility and protection consumers face as they navigate the bank-fintech ecosystem needs to be brought under control and flattened. To allow data (and maybe transactions) to traverse peaks and valleys of high regulation or total absence of regulation cannot be the way forward. Solving this requires a focus on two main areas: a way to ensure that all the players in the ecosystem are under similar rules, and a fair and sustainable distribution of liability. The latter is the topic of Chapter 3, in which Steven Boms and Sam Taussig ask: "Who is responsible for making the customer whole?"

Banks spend billions of dollars a year to ensure they are in compliance with regulations which run into thousands upon thousands of pages. Requiring young fintech startups to do the same would be to decree their extinction. Neither should they get a complete pass. A reasonable compromise would be to ensure that anything or anyone that wants to connect into the bank-based data ecosystem meets certain basic criteria. As in amusement park rides that display "you must be *this tall* to ride," a set of basic requirements could include signing up for essential cyber-protection and information security practices, committing to standard privacy policies, making operations auditable, and offering full transparency as to who is behind the app.

In the European Union, the PSD2 mentioned earlier in this chapter makes it obligatory for banks to grant access to customer-mandated payment services providers and other fintechs, as long as the third-party seeking access has been vetted and licensed by the government in its EU state of domicile. Mexico, in its wide-ranging Ley Fintech law of 2018, takes a similar approach, as do many other jurisdictions.

There are no such provisions in the United States' fragmented, layered state and federal regulatory lattice for financial services—a complexity widely acknowledged by everyone, from policymakers and regulators themselves to the US Congress Government Accountability Office, which illustrated it this way in a 2016 report[10] (see Figure 1.3).

---

[10] Government Accountability Office, "Financial Regulation: Complex and Fragmented Structure Could be Streamlined to Improve Effectiveness" GAO-16-175 (Feb. 25, 2016). https://www.gao.gov/products/GAO-16-175.

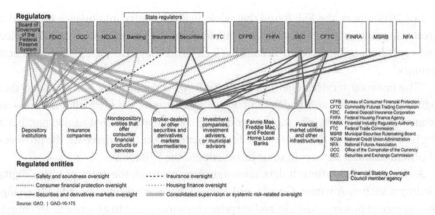

Figure 1.3 US regulators.

One possible solution lies in the market-based approach espoused by the TCH and its member banks with their Connected Banking program. Connected Banking was designed to include a one-stop-shop vetting facility to spare fintechs the excruciating "death by a thousand due diligences" they face if they attempt to undergo reviews and approval by each of the banks to which they aspire to connect for data access via APIs. Another approach would be a federal nondepository license for fintech payments or lending companies, as intended by the OCC. Such a license, however, would be available only to large, well-funded companies with the broad regulatory compliance programs required to earn the OCC's endorsement. This would leave out the vast majority of fintech undertakings, potentially making it impossible for them to ever gain critical mass in a vicious circle of subqualification.

7. Look at Fintech . . . Look at BigTech?

Since the fintech venture-capital funding wave started to build in earnest in the mid-2010s, incumbent banks have spent a lot of time focusing on their interaction mode with fintech startups. But they have also been looking at the ecosystem more broadly, aware of the growing role of "BigTech" platforms in financial services—now a major focus area for regulators around the world, and with good reason.

Part of the challenge for regulators is that whereas fintech startups are easy to spot (if not always to classify and regulate), BigTech companies' entry into financial services has been comparatively low-key by design, difficult to measure, and challenging to define. You will come across this common theme in the other chapters, particularly Chapter 8, in which Douglas W. Arner, Ross P. Buckley, and Dirk A. Zetzsche raise antitrust issues posed by Big Data.

The Basel-based Financial Stability Board (FSB), sometimes called "the fourth pillar of world economic governance" alongside the International Monetary Fund, the World Bank, and the World Trade Organization, is the global community's forward radar to spot and prevent any crises like the one in 2008 that led to its creation by the G20 the following year.

In a 2019 report, the FSB found that while BigTech's entry into finance may lead to greater innovation, diversification, and efficiency in the provision of financial services and contribute to financial inclusion, BigTech firms may also pose risks to financial stability.[11]

"The financial services offerings of BigTech firms could grow quickly given their significant resources and widespread access to customer data, which could be self-reinforcing via network effects. An overarching consideration is that a small number of BigTech firms may in the future come to dominate, rather than diversify, the provision of certain financial services in some jurisdictions," the FSB found.

As far as the bank-fintech data ecosystem is concerned, the entry of major digital platforms such as Amazon, Google, or Facebook has the potential to radically change the balance of power, to delight and surprise consumers, and to give rise to an entirely new set of questions regarding open banking.

At the outset, when fintechs were small, banks were clearly the larger and more powerful party in data exchanges. Data aggregators like Plaid and others in the United States began to alter this equation because as they aggregated data and increased the volume of their data, they also grew in market significance. This became evident in January 2020 when Visa, the credit card network, announced it would spend $5.3 billion to acquire Plaid, the most aggressive of the consumer data aggregators.[12] Even before the announcement, Plaid was laying claim to having access to the accounts of one in four Americans. Just five months after Visa's announcement, rival network Mastercard said it would acquire Finicity, another aggregator, for $825 million.[13] "Open banking gives people and businesses more control over their financial data," Mastercard said in announcing the deal. "This includes determining how and where third parties—such as fintechs or other banks—can access that information to provide new services like money management programs or initiate payments on their behalf."

Visa's acquisition of Plaid fell through, however, in January 2021, a year to the day after it was announced. Opposed by the US Department of Justice, which had sued to block the deal on competition grounds,[14] the failed purchase left Plaid free to reassess its own worth. It was soon reported to be fielding offers from other investors at a valuation of $15 billion—nearly three times as much as Visa had been prepared to pay just a year earlier.[15]

If Visa's and Mastercard's interest in acquiring major data aggregators for such large sums of money was an indication of the potential of the open banking ecosystem as a

[11] Financial Stability Board, "BigTech in Finance: Market Developments and Potential Financial Stability Implications" (Dec. 9, 2019). https://www.fsb.org/2019/12/bigtech-in-finance-market-developments-and-potential-financial-stability-implications/.

[12] Visa, Press Release "Visa to Acquire Plaid" (Jan. 13, 2020). https://usa.visa.com/about-visa/newsroom/press-releases.releaseId.16856.html.

[13] Businesswire, "Mastercard to Acquire Finicity to Advance Open Banking Strategy" (June 23, 2020). https://www.businesswire.com/news/home/20200623005496/en/Mastercard-Acquire-Finicity-Advance-Open-Banking-Strategy.

[14] US Department of Justice, Press Release: "Visa and Plaid Abandon Merger After Antitrust Division's Suit to Block" (Jan. 12, 2021). https://www.justice.gov/opa/pr/visa-and-plaid-abandon-merger-after-antitrust-division-s-suit-block.

[15] Martin Peers, "When Antitrust Opposition Boosts Value: The Information's Tech Briefing," The Information (Jan. 21, 2021). https://www.theinformation.com/articles/when-antitrust-opposition-boosts-value-the-informations-tech-briefing.

whole, the entry of major digital platforms whose origins are not in financial services, unlike those of the cards networks, heralds an entirely new dimension.

Amazon has been offering a growing palette of financial services over the years, from branded credit cards from JP Morgan Chase for its retail customers to financing facilities for its marketplace sellers. Google and Citi announced a joint initiative in late 2019 to "offer smart checking accounts through Google Pay." The *Financial Times* headlined: "Google-Citi deal could be future of banking … Others likely to follow tie-up between West Coast tech and East Coast finance."[16] Facebook, with some three billion monthly active users as of mid-2020, led the creation of a global private association with other companies, under the name of Libra, to build and commercialize a "stablecoin"— a digital currency whose value would be held stable vis-à-vis those of key currencies (early reactions from regulators and policymakers in major economies were strongly negative). In China, technology conglomerate Tencent launched in 2011 WeChat, an app that offers a combination of social media and messaging capabilities with mobile payments. As of early 2020, WeChat had an estimated 1.2 billion monthly active users.[17] Four years earlier, also in China, Alibaba—often referred to as "the Amazon of China"—launched in 2004 Alipay, a platform for mobile and online payments. Renamed as Ant Financial in 2014, it had garnered some 900 million monthly active users as of mid-2020.[18]

The step change in the open banking ecosystem because of these BigTech moves relates to data asymmetries between the types and volumes of data available to financial institutions and to the digital platforms. With years of records of your product searches in its files, Amazon, for example, knows a great deal about your interests and can infer a great deal more about you and your evolving circumstances. Similarly, Google's own television advertisements have highlighted the way in which a person's searches can plot the course of their lives. As for Facebook, it knows so much about your social and professional networks, in addition to the intelligence you share voluntarily in the form of location, connections, words, and photographs, that it can suggest reconnecting with people who had faded from your memory—in other words, it can know more about you than you do.

8. Ecosystem Asymmetries: Questions for the Coming Years

This chapter opened with the suggestion that open banking should be thought of as one more step in a broader dematerialization of banking. We looked back at the way in which banks had figured out how to bring their services ever closer to their clients by leveraging successive generations of technology. We tracked the four-decade evolution from the first ATMs to online banking on personal computers, then to mobile

[16] Robert Armstrong, "Cache Crunch: Google-Citi Deal Could Be Future of Banking," *Financial Times* (Nov. 15, 2019). https://www.ft.com/content/ac22c4de-078b-11ea-a984-fbbacad9e7dd.

[17] Lai Lin Thomala, "Number of Active WeChat Messenger Accounts Q2 2011–Q4 2020," *Statista* (Mar. 25, 2021). https://www.statista.com/statistics/255778/number-of-active-wechat-messenger-accounts/.

[18] Stella Yifan Xie, "Jack Ma's Fintech Giant Ant to Drop 'Financial' From Its Name," *Wall Street Journal* (June 22, 2020). https://www.wsj.com/articles/jack-mas-fintech-giant-ant-to-drop-financial-from-its-name-11592822997.

banking on smartphones, on to wearable banking on the Apple Watch, and finally to the watershed leap from bank-branded customer touch points, where the customer always needs to come to a bank-run site or app, to a "banking inside" approach in which banks' offerings begin to surface within other domains (e.g., during an online shopping journey on a retailer's website). We recounted the evolution of what has become an ecosystem for consumer-directed data access, from chaotic and risky screen-scraping to well-governed APIs. We previewed consumers' implicit expectations and assumptions as to the safety of such data exchanges, and finally we previewed the growing role of BigTech in financial services, as well as some of the associated implications in the data domain.

To round out this look at the open banking ecosystem, let us take a step back for a broader view of consumers and their data. Why focus only on open banking? There is no debate as to how important money and financial services are in people's lives, and in enabling every person to reach her full potential. But why stop there?

Many other domains of modern life are ripe for a similar approach. How about Open e-Commerce? Why should you not be able to grant some mobile app the right to fetch data on your Amazon searches and purchases, every day, and use that information to recommend other options, or present you with targeted special deals?

How about Open Social Media? Why would you not be able to enable a third-party to come harvest every piece of data about your interactions with acquaintances on Facebook and on LinkedIn, every comment you made, every Like, Sad, or Angry reaction from you? Smart entrepreneurs would no doubt be able to create additional value for you—and for themselves, in the process—if only you could give them access to that data.

How about Open Energy? If you could let someone else access in real time your electricity consumption patterns, surely, they would be able to provide smart insights and help you save money (and the planet).

How about Open Search? Google's search engine knows so much about you, it can accurately guess what you are looking for on Google Maps with just a couple of characters when you start to type in a place. What could others do if they were able to tap into that trove of information on your behalf—how much would you be able to learn about yourself?

How about Open Telecoms? How about Open Social-Media Messaging? How about Open Health data? And how about Open Fintech and Open Data Aggregation? If it is your right to share your bank data with third-parties, why would it not be just as much as a right for you to be able to share your data from those third-parties—whether fintech apps or data aggregators—with *other* third-parties, or back with your bank? Why would your bank or your credit card issuer not be able to access your social media, or e-commerce, or health, or search data, if you wanted them to be able to do so? The question of asymmetries in data access, and their impacts on consumers, is discussed in more depth in the final chapter by Brad Carr of the Institute of International Finance.

The bottom line is this: there is no real reason why open banking should remain a domain-restricted phenomenon. Banking has been around for centuries, and it is an important part of people's lives. It is natural for consumer-directed data-sharing to have begun there. In the decade to come, consumers ought to be able to mandate the same kind of data access from other domains. Entrepreneurial minds would be able to create great life-enhancing value from data mashups from across different industries and from across the many facets of our lives. As you begin Chapter 2 by Kaitlin Asrow on data rights and the role of the consumer, do not think narrowly about open banking. Think about *Open Data*, across all domains.

2

Defining Data Rights and the Role of the Individual

Kaitlin Asrow[*]

1. Introduction

At its core, open banking establishes and facilitates a bundle of individual data rights around financial information in order to promote policy goals, such as increased competition. While data rights in open banking can be tools to achieve policy, codifying them more broadly can also be a standalone goal for countries that view them as tied to human rights and individual dignity.[1] The more tactical approach to data rights as tools for open banking has both benefits and drawbacks. The broadest benefit has simply been the increased attention that open banking has brought to the actions that individuals can take around data, in addition to the protections they may receive. Increasing calls for data privacy and data protection are being balanced with an acknowledgment that continuing to use, and share data, is fundamental to future innovation and the well-being of individuals. Open banking has also placed an important emphasis on the development of technical systems and digital infrastructure to facilitate greater data protection and the actual uptake of rights such as portability. Beyond financial services, some countries are already shifting toward a national approach to data governance, which speaks to the broad potential of data rights.

This chapter focuses on redefining data privacy as a combination of data protection and active data rights, and how various data rights have been discussed, and implemented, in financial services to date. These approaches may serve as a model for other economic sectors and an economy based on open data as mentioned in the first chapter by Andres Wolberg-Stok. This chapter begins with a brief history of the evolution of data privacy into data rights in the United States; identifies key data issues in open banking, the current legal and regulatory framework for data protection, and data rights in financial services; and concludes with policy proposals for a broader data rights framework for protecting our personal financial data while balancing economic interests in fostering a dynamic open data framework. For the purposes of this chapter,

[*] Fintech Policy Advisor, Federal Reserve Bank of San Francisco.
The opinions expressed in this chapter are the author's and are intended only for informational purposes; they are not formal opinions of, nor binding on, the Federal Reserve Bank of San Francisco or the Board of Governors of the Federal Reserve System.

[1] Oliver Diggelmann and Maria Nicole Cleis, "How the Right to Privacy Became a Human Right," *Human Rights Law Review* (2014). https://academic.oup.com/hrlr/article-abstract/14/3/441/644279?redirectedFrom=fulltext.

Kaitlin Asrow, *Defining Data Rights and the Role of the Individual* In: *Open Banking*. Edited by: Linda Jeng, Oxford University Press.
© Oxford University Press 2022. DOI: 10.1093/oso/9780197582879.003.0003

"data" is defined as any information related to an individual that serves a commercial purpose.

2. A Brief History of Data Rights in the United States

The concept of data rights for individuals in a digital economy was first introduced in the United States in 1970 under the rubric of Fair Information Practices (FIPs) presented within US federal agency reports.[2] The original FIPs touched on both data protection as a right and the rights of transparency or visibility into data activities, consent, and correction. The FIPs were partially adopted into law in the United States through regulations such as the Fair Credit Reporting Act (FCRA) of 1970, the Privacy Act of 1974, and the Gramm-Leach-Bliley Act of 1999. These laws incorporated only some of the FIPs ideas, though, and took a sector-specific approach.

Outside of sectoral laws in the United States, the FTC encouraged businesses to disclose, and seek consent for, their digital activities in a series of public workshops in the 1990s.[3] While these workshops did result in comprehensive digital protections for children through the Children's Online Privacy Act,[4] broader, more comprehensive data governance was never enacted. The United States has maintained this sector-specific, and now state-specific, approach to data rights through the modern era. In 2010, following the financial crisis, Section 1033 of the Dodd-Frank Wall Street Reform and Consumer Protection Act established the right of individuals to access their digital financial records.[5] In 2012, the Obama administration attempted to create a privacy bill of rights, but it was never taken up by Congress.[6] Most recently, California introduced the California Consumer Privacy Act (CCPA), which incorporates newer information practices introduced overseas, such as the right to deletion.[7] See Figure 2.1 for a general timeline.

Outside of the United States, the FIP concepts gained greater traction, starting with efforts by the Organization for Economic Cooperation and Development (OECD). The OECD recommended Fair Information Practice Principles in 1980 that added detail and specificity to the original US concepts. This variation on the original FIPs spread throughout the world and has served as the foundation for broadening data governance frameworks such as Europe's General Data Protection Regulation (GDPR).

[2] Pam Dixon, "A Brief introduction to Fair Information Practices," *World Privacy Forum* (Jun. 5, 2006). https://www.worldprivacyforum.org/2008/01/report-a-brief-introduction-to-fair-information-practices/.

[3] "Privacy Online: A Report to Congress at 7-14," *Federal Trade Commission* (Jun. 1998). https://www.ftc.gov/sites/default/files/documents/reports/privacy-online-report-congress/priv-23a.pdf;   "Privacy Online: December 1996 Staff Report at 8-12," *Federal Trade Commission* (Dec. 1996). https://www.ftc.gov/reports/staff-report-public-workshop-consumer-privacy-global-information-infrastructure

[4] Children's Online Privacy Protection Act of 1998 (15 U.S.C. 6501–6505 2018). https://www.ftc.gov/enforcement/rules/rulemaking-regulatory-reform-proceedings/childrens-online-privacy-protection-rule.

[5] Dodd-Frank Wall Street Reform and Consumer Protection Act, US Congress (July 21, 2010). https://www.congress.gov/111/plaws/publ203/PLAW-111publ203.pdf

[6] "We Can't Wait: Obama Administration Unveils Blueprint for a 'Privacy Bill of Rights' to Protect Consumers Online," *National Archives and Records Administration* (Feb. 2012). https://obamawhitehouse.archives.gov/the-press-office/2012/02/23/we-can-t-wait-obama-administration-unveils-blueprint-privacy-bill-rights.

[7] Yoni Bard and Scott Bloomberg, "CCPA: The (Qualified) Right to Deletion," *Security, Privacy and the Law* (July 2019). https://www.securityprivacyandthelaw.com/2019/07/ccpa-the-qualified-right-to-deletion/.

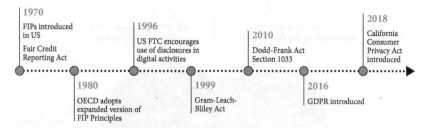

Figure 2.1 General timeline of data protections and data rights.

3. Data Protection vs. Data Rights

The FIP concepts, along with many formal open banking and data rights structures in use today, highlight the important distinction between "passive rights," or protection from external attacks or the misuse of information, and "active rights," or the ability for individuals to take direct actions around information related to themselves. Drawing a distinction between passive data protection and active data rights borrows from the philosophical distinction between negative and positive liberties. The concept of negative liberty (protection) is the idea that individuals have a right to be free from interference, in this case risk and harm relative to data. Positive liberty (rights) is the idea that individuals will be entitled to act independently, in this case asserting various forms of control over data.

In a data rights framework that addresses both passive protection and active rights, organizations would have a responsibility to uphold both sides, but it is important to note that negative rights do not require any affirmative action on the part of individuals. Examples of systems that uphold negative rights, or data protection, include cybersecurity and conduct standards. Cybersecurity protects individuals from data harms related to external attacks or data breaches, while conduct standards, such as controls that restrict employee access to data, can protect individuals from harms related to internal misuse of data by an employee or the company. In contrast, positive data rights are usually enabled by businesses, but they assume action on the part of individuals. Examples of positive data rights include the ability to request data transfers between entities, highlighted by open banking, as well as new types of active rights, such as deletion of data held by companies.

These two sides of protection and data rights are also intrinsically linked and therefore they have been commonly implemented together. Passive rights, or data protection, is a necessary foundation for active data rights. Individuals need to be confident that their use of rights will not expose them to new risks. For example, if entities are held to variable cybersecurity or conduct standards, individuals may not be confident in using an active right such as porting data between companies. The active rights available to individuals could also be limited by companies if they do not have a clear understanding of their own responsibilities and conduct expectations. For example, an individual may not be able to truly use their right to transparency if companies do not disclose their practices in sufficient detail. In addition to facilitating each other, certain elements of data protection complement active data rights. For example, a business responsibility of data accuracy and a right for individuals to correct errors in data. There

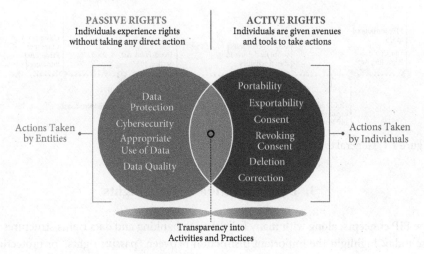

Figure 2.2 Passive and active rights.

may be proactive opportunities for individuals to correct information, but entities would still be expected to maintain policies and procedures to monitor and promote accuracy, and investigate evidence of data errors as a normal part of doing business. An individual correcting errors would not imply that a conduct standard of accuracy was not upheld, instead it is a subsequent opportunity to improve data quality. And as stated before, an individual does not need to act in order for businesses to uphold protection, in this case an expectation of accuracy, but if individuals would like to participate by reviewing for errors, that right is available. Finally, there are also situations where data protection could conflict with active data rights. If there is a conduct expectation that businesses delete data that are no longer being used, that information would no longer be available for an individual to view, or transfer between entities. These interactions between an overarching bundle of both passive and active data rights are important to consider as these kinds of governance structures are designed and implemented.

In the remainder of this chapter, the term "data protection" will be used to indicate "negative"/passive data rights, and "data rights" or "active data rights" will indicate "positive"/active data rights. See Figure 2.2 for a diagram of general passive and active data rights.

a. Facilitating Data Protection in Open Banking

Data protection and data rights are easy to describe and consider in theory, but implementation structures and oversight systems are essential to making them a reality. Open banking has a particular focus on the active data right of porting data between entities, but it can also establish important structures for data protection across the digital ecosystem. The most formalized open banking system in the United Kingdom, administered by the Open Banking Implementation Entity (OBIE), extended the perimeter of regulatory oversight to include all third-party service providers that could receive data from traditional financial institutions. In addition to levying the same expectations across all companies handling financial data, this system established a certification program for any new entities that would like to participate in the data transfer ecosystem. This expanded group of regulated entities is an example of how stronger data protection facilitates a broader use of active data rights.

It is important to note that data protection and data rights provided solely through open banking structures may not cover companies that engage in data activities, but do not participate in the system for financial data portability. Because open banking is sector-based rather than economy-wide, this still leaves the potential for companies that engage in data activities to fall outside both direct and indirect regulatory oversight. On the other hand, the United Kingdom's system for open banking does not have to face the trade-off of data activities that may fall outside of the financial system due to GDPR. The United Kingdom passed the Data Protection Act[8] as its implementation of GDPR, which covers companies both within and outside of the open banking system.

What Is Data Privacy?

It is common to hear calls for data privacy as more and more information flows, but what does it mean? "Data privacy" is defined as "the quality of being apart from observation or intrusion," and the term first appears in English Common Law. The original use of the term "privacy" defined areas where an individual was free, and separate from the state. Stemming from this concept, privacy was declared a human right by the United Nations following the state-led atrocities of World War II.[9]

While the term "privacy" is beneficial because it is broadly recognizable, the word alone is not nuanced enough to capture the concepts and implementation of data governance. Precedent surrounding data privacy is typically focused on intrusion by the state, or by other individuals. Now, many companies and nonprofit entities have unprecedented access to information about individuals that was not previously considered. The emergence of this new category of actors is not addressed under historic concepts of privacy. Furthermore, companies increasingly use automated systems to provide products and services, and many personal interactions with technology, by their digital nature, generate data about individuals. This ability to constantly observe individuals and intervene at moments of decision-making has powered innovation and benefit, but it is challenging to clearly define when data activities become intrusive and objectionable.

Additionally, data privacy may imply data protection to some, and for others there is a necessary element of individual choice around what should be protected or kept private. For these reasons, additional terms, such as *data protection* and *data rights* are helpful in articulating what is meant by "privacy."

---

[8] The Data Protection Act, Government of the United Kingdom (May, 23, 2018). https://www.legislation. gov.uk/ukpga/2018/12/contents/enacted .

[9] Diggelmann and Cleis, *supra* note 2.

4. Active Data Rights in Open Banking

There are a number of active data rights that have been proposed over the past half century, and there may be others that have not been thought of yet. This section will review this universe of active data rights, with particular attention to those that may be part of open banking systems.

a. Right to Transparency

The right to pierce the veil over individuals' data held by companies is part of the original FIPs and, like data protection, can be a necessary precondition for acting upon other data rights. For individuals to take up other active rights, such as correcting or transferring data, they must first be able to see what data to act upon. The right to transparency could be at an aggregate level, just informing individuals broadly of the types of data collected and stored, or it could be enacted at a granular level, with individuals able to see each data point collected over time. Transparency is challenging because people may have different levels of awareness and capacity to understand their digital interactions. For example, if this right to transparency were enacted at a granular level, many individuals may find it difficult to parse through what their information means, especially if the format and presentation are not intuitive or consistent.

b. Right to Portability and Exportability

Data portability and exportability are new additions to the original FIP concepts, and refer to the ability to transfer data between entities. These are the rights most commonly associated with open banking and are discussed further in Chapter 6, by Zee Kin Yeong and David Roi Hardoon.

The right to transfer data is separated here into two distinct but equally important concepts. Portability indicates a right to transfer data from one business to another at a single point in time. This could be for switching between service providers, and ideally enables businesses to compete irrespective of the length of a relationship, and therefore the amount of information they may have collected from individuals. Exportability refers to ongoing transfers of information between two connected entities, both of which have relationships with the individuals of whom the information pertains. This distinct type of transfer right enables new services to connect to information where it is already stored, rather than separately collecting or replicating it.

c. Right to Consent

Consent was one of the original FIPs and refers to an individual agreeing to data activities, such as the initial collection of data, the processing of data (such as cleaning or standardizing formats), the use of data to create information about individuals and make decisions, and the transfer or sale of data to new entities. Consent is arguably the most recognizable "right" that individuals in the United States have around data, but for a wide array of companies it is a voluntary practice stemming from encouragement by the FTC in the 1990s.

There are sectors, such as financial services, where some forms of consent are required. Today, the consent available to individuals in digital interactions is typically "opt-out" consent. This means that simply by using the service with its default settings, individuals are agreeing to data-sharing activities. Some data governance structures are shifting to call for "opt-in" consent, which requires that an individual take action, such as selecting among different options, in order to demonstrate agreement. Consent may also be required for all data activities, or only for certain activities, or only at certain times. For example, under GDPR in the European Union, consent is one of the lawful bases for collecting and processing data, and if that basis is used, consent must be obtained prior to collection. In California, under CCPA, consent is not required for the initial collection of data, but it is required if companies want to sell that information to other parties. There is ongoing debate around what constitutes a "sale" of data, but so far it is interpreted to encompass any transfers of value. Under the UK Open Banking regime, individuals must give consent twice—to allow for third-parties to collect data and to allow for financial institutions to share data.

d. Right to Revoking Consent

Rescinding previously provided consent may be thought of as part of the right to consent, and while it is tied to what is originally agreed to by individuals, it has its own unique considerations. Revoking consent typically means that no additional information is collected about an individual, and information tied to that individual is no longer processed and used. This right does not mean that companies have to destroy previously collected information, and depending on the interpretation and implementation of this right, entities may still be allowed to process and use previously collected information if it is considered "de-identified" or no longer linked to a specific individual.

e. Right to Correction of Data

The right to correct errors in data is part of the original FIPs and, like portability and exportability, is dependent on other rights already being available to individuals. Individuals need to be aware of data collection, and have transparency into what information has been collected, in order to review and identify errors independently. A right regarding error correction has not typically been a focus of open banking structures, though there is an important emphasis on the related issue of data accuracy.

f. Right to Deletion of Data

The final right that has been conferred to individuals in various jurisdictions is the right to request that entities delete previously collected data. Like portability, this is a new addition to the original FIPs. This right is not typically part of open banking specific governance, but it is included in broad data governance regimes, such as GDPR and CCPA. One of the core challenges regarding the right to deletion is the ability for individuals to know where data are stored in the first place. Businesses practices and new active rights, such as portability, can result in data being copied and stored across many different companies. Individuals need transparency into where information related to them is stored and processed in order to act on this right.

5. US Data Protection and Data Rights Frameworks

Today, in the United States, many of the laws at the federal level that govern the management of data related to individuals cover only the financial services sector. There are also new state laws emerging, such as CCPA, which take a broader perspective and are not sector-specific, but often carve out data that is already governed by more specific federal statutes.

These laws can provide examples of what has worked well in data policy and where there may be room for improvement. Most of these laws incorporate elements of both data protection and data rights, which underscores the important combination of these two concepts. Another theme that is apparent through these laws is the importance of clear interpretation for businesses and regulators, and awareness on the part of consumers. Many of these laws were created prior to the ubiquity of modern digital interactions and interconnections, which has left open questions as to their applicability. See Figure 2.3 for a table briefly comparing some of these laws.

	FCRA	GLBA	Dodd-Frank 1033	CCPA	GDPR
Data Protection Focus		X			X
Right to Transparency	X		X	X	X
Right to Portability and Exportability*	Not a primary focus	Not a primary focus	X	X	X
Right to Consent	Rarely required	Opt-out right only for certain transfers	Always required	Opt-out right only for onward sale of data	X
Right to Revoke Consent**					X
Right to Correction of Data	X				X
Right to Deletion of Data				X	X

Figure 2.3 Brief survey of data protection and active data rights concepts in US law.

*Portability and exportability are not delineated in current law.

**Revocation of consent is not delineated from consent in current US law.

a. Gramm-Leach-Bliley Act

The Gramm-Leach-Bliley Act (GLBA; also known as the Financial Modernization Act of 1999) was enacted in 1999 and repealed parts of the Glass-Steagall Act. Title V of GLBA requires financial institutions to disclose how they share and protect customers' private information. GLBA focuses on information disclosures, data-sharing, and information security requirements. The law is divided into two provisions, the Safeguards Rule and the Privacy Rule. The Safeguards Rule regulates information security requirements, while the Privacy Rule establishes boundaries around data-sharing and enables individuals to halt certain activities.

GLBA's Safeguards Rule, or data protection component, covers data related to customers who have an ongoing relationship with a financial institution. This definition of customers can extend beyond direct relationships, for example, consumer reporting agencies. The GLBA Privacy Rule is slightly broader and also covers individuals who may have applied for a one-time service, such as credit, but do not have an ongoing relationship with an entity.

GLBA applies broadly to "financial institutions," which includes any company that engages in financial activities as defined under the Bank Holding Company Act. This extends the purview of GLBA beyond just depository institutions to include securities, insurance, retail banking products, financial advisory activities, and the processing and transmission of financial data broadly. Many data aggregators and fintech companies consider themselves subject to GLBA through their provision of services and relationships to financial institutions. Despite this assumption, those entities are not directly supervised for compliance with this regulation, and therefore it is upheld through their contracts with financial institutions and through the potential of enforcement action brought by the Consumer Financial Protection Bureau (CFPB).

GLBA emphasizes data protection and provides for limited active data rights, including the receipt of disclosures and the ability to opt out of certain data-sharing by businesses. The law requires that financial institutions adopt "information safeguards" to protect the security of identified data, regardless of any action by individuals. Specifically, the law protects, and restricts the sharing of, "nonpublic personal information" obtained through the provision of a financial product or service. This category of information is typically defined as financial information that is associated with a specific individual and has been provided or collected in order to obtain a financial product or service. This also covers information that results from a financial transaction, such as information on a bank statement. Data that are "anonymized," or no longer explicitly associated with an individual, are not covered by GLBA.

GLBA also requires financial institutions to provide notice and an opportunity for individuals to opt out of certain activities, such as marketing by third-parties. These already limited rights to transparency and opt-out consent are subject to a number of exceptions, so they are not available in all circumstances.

The prudential financial regulators, the FTC and the CFPB, all enforce GLBA, but differences among these agencies and their jurisdictions mean that financial institutions may be subject to additional scrutiny through ongoing supervision compared to nonbank entities. Prudential regulators and the FTC are both responsible for the Safeguards

Rule. Prudential agencies, the FTC, and the CFPB all have the authority to enforce the Privacy Rule.

A key challenge of this law has been the variation in oversight capacity among these entities, despite being responsible for the same law. Financial institutions fall under ongoing supervision, while nonbank entities do not undergo the same level of monitoring. For example, the CFPB can examine and enforce the GLBA Privacy Rule for nonbank entities, but not the Safeguards Rule. The FTC does have enforcement authority over the GLBA Safeguards Rule for nonbank entities, but has limited staff and no prudential supervision authority.

b. Fair Credit Reporting Act

The FCRA was passed in 1970 and was one of the first examples of US regulation that incorporated concepts of data governance. The FCRA is broader than GLBA and touches on data protection, data accuracy, disclosures, and active rights to dispute and correct information.

The majority of the Fair Credit Reporting Act applies only to information contained in "consumer reports," which is defined as any communication by a "consumer reporting agency" that has a bearing on a consumer's creditworthiness, character, or reputation, and is collected for the purpose of determining the consumer's eligibility for credit, insurance, employment, or other authorized purposes. This definition extends the reach of the FCRA beyond financial services and into data that is used in connection with employment and housing.

The FCRA generally defines a consumer as an individual, while it uses the term "person" more broadly to encompass individuals, partnerships, corporations, and various other types of entities. Although the FCRA does not apply to credit reports about businesses, it has been interpreted to apply in situations in which a lender obtains a personal consumer report about a business owner in conjunction with extensions of commercial credit. The law has been interpreted to not apply to de-identified, "anonymized" data only when it is used for general research purposes. Any data that could be linked back to an individual but is used only for internal business purposes is still covered by the FCRA.

The FCRA requires disclosures on a broad range of topics, but it does not require consumers' consent to collect data in the first instance. Transmission and use of data for purposes that are designated as permissible under the statute also do not generally require consumer permission, with the exception of certain employment-related situations and new rights that allow individuals to place "freezes" on their reports in order to manage concerns about identity theft in the credit context. The law isn't typically thought of as a portability regime, though it does allow consumers to share consumer reports if they provide written permission to firms, even for purposes that would not otherwise be permitted by the statute. However, the consumer reporting agency is not required to disclose the information even if the firm has written permission and there is relatively little regulatory guidance governing such situations.

The law provides consumers with a general right to dispute the accuracy or completeness of information in their consumer reports and helps to facilitate the exercise of this right in situations in which lenders or certain other parties take an "adverse action" based on information in a consumer report, by mandating that individuals be provided with certain disclosures and an opportunity to review the underlying information.

The FCRA was enforced only by the FTC through 2011, when the Dodd-Frank Act gave the CFPB joint enforcement authority with the FTC. The CFPB can examine consumer reporting agencies used for financial services that meet specified size thresholds for all FCRA requirements, except for certain rules concerning identity theft "red flags" and records disposal. The CFPB cannot examine activities related to employment or tenant background checks. Banks and credit unions are subject to examination for compliance with furnisher and user requirements, and some nonbanks are also subject to CFPB examination for most of the same provisions. The definitions of what constitutes a "consumer reporting agency" are blurring though, and there is active debate around how to effectively regulate these kinds of entities.

i. Section 1033 of the Dodd Frank Act and CFPB Authorized Access Principles

Section 1033 was passed in 2010 as part of the larger Dodd-Frank Wall Street Reform and Consumer Protection Act. This section of the law creates a right for consumers to access digital accounts and transaction information related to financial products or services and is the statute that most closely resembles open banking concepts in the United States.

The law requires covered persons, defined broadly to include corporations, partnerships, or other types of entities, to provide information that can be retrieved in the ordinary course of their business, in usable electronic form, upon the request of a consumer, but the law does not address consumer disclosures or transfer request procedures. "Consumer" is generally defined to include not only individuals who are obtaining financial products and services for personal, family, or household purposes but also agents, trustees, and representatives acting on behalf of such individuals. The law does not explicitly cover data aggregation activities, but entities who gather data at the request of consumers consider themselves as representatives of the individual.

Section 1033 directs the CFPB to prescribe "standards . . . to promote the development and use of standardized formats for information," but as of March 2020 the CFPB has not prescribed rules. In October 2017, the CFPB released nonbinding principles on consumer-authorized financial data-sharing and aggregation.[10] These principles touched on data access, data usability, control and informed consent, authorizing payments, information security, transparency, accuracy, dispute resolution, and accountability or liability mechanisms. In spite of this guidance, market stakeholders continue to debate the scope and impact of this law. In February 2020, the CFPB held a public hearing to discuss what additional steps may be needed,[11] and in October 2020,

---

[10] "Consumer Protection Principles: Consumer-Authorized Financial Data Sharing and Aggregation," *Consumer Financial Protection Bureau* (Oct. 18, 2017). https://www.consumerfinance.gov/data-research/research-reports/consumer-protection-principles-consumer-authorized-financial-data-sharing-and-aggregation/.

[11] "CFPB Symposium: Consumer Access to Financial Records," *Consumer Financial Protection Bureau* (Feb. 26, 2020). https://www.consumerfinance.gov/about-us/events/archive-past-events/cfpb-symposium-consumer-access-financial-records/.

an announcement of proposed rule-making was released for comment on Consumer Access to Financial Records.[12]

Section 1033 is an important step toward a more structured open banking regime in the United States because it establishes that individuals should be able to access transaction and account information in an electronically usable form upon request. However, the statutory provision is quite short and is silent on sharing data with third-parties such as data aggregators, and until the CFPB provides more guideposts it is not clear how the law will be implemented and enforced.

c. California Consumer Privacy Act

In June 2018, the State of California passed CCPA, which went into effect on January 1, 2020. This is the broadest data-focused law in the United States today because it extends beyond specific sectors, such as financial services, to more broadly focus on increasing the agency of the individual relative to his or her data. The California attorney general has provided detailed implementation rules for the law, though there continue to be strong debates around what is reasonable and necessary.

The law covers for-profit entities doing business in California that either collect the personal information of at least 50,000 individuals, households, or devices, directly or through third-parties; have an annual gross revenue in excess of $25 million; or derive 50 percent or more of their revenue from selling data. There is significant debate as to what constitutes "sale" of data, and while the law defines sale beyond just a monetary exchange, there may be transfers between businesses where an exchange of value is not clearly delineated.

CCPA defines a broad scope of coverage with regard to "consumers." The law applies to all natural persons who are residents of California, it does not require that individuals are in a business relationship with firms collecting, processing, or using data, and protections and rights provided cannot be waived through contract.

The law applies to any data that identifies, relates to, or can reasonably be associated with an individual or household. This is an expanded definition of covered data relative to most other privacy regimes because it applies to data that is not currently associated to an individual, but could reasonably be re-associated. The law names particular data points that have historically been excluded from the definition of personally identifiable information under other regimes, such as IP address, to illustrate this point. The law also explicitly covers information that has been inferred about individuals. CCPA does exempt "de-identified" information, which is defined as information that cannot reasonably identify, relate to, describe, be capable of being associated with, or be linked, directly or indirectly, to an individual. Businesses that use de-identified information are required to have technical and organizational structures in place to prevent

---

[12] "Consumer Financial Protection Bureau Releases Advance Notice of Proposed Rulemaking on Consumer Access to Financial Records," *Consumer Financial Protection Bureau* (Oct. 22, 2020). https://www.consumerfinance.gov/about-us/newsroom/consumer-financial-protection-bureau-releases-advance-notice-proposed-rulemaking-consumer-access-financial-records/.

re-identification. The law does not cover data that are subject to other existing privacy laws such as GLBA and the Health Information Protection and Portability Act.

CCPA provides a number of clear individual data rights and establishes certain data protection standards for businesses. California residents can now request access to the information that a company has collected about them, and as part of that request, they also have a right to know which third-parties a company has previously obtained information from or sold it to. Under the law, individuals may also request that entities delete information related to them, but that is limited to identifiable information and is subject to exceptions, such as certain types of research. Individuals can also opt out of data being sold, and, for children under the age of thirteen parental authorization is required for the sale of data. The right of individuals to initiate direct transfers of data between entities is not explicitly called out in the law, but companies that respond to access requests electronically are required to provide the information in formats that can be transferred.

In November 2020, California voters approved a proposition creating a follow-on law called the California Privacy Rights Act, which augments the rights that CCPA provides to state residents. The new law adds rights including the ability to correct inaccurate information, minimization and purpose limitation at the time of initial data collection, and the ability to receive notices around the use of particularly sensitive information. The law also expands some of the original rights provided in CCPA and creates a new enforcement authority, the California Privacy Protection Agency.[13]

d. Additional and Related Law

There are a number of other laws in the United States that interact with data protection and active individual rights in some way. These include additional financial regulation such as third-party service provider guidance, broader laws such as Unfair, Deceptive, or Abusive Acts or Practices, other sector-specific laws such as the Health Insurance Portability and Accountability Act of 1996, youth-specific laws such as the Children's Online Privacy Protection, and many more.

A number of US states besides California are also considering or have passed privacy legislation. For example, in March 2021 Virginia passed a Consumer Data Protection Act, which includes many components of CCPA.[14]

As this section outlines, the United States does have existing data protection and conduct standards, as well as some codified individual data rights. In addition to these laws, courts have established a broad precedent for privacy.[15] Unfortunately these regulations and precedents are fragmented across sectors and states and are inconsistent in their definitions of the information, individuals, and entities covered by the law. These laws also fall between and among overlapping agency jurisdictions, which can create both redundancies and gaps in oversight.

---

[13] "California Privacy Rights Act: An Overview," Privacy Rights Clearinghouse (Dec. 10, 2020).
[14] "HB 2307 Consumer Data Protection Act; Personal Data Rights of Consumer, Etc.," Virginia's Legislative Information System.
[15] "Privacy Rights and Personal Autonomy," *Justia* (Aug. 2018). https://www.justia.com/constitutional-law/docs/privacy-rights/.

6. Global Approaches to Data Rights

There is a global shift occurring to provide citizens across a number of countries with comprehensive data protection and data rights. The movements described below go beyond open banking and sector-specific structures and take a nationwide approach to creating data governance.

a. General Data Protection Regulation—European Union

GDPR is the first law of its kind and has served as model for other countries developing data protection laws. GDPR is a pan-European law that went into effect on May 25, 2018, and is intended to create consistent governance of data privacy across Europe.[16] Data protection authorities were established to oversee and enforce the law. A key element of the law is that it addresses both data protection through security and conduct expectations and also provides individuals with a number of active data rights.

The protections and rights that GDPR affords is based on citizenship rather than use of a product, like GLBA, or physical residency, like CCPA. This enables European regulators to address data issues that occur outside of their borders but are related to information concerning their citizens. Europe also established commensurate oversight capabilities through their new data protection agencies to oversee the wide spectrum of new companies within this regulatory perimeter.

GDPR establishes a number of expectations for companies around how they handle data. This includes security expectations, but also conduct standards. One of the most important standards to come out of GDPR is the expectation that entities have a legitimate purpose for engaging in data collection, processing, and use before those activities occur. In addition to robust data protection, GDPR also provides a bundle of active data rights which incorporate original FIPs concepts as well as providing for new types of individual agency over data. Through GDPR, EU citizens' data rights include transparency into firm's data activities, direct access to data collected, the ability to correct data, the ability to port data between entities, and the right to delete information held. GDPR also includes additional rights which give individuals the ability to object to certain activities, including automated decision-making and profiling.

b. Personal Data Protection Bill—India

In July 2018, the Indian parliament proposed the Personal Data Protection Bill,[17] which was subsequently amended and reproposed in 2019. As of May 2020, the bill is still under parliamentary review and has not formally gone into effect. Like GDPR, the proposed law is broad and establishes comprehensive data protection for all Indian

---

[16] "General Data Protection Regulation," *European Union* (Apr. 27, 2016). https://eur-lex.europa.eu/legal-content/EN/TXT/PDF/?uri=CELEX:32016R0679.

[17] The Personal Data Protection Bill, 2018, Ministry of Electronics and Information Technology. https://meity.gov.in/writereaddata/files/Personal_Data_Protection_Bill,2018.pdf.

citizens, as well as providing for specific data rights. The bill also establishes a Data Protection Agency to implement the new law and to provide oversight.

Like GDPR, the Indian proposal establishes security and conduct expectations for businesses that handle data. The bill also enables individuals to access information and port it to new entities, correct errors, and request that information be deleted. There are a number of important distinctions between this law and the EU approach. India's framework is more state-focused and adds requirements around "data localization." This requires that entities physically maintain copies of data related to Indian citizens in the country. The newly updated Personal Data Protection Bill also exempts the government from needing to comply with certain data rights around revealing and sharing data. It is important to note that, like in Europe, this law is bolstered in India by the Supreme Court's formal designation of privacy as a human right. This decision established that being left alone is part of a fundamental right of life for individuals.[18] A final unique characteristic of India is their implementation of a national digital identity system called Aadhaar.[19] This is part of a larger focus on digital infrastructure in India known as the India Stack,[20] which, combined with a codification of data protection and data rights, could enable individuals to manage data and digital interactions in new ways. (See Chapter 11, by Yan Carrière-Swallow, Vikram Haksar, and Manasa Patnam, for a description of India's open banking framework.)

c. Consumer Data Right—Australia

An initiative was launched by the Australian government in July 2017 to improve individual's access to, and control over, data. This work began with a focus on open banking structures in the financial services sector, but the government elected to expand the proposed regulation to cover all economic sectors of the country.

Implementation rules and processes are currently being developed by the Australian Competition & Consumer Commission.[21] Like other international approaches, the Australian proposal includes both data protection and active data rights provided to individuals. The main individual data right in this case though, remains data portability, or moving information between entities in a secure way and is discussed in more detail in Chapter 6. A unique element of the Australian approach is their focus on information as a resource for the country as a whole, with the goal of more effectively harnessing that resource through improved portability. Chapter 10, by Jamie Leach and Julie McKay, describes Australia's journey from open banking to open data.

---

[18] Julie McCarthy, "Indian Supreme Court Declares Privacy a Fundamental Right," *NPR* (Aug. 24, 2017). https://www.npr.org/sections/thetwo-way/2017/08/24/545963181/indian-supreme-court-declares-privacy-a-fundamental-right.

[19] "Digital Locker: Ministry of Electronics and Information Technology, Government of India," Ministry of Electronics and Information Technology. https://meity.gov.in/digital-locker.

[20] "What Is Aadhaar—Unique Identification Authority of India: Government of India," Unique Identification Authority of India. https://uidai.gov.in/what-is-aadhaar.html.

[21] Consumer Data Right (CDR), Australian Competition and Consumer Commission (Dec. 2019). https://www.accc.gov.au/focus-areas/consumer-data-right-cdr-0.

d. Brazilian General Data Protection Law—Brazil

The Brazilian General Data Protection Law, published in August 2018, provides both individual data protection and certain data rights.[22] This law is modeled on the EU's GDPR and has a broad scope of applicability to all Brazilian citizens and all entities handling information about these citizens. Brazil, like the United States, already had a number of sector-based data governance laws, which this new regulation replaces or supplements. This law requires that entities have a legal basis for collecting, processing, and using data, and establishes a number of additional security and conduct expectations. The law includes the ability to directly access data collected, transparency into entities' data activities, the right to correct errors, and the ability to revoke previously provided consent.

These examples represent only a handful of the active efforts that are in motion around the world.[23] For example, countries such as New Zealand and Singapore are providing fundamental data infrastructure around digital identity[24] and Know Your Customer (KYC) utilities,[25] while other countries, such as Japan, are encouraging data portability through nonbinding API standards.[26] Additionally, there are regulatory efforts underway in Europe to create blended, synergistic approaches[27] to the myriad of intersecting policy goals around data governance.

7. Considerations for Broad Data Protection and Data Rights Frameworks

As open banking and these broader global initiatives have demonstrated, there can be benefits to extending the expectation of data protection to new entities and codifying active individual rights around data. While these benefits are exciting, they are also challenging to achieve, and there are a number of considerations that must be taken into account in order to effectively design and implement broad data governance.

a. Considerations for Individual Data Protection

Requirements around information security and business conduct that extend to all entities that handle information, subject to reasonable thresholds, can lay the

---

[22] Renato Leite Monteiro, "The New Brazilian General Data Protection Law—A Detailed Analysis," *IAPP* (Aug. 15, 2018). https://iapp.org/news/a/the-new-brazilian-general-data-protection-law-a-detailed-analysis/.

[23] Kathleen McGowan et al., "Personal Data Empowerment: Restoring Power to the People in a Digital Age," Pathways for Prosperity Commission, Technology & Inclusion Development (Sept. 2018). https://pathwayscommission.bsg.ox.ac.uk/sites/default/files/2018-11/personal_data_empowerment.pdf.

[24] "About Us," Digital Identity New Zealand. https://digitalidentity.nz/about/#:~:text=Digital%20Identity%20NZ%20is%20a,future%20for%20all%20New%20Zealanders.

[25] "Digital ID and e-KYC," Monetary Authority of Singapore. https://www.mas.gov.sg/development/fintech/technologies---digital-id-and-e-kyc.

[26] "Report of Review Committee on Open APIs: Promoting Open Innovation," *Japan Banking Association* (July 13, 2017). https://www.zenginkyo.or.jp/fileadmin/res/en/news/news170713.pdf.

[27] Digital Clearinghouse. https://www.digitalclearinghouse.org/.

groundwork for subsequent active data rights. A broad data protection regime does require significant resources from entities in order to comply and from regulators to provide sufficient oversight. This resource outlay could make it more challenging for new innovators to enter markets and scale quickly. Conversely though, a broad data protection regime could also enable companies to partner with greater confidence in each other's security and compliance systems. This kind of broad approach can also help protect individuals from a wide spectrum of risks and create confidence in new digital systems and tools.

1. *Protect all individuals*: The lines between entities, sectors, and jurisdictions are blurring, but this is not always apparent to individuals who seek services. It is already difficult for individuals to discern when they are covered by traditional financial protections when using new digital tools,[28] and there are cases when an individual's access to technology changes simply because they step over a state border.[29] Furthermore, increasingly, there are technologies and digital interactions that incorporate data collection in their fundamental design, and a vast amount of data handling occurs among companies without a direct relationship to an individual.[30] Because of these blurring boundaries and how individuals interact with technology today, a data protection regime that applies to all entities within a country and covers all individuals, irrespective of an active "customer" relationship, could help reduce complexity and ensure there are no gaps in protection.

2. *No requirement for proof of tangible harm*: Individuals can experience a wide array of harms due to data activities. Harms can take the form of direct monetary loss, or be more opaque, such as cognitive or social stress due to the revelation of sensitive information. Monetary loss, or money and time spent to resolve issues, can be quantified, while it is much more difficult to quantify other harms such as stress. Additionally, the potential risk to individuals can extend for years after an event has occurred. Because of this, it may be beneficial to not require evidence of tangible harms in order to take regulatory action or compensate individuals for the harm done.

3. *Adoption of different types of protection*: Data harms to individuals can occur because of an external attack resulting in a data breach, or through the internal misuse of data at companies. Due to this reality, a data protection framework should include both cybersecurity and conduct expectations. Conduct standards could include business practices that ensure entities can adequately respond to risks and errors, such as audit schedules and insurance, as well as familiar concepts like demonstrating legitimate interest under GDPR.

4. *Scope of data forms to be protected*: The definition of the data forms that fall within the scope of new data protection laws has been broadening to reflect the failure

[28] David Pommerehn, "Robinhood's Stumble Is a Wake-up Call," *American Banker* (Dec. 21, 2018). https://www.americanbanker.com/opinion/robinhoods-stumble-is-a-wakeup-call.

[29] "Why Google's Arts & Culture App Face Match Doesn't Work in Illinois," *ABC Eyewitness News* (Jan. 17, 2018). https://abc7chicago.com/2959613.

[30] "Update Report into Adtech and Real Time Bidding," United Kingdom Information Commissioner's Office (June 20, 2019). https://cy.ico.org.uk/media/about-the-ico/documents/2615156/adtech-real-time-bidding-report-201906-dl191220.pdf

of so-called "anonymized" data.[31] Information ranging from demographics,[32] to metadata,[33] to location, and more[34] that has had "identifying information" removed can still be easily attached to individuals and even used to determine extremely sensitive details about their lives.[35] A deeper examination of "de-identification" began in the 1990s led by Professor Latanya Sweeney, PhD, Professor Sweeney found that 87 percent of the US population could be uniquely identified using only date of birth, gender, and zip code by combining it with other publicly available data sets.[36] This risk has only increased as more and more sensitive data sets have been exposed through data breaches. Despite the reality that almost all information related to an individual can be "identifiable," murky distinctions are commonly used in data protection laws, such as data that cannot be "reasonably" linked to an individual. While these definitions encourage anonymization techniques and enable businesses to innovate with data, they should be carefully considered in light of the risks that remain to individuals despite any "de-identification."

b. Considerations for Active Data Rights

Building on a foundation of individual data protection, there are important considerations for creating an active data rights regime that extends beyond open banking. One of the most important factors is the consistency and simplicity of mechanisms to enable individuals to act on data preferences. Under an active data rights framework, individuals would have more access to information and increased choice, but they may struggle to effectively act. In particular, populations with less access to education and technological resources may be at a disadvantage in understanding and acting upon information. This dynamic could be exacerbated if active rights, such as the ability to request, correct, or delete information, are implemented without accounting for the cognitive and resource management burden that this could place on individuals. In particular, if systems are not well designed and consistent and do not work together, it requires a much greater effort for individuals to manage information and take actions.

Additionally, while the experience of users is important, friction for individuals is not always bad. There may be situations, such as authenticating an individual's identity, which can be especially sensitive. The security that needs to go along with these kinds of processes may mean that it is not frictionless for the individual.

---

[31] Paul Ohm, "Broken Promises of Privacy: Responding to the Surprising Failure of Anonymization," *UCLA Law Review*. https://www.uclalawreview.org/pdf/57-6-3.pdf.

[32] Latanya Sweeney, "Simple Demographics Often Identify People Uniquely," *Data Privacy Lab* (Jan. 2000). https://dataprivacylab.org/projects/identifiability/index.html.

[33] Jonathan Mayer, Patrick Mutchler, and John C. Mitchell, "Evaluating the Privacy Properties of Telephone Metadata," *National Academy of Sciences* (May 17, 2016). https://www.pnas.org/content/113/20/5536.

[34] Alessandro Acquisti and Ralph Gross, "Predicting Social Security Numbers from Public Data," *National Academy of Sciences* (July 2009). https://www.pnas.org/content/106/27/10975.

[35] Stuart A. Thompson and Charlie Warzel, "Twelve Million Phones, One Dataset, Zero Privacy," *New York Times* (Dec. 2019). https://www.nytimes.com/interactive/2019/12/19/opinion/location-tracking-cell-phone.html.

[36] "Policy and Law: Identifiability of de-identified data" LatanyaSweeney.com. http://www.latanyasweeney.org/work/identifiability.html.

1. *Right to transparency and data portability*: Important considerations for the right to transparency are how and where individuals will be able to see information. For example, individuals could review information through a dashboard that is always available,[37] or through sending individuals information directly. Building out structure and guidance around this right is necessary so individuals are not alone in navigating and ingesting a new flood of information, either when viewing it in a dashboard or when receiving it directly. For example, currently, many transparency requests must be sought out, and requested of, each entity separately. This system is onerous for all parties. Individuals have no way to standardize and parse information in different formats, and companies are dealing with a flood of new requests. European companies have also experienced a number of falsified information requests that are challenging to navigate while also responding to new valid requests.[38] The concern has also been raised that providing a right to granular transparency would force companies to rematch data to individuals that they otherwise could keep more secure. An option to consider is enabling this right to be fulfilled through both summary information around what has been collected, processed, and used, and revealing full data sets. Summary information may be easier for individuals to interpret and can differentiate the right to transparency from a portability right that requires full data. Conversely, though, the FCRA originally required credit bureaus to reveal only summary information, but there have been subsequent efforts to provide more comprehensive information to individuals.[39] This highlights the need for a bundle of active data rights that can enable individuals to take action based on their specific needs and capacities. If an individual prefers summary information, this could be an option through a transparency right, while full data could be viewed through a portability right.

2. *Right to consent*: While consent is part of the original FIPs and is fundamental to how many formal, and informal, data governance systems work today, it is challenging to make consent meaningful for individuals. Currently, consent is typically sought alongside disclosures provided for transparency. While this gives individuals more information to base their decision on, information can be frustrating to access, and the paths and prompts to do so are presented inconsistently across entities. Disclosures appear in different locations and are presented at different times.

If individuals are able to find a company's disclosed policies, they are almost impossible to understand for a variety of reasons. Disclosures are typically too long to reasonably

[37] Penny Crosman, "JPMorgan Chase Moves to Block Fintechs from Screen Scraping," *American Banker* (Jan. 2020). https://www.americanbanker.com/news/jpmorgan-chase-moves-to-block-fintechs-from-screen-scraping; "Control TowerSM," *Wells Fargo*. https://www.wellsfargo.com/online-banking/manage-accounts/control-tower/.

[38] Catherine Stupp, "Companies Scramble to Respond to Spam GDPR Requests," *Wall Street Journal* (Nov. 25, 2019). https://www.wsj.com/articles/companies-scramble-to-respond-to-spam-gdpr-requests-11574677802.

[39] Maxine Waters, Proposed Amendment to the Fair Credit Reporting Act, US House Committee on Financial Services (Feb. 2019). https://financialservices.house.gov/uploadedfiles/comprehensive_consumer_credit_reporting_reform_act_02262019.pdf.

read, with some researchers estimating that twenty-five full days are needed to read every disclosure agreement for the websites visited by an individual over a year.[40] That estimate does not account for mobile-phone applications and the increasing ubiquity of internet connected devices that also collect significant amounts of information.[41] If individuals find and elect to take the time to read every disclosure, the content would be largely incomprehensible. Tests show that readability scores for common disclosures are lower than dense philosophical texts, and even lawyers would struggle to understand them.[42] In addition to using jargon and legal phrasing, information about activities and practices are typically described in vague terms, such as for "business purposes" or "service improvement," which could span a huge spectrum of activities. Finally, if individuals did understand the complexity and density of disclosures, there is no opportunity to negotiate for different terms of the relationship. Notice and choice is typically a contract of adhesion,[43] meaning that the only option that an individual has if they do not agree with the outlined terms is to not use the service at all.

Consent is also heavily influenced by the digital context and format in which it is presented. Research has shown that it is easier for individuals to interact with, and consent to, binary choices rather than complex choices, but granular consent is more effective at revealing preferences.[44] If detailed choices are presented to individuals, they are commonly opt-out rather than opt-in decisions, and research has demonstrated repeatedly that individuals rely on default settings and rarely proactively opt out of presented activities.[45] Evidence has also shown that the ways in which consent requests are phrased can change responses, and digital context such as the professionalism of a website can have unexpected effects. For example, researchers found that individuals were more likely to disclose sensitive information in less professional digital settings, while more professional-looking websites cued them to think about potential risk.[46]

In addition to the digital context in which disclosure and consent is displayed, it is also heavily influenced by human psychology and the physical environment, such as time pressures. There is a phenomenon known as "information avoidance," which results in individuals becoming overwhelmed and avoiding details altogether if they run contrary to their preferences.[47] There are also phenomena that have been identified in social science research such as "risk discounting," "optimism bias," and the desire to

---

[40] Alexis C. Madrigal, "Reading the Privacy Policies You Encounter in a Year Would Take 76 Work Days," *Atlantic Media Company* (Mar. 1, 2012). https://www.theatlantic.com/technology/archive/2012/03/reading-the-privacy-policies-you-encounter-in-a-year-would-take-76-work-days/253851/.

[41] Bill Budington, "Ring Doorbell App Packed with Third-Party Trackers," *Electronic Frontier Foundation* (Jan. 27, 2020). https://www.eff.org/deeplinks/2020/01/ring-doorbell-app-packed-third-party-trackers.

[42] Kevin Litman-navarro, "We Read 150 Privacy Policies. They Were an Incomprehensible Disaster," *New York Times* (June 2019). https://www.nytimes.com/interactive/2019/06/12/opinion/facebook-google-privacy-policies.html.

[43] "Adhesion Contract (Contract of Adhesion)," *Legal Information Institute*. https://www.law.cornell.edu/wex/adhesion_contract_(contract_of_adhesion).

[44] Barry Schwartz, "The Paradox of Choice: Why More Is Less," *Harper Perennial* (Jan. 2005).

[45] Hana Habib et al., "An Empirical Analysis of Data Deletion and Opt-Out Choices on 150 Websites," *USENIX* (2019). https://www.usenix.org/conference/soups2019/presentation/habib.

[46] Leslie K. John, Alessandro Acquisti, and George Lowenstein, "Strangers on a Plane: Context-Dependent Willingness to Divulge Sensitive Information," *Journal of Consumer Research Carnegie Mellon University* (Feb. 2011). https://www.cmu.edu/dietrich/sds/docs/loewenstein/StrangersPlane.pdf.

[47] Dan Svirsky, "Why Are Privacy Preferences Inconsistent?," Harvard Law School, John M. Olin Center for Law, Economics, and Business Fellows' Discussion Paper Series (June 2018). http://www.law.harvard.edu/programs/olin_center/fellows_papers/pdf/Svirsky_81.pdf.

take the path of least resistance. Risk discounting refers to the struggle for individuals to calculate risks in the future.[48] Optimism bias is the tendency for individuals to over-anticipate positive outcomes and under-anticipate negative outcomes.[49] Therefore if disclosed information is hard to find, read, or understand, or it runs contrary to an individual's preferences, the disclosure may be ignored in favor of simply accepting the terms.

Broadly, this indicates that it is extremely difficult to enable meaningful consent given the complexity of technology and the volume of daily digital interactions. That is not necessarily a reason to do away with consent, but it has raised the idea among stakeholders of a baseline legitimate purpose requirement for the collection, processing, and use of data that would apply prior to an entity performing any activity on data or establishing a relationship with individuals, and could not be superseded by consent. For example, the Consultative Group to Assist the Poor (CGAP) released a report in late 2019[50] calling for either a legitimate purpose requirement or a fiduciary duty standard. This approach is distinct from GDPR, which outlines multiple lawful bases for processing information, and either consent or legitimate interest can be used.[51] Under a legitimate purpose requirement, consent alone cannot be a lawful basis for collecting, processing, or using data. "Legitimate interest" is also a more broadly defined concept and centers on the interests of the entity as long as those meet certain criteria, rather than what may be considered legitimate for the individual.

Another important consideration relative to consent is how that consent is shared among partners and data-sharing systems to ensure that all parties are aware of what has been agreed to, and are prepared to act on that. To address this, the United Kingdom's OBIE introduced the concept of "consent codification," which would be attached to data as it flows through processing and portability systems.[52]

1. *Right to correction and consent revocation*: As described earlier, it is important to consider how correcting errors and revoking previously provided consent would work in tandem with other rights, such as transparency and consent. As with the right to transparency, the mechanisms that are available to individuals to review data and flag errors should be consistent and simple to use across diverse populations. It is also essential that there are procedures in place to process these kinds of requests in a way that is secure, is not onerous for the individual, and ideally does not require significant additional data collection to fulfill. For example,

[48] G.J. Madde and W.K. Bickel, "Impulsivity: The Behavioral and Neurological Science of Discounting," *American Psychological Association* (2010). https://doi.org/10.1037/12069-000; Shane Frederick, George Loewenstein, and Ted O'Donoghue, "Time Discounting and Time Preference," *Advances in Behavioral Economics* (June 2002), 162–222. https://www.aeaweb.org/articles?id=10.1257/002205102320161311.

[49] Tali Sharot, "The Optimism Bias," *Current Biology* 21(23) (Dec. 6, 2011). https://doi.org/10.1016/j.cub.2011.10.030; Dylan Evans, "Your Judgment of Risk Is Compromised," *Harvard Business Review* (June 21, 2012). https://hbr.org/2012/06/recognize-the-limits-of-judgme.

[50] David Medine and Gayatri Murthy, "Making Data Work for the Poor," *CGAP* (Jan. 2020). https://www.cgap.org/research/publication/making-data-work-poor.

[51] "Lawful Basis for Processing," *Information Commissioner's Office*. https://ico.org.uk/for-organisations/guide-to-data-protection/guide-to-the-general-data-protection-regulation-gdpr/lawful-basis-for-processing/.

[52] "Open Banking, Preparing for Lift Off," United Kingdom Open Banking Implementation Entity (July 2019). https://www.openbanking.org.uk/wp-content/uploads/open-banking-report-150719.pdf.

the identification and correction of true data errors benefits both individuals and businesses, but if systems are not accessible and easy to use, uptake will likely be limited. Individuals should also ideally be aware that the option to revoke consent is available at the initial moment of agreement to the service and activities.

2. *Right to portability*: One of the most important considerations for portability is how secure transfers will occur, which is the basis for many formal open banking structures that mandate API protocols, data formats, and certification programs. Two other fundamental considerations for the right to portability are the data formats and data types available for this transfer. Like many of the other rights, typically data that have been "de-identified" are not considered available for porting. As discussed earlier, "de-identification" can be easily reversed, therefore using this as the only distinction between what can or cannot be ported is challenging. In addition to needing to determine the fields of data that are available for individuals to port to new entities, it is essential to come to broad agreement on which data points are available. A key debate in the United States is around which data are considered proprietary to an institution, like variable fees, and therefore porting it to new entities could place companies at a competitive disadvantage.[53] Singapore is adopting an extensive data portability framework based on data portability as an individual right (see Chapter 6, by Zee Kin Yeong and David Roi Hardoon, for more on Singapore's policies on data portability). There is likely value in maintaining intellectual property rights over some information for companies, but it is important to distinguish what data are available for an individual to port directly through technological means and what information may be sensitive to a company's interests and therefore this digital-based movement would not be allowed. Individuals could still move this kind of information themselves by requesting access and providing it directly to a new firm, but the scale and scope of that kind of movement is inherently limited.

3. *Right to deletion*: Like the rights of transparency and correction, the right to delete data is inherently tied to an individual's ability to comprehensively view what information has been collected and is currently held by entities. Having this visibility in one place instead of multiple places and being able to take action in one central location instead of multiple locations is also beneficial for this right. The right to deletion is important for many individuals and can help stem the intense data proliferation that is occurring, but there may also be value in limiting this right based on certain factors. Many financial consumer protection requirements, such as identity verification and fraud monitoring, require the retention of data. Implementing a blanket right to deletion could immediately come into tension with these regulatory requirements and security needs. Additionally, current technological innovation, such as machine learning, requires large stores of data for continuous retraining, and there may be benefits to revisiting original data that an algorithm was trained on.

---

[53] "CFPB Symposium: Consumer Access to Financial Records," *Consumer Financial Protection Bureau* (Feb. 26, 2020). https://www.consumerfinance.gov/about-us/events/archive-past-events/cfpb-symposium-consumer-access-financial-records/.

8. Conclusion

Implementing data frameworks that provide for both individual data protection and active data rights is important, but there are also situations where other policy goals, such as competition, innovation, and stability, may have to be balanced. Promisingly, there are also situations where policy goals could work in tandem with each other to achieve even better outcomes.

Evidence does suggest that approaches to data governance that only focus on protection, or only on actions like portability, could have suboptimal effects. For example, policymakers and citizens may limit the amount of information that can flow in order to achieve more privacy for individuals, which in turn could reduce opportunities to improve financial inclusion and competition. Maintaining large flows of information to feed innovation may improve the global competitiveness of US technology, but it could also have cybersecurity, concentration risk, and stability implications for the country. It is important to acknowledge and weigh the potential externalities of data governance across policy areas in order to identify areas of harmonization, mitigate negative impacts, and ensure we are triangulating to the desired outcome. In order to balance these policy goals, there are important questions that researchers, policymakers, and the market need to explore further:

- The development of better systems to quantitatively measure the cost of data-related harms to individuals and society. As discussed earlier, the risks of data are both tangible and intangible, and to appropriately protect individuals, policymakers would likely benefit from a greater understanding of how data breaches and data misuse impact lives.
- Whether data governance frameworks can be more effectively designed through a broad approach, like GDPR, or through a sector-based approach. In either case, work is required to either narrow broad frameworks to meet sector-specific needs or to adapt sector-specific structures to other parts of the economy.
- The use of principles-based regulation versus prescriptive regulation. Principles can give companies the confidence to innovate and go beyond suggested implementation in order to provide more secure and functional products. Principles-based regulation can also be challenging because it requires more intensive and qualitative oversight to ensure compliance, and that can be variable depending on the regulators. Prescriptive regulation can create consistent experiences and protection for individuals and provide clarity for business, but it is essential that those guidelines are constantly reviewed and updated to ensure they don't quickly fall behind technologically.
- Finally, there needs to be effective but realistic regulatory models to implement a comprehensive data protection and data rights regime. It is important to delineate the responsibility for oversight among regulators or consider new entities that can take a holistic approach without coming into tension with existing mandates. Additionally, it is important to consider whether compliance will be incentivized through enforcement actions alone, ongoing supervision, or some combination. Ongoing supervision requires significant resources, especially given the breadth

of digital companies and activities. Enforcement can be efficient, but it also doesn't address issues and harms until they have already become significant. There likely is a middle ground where there can be risk-based assessments of companies that can trigger ongoing reviews[54] and certain designations for larger companies that would have a larger impact should something go wrong.[55]

54 "Data Protection Impact Assessments," United Kingdom Information Commissioner's Office. https://ico.org.uk/for-organisations/guide-to-data-protection/guide-to-the-general-data-protection-regulation-gdpr/accountability-and-governance/data-protection-impact-assessments/.

55 Daniel Liberto, "Systemically Important Financial Institution (SIFI)," *Investopedia* (Nov. 2019). https://www.investopedia.com/terms/s/systemically-important-financial-institution-sifi.asp.

3

Customer Protection and the Liability Conundrum in an Open Finance Ecosystem

Steven Boms and *Sam Taussig***,****

1. Introduction

Customers are protected from financial harm for which they are not responsible. This simple tenet of the US financial system, matured over the last century, enacted through both statute and regulation, and bolstered by decades of customer expectation and assumption, remains steadfast and true. Institutions bear risk, not customers. To build a more innovative financial system that fosters greater financial access and inclusion, increases competition, lowers prices, and puts the customer at the center of the ecosystem—an open finance ecosystem—policymakers must modernize the implementation of the various rules that dictate liability, and key underpinnings to adjudicate liability, in the US financial system.

Historically, the notion of institutions bearing risk for their customers has been straightforward. For example: a bank customer who notices a fraudulent withdrawal from their account by a nefarious actor is generally entitled to a refund under the implementing regulations emanating under the Electronic Funds Transfer Act (EFTA) of 1978. A customer of a failed bank may rest assured that the Federal Deposit Insurance Corporation (FDIC) insures up to $250,000 in deposits per depositor, per insured bank, per account category. Credit union customers similarly are protected by the National Credit Union Administration. The holder of a brokerage account is entitled to financial restitution of up to $500,000 from the Securities Investor Protection Corporation in the event their brokerage house fails. The sum of the various financial institution customer protections enacted into law have, over decades, facilitated an assumption on the part of many market stakeholders—regulators, customers, and traditional financial institutions themselves—that it is ultimately the responsibility of a customer's financial institution to protect them from financial harm.

While this paradigm may have historically served US financial customers well, it has emerged as an unintended obstacle to the realization of an "open banking environment"

---

* Steven Boms is the President of Allon Advocacy, LLC, a fintech and financial services consulting firm, and Executive Director of the Financial Data and Technology Association of North America.

** Sam Taussig is the former Head of Global Policy and Special Product Development at Kabbage Inc., an online small business cash-flow management platform company.

*** Additional thoughts from the authors are available in Financial Data and Technology Association (FDATA) North America's comments to the US Consumer Financial Protection Bureau in response to its Advanced Notice of Proposed Rulemaking regarding consumer access to financial records, or Section 1033 of the Dodd-Frank Wall Street Reform and Consumer Protection Act. https://fdata.global/blog/2021/02/03/fdata-north-america-responds-to-us-cfpb-anpr-on-consumer-access-to-financial-records/.

Steven Boms and Sam Taussig, *Customer Protection and the Liability Conundrum in an Open Finance Ecosystem* In: *Open Banking.* Edited by: Linda Jeng, Oxford University Press. © Oxford University Press 2022. DOI: 10.1093/oso/9780197582879.003.0004

or the "open finance ecosystem" in the United States under which consumers and small businesses (customers) may freely choose to conduct their financial business with financial institutions or financial technology (fintech) firms acting as partners to institutions or standalone traditional financial institutions themselves. Indeed, the concept of a shared liability framework, along with a legal right to one's own data, unified technology standard, and the ability to "trace" data as it is permissioned throughout an open finance regime, represents a pillar of a true, innovative customer-directed finance framework that facilitates complete customer choice of service provider. In the absence of any of these building blocks, however, today, financial institutions, operating in an environment in which they hold liability to their customers for financial losses related to fraud, are understandably reticent to welcome a true open finance framework under which their customers may permission access to the data their financial institution holds about them to any affiliate institution, business partnership, or truly independent third-party provider or competitor. To the extent that a third-party provider fails or experiences a data breach, the financial institution—and not the third-party provider—is, in the eyes of regulators and customers, the likeliest source of financial restitution.

Compounding this now outdated regulatory and market assumption is the reality that, as data has become more ubiquitous in powering financial tools delivered by incumbents and new entrants alike, its value is highly variable and largely dependent on the circumstances of the individual to which it belongs. For example: when a large credit bureau experienced a data breach in 2017, it is estimated that private records were exposed for as many as 147.9 million Americans, in addition to millions of Brits and thousands of Canadians.[1] The financial harm of this event understandably varied for each impacted individual and is difficult to quantify in sum. For example: an individual applying for a mortgage who discovers that multiple credit accounts had been opened fraudulently using their personal data and, accordingly, no longer qualifies for a prime interest rate arguably derived a larger financial loss (harm) from the data breach than did a retiree with no debt and no intention of applying for additional credit. Moreover, given the persistent value of the data exposed, continued fraudulent usage of the exposed data could facilitate fraud for years after the breach, creating significant difficulty in quantifying the scope of potential customer damages and, in turn, the monetary responsibility of the entity that experienced the data breach.

Transitioning the US financial marketplace to a more innovative, technology-enabled environment will require a modernization of existing customer protection frameworks and a concerted effort toward addressing these important, but difficult, customer protection principles under an open finance ecosystem. Such an open finance ecosystem provides customers a level of control and financial intelligence unmatched by a single or concentrated point of financial services where users[2] may freely conduct their financial business across firms[3] acting as partners across the networks of products and services.

---

[1] "Equifax to Pay $575 Million as Part of Settlement with FTC, CFPB, and States Related to 2017 Data Breach," *Federal Trade Commission*, (July 19, 2019). https://www.ftc.gov/news-events/press-releases/2019/07/equifax-pay-575-million-part-settlement-ftc-cfpb-states-related.

[2] Used interchangeably in various texts as financial service provider's "customers," "consumers" in regulation, and also to include "small business owners and operators."

[3] Used here in this chapter to mean "traditional deposit bearing financial institutions," "banks," "credit unions," "FinTech platforms and providers," "neo-banks and challenger banks," "registered trading and brokerage platforms," financial "service providers," and "apps."

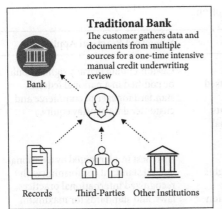

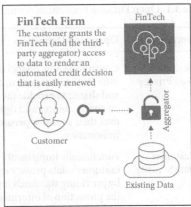

Figure 3.1 Comparing a fintech and a bank underwriting experience where user-permissioned aggregated financial data is used to render a continual underwriting decision without the need for the customer to gather disparate documents and records from multiple sources.

For example, a commercial financing fintech provider may offer a prospective small business customer a competitive financing offer in a single streamlined online experience that takes minutes compared to the days that it may take the same customer to receive an offer from a traditional bank to which they have a banking relationship. The fintech provider uses a variety of relevant user-permissions commercial data channels to aggregate business information, generate a proprietary cash-flow-based credit score, and create a dynamic offer using real-time data directly from the business compared to passive and aged commercial credit bureau scores or other similar proprietary bank scores (Figure 3.1 offers a basic comparison to a traditional financial institution process). The customer is afforded invaluable time and ease with a new ability to shop for products and offers that may be more or equally competitive to traditional financial institutions offering similarly scored financial products.[4]

For more on alternative data, Matthew Adam Bruckner explores consumer protection issues in alternative data in Chapter 4.

The open finance ecosystem (and overall ability to assign liability acutely examined in this chapter) rests on critically related but distinctly separate assumptions (detailed in Table 3.1) that users are fundamentally protected across well-defined[5] supporting consumer protection regimes: privacy, data security,[6] basic interoperability technology

---

[4] The FinRegLab found that "the predictiveness of the cash-flow scores and attributes [for alternative cash-flow-based fintech models] was generally at least as strong as the traditional credit scores and credit bureau attributes studied." "Six-Lender Study Finds Cash-Flow Data Useful for Extending Credit to Consumers and Small Businesses," *FinRegLab*, Washington, DC, (2019). https://finreglab.org/press-release-cash-flow-empiri cal-research/.

[5] The United States does not recognize clear and concise operating definitions for security and data protections like other regimes, such as the General Data Protection Regulation in the European Union. See Chapter 2 by Kaitlin Asrow for a description of the US data protection regime.

[6] Overall, the authors subscribe to the Candace Ranglin/Sam Taussig "Customer Data Triangle" developed in 2018 at Kabbage, Inc., for US federal privacy legislation reform discussions where: *Data Privacy* is concerned with establishing practices and policies around how information is collected, stored, used, shared, and retained in order to protect such sensitive personal information. Privacy affords individuals control over their information, such as opting out of marketing use cases. Privacy also means the right to be left alone or

Table 3.1 Open Finance Ecosystem Assumptions

Assumption	Operating Definition	Suggested Practical Application
1. Customer Data Privacy	Controlling how financial information is collected, used, and shared to provide the customer choices and rights over their sensitive personal information.	Customer data privacy rights should be codified in a national federal standard for ease of commerce and customer data privacy equity.
2. Customer Data Security	Functionally implements customer's data privacy rights by providing standards for the protection of information and information systems, through use, access, disclosure, disruption, alteration, loss, or destruction controls to provide confidentiality, integrity, and data availability.	Also best implemented by a national federal standard conforming with recognized international practices, laws, and standards for maximum interoperability.
3. Cybersecurity Standard	Implements customer security to protect information against threats and attacks.	Best implemented as an agile and evolving industry-led set of practices that supports (legally mandated) customer data privacy and security standards.
4. Interoperable Technology Standard for Secure and Permissioned Customer Data-Sharing	Creates a common, interoperable, and royalty-free standard for the secure access, authentication, and sharing of user-permissioned financial data by means of a recognized and transparent API.	Best executed at an international level with equal input from financial institutions, financial data aggregators, fintechs, payment networks, and other relevant permissioned parties.[a]
5. Liability Framework	In the event of a breach of customer data privacy, security, cybersecurity, or data leakage from an API, liability determines who and to what extent a party or parties to the transaction or exchange provides customers restitution.	The liability framework relies substantially on assumptions 1–4 and must also consider concepts such as customer harm, scope of the offense, traceability (included as a technology standard or otherwise), financial disclosures, electronic transaction rules and obligations, automated clearing house (ACH), card and payment network rules, credit reporting obligations, and provider's size and solvency.

[a] One example is the Financial Data Exchange (FDX), which exists as an independent subsidiary under the umbrella of the Financial Services Information Sharing and Analysis Center (FS-ISAC).

forgotten. *Data Security* is the means by which privacy is implemented. The protection of sensitive personal information and information systems, through controls, from unauthorized use, access, disclosure, disruption, alteration, loss, or destruction in order to provide confidentiality, integrity, and availability. *Cybersecurity* as a practice is concerned with implementing security to protect information against cyber threats or attacks (unauthorized access).

standards for data-sharing, and cybersecurity. For more reading on these topics, see Chapter 2 on data privacy and data protection rights, Chapter 5 on technology access standards, and Chapter 6 on interoperability.

Taken together, policymakers can realize a more inclusive market for customers and institutions alike, but not without targeted investment in understanding the market, updating foundational regulations, and experimenting with new methodologies and technologies to solve complex derivative policy issues. For example, most security experts will agree common authenticating customer information is likely compromised but vigilant surveillance of financial account activity and good cyber hygiene are key to catching and preventing nefarious activities. Independent third-party applications and solutions, decentralized finance (DeFi) products, and regulatory technologies (regtech) that put customers in control of their information increase the likelihood that systems on a uniform technology standard will identify, prevent, and derisk financial harm before an event. Today, prudential regulators do not formally recognize many of these opportunities and solutions.

While, fortunately, policymakers and market participants in the United States have the benefit of observing how other jurisdictions address this important issue, which is not unique to the US financial system, as they contemplate a maturation into an open finance ecosystem, updating existing statutory and regulatory expectations in addition to underlying open finance ecosystem assumptions with regard to liability in the US financial services framework is a daunting but necessary task.

2. The US Financial Statutory and Regulatory Customer Liability Regimes Today

A litany of laws, regulations, and regulatory expectations make clear that financial institutions are, under the current market structure, responsible for protecting their customers from financial loss as a result of fraud. The Gramm-Leach-Bliley Act (GLBA) represents the foundational statute making clear financial institutions' responsibility regarding customer data protection. The act provides information security requirements for financial institutions and prescribes customer-facing disclosures regarding the usage and safekeeping of customer data. While GLBA permits financial institutions to share nonpublic personal information with third-parties at the direction of the consumer necessary to affect a transaction requested or authorized by a consumer,[7] it also requires financial institutions to empower their customers to opt out prior to doing so.[8] However, GLBA has not represented a significant blocker to customer-directed data-sharing, largely due to proactive interagency guidance promulgated as early as 2001. The guidelines provide "[w]hen a customer gives consent to a third party to access or use that customer's information, such as by providing the third party with an account number, PIN, or password, the guidelines do not require the financial institution to prevent such access or monitor the use or redisclosure of the customer's information by

---

[7] *Id.* § 6802(e).
[8] 15 U.S.C. § 6802(a). For more reading on GLBA, see Chapter 2 by Kaitlin Asrow.

the third party."[9] As growing numbers of large financial institutions transition from enabling customer data access through the use of account number, PIN, or password to application programming interfaces (APIs), however, regulatory guidance regarding financial institution responsibilities becomes more onerous.

Arguably the most significant legal obstacle to the deployment of an open finance ecosystem in the United States is the EFTA. The EFTA and its implementing Regulation E limit customers' liability for fraudulent electronic withdrawals from their account "initiated by a person other than the consumer without actual authority to initiate the transfer."[10] Under Regulation E, generally, so long as the customer informs their financial institution of an unauthorized transaction in a timely manner, their total potential liability is limited to $50, with some exceptions, with their financial institution holding responsibility for restituting to the customer the remainder of the financial loss.[11]

The EFTA was hastily enacted in 1978, nine years after the first ATM machine was installed in the United States and made available to the public on Long Island in New York. Accordingly, much of the act's focus is on customer protections in the event of fraudulent transactions conducted using lost or stolen debit cards. The authors, primarily concerned with centralizing disparate state laws and industry-driven consumer protection standards for lost or stolen debit cards, could not possibly have imagined a US financial services system with massive customer-permissioned transfers of data to and from financial institutions and third-party service providers alike.

A decade of consumer protection discourse on the role of federal legislation in the payments space, moral hazard debates, and technology education in Washington, DC, preceded the EFTA's passage with just over one-third of states at the time having enacted some form of their own protections for electronic fund transactions. The very definition of an electronic transfer was elusive in the late seventies. The *Ohio State Law Journal* entry[12] from 1979 quickly makes the caveat that "[a]ny attempt to define the elements of an electronic fund transfer quickly leads one to the realization that the phrase encompasses an almost infinite variety of modern payment services" but only defined six primary transaction types: "the ATM, the point-of-sale ('POS') system (now also the mobile point-of-sale system—mPOS), the 'electronic check guarantee system' (now known as a debit card), ACH, dial entry telephone banking, and the wire transfer." Though Congress and the *Ohio State Law Journal* authors recognized the value and some inherent risk of automated telephone banking, they did not consider a purse or pants pocket–born, centralized, omni-connected personal computer capable of becoming an access device, portfolio management strategy machine, complex calculator, virtual card wallet, and of course, a live-connection access device initiating nearly limitless ACH payment instructions.

The EFTA's stated congressional intent is "to provide a basic framework establishing the rights, liabilities, and responsibilities of participants in electronic fund transfer

[9] Interagency Guidelines Establishing Standards for Safeguarding Customer Information and Rescission of Year 2000 Standards for Safety and Soundness, 2001, 66 Fed. Reg. 8616, 8620.

[10] 12 C.F.R. § 1005.2(m).

[11] "FDIC Law, Regulations, Related Acts," *Federal Deposit Insurance Corporation* (2016). https://www.fdic.gov/regulations/laws/rules/6500-580.html.

[12] Roland E. Brandel and Eustace A. Olliff III, "The Electronic Fund Transfer Act: A Primer," *Ohio State Law Journal* 40(3) (1979) (Nov. 3, 1979). https://kb.osu.edu/bitstream/handle/1811/65105/OSLJ_V40N3_0531.pdf.

systems."[13] The costs to financial institutions for protecting their customers from fraudulent transactions under Regulation E are substantial. In 2018, US financial institutions reported a total of $9.47 billion of fraud-related losses from their credit and debit card customers.[14] But this figure alone does not represent the totality of the significant expense financial institutions commit to making their customers whole in the event of fraud. In its "True Cost of Fraud" study, LexisNexis determined that, for every dollar of fraud loss, US financial institutions in 2019 incurred $3.25 in costs, which includes the direct loss associated with a fraudulent transaction in addition to the legal, investigatory, and compliance costs related to institutions' responsibilities under Regulation E.[15] This data therefore indicates that US financial institutions' actual financial obligations under Regulation E are currently closer to approximately $30 billion annually for their credit and debit card businesses. As growing numbers of US consumers and small businesses turn to third-party financial tools to assist them in managing their financial well-being, and as digital criminal activity becomes more sophisticated, one may logically assume that absent modernization of the EFTA or Regulation E, these costs will continue to rise in the years ahead.

Beyond the substantial financial cost of Regulation E, there exists significant complexity and ambiguity in applying the requirements of both the rule and its underlying statute to a financial ecosystem that looks quite different from the one that existed when the EFTA was first enacted in 1978. Though the Consumer Financial Protection Bureau in 2018 extended to digital wallets many of the protections afforded to consumers under Regulation E,[16] the rule makes clear that when customers furnish "access devices" (which, in 1978, primarily referred to debit cards; digital credit card machines would not be invented for another year[17]) to another party, such transactions shall be considered authorized, and the financial institution therefore is typically no longer responsible for financial restitution. This "access devices" language, now approaching its fiftieth anniversary, today is interpreted to apply to customers providing authorization to a third-party to access data held by their financial institutions. Financial institutions argue that adhering to this standard in the current context and informing a customer that they are not entitled under Regulation E to restitution from the institution in the event of fraud as a third-party provider presents risk of a negative customer experience. Yet, the EFTA, like many of its regulatory body cousins like the Truth in Lending Act and the Fair Credit Reporting Act (FCRA), relies on strong customer disclosures intended to adapt to the specific transaction situation[18] but backed by robust and specific steps for financial institutions to follow to resolve a dispute or error. To avoid the costly prescribed steps and overhead of dispute resolution, some financial institutions

---

[13] EFT Act, § 902, 15 U.S.C. § 1963.

[14] "Card Fraud Losses Reach $27.85 Billion," *Nilson Report* (Nov. 2019). https://nilsonreport.com/ment ion/407/1link.

[15] LexisNexis Risk Solution, "2019 True Cost of Fraud Study." (Nov. 2019).

[16] Rules Concerning Prepaid Accounts Under the Electronic Fund Transfer Act (Regulation E) and the Truth in Lending Act (Regulation Z).

[17] Emily Sorensen, "The Detailed History of Credit Card Machines," *Mobile Transaction* (July 26, 2019). https://www.mobiletransaction.org/history-of-credit-card-machines/.

[18] EFTA Title VI—Electronic Fund Transfers, SS 904, Regulations allows for modifications to disclosure requirements and procedures: "In prescribing such regulations, the Board shall: (1) consult with the other agencies. . . . and allow for the continuing evolution of electronic banking services and the technology utilized in such services."

will heavily discourage their customers from using third-party tools[19] or worse, restrict or thwart their customers' ability to utilize some third-party tools,[20] arguing that in so doing they are protecting their customers from potential financial harm and, in so doing, complying with Regulation E.

On the other hand, the EFTA (Section 904) not only allows for the "continuing evolution of electronic banking services and the technology utilized in such services" but mandates that regulators consider "the effects upon competition in the provision of electronic banking services among large and small financial institutions and the availability of such services to different classes of consumers, particularly low-income consumers." This includes the use of model clauses indented for use by the primary institution and third-parties where regulators "by regulation assure that the disclosures, protections, responsibilities, and remedies created by this title are made applicable to such persons and services."[21]

Congress clearly felt that the system needed modernization. Though the Dodd-Frank Wall Street Reform and Consumer Protection Act of 2010 (Dodd-Frank) generally transferred rulemaking authority under the EFTA from the Federal Reserve to the Consumer Financial Protection Bureau (CFPB, or the Bureau), Congress also added Section 1033 of Dodd-Frank, which provides that financial institutions shall "make available to a consumer, upon request, information in the control or possession of the [institution] concerning the consumer financial product or service that the consumer obtained from such [institution], including information relating to any transaction, series of transactions, or to the account including costs, charges and usage data. The information shall be made available in an electronic form usable by consumers."[22] Section 1033 is not an anomaly and has parallels in other parts of the financial services ecosystem. Consumers have the right to access aspects of their credit information in consumer reporting agency files under the FCRA[23] and access disclosures on fees, transactions, and use of personal data.[24] The Securities and Exchange Commission (SEC) asks Form N-1A[25] applicants to prepare an "Interactive Data File"[26] for the

[19] S. 910: EFTA provides for a liability safe harbor if the institution disclosures the possibility of "technical malfunctions" or errors "which was known to the consumer at the time he attempted to initiate an electronic fund transfer or, in the case of preauthorized transfer, at the time such transfer should have occurred" that can be extrapolated to mean that a customer transacting outside of the core "approved" system is liable for any loss or harm.

[20] K. Rooney, "PNC's Fight with Venmo Highlights Bigger Issue over Who Owns Your Banking Data," *CNBC* (Dec. 16, 2019). https://www.cnbc.com/2019/12/16/venmo-and-pncs-fight-over-sharing-consumer-financial-data.html.

[21] Electronic Fund Transfer Act (EFTA) (15 U.S.C. 1693 et seq.) of 1978.

[22] 12 U.S.C. § 5533(a).

[23] Fair Credit Reporting Act, 15 U.S.C. 1681g(a). Fair Credit Reporting Act, 15 U.S.C. 1681g(a).

[24] Regulation Z, 12 CFR 1026.5(b)(2) and 1026.7(b) (implementing the Truth in Lending Act with respect to periodic statements for credit cards); Regulation E, 12 CFR 1005.9(b) (implementing the Electronic Fund Transfer Act with respect to periodic statements for traditional bank accounts and other consumer asset accounts); Regulation DD, 12 CFR 1030.6(a)(3) (implementing the Truth in Saving Act with respect to periodic statements for deposit accounts held at depository institutions); Gramm-Leach Bliley Act, 15 U.S.C. 6803, and its implementing regulations.

[25] Form N-1A is used to file for the creation of open-end management companies; both open-end mutual funds and open-end exchange-traded funds.

[26] See General Instruction C.(3).g of Form N-1A under the Securities Act and Investment Company Act (requiring electronic machine-readable information about mutual funds as defined in 17 CFR § 232.11—Definitions, and as required by Rule 406 of Regulation S-T (17 CFR 232.406), and in the manner provided by the EDGAR Filer Manual.

Commission and for it to be publicly available on the Fund's website using Inline XBRL to provide a benefit to data users for "an easier way to view, access, and explore the contextual information of the underlying data."[27,28] The SEC has required electronic filing on the Electronic Data Gathering, Analysis, and Retrieval (EDGAR) system since 1993 with significant updates to what must be encoded as machine readable through 2003, 2007, and 2009.

A report issued by the Department of the Treasury in 2018 determined that the definition of "consumer" under Dodd-Frank Section 1033, consistent with the definition of the term throughout the statute, "is best interpreted to cover circumstances in which consumers affirmatively authorize, with adequate disclosure, third parties such as data aggregators and consumer FinTech application providers to access their financial account and transaction data from financial services companies."[29] Accordingly, significant tension, partially due to a lack of periodic updates and rulemakings after 1978, exists between the regulatory requirements prescribed under the EFTA and the requirements of the Dodd-Frank Act with regard to customer-permissioned data access.

In addition to the EFTA and its implementing Regulation E, regulatory guidance has made clear over the last twenty years that financial institutions are required to exert third-party service provider oversight obligations over parties that connect to or access customer data they hold. While the Office of the Comptroller of the Currency (OCC) first published guidance regarding customer-permissioned data aggregation in February 2001, it released as recently as March 2020 additional guidance on third-party oversight that specifically addresses data aggregators and sets forth expectations regarding enhanced governance of aggregators' activities.[30] Generally, the guidance seeks to make clear supervised banks' responsibilities to ensure that aggregators that access bank-held data are subject, in many cases, to the OCC's third-party relationship risk management program. Consistent with the perspective US financial regulatory agencies have taken over the last century, the implication of the OCC's guidance has been to provide to financial institutions—the holders of their customer's data—significantly more control over instances in which their customers may or may not grant permission to third-parties to access their data. No financial technology tool can provide its service in the absence of access to data held by a customer's financial institution. Although the CFPB was granted sole statutory authority under Dodd-Frank in 2010 to assure financial institution customers can permission data access to third-party providers,[31] ownership of third-party relationship risk management requirements by

[27] "Inline XBRL," US Securities and Exchange Commission (2020). https://www.sec.gov/structureddata/osd-inline-xbrl.html.

[28] The SEC continues to describe the benefit of machine readable data: "For example, users can hover over values in the filing to find more information about the data, such as citations and hyperlinks to the relevant accounting guidance, narrative definitions for the values, and reporting period information associated with each value."

[29] US Department of the Treasury, "A Financial System that Creates Economic Opportunities: Nonbank Financials, Fintech and Innovation" (July 2018).

[30] See John C. Lyons, Jr., "Third-Party Relationships: Risk Management Guidance," Office of the Comptroller of the Currency, 2013, OCC Bulletin 2013-29. https://www.occ.gov/news-issuances/bulletins/2013/bulletin-2013-29.html; *supra* note 28.

[31] In July 2020, the CFPB announced its intention to issue an Advance Notice of Proposed Rulemaking utilizing the authority vested in it under the Dodd-Frank Act to promulgate a rule that would provide bank customers with this ability.

the prudential regulators makes for a significantly more fractured jurisdictional land-scape in practice. That said, while arrangements between aggregators and financial institutions can vary in certain circumstances, in the case of customer-directed access to financial information, the relationship is generally at the low end of third-party risk for the institution. The OCC's March 2020 guidance, for example, recognizes a sliding scale when banks deal with aggregators accessing consumer-permissioned data. It notes that, "[i]n many cases, banks may not receive a direct service or benefit from these arrangements. In these cases, the level of risk for banks is typically lower than with more traditional business arrangements."[32] In contrast, obligations are higher when the bank engages a third-party in a contract to perform some bank function—for example, to use data aggregators to obtain data from other sources to help offer services to their existing customers.

There's some debate that customer-directed data-sharing may be restricted, at least in part for credit decisions, by the FCRA. The FCRA generally imposes obligations on "consumer reporting agencies" (CRAs) that provide defined "consumer reports" for certain purposes. It also imposes obligations on recipients of those consumer reports and furnishers of information to CRAs. One "permissible purpose" covered by the FCRA is for use in connection with a credit transaction.[33] However, upon closer ex-amination, data aggregators themselves are not functioning as "consumer reporting agencies." Section 603(f) of the FCRA provides, in part, that a "consumer reporting agency" is "any person which . . . regularly engages in whole or in part in the prac-tice of assembling or evaluating consumer credit information or other information on consumers for the purpose of furnishing consumer reports to third parties."[34] The FTC has released informal guidance that entities that perform "conduit functions" do not fall within this definition. In particular, the guidance notes that "[a]n entity that performs only mechanical tasks in connection with transmitting consumer informa-tion is not a CRA because it does not assemble or evaluate information," and "a business that delivers records, without knowing their content or retaining any information from them is not acting as a CRA" even if the recipient uses the information for a permissible purpose under the statute.[35] Financial institutions are also not "furnishers" of infor-mation under the FCRA, even if aggregators were deemed to be CRAs. In the case of permissioned consumer data access, the consumer is effectively providing the infor-mation, by authorizing its release directly from the financial institution in the digital equivalent of delivering a shoebox full of receipts and bank statements to, say, their ac-countant. Instead, the statute requires some affirmative act by an entity to "furnish" in-formation to qualify as a furnisher. (For more reading on the FCRA, see Chapter 4, by Matthew Adam Bruckner.)

[32] Lyons Jr., *supra* note 34.
[33] 15 U.S.C. § 1681 et seq.
[34] *Id.* § 1681a(f),
[35] FTC, "40 Years of Experience with the Fair Credit Reporting Act," at 29 (July 2011). https://www.ftc.gov/sites/default/files/documents/reports/40-years-experience-fair-credit-reporting-act-ftc-staff-report-summ ary-interpretations/110720fcrareport.pdf.

3. Market Attempts to Address Liability are Inadequate

In an effort to create a customer data-sharing methodology that does not offend regulators or upset the current (and confusing) liability and data-sharing dynamic, several large financial institutions have executed and continue to negotiate bilateral data access agreements with financial data aggregators—the intermediaries between financial institutions and third-party financial tools that facilitate the flow of permissioned financial data become affiliated business engagements of the financial institution. These agreements include, among many other provisions, nondisclosure indemnification and liability clauses that make clear to contracting parties, but not necessarily the regulators, that the counterparties' responsibilities in the event of financial harm that befalls end customers due to a data breach. While, in the absence of a set of legally binding open finance standards or clauses,[36] these contractual terms may be the only tool available to market stakeholders to address such a critical issue, they are an imperfect resolution.

First, the breadth of the US financial system makes impossible the idea that such contractual terms will be implemented uniformly across the various market participants. As of the end of March 2020, the FDIC reported more than 5,100 active insured financial institutions in the US market.[37] The National Credit Union Administration reported a similar number of federal insured credit unions during the same period,[38] which would mean that, under a framework in which customer liability is determined solely under bilateral contractual terms, more than 10,000 depository institutions would each be responsible for executing data access agreements with each financial data aggregation firm or direct data consuming fintech application in the marketplace, to say nothing of the thousands of additional nondepository financial institutions in the United States that rely on aggregated data for various product functions. Such an outcome would surely provide for starkly different liability and indemnification clauses from one agreement to another, leading to an environment under which end customers have varying levels of protection based on the terms of a bilateral agreement their financial institution executed to which they were not party to. A tenet of a true open finance system is that customers receive uniform protections regardless of which financial providers they choose.

Second, agreements negotiated and executed between financial institutions and data aggregation firms excludes the third-party providers with which the customer directly interacts, from the negotiations or the agreements themselves. The third-party providers, however, would be required to meet significant obligations under the data access agreements that their aggregation platforms execute with financial institutions.[39]

---

[36] Policymakers could look to standard contractual clauses (SCC) for secure data transfers between EU and non-EU countries for parallels that could be applied to an open finance ecosystem. The European Commission created safe harbor SCCs to be completed by the data importer and data exporter that set out obligations for both parties and define the data subject's rights in a way that covers the specific business use case. The SCC model could be adapted so US regulators prescribe basic safe harbors to cover the "Customer Data Triangle (see chapter introduction) assumptions and bilateral liability without inherently restricting the data or business use cases.

[37] "FDIC Statistics at a Glance." https://www.fdic.gov/bank/statistical/stats/2020mar/industry.pdf.

[38] "Summary of Federally Insured Credit Union Call Report Data: 2020 Q1." https://www.ncua.gov/files/publications/analysis/quarterly-data-summary-2020-Q1.pdf.

[39] For example: a "model data access agreement" released in November 2019 by The Clearing House, a consortium of the largest financial institutions in the United States, includes up to twenty separate enforceable

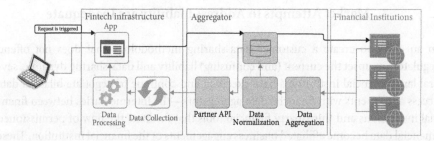

Figure 3.2 Sample technical diagram of a fintech application interacting with an aggregator to import bank information for metric analysis. In this case, to qualify for a product or service. Note: Partner API refers to the manner in which the data recipient (the fintech) receives the data.

These third-parties, which, in some cases, may grant access to customer data, with their permission, to additional parties, represent the customer-facing platforms and services that enable customers to access financial tools and products in an open finance framework (Figures 3.2 and 3.3 demonstrate how aggregations platforms interact with industry actors on behalf of end users/ customers) and would, in all likelihood, be responsible for making restitution to their customers in the event their platforms enabled or facilitated erroneous account withdrawals.

That these critical stakeholders are not party to data access agreements represents a significant and impactful shortfall of the status quo. Moreover, the EFTA could not have envisioned in 1978 a financial system in which an "access device" potentially grants, with the customer's permission, access to their financial institution–held data to numerous additional service providers and has not sufficiently evolved since to recognize this new world order and customer demand. Indeed, US financial institution customers would not themselves even have access to their own financial data electronically for another twenty years, when online banking portals begin to be deployed in the late 1990s.

Finally, even in the absence of the other critically important decencies of a system that relies on bilateral data access agreements to dictate liability in an open finance framework, the reality exists that, even with an executed agreement that prescribes where a financial institution's financial responsibility to its customer ends in the context of a data breach at a third-party provider, a fundamental, simple truth presents a very real risk of undermining the terms of any indemnification and liability provisions contained such contracts: *it remains impossible to quantify the maximum potential consumer losses associated with a significant data breach.* Even within a bilateral agreement, it remains insurmountably difficult to determine liability when there is no standard of data traceability for regulators or market participants on which to rely, particularly when harm and injury can occur removed from the original data breach, leakage, or misuse event.

The concept of traceability to reconstruct how users authorize data and how parties use and access data after consent is broad and nascent. Traceability methodologies can encompass, for example, data registers, like those initially embraced under the

---

clauses with which third-party providers would be required to comply as a prerequisite to accessing customer-permissioned data, though the third-party itself would not be party to the contract.

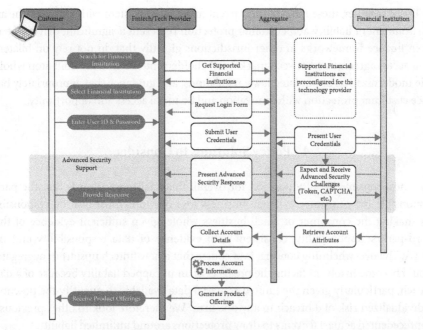

Figure 3.3 Sample technical diagram of how a fintech, an aggregator, and a bank verify customer credentials for accessing read-only, user-permissioned account data.

United Kingdom's Open Banking regime by the United Kingdom's Open Banking Implementation Entity. Encoded headers, and even the blockchain, are among many other tools also available to trace the data path. The goal of such functionality is to assign fault more effectively so regulators or courts may assign liability for a data event like a breach. While no comprehensive solution to this intractable dilemma has been widely introduced in any market, many other jurisdictions that enjoy more open finance regimes have implemented incremental traceability frameworks that provide meaningfully more ability for regulators, customers, financial institutions, aggregators, and fintechs to monitor the permissioned flows of data throughout the ecosystem. The absence of any federated traceability framework in the US data access regime also makes it nearly impossible for market participants to discern whether the customer themselves enabled, deliberately or inadvertently, a fraudulent transaction. Reg E makes clear that in such cases the customer, not the financial institution, is responsible for bearing the burden of any financial loss.

In the United States, financial institutions, regulatory agencies, and customers have little or no ability to assess whether third-parties in the ecosystem have the financial capacity to abide by the terms included in agreement. Accordingly, bilateral data access agreements may best be viewed in this regard as providing some transfer of liability from financial institutions to third-party technology providers but should not be contemplated as a long-term equitable or sustainable solution in a competitive and innovative financial ecosystem as the EFTA does not provide any clear justification for overriding customer preferences or limitations on otherwise permissible electronic transfers and data-sharing.

Taken together, these flaws of the current financial ecosystem with regard to the apportionment of liability and customer protection represent a significant driver of true open finance frameworks in other jurisdictions globally that do not rely on bilateral data access agreements between market stakeholders, but instead are built atop wholesale modernization of outdated laws, regulations, and guidance that appropriately balance customer protection with innovation and financial access and opportunity.

4. Policy Solutions to Consider

The most sensible liability position for overall financial innovation is that the party responsible for consumer or small business loss of funds must also be responsible for making the consumer or small business whole, given sufficient evidence of that third-party's responsibility, consistent with evidence of data responsibility and the EFTA. The overwhelming concern is of course that a new fintech upstart or aggregator would become insolvent facing the prospect of an uncapped liability because of a data breach, particularly given the limited actuarial data available to quantify the potential individualized risk of a breach to any one firm. We therefore look to other previously unprecedented actuarial events to draw protections around unlimited liability.

One such example comes from terrorism risk insurance. In many ways security events in the physical world provide great insight into preparing for security events in the virtual world. One must constantly evaluate opportunity, threat vectors, available and developing means, understand motivations and capabilities of suspected and potential adversaries, and continually assess and push the collective imagination to discover and prevent avenues of harm. Also, like events in the physical world, cyber and virtual-based vectors have the potential to be perpetrated by state actors or nonstate actors beyond the reach of traditional law enforcement. Similarly, yet unfortunately, these virtual vectors contain "unknown unknown" means, motives, and opportunities and corresponding harm and costs only seen in hindsight followed by unforeseen lingering impacts of events on people, communities, infrastructure, markets, and society at large with associated negative externalities, irrational responses, and market failures. Recent large credit bureau data breaches exposed the nascent liability framework and immature market for data protection insurance due to an inability to fully price risk much like insurance markets responded after the 9/11 attacks. Fortunately, we can look at how the federal government responded to bolster firms' ability to price risk, prevent future attacks, and protect their productive assets and people.

Prior to the September 11, 2001, terrorist attacks, coverage for losses from such attacks was included in general business and business interruption insurance policies without additional costs or coverage to the policyholders as policyholders and issuers had only accounted for overall minimal physical damage and personal harm based on prior terrorist activities. Unsurprisingly, in the wake of 9/11, such coverage was sparely offered or completely unavailable for "soft target" firms and properties.

Congress authored the Terrorism Risk Insurance Act of 2002 (TRIA), which initially created a Terrorism Insurance Program for three years, which at the time, Congress believed would pacify the market's concerns about another large-scale terrorism event. TRIA has subsequently expanded as a continuing program administered by the US

Treasury.[40] The core tenets of TRIA, under which the government provides a liquid re-insurance pool that shares the losses on commercial property and casualty insurance above certain catastrophic loss threshold and requires insurers to make coverage but does not require policyholders to purchase the coverage, can be considered as a structural example for open finance liability insurance. Unlike TRIA, though, the offending party may be available to bring claims against.

As with TRIA, under a proposed *data-sharing liability policy* (DSLP), in general terms, if a covered data event occurs, the issuer initially covers the entire amount for relatively small aggregate losses under a maximum statutory dollar threshold, but unlike TRIA, issuers and the government can approach the liable or offending party for damages if regulators or a court can determine said party is in fact willfully or legally at fault. For a medium-sized loss, the government initiates a rapid review to assist insurers that initially make a consumer whole but gradually recoups losses from liable parties, not issuers like TRIA, over time, spreading losses as to not create a "liability cliff" and avoid rampant moral hazard. For major losses, the federal government would immediately step in and address any broader emergent public policy issues (such as a coordinated attack or massive intellectual property theft), support the insurance market, and make impacted consumers or associated cyber victims whole.

The goals of a DSLP would broadly be to: (1) create a public and private regime for consumer compensation for insured data event losses that allows the private market to continue to advance with modern, competitive, and innovative solutions that rely on an open and free data ecosystem; (2) protect consumers by ensuring the availability and affordability of insurance for data-related and privacy risks; (3) to create a regulated arbitration system for determining loss and liability where the liable party is available;[41] and (4) allow insurers the ability to offer related policies around the world and across a federated system of state-based financial and insurance regulations by capping their potential exposure to losses of events for which they do not yet have the ability to build actuarial tables.

Under DSLP, with growing losses, more likely to be realized with time as evident in large credit bureau breaches, the government covers a greater percentage of losses up to a statutory cap after which there is no mandate to recoup losses from the offending liable

---

[40] On November 26, 2002, the president signed into law the Terrorism Risk Insurance Act of 2002 (Pub. L. 107-297, 116 Stat. 2322) [TRIA].

On December 22, 2005, the president signed into law the Terrorism Risk Insurance Extension Act of 2005 (Pub. L. 109-144, 119 Stat. 2660) [TRIEA 2005]. TRIEA extended TRIP through December 31, 2007.

On December 26, 2007, the president signed into law the Terrorism Risk Insurance Program Reauthorization Act of 2007 (Pub. L. 110-160, 121 Stat. 1839) [TRIPRA 2007], which further extended TRIP through December 31, 2014.

On January 12, 2015, the president signed into law the Terrorism Risk Insurance Program Reauthorization Act of 2015 (Pub. L. 114-1, 129 Stat. 3) [2015 Reauthorization Act], which extended TRIP through December 31, 2020.

On December 7, 2016, Treasury published an interim final rule regarding the process of certifying an act of terrorism. On December 21, 2016, an additional final rule was published as part of Treasury's implementation of changes to the Program required by TRIPRA 2015.

On December 20, 2019, the President signed into law the Terrorism Risk Insurance Program Reauthorization Act of 2019 (Pub. L. 116-94, 133 Stat. 2534) [2019 Reauthorization Act], which extended TRIP through December 31, 2027.

[41] An example of an "unavailable" offending liable party would be a nation-state attack like the 2014 North Korean state-sponsored hack of Sony Pictures that resulted in the loss of proprietary content and exposed sensitive personal data.

party, or if their assets are exhausted. It would be the Treasury Secretary's responsibility to certify that an event, or related events, breaches the statutory cap, or to certify "excessive damages" even if below the statutory maximum, including emergency powers.[42] The idea is that above some critical loss threshold it is in the taxpayer's interest to enact a floor on a negative externality and draw from the general treasury to pay for damages but avoid elastic moral hazard on behalf of policyholders and issuers. Likewise, the government would need to assist insurers in making consumers and businesses whole if the offending party becomes insolvent during the liability claims process or as another result of the covered data event. Much like TRIA, the thresholds are dependent on how losses are distributed among insurers and the size of the insurers themselves and the size of the responsible party. This framework has the added benefit, as has been the case in the terrorism insurance market, of making private coverage more widely available and affordable.

Covered events are far more vast and difficult to determine in the digital world compared to the types of events covered by TRIA. While an event under TRIA may have lagging effect and injuries, for example, health impacts suffered from toxic exposures around the World Trade Center "ground-zero" site, consumers and small businesses may continue to suffer immense financial harm years after a seemingly innocuous exposure of production data to a trusted but unauthorized third-party in the course of a business relationship if such third-party subsequently leaks data or uses data in a derogatory manner, such as an improperly reported credit score factor. The industry would likely need to first decide on a traceability standard before it can reasonably create a comprehensive list of covered events and trigger threshold and define instances, such as when, as verified by the traceability regime, the customer themselves bears responsibility for a fraudulent event. Like TRIA, DSLP would only be activated under an aggregate insured loss threshold each year, which could possibly be triggered by a single catastrophic event.

Under TRIA (and the extensions), the insurer must allow the policyholder to decide whether they want coverage in part or in full. A DSLP proposal should allow for similar policyholder choices based on the commensurate risk profile and context of data activities but must carry a mandatory minimum level of coverage as the end customer shoulders the potential burden where TRIA would not otherwise place potential future burdens on individuals. There is a considerable amount of work to be done to consider an appropriate minimum level of coverage and where applicable, corresponding statutes of limitations, enforceability of long-term liability, and a court's acceptance of traceability standards.

Realistically, TRIA would have to intersect with a DSLP program to determine what covers the possibility of damage from cyberterrorism and should also be housed in the US Treasury Department. Major cyber major events have extensive national security, intelligence, defense, criminal, and public safety related concerns and nexus points that transcend certain state and local interests and need a strong federal executive sponsor accustomed to multilateral foreign engagements, broad federal government

---

[42] It is advisable that expanded DSLP provisions be included as part of Executive Office Emergency Declarations and Major Disaster Declarations and considered as amendments to the National Emergencies Act and the Stafford Disaster Relief and Emergency Assistance Act.

coordination—including the White House, Federal Reserve, Department of Health and Human Services (where HIPAA covered data is of concern), and Department of Justice, in addition to the Intelligence Community[43]—and strong state-level partner organizing capacity. Though TRIA does not directly contemplate cyberterrorism, a similar existing framework is broadly captured under property and casualty and many state insurance regulators consider cyber liability coverage in their examinations. The Treasury Secretary will need to work closely with state partners as insurance is typically a state-regulated affair. Recognizing the national importance of customers' financial data and the need to protect consumers and small businesses equally, the Treasury should maintain federal preemption on otherwise devolved regulatory, ruling, enforcement, and response actions but include state regulators in the decision-making process. Like many regulatory boards and organizations, it is advisable that a group like the Conference of State Bank Supervisors have a significant role in governing the DSLP and developing day-to-day policies as they can provide insight into emerging insurance market issues and trends and contribute real-time intelligence on events and problematic actors in coordination with their member institutions and attorneys general. Policymakers and industry will undoubtedly consider many of the same issues discussed during TRIA considerations given the national importance of the sector and the sensitivity of Americans' data.

Another possibility borrowed from the early terrorism insurance debates and initial contemplation in the US House of Representatives regarding what ultimately became the Dodd-Frank Act is the concept of an industry-operated catastrophic event pool. However, Congress decided to set up an *ex post* fund instead.[44] Irrespective of an overarching government-backed program, industry may wish to consider an alternative liability scheme that builds a shared policy pool for liability-related payouts for catastrophic financial data–related events. The core concept is simple: related but not systematically dependent businesses with a critical mass of data custody responsibilities pay into a jointly owned but independently managed nonprofit risk compensation vehicle. Payments are proportionate to the data exposure risk (where members likely carry the same probability of exposure and liability possibility) based on volume tiers. Payouts for uncontrolled liabilities are released when a member reaches sufficient vesting rights (to avoid new entrant moral hazard) and liability claims exceed a predetermined percentage of "shares" or other agreed-upon metrics. Such a proposal should be mutually exclusive to a comprehensive DSLP that would create a robust insurance market below the enumerated event threshold, but recognizing the complexities of data markets, a shared risk pool may make sense as a complement to DSLP for market engagements not well covered by a federally backed DSLP, such as international data exchange environments (US to EU standard contractual clauses) or quasi-legal markets like marijuana-related business banking markets.

The general structure of a shared risk pool governed in full or in part by specific industry subsets is commonplace in the United States and could be operationalized inside

---

[43] Treasury's Office of Terrorism and Financial Intelligence is part of the United States Intelligence Community and includes the Office of Terrorist Financing and Financial Crimes, the Office of Intelligence and Analysis, the Office of Foreign Assets Control, the Financial Crime Enforcement Network, and the Treasury Executive Office for Asset Forfeiture.

[44] See Title II of the Dodd-Frank Act.

of a number of existing self-regulatory organizations such as the Securities Investor Protection Corporation or the Financial Industry Regulatory Authority or more generally in member-based associations like the Bank Policy Institute or the Financial Data and Technology Association (FDATA).[45] As the mean cost of a data breach increases each year, passing $8 million in the United States in 2019 for exposing an average of 25,000 records,[46] companies with sensitive personal data specifically enumerated by preexisting regimes like General Data Protection Regulation (GDPR) and the California Privacy Rights Act[47] may benefit the most from a liability defense designed internal to industry best practices.

5. Next Steps for US Policymakers

The United States' regulatory framework is unique among the more robust financial services marketplaces in that it is decidedly fragmented. As many as eight different federal agencies have at least some statutory authority over consumer and small business financial data, and, of course, each state asserts its right to protect its citizens from harm arising from data breaches. A transition to an innovative, twenty-first-century open finance framework, however, requires a consistent approach to both customer empowerment and customer protection that only the federal system can implement uniformly. Moreover, Congress has already afforded the relevant regulatory agencies—namely, the CFPB, the OCC, the FDIC, and the Federal Reserve—the required statutory authority to move forward through the EFTA, the Dodd-Frank Wall Street Reform and Consumer Protection Act, and other enacted laws.

The US federal regulatory apparatus has several options to clarify the liability obligations for an open finance ecosystem regardless of a catastrophic breach pool or DSLP proposal based on TRIA. One such example is employing the CFPB's "larger participant rule" to supervise third-party data custodians more directly, like data aggregators. One of the Bureau's responsibilities under the Dodd-Frank Act is the supervision of nonbank-covered persons and large institutions' affiliates. The CFPB also has supervisory authority over "larger participant[s] of a market for other consumer financial products or services,"[48] through the rulemaking process. As with debt collectors and credit reporting agencies, the CFPB can collect and examine evidence for compliance with consumer financial law and assess risks to consumers and consumer financial markets through enforcement actions, confidential examination reports, supervisory letters, and ratings.

The CFPB could use the rule to create a defined class of third-party aggregators, service providers, or other financial data custodians that surpass a quantifiable risk

---

[45] The authors are founding members of FDATA North America.

[46] "How Much Would a Data Breach Cost Your Business?," *IBM*, https://www.ibm.com/security/data-breach.

[47] The California Privacy Rights Act of 2020 revised the California Consumer Privacy Act (CCPA), expanding the law to cover new consumer privacy rights, obligations, and enforcement means.

[48] 12 U.S.C. 5514(a)(1)(B), (a)(2). The Bureau also has the authority to supervise any nonbank covered person that it "has reasonable cause to determine, by order, after notice to the covered person and a reasonable opportunity * * * to respond * * * is engaging, or has engaged, in conduct that poses risks to consumers with regard to the offering or provision of consumer financial products or services." 12 U.S.C. 5514(a)(1)(C).

threshold for consumer protection, trust, and overall financial ecosystem integrity and begin the process of building a compliance manual for regulatory standards. Such a rule may, for example, capture data stewards with more than ten million specific consumer financial data attributes and subject them to CFPB supervision and create a baseline for data, cybersecurity, and information security practices as well as corporate governance standard assessments that if followed, could provide a safe harbor for infinite liability claims or even mandate coverage like a DSLP or catastrophic liability pool.

* * *

The authors were heartened by the CFPB's announcement of its intention to issue an Advance Notice of Proposed Rulemaking (ANPR) regarding Section 1033 of the Dodd-Frank Act. In its July 24, 2020 announcement, the Bureau noted that "some emerging practices may not reflect the access rights described in Section 1033"[49] of the Dodd-Frank Act. This announcement, and the subsequent release of the ANPR requesting information related to consumer access to financial records, unquestionably represents a victory for consumers and small businesses in the United States. The October 22, 2020 ANPR[50] and subsequent rulemaking has the potential to usher in a true open finance ecosystem in the US marketplace, but to be successful, any such regulatory action must include, in tandem, a wholesale review of the various rules that dictate liability in the financial services ecosystem, including the EFTA and Regulation E, that begins the process of meaningfully adopting a DSLP or catastrophic liability pool as a means of eliminating the need for bilateral data access agreements between financial institutions and data aggregation platforms. The entity responsible for customer loss of funds related to an event ought to be responsible for making that customer whole based on custody and responsibility. Though the market's efforts to address liability concerns in the permissioned data access space are laudable, they are, and will continue to be, if unsupported by a federal framework, inadequate in providing the underpinnings of a functioning, more innovative open finance regime in the United States.

---

[49] "CFPB Announces Plan to Issue ANPR on Consumer-Authorized Access to Financial Data," *Consumer Financial Protection Bureau*, Washington, DC, 2020. https://www.consumerfinance.gov/about-us/newsroom/cfpb-anpr-consumer-authorized-access-financial-data/.

[50] "Consumer Access to Financial Records," *Bureau of Consumer Financial Protection* (2020). https://files.consumerfinance.gov/f/documents/cfpb_section-1033-dodd-frank_advance-notice-proposed-rulemaking_2020-10.pdf.

4

Artificial Intelligence and Machine Learning: The Opportunities and Challenges of Using Big Data

Matthew Adam Bruckner[*]

1. Introduction

Open banking[1] offers the promise of innovative financial services and products through the sharing of customer-permissioned data by banks with nonbank financial technology firms and, thus, through increased competition. These nonbank financial services firms also have access to data sources not used by banks in traditional credit underwriting. In recognition, five financial regulators issued a joint statement in December 2019, acknowledging for the first time "alternative data's potential to expand access to credit and produce benefits for consumers," including "improving the speed and accuracy of credit decisions," "additional products, and/or more favorable pricing/terms.[2] But the growth of open banking and credit underwriting models that rely on artificial intelligence (AI) and/or machine learning (ML) is not an unalloyed good.[3]

The promise of financial technology firms using AI might be best exemplified by Upstart Network, Inc. Upstart's credit-underwriting data was recently reviewed by the Consumer Financial Protection Bureau (CFPB), which reported that the company's AI/ML algorithms increased access to credit by approving "27% more applicants than the traditional model, [with] 16% lower average [interest rates] for approved loans."[4]

[*] Associate Professor, Howard University School of Law. This book chapter builds on three earlier pieces that I wrote on fintech lending: "The Promise and Perils of Algorithmic Lenders' Use of Big Data," *Chicago-Kent Law Review* 93(3) (2018), "Regulating Fintech Lending," *Bank. & Fin. Srvcs. Pol'y Rep.* 37 (2018), and "Preventing Predation & Encouraging Innovation in Fintech Lending," *Consumer Fin. L.Q. Rep.* 72 (370) (2018). Portions of the text may have been taken directly from these previous works without additional attribution or the use of quotation marks. Research assistance was provided by Elizabeth Gabaud, Paul Lisbon, Alexander Scott McGee, and Zoe Nwabunka. Thanks also to participants at the 2020 virtual National Business Law Scholars Conference and the Machine Learning and Consumer Credit workshop for their comments and suggestions. I'm grateful to Linda Jeng, Rory Van Loo, and Anya E.R. Prince for providing comments on an earlier version of this chapter. As always, this work would not have been possible without my wife's support (thanks, Morgan!).

[1] Earlier in this book, we defined open banking as a part of the process of allowing third-party financial service providers access to the consumer financial data stored with financial institutions, mostly through the use of APIs. See the Introduction, by Linda Jeng and Chapter 1, by Andres Wolberg-Stok.

[2] Interagency Statement on the Use of Alternative Data in Credit Underwriting (Dec. 2, 2019). https://www.federalreserve.gov/newsevents/pressreleases/files/bcreg20191203b1.pdf.

[3] See Matthew Bruckner and Christopher K. Odinet, Comments to Advance Notice of Proposed Rulemaking regarding National Bank and Federal Savings Association Digital Activities (Docket ID OCC-2019-0028) (July 31, 2020) (commenting on the need for a greater focus on consumer protection when AI/ML is deployed for credit underwriting).

[4] In return for a no-action letter, Upstart was obligated to "share certain information with the CFPB regarding the loan applications it receives, how it decides which loans to approve, and how it will mitigate risk

Matthew Adam Bruckner, *Artificial Intelligence and Machine Learning: The Opportunities and Challenges of Using Big Data* In: *Open Banking*. Edited by: Linda Jeng, Oxford University Press. © Oxford University Press 2022. DOI: 10.1093/oso/9780197582879.003.0005

The CFPB found that credit access increased "across all tested race, ethnicity, and sex segments," with significant benefits for so-called "near prime" consumers, younger consumers, and lower-income consumers.[5] The CFPB also found that Upstart's lending model did not show any disparities for minority, female, or older applicants.[6] This was a ringing endorsement of Upstart's efforts to incorporate alternative data and AI/ML techniques into financial services.[7]

However, the problems of using AI in financial services might *also* be best exemplified by Upstart. In late 2019, the Student Borrower Protection Center (SBPC) made a series of applications for a $30,000 private student loan refinancing product offered by Upstart. Applications for the prospective borrowers "were identical in every respect, except for the [educational] institution attended by the applicant."[8] When refinancing with Upstart, a hypothetical Howard University[9] graduate was offered a loan that cost approximately $3,500 more than a similarly situated New York University (NYU) graduate.[10] Similar results were found when comparing these hypothetical student borrowers at other minority-serving institutions to identical students attending predominantly white institutions. The findings in this report prompted US Senators Cory Booker, Sherrod Brown, Kamala D. Harris, Robert Menendez, and Elizabeth Warren to send a letter to six companies that use educational data for underwriting requesting more information about its algorithm's potential impact on minority borrowers, among other things.[11] Based on their responses, two concerning underwriting practices were identified.[12]

to consumers, as well as information on how its model expands access to credit for traditionally underserved populations." See Press Release, "CFPB Announces First No-Action Letter to Upstart Network" (Sept. 14, 2017). https://www.consumerfinance.gov/about-us/newsroom/cfpb-announces-first-no-action-letter-upst art-network/; see also Patrice Alexander Ficklin and Paul Watkins, "An Update on Credit Access and the Bureau's First No-Action Letter" (Aug. 6, 2019). https://www.consumerfinance.gov/about-us/blog/update-credit-access-and-no-action-letter/.

[5] Ficklin and Watkins, *supra* note 4.
[6] See *id.*
[7] The CEO of First Federal Bank of Kansas City asserted that using Upstart's model allowed the bank to approve "'loans that we would have traditionally denied without the extra data points that they have,' so the bank can extend credit to more customers and, hopefully, put them on the path to savings and home ownership." Amber Buker, "How Innovative Banks Scale Consumer Loans," *BankDirector.com* (Jan. 8, 2020). https://www.bankdirector.com/issues/retail/how-innovative-banks-scale-consumer-loans/.
[8] "Each hypothetical applicant is a 24-year-old New York City resident with a bachelor's degree. Each applicant works as a salaried analyst at a company not listed among those offered by Upstart. Applicants have been employed by their current employer for five months, earn $50,000 annually, and have $5,000 in savings. Applicants have no investment accounts or additional compensation and have not taken out any new loans in the past three months. Each applicant requested a $30,000 student loan refinancing product." "Student Borrower Protection Center, Educational Redlining," at 16 (Feb. 2020). https://protectborrowers.org/wp-content/uploads/2020/02/Education-Redlining-Report.pdf. But see Paul Gu, "Upstart's Commitment to Fair Lending." https://www.upstart.com/blog/upstarts-commitment-to-fair-lending ("The applications had many differences among them, including changes to the applicant's credit report.").
[9] Howard University is a private, federally-chartered, historically Black university in Washington, DC. See https://home.howard.edu/.
[10] "Student Borrower Protection Center," *supra* note 8, at 17 ("In this example, borrowers who attended the HBCU pay higher origination fees and higher interest rates over the life of their loans. Similar results are observed for applicants who attended NMSU, an HSI. In effect, borrowers who attend certain MSIs are penalized simply because of where they went to college.").
[11] Letter from Senator Sherrod Brown et al., to Dave Girouard, CEO, Upstart Network, Inc. (Feb. 13, 2020). http://brown.senate.gov/download/21320-upstart.
[12] "Use of Educational Data to Make Credit Determinations." https://www.banking.senate.gov/imo/media/doc/Review%20-%20Use%20of%20Educational%20Data.pdf ("Based on the information we received from the six respondents, we identified two underwriting practices that may result in violations of ECOA and

Are fintech lenders[13]—those predominantly online, nonbank financial companies using AI/ML techniques to parse unconventional data[14]—increasing credit access, lowering costs, and improving customer experiences?[15] Or are they going to "perpetuate, exacerbate, or mask harmful discrimination"?[16] What risks exist for fintech lenders under the current regulatory framework, and does the extant framework encourage the development of nondiscriminatory AI/ML-based credit algorithms and underwriting models?[17] This chapter takes up these questions after briefly explaining how fintech lenders' use of Big Data and AI/ML differentiates them from conventional lenders.

2. Fintech Lenders Embrace Alternative Data and AI/ML

Fintech lenders first appeared in the United States in 2006.[18] They have quickly grown to dominate the market for small-dollar, unsecured loans.[19] Some of the largest fintech

Regulation B: (1) considering the school an applicant attended to determine creditworthiness; (2) considering an applicant's major or program to determine creditworthiness. In addition, we found that the respondents had inconsistent and often inadequate programs to ensure compliance with fair lending laws. These three issues are discussed below.").

[13] By fintech lending, I mean to exclude robo-advisors, money transmitters, blockchain-based companies, and cryptocurrencies. See Kristin Johnson, Frank Pasquale, and Jennifer Chapman, "Artificial Intelligence, Machine Learning, and Bias in Finance: Toward Responsible Innovation," *Fordham Law Review* 88 (2019), 499, 499 n.3 (discussing varying definitions of fintech).

[14] Eric Bank, "How Marketplace Lenders Decide If You're a Good Risk," *Credible* (Feb. 10, 2017). https://www.credible.com/blog/marketplace-lenders-decide-good-risk [https://perma.cc/R737-7EQ4]; David F. Freeman, Jr. et al., "FTC Report on Big Data Could Foreshadow Big Compliance Issues: Implications for Unfair Lending, Credit Reporting, and Unfair and Deceptive Practices Compliance," *Arnold & Porter Kaye Scholer* (Jan. 20, 2016). https://www.apks.com/en/perspectives/publications/2016/1/ftc-report-on-big-data [https://perma.cc/C5UY-M4L8] (noting the "emerging array of new FinTech companies offering loan products or services based on the use of non-traditional methods for assessing creditworthiness, largely through the use of Big Data").

[15] "Crossing the Lines: How Fintech Is Propelling FS and TMT Firms out of Their Lanes," *PwC*, at 3 (2019). https://www.pwc.com/gx/en/industries/financial-services/assets/pwc-global-fintech-report-2019.pdf (Financial services firms have embraced fintech "to sharpen operational efficiency, lower costs, improve customer experience and heighten the appeal of their products and services.").

[16] Exec. Office of the President, "Big Data: A Report on Algorithmic Systems, Opportunity, and Civil Rights," at 5 (2016). https://obamawhitehouse.archives.gov/sites/default/files/microsites/ostp/2016_0504_data_discrimination.pdf [https://perma.cc/4JNR-LDNS]. Big Data may be used to purposefully discriminate against low-income, minority, and underserved populations using "legally protected characteristics in hiring, housing, lending, and other processes" as proxies for variables that could not be used. See Odia Kagan et al., "Use of Big Data May Violate Federal Consumer Protection Laws, FTC Report Warns," *Ballard Spahr* (Jan. 13, 2016). http://www.ballardspahr.com/alertspublications/legalalerts/2016-01-13-use-of-big-data-may-violate-consumer-protection-laws-ftc-report-warns.aspx [https://perma.cc/5ZYH-TQBX] (reporting that the FTC has expressed concern about "how [B]ig [D]ata could be used in the future to the disadvantage of low-income and underserved communities and adversely affect consumers" (citation omitted)); Solon Barocas and Andrew Selbst, "Big Data's Disparate Impact," *California Law Review* 104 (2016), 671, 674 (noting that "because the mechanism through which data mining may disadvantage protected classes is less obvious in cases of unintentional discrimination, the injustice may be harder to identify and address").

[17] As framed by the CFPB, "[t]he use of alternative data and modeling techniques may expand access to credit or lower credit cost and, at the same time, present fair lending risks." CFPB, "Fair Lending Report of the Bureau of Consumer Financial Protection," at 11 (June 2019). https://files.consumerfinance.gov/f/documents/201906_cfpb_Fair_Lending_Report.pdf [hereinafter CFPB, "Fair Lending Report"].

[18] See "A Temporary Phenomenon? Marketplace Lending," *Deloitte*, at 4 (2016). https://www2.deloitte.com/content/dam/Deloitte/uk/Documents/financial-services/deloitte-uk-fs-marketplace-lending.pdf [https://perma.cc/FV7B-TNN5] (reporting that "[t]he world's first [marketplace lender], Zopa, was founded in the UK in 2005. The first in the United States, Prosper, was founded in 2006").

[19] From nothing in 2006 to 22 percent in 2015, and then more than doubling to almost half of the loan volume in 2019. See "Fintech vs. Traditional FIs: Trends in Unsecured Personal Installment Loans," *Experian*,

lenders include Lending Club, OnDeck Capital, and Prosper. The key to their growth has been access to Big (or at least alternative) Data, and their development of new credit-underwriting models, powered by this data and AI/ML techniques.[20] Fintech lending promises to make underwriting both more efficient and more accurate.[21] In turn, this promises to expand credit access, particularly for consumers without traditional credit scores by, among other things, identifying which consumers are better credit risks than their conventional credit score indicates.[22] But the methods to achieve these promises threatens to unfairly discriminate against prospective borrowers and, simultaneously, to make it harder to prevent unfair discrimination.[23]

a. Alternative Data

Fintech lenders have differentiated themselves from conventional lenders[24] by using AI/ML techniques to analyze alternative data.[25] "Examples of alternative data include

at 3 (2019). http://go.experian.com/IM-20-EM-AA-FintechTrendseBookTY ("A year over year comparison shows that in March of 2015 fintechs made up only 22% of the market, whereas in March of 2019 fintechs made up nearly half of loans originated."); see also Lawrance Lee Evans, Jr., "Financial Technology: Agencies Should Provide Clarification on Lenders' Use of Alternative Data," *Gov. Accountability Office* (2019). https://www.gao.gov/assets/700/696149.pdf ("For example, personal loans provided by lenders GAO interviewed grew sevenfold from 2013 through 2017 ($2.5 billion to $17.7 billion).").

[20] Nikita Aggarwal, "The Norms of Algorithmic Credit Scoring." 80(1) Cambridge Law Journal (2021) 42–73 (discussing how algorithmic credit scoring differs from conventional credit scoring); Kristin N. Johnson, "Examining the Use of Alternative Data in Underwriting and Credit Scoring to Expand Access to Credit," Written Testimony Before the United States House Committee on Financial Services Task Force on Financial Technology, 2 (July 25, 2019). https://papers.ssrn.com/sol3/papers.cfm?abstract_id=3481102 ("Unlike legacy credit scoring businesses such as Equifax, Experian and Transunion that rely on commercially available credit scoring models like the Fair Isaac Corporation Lenders ('FICO') methodology fintech firms increasingly rely on alternative credit scoring models and nontraditional source data.").

[21] Aggarwal, *supra* note 20, at 1–2 ("The enthusiastic emphasise the prospect of greater efficiency and accuracy in lending decisions, particularly in assessing credit risk.").

[22] Julapa Jagtiani and Catharine Lemieux, "Do Fintech Lenders Penetrate Areas That Are Underserved by Traditional Banks?," Federal Reserve Bank of Philadelphia Working Paper No. 18–13 (2018). https://papers.ssrn.com/sol3/papers.cfm?abstract_id=3178459; Tobias Berg, Valentin Burg, Ana Gombović, & Manju Puri, "On the Rise of FinTechs—Credit Scoring Using Digital Footprints," FD CFR Working Paper 2018-04 (Sept. 2018). https://www.fdic.gov/bank/analytical/cfr/2018/wp2018/cfr-wp2018-04.pdf.

[23] Aggarwal, *supra* note 20, at 2 ("The fearful, on the other hand, emphasise the dangers of *inaccuracy*, opacity, and unfair discrimination due to algorithmic credit scoring, and more broadly, the loss of privacy, autonomy, and power in a society dependent on algorithmic decision-making."); see also Johnson et al., *supra* note 13.

[24] Of course, there has been a convergence between conventional lenders (such as Citibank) and fintech lenders because of the recent success of fintech companies. Conventional lenders are partnering with fintech lenders. And fintech lenders are using both conventional credit scoring and algorithmic credit scoring techniques. See Aggarwal, *supra* note 20, at 4; see also Evans, L., *supra* note 19 ("Fintech lenders are partnering with banks to originate loans. Generally, loan applicants are evaluated using the fintech lenders' technology-based credit models, which incorporate the banks' underwriting criteria. The fintech lenders then purchase the loans from the banks and sell them to investors or hold them on their balance sheets.").

[25] Aggarwal, *supra* note 20, at 3–4; see also Harry Surden, "Machine Learning and Law," *Washington Law Review* 89 (2014), 87, 88–89 (describing "machine learning" as "a subfield of computer science concerned with computer programs that are able to learn from experience and thus improve their performance over time"); Eva Wolkowitz and Sarah Parker, "Big Data, Big Potential: Harnessing Data Technology for the Underserved Market," *Ctr. for Fin. Servs. Innovation*, at 3 (2015). http://www.morganstanley.com/sustainableinvesting/pdf/Big_Data_Big_Potential.pdf [https://perma.cc/9WY8-WZMG] (Big Data has been defined "as the collection and use of large data sets that can be broadly combined and distributed to identify patterns and create new data based on these insights—known as metavariables—to increase the effectiveness and efficiency of consumer finance products."); Freeman, *supra* note 14 (suggesting that Big Data "can be loosely defined as the amassing and analysis of large consumer data sets and the incorporation of analytical results and conclusions

utility payments, cash flow statements, education information, social media activity, and internet browser history."[26] In theory, a fintech lender could accumulate every scrap of information they can about a person and then feed that information into its credit-underwriting models to determine whether or not to lend money to the consumer. This is the approach that some early fintech lenders claimed to use. For example, ZestFinance previously claimed that "all data is credit data, we just don't know how to use it yet. . . . More data is always better," even if some of that data is inaccurate.[27] Similarly, Branch—a fintech lender operating in Sub-Saharan Africa—claimed to use "text message logs, social media data, financial data, and handset details including make, model, and browser type" to assess a prospective borrower's creditworthiness.[28] And in China's new "social credit system," the government even proposed incorporating data about "filial piety . . . into the scoring system, assessed, for example, by the frequency with which an individual visited his or her parents and by whether an individual's parents had enough food."[29]

In the United States, fintech lenders need to be more discriminating than their foreign counterparts because of our fair lending laws.[30] Rather than using every scrap of available data about a borrower, fintech lenders often use a more limited subset of possible "alternative data" points.[31] Still, alternative data might include vastly more data

into marketing and lending decisions"). But see Evans, L., *supra* note 19, at 2 (reporting that only "[f]ive of the 11 fintech lenders we interviewed for our December 2018 report said they used alternative data to supplement traditional data when making a credit decision.").

[26] Evans, L., *supra* note 19; see also Aggarwal, *supra* note 20, at 4; Johnson Testimony, *supra* note 20, at 4–6 (discussing various types of alternative data).

[27] Quentin Hardy, "Just the Facts. Yes, All of Them.," *N.Y. Times* (Mar. 25, 2012). https://archive.nytimes.com/query.nytimes.com/gst/fullpage9A0CE7DD153CF936A15750C0A9649D8B63.html; Joe Deville, "Digital Subprime: Tracking the Credit Trackers" (chapter from *The Sociology of Debt*, Mark Featherstone ed.) (forthcoming Dec. 2020), at 153. https://policy.bristoluniversitypress.co.uk/the-sociology-of-debt ("wrong information, in isolation, may not in itself be a barrier to prediction. To reprise Merrill: '. . . And of those thousands [of data points] many are missing, many are wrong, etc, *but regardless you build a score*' (emphasis added).").

[28] Gregory Roberts, "Regulator Wades into Big Data Credit Swamp," *Bloomberg Law: Banking* (Apr. 20, 2017). https://www.bna.com/regulator-wades-big-n57982086887/ [https://perma.cc/T8VP-JPZR]; see also Deville, *supra* note 27, at 156 (discussing some unusual examples of data points that fintech lenders have used, including location, "browser used to access the site [and] repeat visits."); see generally Berg et al., *supra* note 22 (discussing a 10-point "digital footprint" with the predictive power of traditional credit score data).

[29] Yongxi Chen and Anne Sy Cheung, "The Transparent Self under Big Data Profiling: Privacy and Chinese Legislation on the Social Credit System," *Journal of Comparative Law* 12 (2018), 356, 359; see also Jason Kilborn, "Orwellian Debt Collection in China," *Credit Slips* (Mar. 29, 2018, 10:28 am). http://www.creditslips.org/creditslips/2018/03/orwellian-debt-collection-in-china.html (expressing dismay at the prospect of using this sort of data); see also Aurelie L'Hostis and Meng Liu, "WeBank Is Driving Financial Inclusion at Scale in China," *Forbes* (Nov. 5, 2019, 3:30 pm EST). https://www.forbes.com/sites/forrester/2019/11/05/webank-is-driving-financial-inclusion-at-scale-in-china/#4d22f22d72a8 (discussing how WeBank uses Tencent's alternative data "to develop a disruptive credit profiling system").

[30] See Section 4, *infra*; see also Patrice Alexander Ficklin et al., "Innovation Spotlight: Providing Adverse Action Notices When Using AI/ML Models," *CFPB* (July 7, 2020). https://www.consumerfinance.gov/about-us/blog/innovation-spotlight-providing-adverse-action-notices-when-using-ai-ml-models/ ("Despite AI's potential, industry uncertainty about how AI fits into the existing regulatory framework may be slowing its adoption, especially for credit underwriting."); see also Kathleen Ryan, "The Big Brain in the Black Box," *ABA* (May 4, 2020). https://bankingjournal.aba.com/2020/05/the-big-brain-in-the-black-box/ ("uncertainty about how regulators view alternative data have made lenders hesitant to incorporate alternative data into their decision-making.").

[31] "[A]lternative data means information not typically found in the consumer's credit files of the nationwide consumer reporting agencies or customarily provided by consumers as part of applications for credit." See Interagency Statement on the Use of Alternative Data in Credit Underwriting, *supra* note 2; see also Ryan, *supra* note 30 ("Alternative data include rent and utility payment history, educational attainment, social media use and other behavioral information not traditionally factored into credit decisions.").

points than conventional credit-scoring models.[32] For example, "Upstart's technology [allegedly] uses about 1,600 data points to assess creditworthiness, an eye-popping number compared to traditional lenders, which typically use just 12 data points on average."[33] In other words, fintech lenders in the United States reportedly use vastly more data points than conventional lenders but may use far fewer than fintech lenders outside the United States.

b. Machine Learning

In addition to a limited embrace of alternative data,[34] fintech lenders are widely touted as using highly sophisticated AI/ML processes alongside more conventional methods of underwriting, like FICO scores, to evaluate the creditworthiness of potential borrowers.[35] An AI/ML algorithm is an algorithm that trains itself to make creditworthiness determinations.[36] Instead of human programmers deciding which data points are correlated with creditworthiness and how to weight them, an AI/ML algorithm is usually given a set of data on which to train itself.[37] From the data given to it by programmers, an AI/ML algorithm decides which features are relevant and how to weigh them.[38] In other words, many AI/ML algorithms are often thought of as a black box, where programmers can see what went in (vast amounts of data) and what came out (e.g., a credit determination) but not how or why the algorithm made any particular determination.[39] In addition, AI/ML algorithms are often dynamic rather than static.[40]

---

[32] Bruckner, "The Promise and Perils of Algorithmic Lenders' Use of Big Data," *supra* note *, at 3, 11 ("A FICO score is reportedly derived from fewer than fifty data points.").

[33] Buker, *supra* note 7 ("That amount of data doesn't work with simple regression analyses and spreadsheet calculations, so Upstart uses machine learning and automation to crunch the numbers.").

[34] See Evans, L., *supra* note 19.

[35] See Christopher K. Odinet, "Consumer Bitcredit and Marketplace Lending," *Alabama Law Review* 69 (2018), 781, 787–788; see also Thornton McEnery, "SoFi's 'FICO-Free Zone' Loan Process Was Maybe Actually Rather Full of FICO," *Dealbreaker* (Sept. 14, 2017, 5:06 pm). http://dealbreaker.com/2017/09/sofis-fico-free-zone-loan-process-was-actually-rather-full-of-fico/ [https://perma.cc/LX9Q-ZWTT] ("According to conversations with numerous former SoFi employees, the company's 'FICO-Free Zone' loan product actually relied quite heavily on evaluating applicants by their FICO score.").

[36] "Using ML techniques, a computer system can be trained to ecognize patterns in data and use this experience to predict outcomes in previously unseen data, without being explicitly programmed." Aggarwal, *supra* note 20, at 1.

[37] Surden, *supra* note 25, at 93; see Mikella Hurley and Julius Adebayo, "Credit Scoring in the Era of Big Data," *Yale Journal of Law & Technology* 18 (2016), 148, 181) ("ZestFinance may rely on statistical algorithms to automatically identify the most significant metavariables."). Of course, the choice of which data to give the algorithm usually involves human judgment.

[38] Barocas and Selbst, *supra* note 16, at 678 ("In particular, by exposing so-called 'machine learning' algorithms to examples of the cases of interest (previously identified instances of fraud, spam, default, and poor health), the algorithm 'learns' which related attributes or activities can serve as potential proxies for those qualities or outcomes of interest."); see also Surden, *supra* note 25, at 93. This is not true in every case. In some cases, programmers may continue to manually curate some features of learning algorithms. See David Lehr and Paul Ohm, "Playing with the Data: What Legal Scholars Should Learn About Machine Learning," *UC Davis Law Review* 51, (2017), 653, 664 (describing "the very nature of machine learning" as being "one that takes the human element largely out of embedding correlations and inferences in an algorithm.").

[39] See Bennie Mols, "In Black Box Algorithms We Trust (or Do We?)," *ACM News* (Mar. 16, 2017). https://cacm.acm.org/news/214618-in-black-box-algorithms-we-trust-or-do-we/fulltext; see also Lehr and Ohm, *supra* note 38, at 657 (complicating the view of algorithms as black boxes by suggesting various ways to peer inside of algorithmic black boxes, and also by suggesting that observable data inputs are often more important than less observable data analysis).

[40] Jane Bambauer and Tal Zarsky, "The Algorithm Game," *Notre Dame Law Review* 94 (2018), 1.

An AI/ML algorithm is able to constantly update the relevance and weights of various data points. As a result, if an error occurs with a dynamic AI/ML algorithm, a programmer is unlikely to be able to review the instructions the algorithm followed "to find out why the error occurred and correct it," as they could do with a static algorithm.[41]

The combination of AI/ML algorithms and larger data sets can uncover some nonintuitive connections.[42] For example, some foreign fintech lenders appear to charge different rates based on your phone's screen resolution or your political leanings.[43] Understanding how the screen resolution on a person's mobile phone correlates with that person's creditworthiness can be difficult for some people to grasp.[44] And many connections may not be intuitive at all. AI/ML's ability to make nonintuitive connections is one reason why it is able to surpass human ability in some areas, but it may make it difficult for fintech lenders to comply with the United States' fair lending laws.[45]

3. Regulating Fintech Lending

In "The Promise and Perils of Algorithmic Lenders' Use of Big Data," the primary article from which this book chapter is adapted, I examined how our traditional regulatory framework affects fintech lending.[46] There, I argued that strictly enforcing the four laws that make up the backbone of US consumer financial services regulation—the Equal Credit Opportunity Act (ECOA), the Fair Credit Reporting Act (FCRA), the Federal Trade Commission's Unfair and Deceptive Acts or Practices authority, and the Consumer Financial Protection Bureau's Unfair, Deceptive, and Abusive Acts or Practices authority—do not adequately protect the most vulnerable Americans[47] from the most perilous aspects of fintech lending and do not generally encourage fintech lenders to fulfill their promise.[48] Our traditional regulatory framework is of limited

---

[41] Andrew Tutt, "An FDA for Algorithms," *Administrative Law Review* 69 (2017), 83, 93.

[42] Andrew Selbst and Solon Barocas, "The Intuitive Appeal of Explainable Machines," *Fordham Law Review* 87 (2018), 1085 (distinguishing inscrutable algorithms from nonintuitive algorithmic decision-making and quoting Paul Ohm, "The Fourth Amendment in a World Without Privacy," *Mississippi Law Journal* 81 (2012), 1309, 1318, as writing, "We are embarking on the age of the impossible-to-understand reason, when marketers will know which style of shoe to advertise to us online based on the type of fruit we most often eat for breakfast, or when the police know which group in a public park is most likely to do mischief based on the way they do their hair or how far from one another they walk.").

[43] Deville, *supra* note 27, at 160–161.

[44] As it turns out, "[s]creen resolution reveals a lot about the precise type of device being used." *Id.* At 160. And people who own more expensive devices are likelier to have a higher income. See Marianne Bertrand and Emir Kamenica, "Coming Apart? Cultural Distances in the United States over Time," NBER Working Paper 24771 (Dec. 2018). https://faculty.chicagobooth.edu/emir.kamenica/documents/comingApartOnline.pdf.

[45] But see Ficklin et al., *supra* note 30 (discussing how the "existing regulatory framework has built-in flexibility that can be compatible with AI algorithms.").

[46] Bruckner, "The Promise and Perils of Algorithmic Lenders' Use of Big Data," *supra* note *.

[47] To be clear, I use the word "vulnerable" here to refer to the un(der)-banked, who are often BIPOC, young, and/or low-income. See Cecille Avila, " 'Vulnerable' Is a Public Health Euphemism We Need to Stop Using," *The Incidental Economist* (June 23, 2020). https://theincidentaleconomist.com/wordpress/vulnerable-is-a-public-health-euphemism-we-need-to-stop-using/ (claiming that the word "vulnerable" is often a euphemism that obscures structural issues that go unaddressed because we do not name them); see also Bruckner, "The Promise and Perils of Algorithmic Lenders' Use of Big Data," *supra* note *, at 117 (noting that "the young, the low-income, and minorities" are often "credit invisible").

[48] See *id.* At 25 ("While Big Data's supporters claim that algorithmic decision-making reduces the incidence of human bias, there are several notable examples of human bias bleeding into algorithmic decision-making processes.").

value in regulating fintech lenders because our laws were not drafted in contemplation of lenders' use of Big Data and AI/ML. As a result, I explained how applying outdated consumer financial protection regulations to fintech lenders could inhibit innovation in financial services.[49] This book chapter updates my prior work to account for new guidance from regulators and considers key areas of concern for fintech lenders.

In its 2016 report on Big Data, the Obama White House declared that its goal was "to support growth in the beneficial use of [B]ig [D]ata while ensuring that it does not create unintended discriminatory consequences."[50] Yet there are already many stories about discrimination—particularly discrimination against Black, Indigenous, and people of color (BIPOC)—allegedly caused or exacerbated by AI.[51] One of the ways our fair lending laws try to combat illegal discrimination is by requiring fintech lenders to provide consumers with an "adverse action" notice under certain conditions, including refusing to grant credit at the advertised rate, or at all.[52] This notice must specify the "principal reason(s) for the adverse action."[53] Ideally, these notices help prevent discrimination and educate consumers, while also allowing fintech lenders the freedom to innovate.

There is some dispute about whether fintech lenders—with their reliance on Big Data and AI/ML—can produce the required notices, particularly for credit-scoring algorithms that uncover nonintuitive connections between data points. For example, Andrew Selbst and Solon Barocos suggest that the decisions of some complex AI/ML models cannot be accurately explained in an adverse action notice.[54] But others—including those in industry, academic, and consumer regulation—appear less concerned.

---

[49] For another perspective on how the regulatory framework could inhibit consumer financial innovation, focused on competition enforcement, see Rory Van Loo, "Making Innovation More Competitive: The Case of Fintech," *UCLA Law Review* 65 (2018), 232 (concluding that the CFPB or a new entity is needed to ensure consumers benefit from fintech innovation).

[50] Exec. Office of the President, *supra* note 17, at 4; n.10, at 4; see also Dennis D. Hirsch, "That's Unfair! Or Is It? Big Data, Discrimination and the FTC's Unfairness Authority," *University of Kentucky Law Review* 103 (2014), 345, 346.

[51] See, e.g., Carol A. Evans, "Keeping Fintech Fair: Thinking About Fair Lending and UDAP Risks," *Federal Reserve System, Consumer Compliance Outlook* (2nd issue 2017). https://consumercomplianceoutl ook.org/2017/second-issue/keeping-fintech-fair-thinking-about-fair-lending-and-udap-risks/ (discussing allegations against CompuCredit); Bruckner, "The Promise and Perils of Algorithmic Lenders' Use of Big Data," *supra* note * (or 32), at 3–4, 26 (describing discrimination by Amazon, St. George's Hospital in Britain, and in Google's AdWords).

[52] Sarah Ammermann, "Adverse Action Notice Requirements Under the ECOA and the FCRA," *Federal Reserve System, Consumer Compliance Outlook* (Q2 2013). https://consumercomplianceoutlook.org/2013/second-quarter/adverse-action-notice-requirements-under-ecoa-fcra/; see also Wolkowitz and Parker, *supra* note 25, at 24 (both ECOA and the FCRA and Regulation B require that lenders "provid[e] an applicant with a reason when a loan is not approved.").

[53] 12 C.F.R. § 202.9(b)(2) ("The statement of reasons for adverse action required by paragraph (a)(2)(i) of this section must be specific and indicate the principal reason(s) for the adverse action. Statements that the adverse action was based on the creditor's internal standards or policies or that the applicant, joint applicant, or similar party failed to achieve a qualifying score on the creditor's credit scoring system are insufficient."); 15 U.S.C. § 1691(d)(2); Selbst and Barocas, *supra* note 42, at 1101.

[54] Selbst and Barocas, *supra* note 42, at 1103 ("The difficulty is that there will be situations where complexity cannot be avoided in a faithful representation of the scoring system, and listing factors alone will fail to accurately explain the decision, especially when the list is limited to four."); see also Mols, *supra* note 39 ("Unfortunately, many of these algorithms cannot explain their results even to their programmers, let alone to end-users. They operate like black boxes (devices that can be viewed in terms of their inputs and outputs, without any knowledge of their internal workings)."); Tutt, *supra* note 41, at 107 (describing "black box" algorithms as those that are "difficult or impossible to predict or explain its characteristics.").

At least one fintech lender, ZestFinance claims that its algorithm "produces simple, easy-to-read adverse action reasons."[55] Zest claims to have designed a learning algorithm that surmounts the opacity issues some suggest are inherent to some types of AI/ML (and, thus, to fintech lending).[56] If Zest can truly produce the "intuitive and comprehensible" explanations that it claims to produce, it can probably satisfy the obligations imposed by Regulation B,[57] which implements ECOA and the FCRA.[58]

And there's reason to believe that Zest's claims are accurate. "[C]racking the black box [of lending algorithms] does not seem as impossible as it once did."[59] It remains true that black box algorithms "can be extremely difficult to fully understand" and that they may be understandable to some people, but not to others.[60] But fintech lenders' underwriting models do not necessarily need to be understood entirely to be legally compliant. The law merely requires that a fintech lender provide the principal reason(s) for an algorithmic underwriting decision.[61] And in *The Ethical Algorithm*, Professors Michael Kearns and Aaron Roth explain:

> [O]ne of the benefits of algorithmic decision-making is that we have models that tell us what they would do on any input, so we can explore counterfactuals, such as "What would be the smallest change to your application that would change the decision to acceptance" to which the answers might be things like "Be in your current job for six months longer" or "Have more equity in your home for collateral." Indeed, this type of explanatory understanding at the level of individual decisions or predictions is the basis for some of the more promising research on interpretability.[62]

Thus, it seems that some credit-scoring algorithms may be able to provide comprehensible explanations for why they made a particular decision.[63] For example, if an

[55] See "Machine Learning and Compliance? They Can Coexist," *ZestFinance*. https://www.zestfinance.com/hubfs/Site%20updates%20May%202017/ZAML%20compliance%20case%20study_2017.05.11.pdf?t=1497423189060 [https://perma.cc/R4DH-HKG8].

[56] Cf. Wolkowitz and Parker, *supra* note 25, at 6 (discussing how "[s]ome innovative companies are going beyond legally required minimums of disclosure by transparently conveying the types of data sources they use or explaining to consumers how their behavior can drive profile improvements that lead to better rates and offers.").

[57] "Regulation B protects applicants from discrimination in any aspect of a credit transaction." See https://www.consumerfinance.gov/policy-compliance/rulemaking/regulations/1002/ (discussing 12 CFR Part 1002—Equal Credit Opportunity Act (Regulation B)).

[58] Regulation B is codified at 12 C.F.R. §§ 1002.1–.16 (2018). For more on Regulation B's requirements, see *infra* text accompanying notes 51–52.

[59] Aaron Chou, "What's in the 'Black Box'? Balancing Financial Inclusion and Privacy in Digital Consumer Lending," *Duke Law Journal* 69 (2020), 1183, 1209.

[60] See Michael Kearns and Aaron Roth, *The Ethical Algorithm* (Oxford University Press, 2019), 174, 171 ("the first question that comes to mine when attempting to formulate a theory of algorithmic interpretability is, interpretable to whom?"). But see Selbst and Barocas, *supra* note 42, at 1094–1098 (distinguishing inscrutable algorithms from nonintuitive algorithmic decision-making and expressing concern that some credit-scoring algorithms that uncover nonintuitive connections may not provide comprehensible explanations for its actions.).

[61] See 12 C.F.R. § 202.9(b)(2); 15 U.S.C. § 1691(d)(2); see also CFPB, "Fair Lending Report," *supra* note 17. But see Office of the Comptroller of the Currency, Credit Scoring Models, OCC Bull. No. 97–24, app. At 11 (May 20, 1997) (explaining that, for national banks, the "variables used in a validated credit scoring system" must be "statistically related to loan performance, and has an understandable relationship to an individual applicant's creditworthiness.").

[62] See Kearns and Roth, *supra* note 61, at 174.

[63] See CFPB, "Fair Lending Report," *supra* note 17, at 10 ("Industry continues to develop tools to accurately explain complex AI decisions, and the Bureau expects more methods will emerge. These developments hold

applicant is denied credit because of a prior bankruptcy filing, the applicant can investigate how long the bankruptcy filing will remain on the applicant's credit report and
reapply after it is removed. In this way, adverse action notices may serve a consumer education function. Alternatively, if the applicant never filed bankruptcy, they can inform
the lender and have the error in their credit file corrected.

This type of adverse action may also comport with one sense of fairness. It may seem
fair that a person should wait and rebuild trust before other lenders are required to lend
money to someone who recently failed to repay other creditors. By contrast, if an applicant is offered credit at a higher rate because they graduated from Howard University—
a historically Black college or university (HBCU)—instead of a predominantly white
institution, such as NYU, this should raise red flags because attendance at an HBCU is
likely to be just a proxy for race.[64] And since lenders will almost never be explicit that
they are discriminating on the basis of a protected category (e.g., race), regulators must
remain vigilant and continue to police fintech lenders.

Although some have argued that the optimal level of regulation may be very low
because the pace of financial services innovation will continuously outstrip regulatory capacity,[65] preventing fintech lending from "systematically disadvantaging certain groups" is an important goal that regulators ought to pursue.[66] And there are a
number of potential approaches that could mitigate the problematic aspects of fintech
lending while promoting its promise.[67] For example, just as human decision makers
may receive implicit bias training, it may be possible to offer similar training to AI/ML
lending models.[68] Another promising solution may be to "develop a principle of 'equal
opportunity by design'—designing data systems that promote fairness and safeguard
against discrimination from the first step of the engineering process and continuing
throughout their lifespan."[69]

It's my view, however, that these approaches are unlikely to be pursued absent regulatory intervention. Thus, it remains important that state and federal regulators continue to encourage firms to develop tools to accurately explain otherwise inscrutable

---

great promise to enhance the 'explainability' of AI and facilitate use of AI for credit underwriting compatible
with adverse action notice requirements.").

[64] See SBPC, *supra* note 8; see generally Anya E.R. Prince and Daniel Schwarcz, "Proxy Discrimination in
the Age of Artificial Intelligence and Big Data," *Iowa Law Review* 105 (2020), 1257 (discussing proxy discrimination by automated decision systems).

[65] See, e.g., Jeremy Kidd, "Fintech: Antidote to Rent Seeking?," *Chicago-Kent Law Review* 93 (2018), 165,
166–67.

[66] Exec. Office of the President, *supra* note 17.

[67] The CFPB could work with algorithmic lenders to design their credit-scoring models specifically to
"help mitigate discriminatory results over time and increase inclusion." *Id.*; see also Johnson et al., *supra* note
14, at 523–525 (discussing how explainability requirements can create "algorithmic accountability"); Prince
and Schwarcz, *supra* note 64, at 1306–1318 (discussing various potential strategies for reducing discrimination by AI systems).

[68] See Lehr and Ohm, *supra* note 38, at 704–705 (discussing certain "novel methods for reducing" discrimination during data collection "by, in essence, adding noise to the data.") (citing Michael Feldman et al.,
"Certifying and Removing Disparate Impact," ACM SIGKDD Int'l Conf. on Knowledge Discovery & Data
Mining 21 (2015), 259; Prince and Schwarcz, *supra* note 64, at 1266–1267, 1313–1315 (suggesting the possibility of deploying "'ethical algorithms' that explicitly seek to eliminate the capacity of any facially-neutral considerations to proxy for prohibited characteristics."). Cf. Kearns and Roth, *supra* note 61, at 22–56
(discussing differential privacy). But see Omer Tene and Jules Polonetsky, "Taming the Golem: Challenges of
Ethical Algorithmic Decision Making," *North Carolina Journal of Law and Technology* 19 (2017), 125.

[69] Exec. Office of the President, *supra* note 17, at 5–6.

AI decisions and comply with our other fair lending laws.[70] Regulators must remain attentive to the potential for fintech lenders to harm prospective borrowers, particularly the most vulnerable members in our society.[71] They should investigate reports that emerge about problems with fintech lenders, such as those highlighted by the SBPC's Educational Redlining report.[72]

4. Building Fair AI/ML-Based Fintech Models

This section addresses several fair lending risks that fintech lenders should be alert to and some steps they can take to address these risks. These risks include developing discriminatory underwriting models, which are not mitigated through repeated testing and appropriate data usage. They also include the failure to provide accurate information to consumers, which failure exposes fintech lenders to risk under Regulation B and UDA(A)P statutes.[73] Regulators can and should also be attentive to these issues.

As noted in the introduction to this chapter, there is growing evidence that fintech lending may increase credit access by reducing some forms of discrimination, identifying consumers without traditional credit scores that are good credit risks, and lowering the cost of credit through process-based efficiencies.[74] For example, a recent paper found that "FinTech algorithms discriminate [based on race] 40% less than face-to-face lenders" in the mortgage refinancing market.[75] While this paper did not find that fintech lending completely eliminated illegal discrimination, it found that "FinTech lenders discriminate approximately one-third less than lenders overall in terms of pricing" and "do not discriminate in mortgage accept/reject decision-making."[76]

---

[70] See CFPB, "Fair Lending Report," *supra* note 17, at 10 ("Industry continues to develop tools to accurately explain complex AI decisions, and the Bureau expects more methods will emerge. These developments hold great promise to enhance the 'explainability' of AI and facilitate use of AI for credit underwriting compatible with adverse action notice requirements."); see also Wulf A. Kaal, "Dynamic Regulation for Innovation," in *Perspectives in Law, Business & Innovation* (Mark Fenwick et al. eds., Springer, 2016), 1, 11 ("[B]ut "[o]utdated and ineffectual statutes" cannot adapt to "emerging fact-based changes and innovations.").

[71] Unfortunately, the CFPB appears disinterested in doing so. For example, a recent blog post from members of the CFPB's Office of Innovation recently touted how the "flexibility" and "latitude" of the existing regulatory framework means that fintech lenders need not provide comprehensible reasons to a prospective borrower for a credit denial. See Ficklin et al., *supra* note 30. Yet, the very same blog post suggests that industry will develop and deploy tools that will more "accurately explain complex AI decisions," which will "enhance the explainability of AI and facilitate use of AI for credit underwriting compatible with adverse action notice requirements." *Id.* If fintech lenders need not provide more comprehensible explanations to borrowers, why will they invest in additional research to provide such explanations.

[72] SBPC, *supra* note 8.

[73] This work uses UDA(A)P to collectively refer to both the FTC's UDAP authority and the CFPB's UDAAP authority. For more information about these consumer protection laws, see Bruckner, "The Promise and Perils of Algorithmic Lenders' Use of Big Data," *supra* note */32, at 139–146.

[74] See, e.g., Jagtiani and Lemieux, *supra* note 22; see also Press Release, "CFPB Announces First No-Action Letter to Upstart Network," *supra* note 5; Ficklin and Watkins, *supra* note 4; Prince and Schwarcz, *supra* note 64, at 1310–1311 (hypothesizing that "Ais may, in fact, decrease the incidence of statistical discrimination—by proxy or otherwise—by reducing the costs of acquiring and processing data about directly relevant characteristics.").

[75] Robert Bartlett et al., "Consumer-Lending Discrimination in the FinTech Era" (Nov. 2019), at *6 (unpublished manuscript). https://faculty.haas.berkeley.edu/morse/research/papers/discrim.pdf; Andreas Fuster et al., "Predictably Unequal? The Effects of Machine Learning on Credit Markets" (2018), CEPR Discussion Paper No. 12448, at 3 (mentioning CapitalOne as an example of a lender "with more sophisticated technology [that] more efficiently screen[ed] and provid[ed] credit to members of groups that were simply eschewed by those using more primitive technologies.").

[76] Bartlett et al., *supra* note 75, at 27, 29.

However, there is also growing evidence that fintech lenders can "reinforce[e] and perpetuat[e] historic patterns of unlawful discrimination."[77] For example, a group of scholars found that AI/ML models may price loans to Black borrowers at substantially higher rates than to white borrowers.[78]

To avoid fair lending liability, fintech lenders first need to ensure that their models do not illegally discriminate against members of protected categories, even if the lender doesn't intend to discriminate and their practices appear neutral.[79] Although regulators have not yet brought an enforcement action on this basis against a fintech lender, they regularly bring such lawsuits against other lenders.[80] In many cases, the lenders incented employees to charge "higher fees or interest rates on loans to minorities than to comparably qualified nonminority consumers."[81]

In other words, fintech lenders have fair lending risk if they charge similarly situated minority[82] borrowers more than white borrowers, and evidence suggests that this occurs in at least some instances. Regulators are particularly likely to scrutinize a lender's decision to override its underwriting model. These overrides cannot categorically disadvantage members of protected groups. As noted above, recent analysis of the fintech mortgage refinancing market found racial discrimination in loan pricing.[83] While fintech lenders may be able to defend against a disparate impact lawsuit by arguing that this discrimination is a business necessity, lenders must be prepared to justify their discriminatory practices.[84]

Functionally, this means that fintech lenders need to be prepared to demonstrate that their lending models are accurate and otherwise comply with fair lending laws.[85] Deploying AI/ML-based fintech-lending models "'in the wild', without rigorously testing the results and adjusting the model hyperparameters based on feedback," creates fair lending risk.[86] A recent Government Accountability Office (GAO) report suggests

---

[77] Aggarwal, *supra* note 20, at 12.

[78] Fuster et al., *supra* note 75, at 4–5 ("For White borrowers, the average rate under the machine learning technology rises by a little less than 20 basis points, which is naturally close to the population average, but for Black borrowers, the comparable rise is more than double this number, at 40 basis points."); see also SBPC, *supra* note 8.

[79] Cf. *Texas Department of Housing and Community Affairs v. Inclusive Communities Project, Inc.*, 135 S. Ct. 2507 (2015); see also Evans C., *supra* note 51.

[80] See, e.g., *United States & CFPB v. Provident Funding Assocs., LP*, No. 3:15-cv-02373 (N.D. Cal., Consent order filed May 28, 2015). https://www.consumerfinance.gov/about-us/newsroom/cfpb-and-department-of-justice-take-action-against-provident-funding-associates-for-discriminatory-mortgage-pricing/.

[81] Evans, C., *supra* note 51.

[82] Or members of other legally protected categories.

[83] Bartlett et al., *supra* note 75.

[84] Some commentators have argued that the specter of disparate impact liability won't prevent discrimination by AI/ML models because firms "will typically have little problem showing that this practice is consistent with business necessity and in rebuffing any attempt to show the availability of a less discriminatory alternative." See Prince and Schwarcz, *supra* note 64, at 1305, 1272 ("Where it is available, disparate impact does not require any showing of discriminatory intent, even though such intent may in fact be present. Instead, it requires simply that a facially-neutral practice disproportionately impacts members of a protected group. If so, then the burden shifts to the discriminator to demonstrate that its practice has a legitimate non-discriminatory purpose that is rooted in business necessity. Even if the firm or actor can meet this burden, it may still be in violation of the law if it could achieve its legitimate aims with a less discriminatory alternative.").

[85] Interagency Statement on the Use of Alternative Data in Credit Underwriting, *supra* note 2 ("Robust compliance management includes appropriate testing, monitoring and controls to ensure consumer protection risks are understood and addressed."); Emory Wayne Rushton, "Credit Scoring Models: Examination Guidance," OCC Bulletin 1997–24, Appendix A (May 20, 1997). https://www.occ.treas.gov/news-issuan ces/bulletins/1997/bulletin-1997-24a.pdf ("Banks using credit scoring models purchased from third-party vendors and those using internally developed models must demonstrate that . . . [they] are valid as defined in Regulation B.").

[86] Aggarwal, *supra* note 20, at 11–12.

that many fintech lenders are attuned to this risk, with 100 percent of the interviewed fintech lenders indicating "that they take steps to test their underwriting model for accuracy or compliance with fair lending laws."[87] Models must also be periodically revalidated, otherwise they can become inaccurate and create fair lending risk. Thus, the failure to periodically revalidate models may present a fair lending or regulatory risk.[88] This will be particularly challenging for fintech lenders that use dynamic AI/ML models—models that adjust as new data is obtained. Dynamic AI/ML models would seem to present substantial fair lending risk because it's not clear how a lender would establish that the model was ever fully validated if it is constantly changing in response to new information.[89]

A model's compliance with fair lending laws also depends on the data they use and the assumptions built into the models.[90] Of course, some alternative data, such as cash flow data from bank account ledgers, "are directly related to consumers' finances and how consumers manage their financial commitments."[91] This sort of alternative data "may present lower risks than other data."[92] But lenders may be inclined to use other data without a clear nexus to creditworthiness, such as the "digital footprints"—that information "that people leave online simply by accessing or registering on a website."[93] At least some fintech lenders don't use alternative data for underwriting purposes because of the fair lending risks, and all should think carefully about what data they use and how they use it.

That said, regulators have signaled their approval for the use of some alternative data points. In an "Interagency Statement on the Use of Alternative Data in Credit Underwriting," several regulators that oversee fintech lenders seemingly approved of the use of cash flow data in underwriting decisions.[94] These data are specific to the borrower, are financial in nature, and are derived from reliable sources, and their use "can generally be explained and disclosed to the borrower, as may be required" by certain fair lending laws.[95] By focusing on this sole example, however, these regulators may be signaling that proxy data points, that are nonfinancial in nature, derived from nonfinancial sources, and/or that are harder to explain to consumers present greater

---

[87] Evans, L., *supra* note 19, at 35 (interviewing eleven fintech lenders).

[88] Nat'l Consumer Law Ctr., Fair Credit Reporting § 16.8.4.1 (2017) ("Credit scoring models must be initially validated when they are developed. This means the model must be tested against databases of loan files where the results of the loans (good or bad) are known. The models must also be re-validated periodically. Without re-validation, a credit scoring model can lose its accuracy.").

[89] Fintech lenders may lack sufficient guidance from regulators on what steps they ought to take to ensure compliance. See Evans, L., *supra* note 19, at 35 (describing various ways that lenders said they used to ensure compliance, including using the "CFPB's report on fair lending analysis[,] . . . the federal banking regulators' model risk management guidance [and] third parties, including consulting and law firms specializing in fair lending issues.").

[90] Evans, C., *supra* note 51.

[91] See Interagency Statement on the Use of Alternative Data in Credit Underwriting, *supra* note 2.

[92] *Id.*

[93] Berg et al., *supra* note 22, at 2–3 ("Digital footprints" include information such as whether a mobile device was used, the device's operating system was (e.g., Android vs. iOS), whether the user capitalizes proper nouns, if the user has enabled their "do not track" setting.); see Chou, *supra* note 59, at 1209 (arguing that compliance may be challenging because "owners of AI tools have a difficult time explaining with precision why AI makes certain decisions.").

[94] See Interagency Statement on the Use of Alternative Data in Credit Underwriting, *supra* note 2; see also "The Use of Cash-Flow Data in Underwriting Credit," *FinRegLab* (July 2019). https://finreglab.org/wp-content/uploads/2019/07/FRL_Research-Report_Final.pdf (describing the results of an empirical and policy analysis of the risks and benefits of using cash flow data in "credit underwriting and the hurdles to its wider adoption" by drawing on data from six fintech lenders that have been using this data).

[95] *Id.*

fair lending risks.[96] Thus, a fintech lender that uses, for example, college attendance data may risk fair lending challenges by applicants because this is a nonfinancial data point, derived from nonfinancial sources, and attendance at a HBCU or other minority-serving institution can be a proxy for race.[97] Similarly, some fintech lenders, claim to use "a consumer's online social network . . . , which can raise concerns about discrimination against those living in disadvantaged areas."[98] If lenders' algorithms "make decisions using facially neutral variables that function as proxies in the decision-making process for prohibited criteria," they likely violate fair lending laws.[99] It's important to note, however, that the CFPB granted Upstart a no-action letter, despite it using nonfinancial, proxy data points in its underwriting decisions (e.g., college attendance data).[100]

On a related note, fintech lenders may be considered consumer reporting agencies (CRAs). If so, they are not entitled to use any data they wish in their lending decisions. Instead, "a CRA must delete an item when it has attempted to determine whether the item is accurate and is unable to do so, whatever the reason."[101] They also need to ensure that they are using only accurate information about consumers. There is reason to suspect that they do not always do so.[102] For example, a report from the National Consumer Law Center found that reports from third-party data brokers "were riddled with inaccuracies . . . rang[ing] from the mundane . . . to seriously flawed."[103]

A second fair lending risk for lenders, which was referenced earlier, relates to fintech lenders' need to provide adverse action notices to consumers under certain circumstances. The CFPB's guidance is that fintech lenders need only "disclose a reason for a denial," but they are *not* required to provide a clear and comprehensible reason.[104]

---

[96] Ryan, *supra* note 30 ("By implication, then, banks can assume that regulators would view alternative data that is non-financial in nature and gleaned from non-traditional sources as riskier from a fair lending perspective.").

[97] SBPC, *supra* note 8. Cf. Rushton, *supra* note 85 ("For example, since those who speak Spanish as their primary language are likely to be of Hispanic national origin, a bank using a separate score card for persons who speak Spanish would be scrutinized by the OCC and may risk legal challenges by applicants.").

[98] Evans, L., *supra* note 19, at 37.

[99] Johnson Testimony, *supra* note 21, at *12 (citing Prince and Schwarcz, *supra* note 64; and Selbst and Barocas, *supra* note 42; see also Rushton, *supra* note 85 ("Segmenting the population by any other prohibited basis, regardless of whether the credit scoring system is validated, is illegal. Moreover, factors linked so closely to a prohibited basis that they may actually serve as proxies for that basis cannot be used to segment the population.").

[100] Ryan, *supra* note 30; see also Brown Letter, *supra* note 11 ("In other words, Upstart appears to be assessing creditworthiness based on non-individualized factors, which the CFPB, FDIC, and New York Attorney General have found raise fair lending concerns."); Gu, *supra* note 9 (noting that Upstart's underwriting "model doesn't consider individual schools but groups of schools that have similar economic outcomes and educational characteristics.").

[101] 15 U.S.C. § 1681i(a); Nat'l Consumer Law Ctr., Fair Credit Reporting § 4.2.6 (2017).

[102] Deville, *supra* note 27, at 153 ("The point is not (necessarily) that such companies are unconcerned with accuracy, but that they *are* concerned first, with *combining* information from various sources as a way to make up for missing/inaccurate data and then, second, with building scores that they can then *test*.").

[103] "Big Data: A Big Disappointment for Scoring Consumer Credit Risk," *Nat'l Consumer Law Ctr.*, at 4–5 (2014). https://www.nclc.org/images/pdf/pr-reports/report-big-data.pdf [https://perma.cc/EG78-TLY8].

[104] CFPB, "Fair Lending Report," *supra* note 17, at 9 ("The existing regulatory framework has built-in flexibility that can be compatible with AI algorithms. For example, although a creditor must provide the specific reasons for an adverse action, the Official Interpretation to ECOA's implementing regulation, Regulation B, provides that a creditor need not describe how or why a disclosed factor adversely affected an application, or, for credit scoring systems, how the factor relates to creditworthiness. Thus, the Official Interpretation provides an example that a creditor may disclose a reason for a denial, even if the relationship of that disclosed factor to predicting creditworthiness may be unclear to the applicant.").

In such cases, the adverse action notice may be worth very little to the consumer.[105] For example, what if a fintech lender denies an applicant because the applicant does not visit their family often enough or because the applicant has enabled the "do not track" setting on their web browser?[106] Even if a prospective borrower believes this information is incorrect, they may not be able to prove that the information in their file is incorrect.[107] There are two risks to fintech lenders in this regard. First, it is not free from doubt that every fintech lender, or the banks they partner with, can provide the principal reason(s) for their adverse actions.[108] Second, other regulators may not agree with the CFPB's guidance and might enforce the laws more strictly.[109]

There is a third fair lending risk that fintech lenders and the banks they partner with must pay attention to. They must avoid actively misleading consumers and ensure they disclose adequate information to consumers. Several fintech lenders and a bank that commonly partners with fintech lenders have been sued for failing to do so, including Lending Club,[110] SoFi,[111] and Cross River Bank.[112] These lawsuits all involved allegedly deceptive practices by the lenders. For example, in April 2018, the FTC filed a complaint charging "the LendingClub Corporation with falsely promising consumers they would receive a loan with 'no hidden fees,' when, in actuality, the company deducted hundreds or even thousands of dollars in hidden up-front fees from the loans."[113] Similarly, SoFi claimed to be a "FICO-Free Zone," when its underwriting placed substantial weight on an applicant's FICO score.[114] The solution seems simple on its face: be transparent. Yet

[105] Selbst and Barocas, *supra* note 42, at 54 (noting that our intuitions will sometimes "fail us, even when we've been able to build interpretable models," which would seemingly deprive borrowers of many of the benefits of the adverse action notice).

[106] Chen and Cheung, *supra* note 29 (discussing the potential use of filial piety as a criterion in credit scoring in China); Berg et al., *supra* note 22, at 40, tbl. 3 (discussing "do not track" and its predictive ability).

[107] See Evans, L., *supra* note 19, at 5 n.8 ("Whereas the Fair Credit Reporting Act requires that borrowers have an opportunity to check and correct inaccuracies in credit reports, borrowers could face more challenges in checking and correcting alternative data that some fintech lenders use to make underwriting decisions because alternative data are not typically reflected in credit reports.").

[108] Evans, C., *supra* note 51; see also Lael Brainard, "The Opportunities and Challenges of Fintech" (Dec. 2, 2016). https://www.federalreserve.gov/newsevents/speech/brainard20161202a.htm ("It may not always be readily apparent to consumers, or even to regulators, what specific information is utilized by certain alternative credit scoring systems, how such use impacts a consumer's ability to secure a loan or its pricing, and what behavioral changes consumers might take to improve their credit access and pricing.").

[109] See Rory Van Loo, "Technology Regulation by Default: Platforms, Privacy, and the CFPB," *Georgetown Law Technology Review* 2 (2018), 531 (observing that despite being a data-driven and technologically advanced agency, the CFPB has not aggressively pursued cutting-edge consumer financial technology harms). I agree with Professor Van Loo that the CFPB has not done a great job of adapting consumer financial laws to the algorithmic era and have refrained from pushing the law's boundaries to fulfill congressional intent. I hope state-based regulators will be more ambitious in protecting consumers.

[110] Press Release, "FTC Charges Lending Club with Deceiving Consumers," *FTC* (Apr. 25, 2018). https://www.ftc.gov/news-events/press-releases/2018/04/ftc-charges-lending-clubdeceiving-consumers-0; see also Evans, L., *supra* note 19.

[111] Press Release, "Federal Trade Commission, Online Student Loan Refinance Company SoFi Settles FTC Charges, Agrees to Stop Making False Claims About Loan Refinancing Savings," *FTC* (Oct. 29, 2018). https://www.ftc.gov/newsevents/press-releases/2018/10/online-student-loan-refinance-company-sofi-settles-ftc charges; see also Evans, L., *supra* note 19.

[112] Press Release, "FDIC Announces Settlement with Cross River Bank, Teaneck, New Jersey, and Freedom Financial Asset Management, LLC, San Mateo, California, for Unfair and Deceptive Practices," *Federal Deposit Insurance Corporation* (Mar. 28, 2018); see also Evans, L., *supra* note 19.

[113] Press Release, "FTC Charges Lending Club with Deceiving Consumers," *FTC* (Apr. 25, 2018). https://www.ftc.gov/news-events/press-releases/2018/04/ftc-charges-lending-clubdeceiving-consumers-0; see also Evans, L., *supra* note 19.

[114] McEnery, *supra* note 36.

a GAO report that reviewed the website of fifteen fintech lenders found that key loan terms were not always transparently disclosed, creating fair lending risks.[115]

Fintech lenders may mitigate some of their fair lending risk if they deploy their non-traditional methods and data sources only for applicants who would otherwise fail to receive credit under a conventional approach. These so-called "second-look" programs "may raise fewer concerns about unfairly penalizing consumers than algorithms that are applied to all applicants."[116] While regulators have been sure to note that "Second Look approaches must also comply with applicable consumer protection laws," they appear to be encouraging their use in this regard.[117]

5. Conclusion

Fintech lending leveraging open data does have the potential to "effectively reduce discrimination and promote fairness and opportunity, including expanding access to credit in low-income communities."[118] And regulators should avoid suffocating new developments because of the mere threat of harm.[119] It's not clear to me, however, that fintech lenders will continue to innovate without the urging of regulators. For example, I find it disappointing that the CFPB has made clear that fintech lenders' adverse action notices need only disclose a reason for denying a person credit, "even if the relationship of that disclosed factor to predicting creditworthiness may be unclear to the applicant."[120] While this will alert consumers that an adverse action has been taken, it does nothing to encourage innovation, prevent discrimination, or educate consumers about how to improve the likelihood that they will receive credit in the future.[121] Unfortunately, since Director Richard Cordray left the bureau, the CFPB has gone from being a consumer watchdog to the dog that doesn't bark.[122]

---

[115] Evans, L., *supra* note 19, at *27; see also Barbara J. Lipman and Ann Marie Wiersch, *Uncertain Terms: What Small Business Borrowers Find When Browsing Online Lender Websites*, *Federal Reserve Bank of Cleveland* (Dec. 2019) ("On some sites, product descriptions feature little or no information about the actual products, but instead focus on the ease of applying and qualifying for funding, the speed at which applications are approved, and the array of uses for loan proceeds.").

[116] Evans, C., *supra* note 51.

[117] Interagency Statement on the Use of Alternative Data in Credit Underwriting, *supra* note 2; see also Evans, C., *supra* note 51.

[118] Tene and Polonetsky, *supra* note 68, at 164; see also Jagtiani and Lemieux, *supra* note 22; Bartlett et al., *supra* note 75 (reporting the results of an empirical study finding that "lenders charge otherwise-equivalent Latinx/African-American borrowers 7.9 (3.6) bps higher rates for purchase (refinance) mortgages, costing $765M yearly." The authors find that "algorithmic lenders do reduce rate disparities by more than a third and show no discrimination in rejection rates.").

[119] See generally Bruckner, "Regulating Fintech Lending," *supra* note *.

[120] CFPB, "Fair Lending Report," *supra* note 17, at 9 ("The existing regulatory framework has built-in flexibility that can be compatible with AI algorithms. For example, although a creditor must provide the specific reasons for an adverse action, the Official Interpretation to ECOA's implementing regulation, Regulation B, provides that a creditor need not describe how or why a disclosed factor adversely affected an application, or, for credit scoring systems, how the factor relates to creditworthiness. Thus, the Official Interpretation provides an example that a creditor may disclose a reason for a denial, even if the relationship of that disclosed factor to predicting creditworthiness may be unclear to the applicant.").

[121] See Selbst and Barocas, *supra* note 42, at 1102 ("an explanation of a specific decision may be informative, but it may not reveal an obvious path to an alternative outcome."); see also Evans, C., *supra* note 51 (describing a purpose of adverse action notices as being to "help consumers understand how to improve their credit standing."); Brainard, *supra* note 108.

[122] See Richard Corday, *Watchdog* (Oxford University Press, 2020); Adam Levitin, "Dodd-Frank's 'Abusive' Standard: The Dog that Didn't Bark," *Credit Slips* (June 20, 2017). https://www.creditslips.org/creditslips/2017/06/abusive-the-dog-that-didnt-bark.html.

5

Data Access Technology Standards

A History of Open Banking Data Access

Don Cardinal[*] and Nick Thomas[**]

1. Introduction

A key issue identified for the long-term success of open banking is the need to shift from screen-scraping to using application programming interfaces (APIs) as a more secure way of sharing customer-permissioned data.[1] In the European Union, for example, the European Banking Authority created an API working group that will augment the implementing regulatory technical standards on strong customer authentication and common and secure communication even though the Second Payment Services Directive (PSD2) is tech-agnostic.[2] To achieve this goal, a common, interoperable, and royalty-free standard for the secure access, authentication, and sharing of user-permissioned financial data could help provide a strong foundation for open banking. For such a standard to be widely adopted, there must be agreement within each community in the permissioned data-sharing ecosystem on a common API standard. However, developing and adopting common technical standards is plagued by competing interests among industry stakeholders, between banks, fintech firms, and data aggregators as well as regulators. Given this context, one can easily forget the historical origins of APIs that could inform and guide the development of common standards today.

People often ask: What are APIs, and why are they important to open banking? APIs can be likened to delivery trucks and their payload capacities. You have the connectivity (drive train), you have security and authentication (the truck engine), the customer-facing experience (the gauges on the truck's dashboard), and of course the standardized data (the shipping container being transported). See Figure 5.1.

One could also liken APIs to electric power plugs and sockets. As international travelers know, every region has its own set of technical standards for the AC power plug, socket, voltage, frequency, and electric current capacity.[3] The lack of sufficient

[*] Managing Director at the Financial Data Exchange.
[**] Co-founder @ Finicity (a Mastercard company), Financial Data Exchange, Trust over IP Foundation, & the Bluetooth SIG.

[1] Basel Committee on Banking Supervision, "BIS Report on Open Banking and Application Programming Interfaces," Bank for International Settlements (Nov. 2019). https://www.bis.org/bcbs/publ/d486.pdf.
[2] European Banking Authority, "EBA Working Group on APIs under PSD2," European Banking Authority EBA (Jan. 22, 2018). https://www.eba.europa.eu:443/regulation-and-policy/payment-services-and-electronic-money/eba-working-group-on-apis-under-psd2.
[3] World plugs | IEC (n.d.). International Electrotechnical Commission IEC (Aug. 19, 2020). https://www.iec.ch/world-plugs.

Don Cardinal and Nick Thomas, *Data Access Technology Standards* In: *Open Banking*. Edited by: Linda Jeng, Oxford University Press. © Oxford University Press 2022. DOI: 10.1093/oso/9780197582879.003.0006

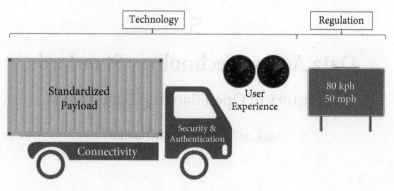

Figure 5.1 APIs as delivery trucks.

international coordination during and after World War II has led to the fourteen types of plugs and sockets in the world today.[4] We have the opportunity now to create a different outcome for open banking APIs.

a. Background

In January 1997, Microsoft, Intuit, and CheckFree announced the creation of a new consortium and technical specification called the Open Financial Exchange (OFX). The purpose of the effort was to standardize and unify use cases, data definitions, and protocols common to Intuit's OpenExchange, Microsoft's Open Financial Connectivity, and CheckFree's electronic banking and payment technology in order to enable financial institutions to exchange financial data over the internet with web users and users of popular software, such as Quicken and Microsoft Money. The initial specification was released on February 14, 1997, and received significant traction over the next eight years. By 2005, over 3,000 financial institutions had deployed some form of OFX.[5]

In 2015, the OFX Consortium was relaunched in 2015 by Intuit, Xero, Enterprise Engineering, Finicity, and Silicon Valley Bank. Leveraging OFX's widespread implementation at over 7,000 financial institutions, the Consortium's renewed mission was to securely and reliably exchange financial data between financial institutions, businesses, and consumers through fintech applications as well as the internet. Starting from a foundation of base installs, OFX was the most credible existing standard to build upon. The renewed OFX organization struggled to attract new interest and attention. On July 23, 2019, OFX merged with the Financial Data Exchange (FDX) with a vision to further unify the financial services ecosystem on a common, interoperable, royalty-free standard.[6]

---

[4] World plugs | IEC (n.d.). International Electrotechnical Commission IEC (Aug. 19, 2020). https://www.iec.ch/worldplugs/why_so_many.htm.

[5] See OFX site. https://www.ofx.net/about-ofx.html.

[6] Financial Data Exchange, "OFX Joins Financial Data Exchange to Accelerate Financial Data Sharing Standards," *Financial Data Exchange FDX* (July 23, 2019). https://financialdataexchange.org/FDX/News/Press-Releases/OFX_Joins_FDX.aspx.

Data becomes valuable information when it is both shared and useful. To that end, there have been many mechanisms over the years to share data. With respect to consumers' personal financial data, the primary mechanism by volume of data accessed has been via credentials-based HTML-harvesting, commonly referred to as screen-scraping. There are more efficient ways of sharing this data, the current best practice being via APIs.

A key question concerning the long-term success of open banking (and, more broadly, open data) is whether API standards will be proprietary or "open." APIs have existed for years and are simply tools for sharing data between software applications. API structure, format, and performance specifications are set out in user agreements, and these specifications can be "open." But what does it mean for API standards to be "open standards"?

There is no single definition for an "open standard." But it is generally agreed that for a standard to be "open" it should be publicly available. By extension, it is fair to also presume that there should be no cost to access or use the API (assuming any appropriate attribution and recognition of the owner's intellectual property). In addition, must an API be formally approved by some committee to be considered a "standard"? That is, must there be some kind of governance and governing/owning body to curate, develop, and maintain the standard? Opinions vary. For instance, the World Wide Web Consortium (W3C) uses the following metrics to determine if standards are "open": "transparency, relevance, openness, impartiality and consensus, availability, maintenance."[7] Another example is the International Telecommunications Union (ITU), which looks for these primary features in an open standard: "available to the general public, developed (or approved) and maintained via a collaborative and consensus driven process, facilitates interoperability and data exchange among different products or services, and intended for widespread adoption."[8] Yet even these two widely regarded bodies are vague around the requirements for consensus-based adoption and requirements for the formal governance of a standard.

It is important to focus on two important elements in these definitions: the first has to do with consensus. Generally, the more parties in the ecosystem that participate in a standard's creation, modification, and maintenance, the better. In addition, the more equal the parties' footing is in this process, the more likely the standard will be approved. For adoption, the easier it is to access and use the standard, the more likely the standard will be used. Thus, consensus and adoption are improved when all the parties in the data chain (i.e., data sources, data access platforms, and data recipients) are included in the creation and maintenance of any open data-sharing standard. In this view, consensus outweighs formal governance in importance. In other words, if everyone agrees, then the mechanism for that agreement is less important.

Another key ease of use feature is "interoperability"—the ability of different systems and applications or products to communicate seamlessly and reliably with each other. A good example of successful interoperability is the Universal Serial Bus

---

[7] W3C, "W3C and Open Standard," *World Wide Web Consortium W3C* (Sept. 29, 2007). https://www.w3.org/2005/09/dd-osd.html.

[8] ITU, "Definition of 'Open Standards,'" *International Telecommunications Union ITU* (Nov. 11, 2005). https://www.itu.int/en/ITU-T/ipr/Pages/open.aspx.

(USB) or Bluetooth devices, which are all interoperable with each other because all the parties using those standards came to a common agreement on how they should work. Thus, these models of other standards indicate that a way to facilitate the adoption of interoperability is to leverage preexisting standards. We will address this in more detail shortly.

2. Screen-Scraping and the History of Early APIs

"Screen-scraping" of financial data via automated scripts acting as the permissioning bank customer originated in the 1990s as data became more widely available via the internet. As screen-scraping became more popular as a way to access and share personal customer data, the first personal financial management (PFM) tools began to emerge. One of the immediate downsides of screen-scraping was that the application needed to maintain a unique script for each data source (e.g., for each individual bank). Therefore, every time the bank's customer display screen was redesigned, the screen-scraping script would fail, necessitating a rewrite of the script. This was expensive and time-consuming. In an attempt to address this problem, a coalition of firms worked to define a data-sharing format in the form of APIs. Thus, the OFX was created to build and maintain this new standard.

a. History of the Open Financial Exchange Standard

Since 1997, OFX has been the dominant direct API standard for financial institutions sharing data with financial applications. As an open standard for exchanging financial data and performing financial transactions among financial institutions and financial applications, the OFX specification is publicly available for use by any financial institution or vendor.[9] Further, OFX allows the exchange of data either directly or via an intermediary like a data aggregation service provider. OFX is now actively used at over 7,000 financial institutions, and remaining institutions have easy access to certified OFX servers via all major technology providers and systems integrators.[10]

On January 16, 1997, Microsoft, Intuit, and CheckFree announced[11] a collaboration to develop a new technical specification called OFX. This specification would enable financial institutions globally to exchange data with web users and users of PFM applications, such as Quicken and Microsoft Money. The OFX specification was the convergence of Microsoft's Open Financial Connectivity, Intuit's OpenExchange, and CheckFree's electronic banking and payment protocols. In addition to promotional statements by the three founding entities, the press release included statements of support from Visa Interactive, Fidelity, Schwab, First Union (now Wells Fargo), Bank One

---

[9] OFX standard is available for review on the OFX website. http://ofx.org.
[10] More information can be found at the OFX website. http://ofx.org.
[11] Microsoft, "Intuit, Microsoft and Checkfree Create Open Financial Exchange," *Microsoft News* (Jan. 16, 1997). https://news.microsoft.com/1997/01/16/intuit-microsoft-and-checkfree-create-open-financial-exchange/.

(now JPMorgan Chase), Citibank, NationsBank (now Bank of America), Wells Fargo, Royal Bank of Scotland, and Bank of Montreal.[12]

Statements by Charles Schwab and Co., Inc. and Citibank in the press release were especially insightful in helping to understand the players' motives for moving to a common standard for consumer-permissioned data access:

> "In terms of development, maintenance, and resources, *a single, consolidated specification removes an expensive burden from the financial institutions. It is a significant milestone in the evolution of the online environment.*"[13]

> "*This is great news for consumers. It gives them access to the provider of their choice, while eliminating the extra costs inherent in multiple proprietary interfaces. Citibank has long advocated open interfaces, and we believe this is a major step forward for the industry.*" (Jerry Rao, division executive, Citibank Development Division.)[14]

With core use cases in financial data access and payment initiation via APIs, the launch of OFX represented the founding event of industry-led, standards-based open banking.

The OFX 1.0 specification was released on February 14, 1997. The standard represented a merging of Intuit's Open Exchange, Microsoft's Open Financial Connectivity, and CheckFree's electronic payment protocols into a single data standard supporting data access and payment use cases. Intuit branded their services as Direct Connect (Express Web Connect) and Web Connect. Web Connect enables consumers to log in to their bank's website and download an OFX-formatted file, while Direct Connect (Express Web Connect) enables Intuit applications to communicate directly with a bank's OFX server. While support for the OFX standard was strong among top banks, data elements and market coverage for data access at banks was limited.[15]

At the time, some organizations maintained multiple consumer logins to different systems under the same roof. For instance, in a March 2001 report, the Gartner Group estimated that customer data within a typical Fortune 1000 company was stored on a

---

[12] T.P. Vartanaian, "The Battle over Data Aggregation," *VerticalOne*. http://www.ffhsj.com/bancmail/bmarts/aba_art.htm. See also Yodlee Press Release (Sept. 28, 1999). http://www.yodlee.com/company/pressreleases/launchfinal.html. Yodlee Press Release, AOL (AOL Personal Finance) (June 7, 2000). http://www.yodlee.com/company/pressreleases/aol.html. CitiBank (MyCiti) Press Release (July 18, 2000). http://www.citigroup.com/citigroup/press/000718b.htm. Yahoo! (Yahoo Finance) Press Release (Aug. 30, 2000). http://docs.yahoo.com/docs/pr/release585.html. eWise company's website. http://www.ewise.com.au/ewise/info/aboutus.asp. AMP (Account Minder): BRW, "Online, It's Harvest Time" (Oct. 23, 2000); Chase Manhattan Bank (Oct. 16, 2000). http://www.yodlee.com/company/pressreleases/chase_launch.html. Merrill Lynch (Feb. 20, 2001). http://www.ml.com/about/press_release/02202001-2_financial_picture_pr.htm. American Express (Feb. 15, 2001). http://home3.americanexpress.com/corp/latestnews/account_profile.asp. Wells Fargo (Mar. 7, 2001). http://www.yodlee.com/company/pressreleases/wellsfargo.html. Fleet Boston (Mar. 12, 2001). http://www.corporate-ir.net/ireye/ir_site.zhtml?ticker=fbf&script=460&layout=-6&item_id=157951. Macquarie Bank (Enrichment): Macquarie Bank Limited Uses Teknowledge's Tekportal (TM) Software to Offer Account Aggregation in Australia and New Zealand, Java Industry Connection (June 19, 2001). Hanvit Bank (e-Clips): E. Cane, "Asian Banks Begin to Embrace Account Aggregation," *FinanceAsia.com* (June 12, 2001). nineMSN (Account Master): "ninemsn, Australia's Leading Portal Launches Net Position Account Aggregation Service," *Parker's Edge News* (July 27, 2001). Monex security (Money Station): *japan.internet.com*, Internet Stock Report (Sept. 22, 2001). Nomura Security: *Nikkei* newspaper (Oct. 24, 2001). E*trade (Money Look) Press Release (Jan. 22, 2002).

[13] *Infra.*

[14] *Infra.*

[15] See A.P. Kamath, "Yodleeing Their Way to the Top," *Rediff* (Oct. 30, 1999). https://www.rediff.com/news/1999/oct/30us2.htm, and "Yodlee," *Immagic* (May 2011). https://www.immagic.com/eLibrary/ARCHIVES/GENERAL/WIKIPEDI/W110405Y.pdf.

minimum of ten different systems. Rangan's technology envisioned a future where a consumer could log in once and retrieve information from multiple sources.

Rangan, together with four co-founders, launched Yodlee and developed an initial financial account aggregation solution using "Web scraping" to harvest account data from bank websites. Yodlee would then present this harvested data to the consumer via a single login in one consolidated view. Famously, only one month after the launch of its Business-to-Consumer (B2C) portal and five hundred connections in the fall of 1999, Yodlee switched to a Business-to-Business (B2B) business model.[16] That year also saw the launch of VerticalOne and Teknowledge, both of which offered an on-premise aggregation platform to compete with Yodlee in the United States.

By 2000, data aggregation was experiencing significant adoption in the United States, with credible installations at AOL, Citibank, and Yahoo!. In addition to the players mentioned, other providers included EZLogin, acquired by 724 Solutions in March 2000; View, acquired by Digital Insight in June 2000; Canadian-based CashEdge; and eWise in Australia.[17]

3. Evolution to Common Standards for Authentication and Data-Sharing

a.   Commonalities

The technical aspects of any open data scheme can be thought of as a three-legged stool: communications, authentication, and payload/functionalities. These features, regardless of policy and legal considerations, are focused on the engineering questions of how to connect two parties, authenticate them to each other, and securely share data at scale. In addition, the reuse of common elements can be a useful way to aid interoperability and speed innovation. In other words, why reinvent the wheel if existing standards and protocols can be leveraged?

b.   Communications

Securely connecting two parties was the primary objective in introducing the secure version of Hypertext Transfer Protocol (HTTPS) and session encryption via Transport Layer Security (TLS), which is the industry standard for session layer security. Additional "defenses-in-depth,"[18] such as Mutual TLS (MTLS),[19] are often used as

---

[16] J. Melnyk and D. Meister, *Yodlee Inc.—The VerticalOne Integration (A)* (Ivey Publishing, Feb. 14, 2003). https://store.hbr.org/product/yodlee-inc-the-verticalone-integration-a/903e02?sku=903E02-PDF-ENG.

[17] Hiroshi Fujii et al., "E-Aggregation: The Present and Future of Online Financial Services in Asia-Pacific," Working Paper CISL# 2002-06, Composite Information Systems Laboratory (CISL), Sloan School of Management, Room E53–320 Massachusetts Institute of Technology (Sept. 2002). http://web.mit.edu/smadnick/www/wp/2002-06.pdf.

[18] P. Mell, J. Shook, and R. Harang (eds.). "Measuring and Improving the Effectiveness of Defense-in-Depth Postures," *Association for Computing Machinery ACM* (2016). https://doi.org/10.1145/3018981.3018986.

[19] Bradley Campbell, N. Sakimura, and T. Lodderstedt, "RFC 8705—OAuth 2.0 Mutual-TLS Client Authentication and Certificate-Bound Access Tokens," *Internet Engineering Task Force IETF* (Feb. 2020). https://tools.ietf.org/html/rfc8705.

well with strong cyphers and access control lists. Ultimately, the two parties sharing data should conduct a risk-based assessment of controls and costs that determine the optimal control stack and revisit this assessment periodically, leveraging industry best practices where possible.

c. Authentication

Authentication and authorization, is a delegated framework for (REpresentational State Transfer) REST APIs. Through OAuth, apps can access in a limited way a user's data without giving away a user's password by decoupling authentication from authorization.[20] "The OAuth protocol was originally created by a small community of web developers from a variety of websites and other Internet services who wanted to solve the common problem of enabling delegated access to protected resources."[21] OAuth was designed to work over HTTPS, and OAuth 2.0 (RFC 6749) "enables a third-party application to obtain limited access to an HTTP service."[22] This limited access can be on behalf of a customer/data owner by constructing an approved interaction between the customer/data owner and the HTTP service, or by allowing a third-party fintech application to obtain access on the customer's own behalf. It also allowed for access without using the resource owner's ID and password, and instead using a substitute object. That object has become known as an OAuth token. So to recap: OAuth solves a crucial need for third-party access and also helps with the issue of credential leakage.

OAuth 2.0's subsequent extension, RFC 8252,[23] specifies how native apps can interact with an authorization endpoint. The authorization endpoint is the interface where the user says what access a given party can have (e.g., "App X would like access to your email account—do you approve?"). A "native app" is just an application that is installed by the user to their device instead of an application running in their browser. Currently, this best practice documents how native apps can implement authorization flows using the browser as the preferred external user-agent as well as the requirements for authorization servers to support such usage.

OAuth 2.0 still did not fully address the security issue of sharing user credentials. The OpenID Foundation proposed in 2014 a method of tokenizing this access so that properly authenticated parties could transact on behalf of users without ever knowing their credentials.[24] OpenID Connect (OIDC) is an interoperable authentication protocol based on the OAuth 2.0 family of specifications. It uses REST/JSON (JavaScript Object Notation) message flows and lets developers authenticate their users across websites and apps without having to own and manage password files. OIDC allows for clients of

---

[20] M. Raible, "What the Heck Is OAuth?," *Okta Developer Blog* (June 21, 2017). https://developer.okta.com/blog/2017/06/21/what-the-heck-is-oauth.

[21] E. Hammer-Lahav, "RFC 5849—The OAuth 1.0 Protocol," *Internet Engineering Task Force IETF* (Apr. 2010).. https://tools.ietf.org/html/rfc5849

[22] D. Hardt, "RFC 6749—The OAuth 2.0 Authorization Framework," *Internet Engineering Task Force IETF* (Oct. 2021).. https://tools.ietf.org/html/rfc6749.

[23] W. Denniss and J. Bradley, "RFC 8252—OAuth 2.0 for Native Apps," *Internet Engineering Task Force IETF* (Oct. 2017). https://tools.ietf.org/html/rfc8252.

[24] D. Thibeau, "The OpenID Foundation Launches the OpenID Connect Standard | OpenID," *OpenID Foundation* (Feb. 26, 2014). https://openid.net/2014/02/26/the-openid-foundation-launches-the-openid-connect-standard/.

all types, including browser-based JavaScript and native mobile apps, to launch sign-in flows and receive verifiable assertions about the identity of signed-in users. Effectively (Identity, Authentication) + OAuth 2.0 = OIDC. Version 2 of OIDC was approved January 8, 2020.[25] According to Ping Identity, OIDC implementers include Google, Microsoft, PayPal, Ping Identity, Nikkei Newspaper, Tokyu Corporation, mixi, Yahoo! Japan, and SoftBank. There are also mature deployments underway by Working Group participant organizations, such as Deutsche Telecom, AOL, and Salesforce.[26] Sign In with Apple also uses OIDC.[27]

When it came to how to move away from credential-based access (e.g., someone besides the end user holding the end user's ID and password to access data) in operational production, the OAuth 2.0 authentication schema with the OpenID Foundation's concept of tokenized access (OIDC) was an established and growing tool set. The parties in the ecosystem could offer strong customer authentication (interchangeably used with multi-factor authentication) and only exchange secure tokens instead of end users' login credentials. Similarly, the concept of REST APIs and JSON had come to define best-in-class practices in data exchange.

Operationally, OAuth 2.0 is not specific enough for interoperability at scale as it allows for many implementation choices. This is by design as OAuth can cover a wide range of use cases, but financial services via the internet necessitate more rigorous and secure choices. Accordingly, OAuth 2.0 used for financial data needed to be tailored to these specific requirements: obtain the OAuth 2.0 tokens in an appropriately secure manner, utilize OIDC to identify the customer, and use the tokens to read out the financial data from the REST endpoints. This stack was consolidated in 2017 by the OpenID Foundation into the financial-grade API authentication specification (FAPI).[28] Most open data implementations use FAPI or a close variant. (See the United Kingdom,[29] Australia,[30] New Zealand,[31] the United States,[32] and Canada[33] on FDX; and Brazil,[34]

[25] M. Jones, "Second Implementer's Draft of OpenID Connect Federation Specification Approved | OpenID," *OpenID Foundation* (Jan. 9, 2020). https://openid.net/2020/01/08/second-implementers-draft-of-openid-connect-federation-specification-approved/.

[26] "Ping Identity. How OpenID Connect Works Tutorial," *OIDC* (2019). https://www.pingidentity.com/en/resources/client-library/articles/openid-connect.html.

[27] N. Sakimura, "Apple Successfully Implements OpenID Connect with Sign In with Apple | OpenID," *OpenID Foundation* (June 29, 2020). https://openid.net/2019/09/30/apple-successfully-implements-openid-connect-with-sign-in-with-apple/.

[28] M. Jones, "FAPI 1.0 Part 1 and Part 2 are now Final Specifications | OpenID," *OpenID Foundation* (Mar. 13, 2021). https://openid.net/2021/03/12/fapi-1-0-part-1-and-part-2-are-now-final-specifications/.

[29] M. Leszcz, "The UK Open Banking Implementation Entity Adopts the OpenID Foundation Financial-Grade API (FAPI) Specification & Certification Program | OpenID," *OpenID Foundation* (July 13, 2018). https://openid.net/2018/07/12/the-uk-open-banking-implementation-entity-adopts-the-openid-foundation-financial-grade-api-fapi-specification-certification-program/.

[30] CSIRO Data 61, "Consumer Data Standards Australia," *GitHub* (Dec. 18, 2018). https://consumerdatastandardsaustralia.github.io/standards/#security-profile.

[31] Payments New Zealand, "NZ Banking Data API Specification v1.0.0—Payments NZ API Standards," Payments NZ (Mar. 6, 2019). https://paymentsdirection.atlassian.net/wiki/spaces/PaymentsNZAPIStandards/pages/374669617/NZ+Banking+Data+API+Specification+v1.0.0.

[32] "Financial Data Exchange, OpenID Foundation Take Step Towards Global Standard for Financial Data Sharing," *Financial Data Exchange (FDX)* (Mar. 26, 2019). https://financialdataexchange.org/FDX/News/Press-Releases/FDX_OpenID_Global_Standard.aspx.

[33] "Leading Canadian Financial Services Firms Moving to Adopt the FDX Technical Standards for Secure Financial Data Sharing," *Financial Data Exchange (FDX)* (July 29, 2020a). https://financialdataexchange.org/FDX/News/Press-Releases/FDX_Canada.aspx.

[34] H. Davies, "TecBan and Ozone bring open banking to Brazil," *Ozone API* (May 17, 2020). https://ozoneapi.com/2020/05/15/tecban-and-ozone-bring-open-banking-to-brazil/.

Mexico,[35] Germany,[36] Japan,[37] as some examples.[38]) FAPI's prevalence is indicative of FAPI being an ideal feature in open API standards that use protocols that are fit-for-purpose in financial data-sharing.

d. Payload/Functionalities

Communications and authentication are not the whole story however. API functionalities and data payloads (while typically all JSON objects) differ between jurisdictions for a variety of regulatory and market-driven reasons. In regulatory schemes, the payloads are often only defined in scope to meet the regulatory minimum functions and nothing more. In market-driven schemes, some functionality that is mandated in regulatory regions is missing altogether. For example: In UK and Mexican requirements, there is a mandate for an API for bank and ATM location, whereas in the FDX spec, there is no API support for it at this time.[39] Similarly there is market demand in North America for consumer investment account data, including tax lots, holdings, pending trades, and so forth, so the FDX specification includes these, whereas the German specification does not at this time.[40]

4. Regulatory Approaches

a. Mandatory Schemes

Markets where regulators have mandated financial data access tend to have a single financial regulator and have a hyperconcentrated banking market; consider the nine major banks in the United Kingdom, four in Australia, four in Mexico, four in Canada, and one in Germany. Often regulatory-led proposals were driven primarily by policy goals. Commonly stated policy goals were increasing competition for services, lowering prices for payments, lowering the bar to entry for new entrants, and improving consumer data control and privacy.

A regulatory approach has the advantage of forcing adoption and conformance, but it also has the potential of superimposing ill-fitting solutions. Incumbents may also treat regulatory compliance as check-the-box exercises, meeting only the bare regulatory

---

[35] Secretaria de Gobernacion, "CIRCULAR 2/2020. DOF—Diario Oficial de la Federación" (Mar. 3, 2020). http://www.dof.gob.mx/nota_detalle.php?codigo=5588824&fecha=10/03/2020.

[36] "PSD2 Access to Bank Accounts | The Berlin Group," The Berlin Group (2019a). https://www.berlin-group.org/psd2-access-to-bank-accounts.

[37] T. Authlete Kudo, "Trends in Banking APIs (or Leveraging OAuth/OIDC)," presented at the Financial APIs Workshop Japan/UK Open Banking and APIs Summit 2018 LinkedIn (July 27, 2018). https://www.linkedin.com/pulse/trends-banking-apis-leveraging-oauthoidc-tatsuo-kudo/.

[38] Notes: Mexico's initial regulation specified REST APIs via JSON, and it is strongly felt that FAPI will be specified for the consumer authentication when released. The German spec (NextGenPSD2) does not mandate JSON, supporting the older XML as well. It also does not mandate tokenized access (OAuth 2.0 or OIDC) and allows for legacy credential sharing in its redirect flow.

[39] Open Banking UK, "ATM Locator API Specification," Open Banking UK GitHub (Apr. 2, 2019). https://openbankinguk.github.io/opendata-api-docs-pub/v2.4.0/atmlocator/atm-locator.html.

[40] "NextGenPSD2 Download Page | The Berlin Group | Core PSD2 Compliancy," The Berlin Group (Mar. 2019). https://www.berlin-group.org/nextgenpsd2-downloads.

minimum. What these regulatory policies sometimes fail to prioritize are the market problems and market needs that open data can and does address. On the other hand, a regulatory approach could ensure highly consistent implementation and common standards.

The European Union's PSD2 (2015/2366) had the intent of allowing third-parties to access consumer financial data and mandated strong customer authentication—also referred to as multi-factor authentication. As a result, the UK Competition and Markets Authority (CMA) issued a ruling in August 2016, mandating the nine largest UK banks—the CMA9: HSBC, Barclays, RBS, Santander, Bank of Ireland, Allied Irish Bank, Danske Bank, Lloyds, and Nationwide—to allow licensed fintech firms acting with the customer's permission access to the customer's financial data (bank accounts and transactions). In addition, the CMA ordered the CMA9 to fund a nonprofit Open Banking Implementation Entity (OBIE) also known as Open Banking Limited, which would issue technical standards, define operating rules, and set up any common utilities, such as a list of approved fintech firms. Implementation was to run from January 2018 through September 2019. You can read more about the UK experience in Chapter 9 by Gavin Littlejohn, Ghela Boskovich, and Richard Prior.

This regulatory-led approach has been followed in several other jurisdictions, including the European Union, Australia, Mexico, and Brazil. Later chapters in this book describe the mandatory open banking regimes of the European Union, the United Kingdom, Australia, and India.

b. Hybrid Schemes

Some jurisdictions have a hybrid approach in which the regulator is involved in the technology as well as policy, but API implementation is voluntary. This seems to be a reflection of the culture and accepted role of regulators—more as coordinators, referees, and facilitators than as market-owners. This allows the specifics of implementation to be managed by the entities directly interfacing with consumers and does not put the responsibility of picking technical architectures and solutions solely on a regulator. For instance:

- Singapore's Monetary Authority has released a suite of API standards in 2019 with the association of banks in Singapore.[41]
- Japan issued updates to the Japanese Banking Act in 2017 and 2020[42] in support of APIs and open data, but with a focus on ecosystem efficiencies and security.
- The Hong Kong Money Authority introduced its framework in July 2018, launching its Open API Framework in January 2019 with a phased approach, increasing data scopes and capability over time.[43]

[41] Association of Banks in Singapore & Monetary Authority of Singapore, "Finance-as-a-Service: API Playbook," *Financial World* (June 2019). https://abs.org.sg/docs/library/abs-api-playbook.pdf.

[42] Atsushi Okada, Takane Hori, and Takahiro Lijima, "The Financial Technology Law Review," *The Law Reviews* (May 3, 2020). https://thelawreviews.co.uk/title/the-financial-technology-law-review/japan.

[43] The Government of Hong Kong Special Administrative Region, "Open API Framework for the Banking Sector: One Year On," The Government of Hong Kong (July 31, 2019). https://www.info.gov.hk/gia/general/201907/31/P2019073100358.htm.

Another advantage of not having a fixed artificial deadline is that it allows solutions to be piloted cautiously and to be implemented organically in an organization's normal change calendar. An important point about financial services and the need for caution with customers' money and data was made by Bank of America's CTO Cathy Bessant in 2017; "The idea of 'fail fast and fail often' does not work in a business where your gross margin in a wildly good year, might be a little bit under two percent. 'Fail fast and big' is not in our lexicon."[44] Chapter 6 describes Singapore's facilitative approach to open banking.

c. Market-Led Schemes

In some jurisdictions, industries have convened data-sharing participants in the ecosystem to address market problems and needs that can be addressed by open banking and open data. Effectively answering the question of: What needs can be addressed by the introduction and adoption of a common, interoperable, royalty-free specification for consumer-permissioned data-sharing? While the mission is altruistic, some participants in these efforts also are likely to be motivated by the desire to introduce these capabilities in advance of any formal rule. Precedents for market-led financial tech innovation include: online banking, mobile banking, and the EMV (EuroPay, Mastercard, Visa) chip replacing the magnetic stripe on cards. Outside the fintech sector—examples like Bluetooth, FIDO, and USB are ubiquitous market-driven solutions built outside of any regulatory mandate.[45]

5. Stakeholders in the Open Banking Ecosystem

So, what would make competing firms with sometimes diametrically opposed views on data-sharing[46] work together on a common framework? The answer is *common purpose*. One of the interesting things is that this common tool can address even different needs of the participants in the ecosystem. We will walk you through some of these different needs and priorities in the following.

a. Banks

Based on an informal poll of financial institutions in the United States: on average, up to 40 percent of their online traffic is from bots and harvesters, up to 40 percent of their online session traffic is from known benign automation (aggregators and fintechs), and

[44] P. High, "The Future of Technology According to Bank of America's Chief Operations and Technology Officer," *Forbes* (Jan. 8, 2021). https://www.forbes.com/sites/peterhigh/2017/06/19/the-future-of-technology-according-to-bank-of-americas-chief-operations-and-technology-officer/#63d4eb1677c5.

[45] For more reading on these different regulatory approaches, see BCBS Report on Open Banking and APIs (Nov. 19, 2019). https://www.bis.org/press/p191119.htm.

[46] D. Huang and P. Rudegeair, "Bank of America Cut Off Finance Sites from Its Data," *Wall Street Journal* (Nov. 10, 2015). https://www.wsj.com/articles/bank-of-america-cut-off-finance-sites-from-its-data-1447115089.

only 20 percent of their session volume is from humans.[47] These percentages are fairly consistent across banks of all sizes and independent of timing (e.g., day of the week or day of the month did not matter).

Consider the millions of dollars needed to provide hardware, software, and support for the known, benign automation. From a cybersecurity perspective—the staff defending the site has to differentiate in real-time between malicious and benign automation—this is a difficult proposition. We also know from polling financial institutions in North America that there were up to 100 million unique sets of customer usernames and passwords being shared with and used by aggregators and fintech firms to access data. Roughly 30 percent of any bank's online customer base has shared their online ID and password with data aggregators and fintechs, according to the same Financial Services Information Sharing and Analysis Center (FS-ISAC) working group survey. Banks could ask themselves:

- What if a firm could move the known, benign automation to a dedicated API that is an order of magnitude more efficient?
- What if as part of that migration that 30 percent of your customer base no longer needed to share their credentials with third-parties?
- What if that API specification was royalty-free to use?

That bank would improve its privacy posture, its cyber-risk posture, and its long-term hardware expense budget as it migrates to this API. The only additional costs would be determining the specifications and setting up the API and enrolling fintechs into the access.

b. Aggregators and Other Fintechs

Accessing data via scraping HTML is very inefficient. It is slow, as each screen must be rendered before data can be accessed. Each financial institution's screens are different—necessitating a custom script for each one. Every time a financial institution changes a screen, the script breaks, meaning a fintech firm must have a dedicated staff to constantly repair broken scripts. Data is inconsistent. Different financial institutions display and describe data in different ways. Often different data is described similarly, for example: "What is the balance on your credit card?" Well, the author of the script has several dollar fields, all described as a balance to pick from: Current Balance, Statement Balance, Promotional Balance, Purchases Balance, Cash Advance Limit Balance, and so on. If the engineer returns the wrong value, it could have negative consequences for the consumer. These firms also must navigate a waterfall of defenses in depth at financial institutions designed to stop fraudsters, often resulting in delayed or blocked access. Finally, the fintechs themselves do not want to have to hold customer credentials as they too wish to minimize their operational risk. Fintechs, in turn, ask themselves:

---

[47] Financial Services Information Sharing and Analysis Center, Spring 2017 FS-ISAC Aggregation Working Group informal poll.

- What if the fintech could have a highly available, efficient, dedicated access portal (an API) to the financial institution?
- What if the data were highly standardized and uniform?
- What if the access no longer required the fintech or an aggregator to hold consumer credentials?
- What if that API specification was royalty-free to use?

Fintechs, accordingly, would improve their privacy posture and their cyber-risk posture and get away from having to spend money on playing whack-a-mole fixing busted scripts as well as have more available, more consistent, and hygienic data products to offer their customers. The only additional costs are also determining the API specifications and setting up the API and enrolling on the financial institution's portal. Notice how the incentives are completely different, yet served by the same tool? Now that the tool is known, the challenge is setting up the ecosystem to adopt and maintain it. One approach has been the one pursued by the FDX.

6. Origins of the Financial Data Exchange

As early as 2013, bank security teams began escalating the concerns from customer-directed automation to their security executives, chief information security officers (CISOs). Most participate in the FS-ISAC. The FS-ISAC convened a working group to understand the issues posed by this access, how the risks have changed since the late 1990s and early days of scripted access, and to propose solutions. Given that the customer demand for this access was about twenty years old, the decision was made to modernize it to an API. HTTPS with TLS was becoming the industry standard for connectivity, and the concepts of REST and OAuth tokenization were new and adopted. For the data payload, advice and content was lent from Intuit and the OFX 2.1 specification. This package was known as the Durable Data API (DDA 1.0) and released in 2015.[48] Despite the promise, few aggregators and fintechs adopted the DDA specification. The FS-ISAC Working Group reconvened in 2016 to update the specification to reflect changes in TLS, OIDC, and Biometrics (FIDO), and further refine and augment the data fields. Version 2.0 was released in February 2018.[49] While banks were starting to adopt DDA and the data payload of version 1.0 of DDA was the initial data specification for FAPI 1.0 (which was adopted by the UK Open Banking Entity), fintech firms were not adopting it. At the same time, a group of fintech firms, parties from the OFX Consortium, and Wells Fargo were looking to create an open banking ecosystem (tentatively called Initiative X) and technical specification in the United States. In this instance, the banks were hesitant to adopt a nonbank standard.

[48] N. Thomas, "How Industry Standardization Will Impact Data Access. ProgrammableWeb" (Mar. 27, 2017). https://www.programmableweb.com/news/how-industry-standardization-will-impact-data-access/analysis/2017/03/27.

[49] W. Ashford, "FS-ISAC Enables Safer Financial Data Sharing with API," ComputerWeekly.Com (Feb. 12, 2018). https://www.computerweekly.com/news/252434931/FS-ISAC-enables-safer-financial-data-sharing-with-API.

In the spring of 2018, the chairs of the FS-ISAC Aggregation Working Group met with the board of Initiative X at Finicity's headquarters in Salt Lake City and agreed to begin the process of merging into what would be launched in October 2018 as the FDX.[50] Both groups of members contributed intellectual property and resources, and worked to agree on common governance principles as an independent subsidiary of the FS-ISAC.

Growth in both the organization and the FDX API has been strong, having grown from 22 founding member organizations to over 180 and expanding into Canada.[51] According to its latest internal member survey, over sixteen million consumers have had their held-away IDs and passwords converted to OAuth tokens. When examining why FDX has seen so much growth in membership and in adoption in a little over two years with no government mandate whatsoever, it is important to consider what makes it different from other open banking sponsors and other technical standards bodies.

FDX is an independent, voluntary, nonprofit technical standards body, with no other commercial interests, that is barred by its charter from lobbying or commenting on policy. As it is not dependent on any government mandated funding scheme, it allows FDX members to set the scope and direction of its work. It also means that any solutions FDX works on must address market needs.

This structure requires a top-to-bottom democracy—examples: leadership at the board, committee, and working group level is always shared (co-chaired) by a Financial Institution (FI) and a non-FI. Technical working groups use a "best idea wins" policy— any member firm can put forward a change, and each organization only gets one vote. Finally, to truly achieve consensus, membership must be open to all ecosystem participants.

When one looks at other jurisdictions and the differences in the structure of their offerings, there is some concern on the sustainability of taxpayer funded efforts over time as well as the participation and adoption by smaller and more varied players in the respective ecosystems. If the members, who are closest to the consumer and dependent on them for their very livelihood, do not manage the organization, how can they be assured that their respective needs and the needs of their customers will be met and that they will receive value commensurate to their participation?

Consider the UK OBIE established by the CMA in 2016. It is composed of and funded by the nine largest banks in the United Kingdom and governed by the CMA.[52] In addition to technical standards (data, technical, and security), it takes on several operational functions: vetting participants and maintaining a Central Register of approved participants as well as a service desk for complaints, disputes, and service levels monitoring.[53] Lacking are small fintechs, academics, consumer groups, and other impacted stakeholders.

---

[50] Financial Data Exchange, "Financial Industry Unites to Enhance Data Security, Innovation and Consumer Control" (Press Release) (Aug. 19, 2020b). https://financialdataexchange.org/FDX/News/Press-Releases/Financial_Industry_Unites_Data_Security.aspx.

[51] Financial Data Exchange, "Leading Canadian Financial Services Firms Moving to Adopt the FDX Technical Standards for Secure Financial Data Sharing" (July 29, 2020). https://financialdataexchange.org/FDX/News/Press-Releases/FDX_Canada.aspx.

[52] Open Banking UK, "Open Banking UK About Us" (n.d.). https://www.openbanking.org.uk/about-us/.

[53] Open Banking UK, "Operational Governance Rules and Guidelines for March 2017 Open Data (1.0)" (Mar. 2017). https://www.openbanking.org.uk/wp-content/uploads/2017/02/Operational-Governance-OB-Rules-and-Guidelines-March-2017-V1.0-Baselined-Web-1.pdf.

7. Current Challenges

Any standard's success has to be measured primarily by level of adoption (both in "endpoints" and in "volume"). In this case, "endpoints" means the number of data sources (banks, brokerages, credit unions, insurance companies, utilities, etc.), the number of aggregators, and the number of fintech apps that support a given standard. The other useful measure is "volume," which refers to the number of API calls and is indicative of the amount of data flowing through an API. "In markets where a standard is mandated, we see large endpoints adopting, but volumes failing to meet expectations. In voluntary markets, adoption is not as fast as mandated markets for a few reasons: everyone is waiting to see that everyone else will adopt, and any adoption projects must compete with other priorities in a firm whose build schedules can often be longer than a year. It is not unheard of for a project with a firm funding commitment to be slated for delivery two years in the future. Other barriers to adoption can be from the policymakers themselves. If there is regulatory uncertainty on key questions, it is difficult to proceed. Engineers in a digital world must code to 1 or 0, not "maybe."

When looking at timing for open banking (as well as open finance and, more broadly, open data), one need only look back to prior innovations: EMV chips, online banking, and mobile banking. We see large firms with ample resources able to deploy minimum viable products ahead of others. Next, the very small firms who have outsourced some or all of their tech stacks will receive these capabilities when their platforms deploy them, a "rising tide lifts all boats" effect. The final group to have adopted these earlier innovations listed above were the midsize organizations that managed most of their tech but more likely did not readily have the expertise or resources to deploy as quickly as larger firms while also not having a larger services firm like a core processor to lean on. However, as in the past, other third-party firms can and will emerge to fill this gap.

A challenge faced in voluntary schemes not faced by mandatory regimes is new entrant vetting. In mandatory regimes, once a firm passes regulatory review and meets organizational requirements (e.g., SOC2-certification, PCI-DSS audit along with a minimum level of insurance or bonding) and demonstrates technical conformance, all firms in that ecosystem can (or must) engage with them. The former is still in a highly customized state where any two parties wishing to share data must complete a bilateral agreement. There is some movement to try to find solutions to each of these issues in a market-driven, sustainable manner, but it is still early stages. The Clearing House, a banking association and payments company owned by the largest commercial banks, for example, has created a common model agreement for firms to use as a basis of their agreement construction. There have been discussions among industry players on what a common open banking audit might look like—perhaps a sort of hybrid of PCI-DSS/SOC2 that is tailored to consumer-permissioned data-sharing. One potential tool is a data-sharing risk assessment piloted by The Clearing House.[54] But for regulated firms to rely on a new sort of common artifact, they will need very clear regulatory guidance indicating that the audit is acceptable. Additionally, while mandatory regimes can

---

[54] The Clearing House, "New Streamlined Data Sharing Risk Assessment Service" (Jan. 26, 2021). https://www.theclearinghouse.org/payment-systems/articles/2021/01/01-26-2021_new-streamlined-data-sharing-risk-assessment-service.

require open banking participants to insure against breaches and other liabilities (one could also argue that in such situations the government becomes the de facto insurer of last resort), such insurance counterparties have yet to make entry into voluntary regimes. The good news is that in the past, markets (whole industries) have created captive reinsurers who can then specialize in underwriting very particular technical risks. The path from ideation to realization for this development is a few years off.

The final barrier for adoption in voluntary schemes is the replacement of all the data and functionalities that exist today via credentials-based access. Firms may be hesitant to provision data, especially data their regulator may have called out for special handling in security or privacy regulation. As mentioned previously, regulatory certainty about data elements, controls, and how to show conformance with regulatory preferences will be needed so that any business requirements can be reflected in the technology.

With global harmonization on communications and authentication becoming a reality (HTTPS with TLS 1.2 and FAPI 1.0)—the remaining areas for technical harmonization will be payload and functionalities. Quality as well as quantity will matter. Standards that get "Swiss Army Knife" syndrome and try to do all things for all needs, especially without very diverse representation from stakeholders as the capabilities are built out, will likely not see much adoption as the market and consumer needs are the ultimate arbiter of what standards will be used. Just look to the past for lessons learned: VHS versus Betamax, and HD versus Blu-ray.

6

Taking Your Data with You

Singapore's Approach to Data Portability

Zee Kin Yeong[*] *and David Roi Hardoon*[**]

1. Introduction

This chapter commences with an introduction to open banking developments in Singapore, which has hitherto focused on technical aspects that are necessary for the transfer of data. Early open banking pilots led to a maturing realization that to achieve a balanced outcome, the open banking conversation needed to instead evolve into one around data portability, centered on enhancing the consumer/data subject's ability to control his or her digital footprint. The evolutionary path of open banking toward data portability can perhaps be seen as proof of the Banking Committee on Banking Supervision's finding that "data privacy laws can provide a foundation for an open banking framework."[1]

The main focus of this chapter is the ongoing policy and legislative developments in data portability, which is the area of data privacy rights that will provide the foundation for open banking.[2] While the objectives behind data portability in Singapore are policy- and regulator-driven, a keen eye is kept on the technical and process details that are necessary for successful implementation. Implementation of data portability in Singapore draws on its open banking experience—for example, in establishing application programming interfaces (APIs) for requesting and transmitting data—in order to ensure that its policy objective of securing the flow of data across its economy to support competition is achieved. Drawing comparisons with ongoing developments in Australia, the European Union, and the United States, the chapter puts forward the Singapore model as an example of how a data portability framework could be designed.

2. Singapore's Approach to Open Banking

There is no official definition of "open banking," but it has been defined by the Basel Committee on Banking Supervision as "the sharing and leveraging of

---

[*] Deputy Commissioner, Personal Data Protection Commission of Singapore.
[**] Senior Advisor, Union Bank of the Philippines. The author would like to acknowledge the Monetary Authority of Singapore, where he was Chief Data Officer and Special Advisor (AI).

[1] See, Banking Committee on Banking Supervision's "Report on Open Banking and Application Programming Interfaces," *Bank for International Settlements* (Nov. 2019), at p 8. https://www.bis.org/bcbs/publ/d486.pdf.
[2] See also the discussion on the broader spectrum of data rights, of which data portability is one, in Chapter 2.

Zee Kin Yeong and David Roi Hardoon, *Taking Your Data with You* In: *Open Banking*. Edited by: Linda Jeng, Oxford University Press.

customer-permissioned data by banks with third-party developers and firms to build applications and services."[3] This right to share data is perhaps best seen as a species of the larger genus that is the right to data portability. This is perhaps the best perspective to take in understanding the developments in open banking and data portability in Singapore.

Open banking in Singapore takes a developmental approach with a focus on facilitating experimentation and enabling public-private collaboration, in order to establish an ecosystem conducive to the development of financial technology (fintech) and regulatory technology (regtech) solutions and companies. This stems from a desire to motivate the industry to base their adoption through the appreciation of commercial and operational benefit of "opening up" access to customer information, without reliance on an obligatory regulatory mandate. This could be due to the high levels of innovation already seen within its financial sector, particularly the growth of fintech solutions in recent years.

Open APIs enable interoperability and supports agile experimentation, thereby reducing the costs of collaboration and co-creation between industry players. Don Cardinal and Nick Thomas undertake a more extensive discussion of open APIs in Chapter 5. In the context of Singapore's open banking efforts, open APIs are intended to accelerate the development of innovative solutions and new business models in the financial ecosystem, and the Monetary Authority of Singapore (MAS)[4] actively promoted the proliferation of APIs in the financial sector. In comparison to traditional means of data access (e.g., electronic data interchange or screen-scraping), where knowledge of the underlying system may be required, APIs provide an easy and dynamic conduit to organizations' data where one only needs to know the standard structure of the API function call and the definitions of data returned.[5]

MAS, working with the Association of Banks in Singapore, published in 2016 its *Finance-as-a-Service: API Playbook*,[6] providing a glossary of recommended API data structure. More recently, MAS also established a Financial Industry API registry featuring transactional and information APIs from five major financial institutions,[7] so as to provide the industry with reference guidelines aimed at encouraging API-enabled innovation.

The combination of open banking efforts on the back of a strong push for fintech has fomented the development of a vibrant fintech startup scene.[8] Specific to fintech solutions that make use of open banking APIs, SoCash is an example of a bank-fintech partnered solution that makes use of the APIs to provide digital cash points at participating merchants, instead of hunting for an ATM.[9] Standard Chartered's Live The Good Life service[10] is an example of how a broader ecosystem is enabled when a

---

[3] *Supra*, note 1, at 5..

[4] Monetary Authority of Singapore is the Central Bank, Integrated Financial Regulator and Financial Development Centre of Singapore.

[5] Chapter 5 discusses APIs and data access standards in more detail.

[6] https://www.mas.gov.sg/-/media/MAS/Smart-Financial-Centre/API/ABSMASAPIPlaybook.pdf.

[7] Namely, NETS, DBS Bank, OCBC Bank, Citi, and Standard Chartered. https://www.mas.gov.sg/development/fintech/financial-industry-api-register.

[8] For example, see "Top 30 Fintech Startups in Singapore." https://fintechnews.sg/top-30-fintech-startups-in-singapore/.

[9] Example taken from "Open Banking Initiatives in Singapore, Australia, Hong Kong and India," *Tecknospire*. https://teknospire.com/open-banking-initiatives-in-singapore-australia-hongkong-and-india/.

[10] https://www.sc.com/sg/promotions/the-good-life-privileges/#438442-sg.

bank partners with fintech and other startups to develop applications that make use of its APIs, in this case offering dining and lifestyle privileges to Standard Chartered card holders.[11] Banks had commenced publishing their available APIs providing software developers and fintech firms a "sandbox" in which to test their solutions, such as Citi's Global API Developer Portal[12] and DBS Bank developer portal[13] among others.

The early successes of open banking can be attributed to a forward-thinking financial regulator working with established financial institutions that were able and willing to provide open access to their data. In open banking conversations, concerns are often raised about the need for reciprocity and the creation of opportunities for both porting and receiving entities.[14] These concerns are also echoed in the data portability discussions discussed in the next part of this chapter.

Specific lessons can be drawn from the open banking experience thus far. First, open banking efforts focused only on moving data within the financial sector alone is sub-optimal, as switching financial services providers is in essence a zero-sum game even though it provides greater consumer choice. Second, unlocking data from only incumbent financial institutions imposes an unfair burden on financial institutions and sets out a unidirectional flow of personal data, thereby establishing an asymmetric data ecosystem.[15] In order to achieve its smart financial center objectives, open banking efforts had to establish demonstrable outcomes that are not confined within a bank's environment or specific bank-fintech collaboration. Open banking in the Singapore context is, in fact, leading the way for broader efforts in facilitating the porting of data across organizations and business sectors.

3. What Is Data Portability?

Data portability is essentially a set of rights and obligations that empowers the consumer to make a request for copies of his or her personal data held by one organization to be transmitted to another organization.[16] Concomitantly, the organization that has possession, custody, or control over that set of data is under an obligation to give effect to the request and make the transfer. When implemented as part of data protection laws, data portability requirements enable a data subject to port his or her data from one data controller to another. This is the most common form of implementation globally, although Australia has framed its implementation of this policy in a broader sense through its Consumer Data Right (CDR).[17]

As discussed by Kaitlin Asrow in Chapter 2,[18] even with more common implementations of data portability in data protection laws, there can be a number of

---

[11] Example taken from Graham Rothwell, "The Brave New World of Open Banking in APAC: Singapore." https://bankingblog.accenture.com/brave-new-world-open-banking-apac-singapore.
[12] https://www.citigroup.com/citi/news/2016/161114a.htm(10 November 2016).
[13] https://www.dbs.com/dbsdevelopers/discover/index.html.
[14] See also "Open Banking around the World," *EMEA Centre for Regulatory Strategy, Deloitte*. https://www2.deloitte.com/cy/en/pages/financial-services/articles/open-banking-around-the-world.html.
[15] See also the discussion in Chapter 14, by Brad Carr.
[16] As discussed in Chapter 2 on data rights.
[17] As further discussed by Jamie Leach and Julie McKay in Chapter 10 on Australia's open data framework.
[18] See Section 4.b, "Right to Portability and Exportability," in Chapter 2.

variations. One key distinction is the difference between data portability (which is a more recent development) and the longer-standing right of a data subject to access a copy of their data controlled by an organization ("data subject access request right").[19] The *data subject access request right* is a common and probably universal feature of all data protection legislation. This can be traced to the individual participation principle in the 1980 OECD Guidelines on the Protection of Privacy and Transborder Flows of Personal Data (OECD Guidelines).[20]

The *data subject access right* should be thought of as a right that gives effect to two related principles: the neighboring data quality principle and the individual participation principle. The neighboring *data quality principle*[21] ensures that data controllers making decisions that affect data subjects do so with information that is accurate, complete, and updated. The *individual participation principle* states that communication to the data subject should be "data relating to him . . . in a form that is intelligible to him."[22] Empowering the data subject with a right of access enables him or her to request the correction of inaccurate data and to require that the data controller provide an account of how his or her data has been used.[23] Building on these principles, data portability goes beyond the data subject access right and the individual participation principle in that it imposes an obligation to effect a request to transmit a copy of the data to another organization and not merely provide a copy to the requestor.

Another key feature is that most implementations of data portability require transmission of information in a machine-readable form.[24] This is unsurprising since data portability is a modern development, and the preponderance of our information is now stored in digital form. Transmission in machine-readable form speaks to the raison d'être for data portability, which is to enable the movement of data across the economy in order to support competition, whether this is through switching to comparable services and products or to support recombinant innovation.[25] It is eminently possible to modernize data subject access rights by requiring that copies of data that the data subject has a right to access should be provided in machine-readable form. Doing so will enable the data subject to personally transfer downloaded data to a new service provider, but this introduces friction in the switching or onboarding process. However, until there is global consensus on how to modernize the data subject access right—whether through reinterpretation of extant implementing legislation or through

---

[19] Section 1033 of the Dodd-Frank Act is such an example. See Chapter 2 for more reading.

[20] Recommendation of the Council Concerning Guidelines Governing the Protection of Privacy and Transborder Flows of Personal Data (Sept. 23, 1980). http://www.oecd.org/sti/ieconomy/oecdguidelinesontheprotectionofprivacyandtransborderflowsofpersonaldata.htm.

[21] *Id.*, at Section 8.

[22] *Id.*, at Section 13.

[23] See also, *In the matter HSBC Bank (Singapore) Limited* [2021] SGPDPC 3, paras 6 – 8 (10 March 2021). https://www.pdpc.gov.sg/-/media/Files/PDPC/PDF-Files/Commissions-Decisions/Decision--HSBC-Bank-Singapore-Limited--10032021.pdf?la=en.

[24] Section 56AI of the Australian Competition and Consumer Act 2010. See Section 5(c) of this chapter and Chapter 2 for more on data portability.

[25] "Data: Engine for Growth—Implications for Competition Law, Personal Data Protection, and Intellectual Property Rights." https://www.cccs.gov.sg/resources/publications/occasional-research-papers/data-engine-for-growth. See Section 4(b) of this chapter and Chapter 7 for a discussion of the economic features of data.

legislative amendments—the requirement of providing data in machine-readable form is a distinctive feature of data portability. Thus the Californian Consumer Privacy Act focuses on obtaining a copy of data in machine readable form and is often referred to as an example of data portability.[26]

A third feature is the scope of data that the data portability right covers and, as a corollary, the types of entities that might be able to exercise this right and to whom this obligation is owed. Most practitioners and scholars will point to the European Union's General Data Protection Regulation (GDPR)[27] as the genesis of this concept, which is being introduced in a number of jurisdictions as their data protection laws are enacted or updated.[28] When implemented as part of data protection laws, the data portability right augments the data subject's personal rights and gives the data subject greater control over his or her data.

In the European Union, this is seen as an extension of the data subject's fundamental rights. Whereas in Singapore, the discussions leading to the introduction of data portability have been driven primarily by competition and consumer protection policies.[29] In contrast to the global trend, data portability is implemented in Australia as a *customer* data right based on consumer protection as opposed to a personal data subject right.[30] This has the twin effects in expanding the scope of data to cover nonpersonal data that would be subject to data portability and expanding the benefits of data portability to businesses that are also consumers (for example, businesses with bank accounts). This is unsurprising, since the impetus in Australia for the introduction of data portability is traced to recommendations of the Productivity Commission's inquiry into data availability and use.[31] There is clear wisdom in taking this approach if the policy objective is to increase competition, particularly since massive volumes of data are generated through commercial transactions and operations in business, manufacturing, and agriculture. These benefits have not gone unnoticed in Singapore as there is a recent law reform proposal advocating the introduction of data portability for businesses over nonpersonal data.[32]

[26] See also Chapter 2 for a discussion of data portability.

[27] Regulation (EU) 2016/679 of the European Parliament and of the Council of April 17, 2016, on the protection of natural persons with regard to the processing of personal data and on the free movement of such data, and repealing Directive 95/46/EC (General Data Protection Regulation). https://eur-lex.eur opa.eu/legal-content/EN/TXT/?uri=uriserv%3AOJ.L_.2016.119.01.0001.01.ENG&toc=OJ%3AL%3A2 016%3A119%3ATOC. For more on the GDPR, see Chapter 8 on the EU approach.

[28] For a comparative study of Australia, the European Union, and Singapore, see *infra*, note 36 and the discussion in the accompanying main text; see also California and Philippines, *infra*, notes 46 & 47 and the discussion in the accompanying main texts.

[29] See, para. 15.8. Personal Data Protection Commission. "Advisory Guidelines on Key Concepts in the Personal Data Protection Act" (issued Sept. 23, 2013, revised Feb. 1, 2021). See also, Section 5(a) of this chapter and Chapter 8 for a discussion of EU data portability.

[30] *Id.*; see also Chapter 10 for a discussion of Australia's open data framework.

[31] Australian Government Productivity Commission Inquiry Report on Data Availability and Use (Overview & Recommendations) (31 March 2017). https://www.pc.gov.au/inquiries/completed/data-access/report/data-access-overview.pdf.

[32] See "Rethinking Database Rights and Data Ownership in an AI World" (July 2020), 33–36, part of the "Report Series: The Impact of Robotic and Artificial Intelligent on the Law." https://www.sal.org.sg/Resour ces-Tools/Law-Reform/Robotics_AI_Series.

4. Development of Data Portability in Singapore

a. Introduction to the Personal Data Protection Act

Data portability is implemented in Singapore through its data protection legislation: the Personal Data Protection Act (PDPA).[33] The PDPA is a general data protection law, covering ten obligations[34] that serve to protect personal data. These obligations adhere to equivalent principles in the OECD Guidelines;[35] and the consent-based approach of the PDPA puts it in the same family as personal data protection regimes in Australia, Canada, and New Zealand.[36]

The obligations can be largely grouped into three categories. First, the set of obligations around consent, purpose limitation, and notification defines the scope within which the data controller can use personal data that is collected. Second, a set of obligations—anchored in accountability—ensures that data controllers put in place policies and practices that protects data within their possession or control from unauthorized access, modification, or disclosure. Overseas transfers are limited to receiving organizations that can protect the transferred personal data to a comparable standard, and that data is properly expunged at the end of their life cycle. The final set of obligations is what has been referred to as *data subject access rights*. These impose obligations on data controllers to provide data subjects access to their personal data and to make corrections should there be any inaccuracies. Data subject rights were recently expanded to include mandatory data breach notification, where likely to result in significant harm posed to the affected individuals.

Data portability is expected to be introduced as a new obligation under the PDPA in upcoming implementing regulations, and will augment this last category of data subject access rights by extending the right to request a copy of one's personal data to a right to request a copy of one's personal data be transmitted to another organization in machine-readable form.[37]

In the following we briefly describe the rationale for introducing data portability in Singapore and the approach adopted for this new data protection obligation.

---

[33] Vide the Personal Data Protection (Amendment) Bill (No. 37/2020). https://sso.agc.gov.sg/Bills-Supp/37-2020/Published/20201005?DocDate=20201005.

[34] These obligations are (1) consent, (2) purpose limitation, (3) notification, (4) access and correction, (5) accuracy, (6) protection, (7) retention limitation, (8) transfer limitation, (9) data breach notification and (10) accountability; see Advisory Guidelines on Key Concepts in the Personal Data Protection Act (Revised 1 February 2021). https://www.pdpc.gov.sg/guidelines-and-consultation/2020/03/advisory-guidelines-on-key-concepts-in-the-personal-data-protection-act.

[35] These principles are (1) collection limitation, (2) data quality, (3) purpose specification, (4) use limitation, (5) security safeguards, (6) openness, (7) individual participation, and (8) accountability; *supra* note 3.

[36] See the Australian Federal Privacy Act 1988, the Canadian Federal Personal Information Protection and Electronic Documents Act (2000), the British Columbian Personal Information Protection Act (2003) and the New Zealand Privacy Act (1993).

[37] *Supra*, note 25.

b. Why Introduce Data Portability?

Discussions on the benefits of data portability can be traced to a 2017 study jointly undertaken by the (then) Competition Commission of Singapore, Personal Data Protection Commission (PDPC) and Intellectual Property Office of Singapore.[38] The origins of the discussion is decidedly rooted in competition policy and regulation, as it was intended to study effects of data analytics and data-sharing on competition, data protection, and intellectual property laws. One of the key issues that the study looked into was the increasing concentration of data in the hands of a small group of companies that have amassed data either as an objective of their business model or as a result of their business model. The competition concerns were around how data may be unlocked from such concentrations. Another issue that was studied was the benefits and competition concerns arising from the promotion of data-sharing between businesses.

The main insights that were derived from the study was that competition law is sufficiently malleable so that it will be effective in unlocking concentrations of data held by dominant players or monopolies. Second, the essential facilities doctrine could potentially apply to unlock data in exceptional cases even when the undertaking does not have market power.[39] Finally, competition law could be effective in addressing collusion between undertakings that shared price-sensitive information. The study concluded that while competition law was able to address market conduct where there is a refusal to provide supply, there remains a need to create the impetus for data to flow across the economy even in the absence of anticompetitive market conduct. Enabling data flows across the economy in a broader sense was conducive toward creating a more competitive environment. The joint study concluded that the introduction of a right to data portability could be potentially complementary to competition regulation in achieving this objective.

This led to the February 2019 discussion paper on data portability that was jointly issued by the (newly renamed) Competition and Consumer Commission of Singapore and the PDPC.[40] The 2019 Discussion Paper identified a number of potential effects on the market with the introduction of data portability right as part of the general personal data protection law.[41] These effects can lead to two tangible outcomes for consumers and the market: supporting innovation and enabling easier switching of services.

---

[38] Personal Data Protection Commission In collaboration with Competition and Consumer Commission of Singapore, "Discussion Paper on Data Portability" (February 25, 2019). https://www.pdpc.gov.sg/-/media/Files/PDPC/PDF-Files/Resource-for-Organisation/Data-Portability/PDPC-CCCS-Data-Portability-Discussion-Paper---250219.pdf

[39] To qualify as an essential facility, the access to the data set must be indispensable and its duplication must be extremely difficult. *Id.*

[40] *Supra*, note 38.

[41] These effects are (1) better use of data to increase output, (2) combining data sources to lower costs, (3) recombinant innovation, (4) price discrimination, and (5) lower transaction costs and market dynamics; *supra*, note 38.

c. Shaping Data Portability Policy

A recognition of the role of data-driven technologies like data analytics and artificial intelligence in driving innovation in the present digital economy had underpinned these discussions since the 2017 joint study. The discussions had recognized the importance of access to data in order to benefit from innovation that makes use of such technologies and had been about how to enable access for the broader benefit of the economy. As explored by Yan Carrière-Swallow and Vikram Haksar in Chapter 7, the economics of data differ from traditional commodities. An example of the type of innovation that can arise when data from different sources are brought together is *recombinant innovation*, which is "the effect that the combination of data (which is currently being held in silos) has on innovation (i.e. the creation of new products and services)."[42] Additionally, the introduction of data portability is expected to have an immediate economic effect of lowering transaction costs and market dynamics. Requiring existing service providers to transmit a copy of the data subject's data to another service provider can support the supply of new services that the existing service provider is reluctant or slow to provide. In the context of switching, a new customer who brings along data of past transactions can enable the new service provider to device a more compelling offer or provide a more personalized user experience to the new customer.[43]

The February 2019 Discussion Paper was followed closely by the PDPC consultation in May 2019 proposing the introduction of data portability in its review of the PDPA.[44] The consultation took the discussion beyond the expected positive impact of data portability for consumers and the market, and focused on the issues around the implementation of data portability. The range of personal data that should be ported and the categories of organizations to grant data portability requests were identified. It was proposed that data provided by users and generated by user activities can be ported, but in recognition of the investment and business-specific rules that went into the creation of the data, it was proposed that derived data will not be subject to data portability. The section on handling data portability requests covered implementation details like how requests are to be made and received, how the identity of the data subject and veracity of the request could be verified, and other technical details pertaining to data formats, transmission protocols, and verification of the transferred dataset.

Significant progress in policy development was made in the consultation process, which were summarized in the Response to Feedback issued in January 2020.[45] Outlined below are the key policy positions adopted by Singapore. These policy positions were pragmatic for the following reasons:

[42] *Supra*, note 38, at para. 3.12.

[43] *Supra*, note 38, at para. 3.15 *et seq.*; see also *infra*, para. 2.2 *et seq.*

[44] "Public Consultation on Review of the Personal Data Protection Act 2012—Proposed Data Portability and Data Innovation Provisions" (22 May 2019). https://www.pdpc.gov.sg/-/media/Files/PDPC/PDF-Files/Legislation-and-Guidelines/PDPC-Public-Consultation-Paper-on-Data-Portability-and-Data-Innovation-Provisions-(220519).pdf.

[45] "Response to Feedback on the Public Consultation on Proposed Data Portability and Data Innovation Provisions" (20 January 2020). https://www.pdpc.gov.sg/-/media/Files/PDPC/PDF-Files/Legislation-and-Guidelines/Response-to-Feedback-for-3rd-Public-Consultation-on-Data-Portability-Innovation-200120.pdf?la=en.

White-list approach: first, instead of introducing data portability as a general requirement, it will be introduced for white-listed data sets as a way of providing regulatory clarity and certainty for data controllers and thereby assisting in managing
their compliance and implementation costs.[46] Singapore's approach is a significant departure from the global trend of industry-led efforts in jurisdictions that
have introduced data portability as a comprehensive scheme covering all types
of personal data (e.g., Data Transfer Project).[47] Given the policy objectives that
underpinned the data portability discussions in Singapore, the white-list approach should have the desired effect in ensuring that compliance costs are
incurred only for those data sets that will bring about one or both of the twin
policy goals of supporting innovation and reducing switching costs.

Public-private collaboration: second, data portability will be introduced in phases
through regulatory requirements co-developed with industry stakeholders. These
regulations will apply to organizations that hold—and therefore have to port—the
white-listed data set, as well as those that desire to receive the white-listed data set.
They will be designed around either the "push model" or "pull model" for making
and responding to data porting requests.[48] They will specify technical and process
details (e.g., porting time frame, data format, transmission and authentication
protocols and security standards) to enable interoperability, as well as measures
to ensure consumer protection (e.g., cooling-off periods) and measures to reduce
market risks (e.g., blacklists).[49] This approach recognizes that, unlike data subject
access requests (which are primarily intended to correct individual records), the
systems designed to implement data portability cannot be stand-alone solutions,
but interoperability is a requisite. The policy outcomes of supporting innovation
and reducing switching are dependent on market dynamics, which are driven by
transaction costs. The establishment of standards for both technical porting and
market conduct will serve to lower transaction costs in the long term.[50]

Third, the PDPC recognized that while data portability can increase competition, the
data portability obligation should not be abused by "fast followers" (those that move
and copy services and products quickly) to access confidential commercial information
that unfairly competes with "first movers" ability to reap the fruits of bringing innovative products and services to market. Accordingly, there are plans to provide regulatory guidance in the form of advisory guidelines on the relevant considerations of the
confidential commercial information exception.[51] Once more, the economic and competition policy origins of data portability can be seen shaping the implementation of
data portability. The administration and enforcement of the data portability obligation

---

[46] *Id.*, para. 3.9.

[47] The Data Transfer Project is a collaboration among US tech giants to create an open-source, service-to-
service data portability platform. https://datatransferproject.dev/.

[48] "An example of the pull model is when an individual wishes to use a new service. The new service provider explains to him the categories of data required, how it will be used and where it can be ported from. The
individual proceeds to authorise the new service provider (i.e. receiving organisation) to make the porting
request on their behalf. The push model may be appropriate if there is an established industry practice for a
standard set of data to be pushed to the receiving organisation." See footnote 11, *supra*, note 45.

[49] *Supra*, note 45.

[50] *Supra*, note 45 and the discussion in the accompanying main text.

[51] See para. 3.10, *supra*, note 45.

will attempt to preserve market lead time for innovative products and services, while recognizing the axiom that today's innovation is tomorrow's baseline.

d. Public Consultation and Draft Amendment Bill

Discussions on introducing data portability led to a consultation paper in May 2020 on the draft PDPA amendment bill.[52] The broader amendments to the PDPA are grouped into four categories: (1) strengthening the accountability of organizations by introducing mandatory breach notifications and violations related to egregious mishandling of personal data; (2) enhancing the consent framework through the introduction of deemed consent by contractual necessity[53] and deemed consent by notification[54] as well as new exceptions to the consent requirement where there are legitimate interests or business improvement purposes (while reviewing the research exception), so as to enable meaningful consent where necessary; (3) providing greater consumer autonomy over their personal data through the introduction of a new data portability obligation and revisions to the Do-Not-Call provisions and the Spam Control Act to provide consumers with greater protection and control over unsolicited marketing messages; and (4) strengthening enforcement powers and improving deterrence by raising the cap on financial penalties.

The features of the data portability obligation remain largely unchanged from those that had been set out in the consultation paper and subsequent response. In summary, data portability will cover user provided and user activity data held in electronic form, but will exclude derived personal data.[55] Individuals with existing, direct relationships may make porting requests, and the data controller has to port data to receiving organizations that have a presence in Singapore. Interestingly, there is the first hint of the potential cross-border application of data portability: "PDPC may also extend data portability to like-minded jurisdictions with comparable protection and reciprocal arrangements."[56] As intimated before, the data portability obligation will take effect once regulations, developed in collaboration with industry stakeholders, provide the white list of data categories subject to data portability obligations, along with technical and process details, relevant data porting request models, and safeguards for individuals. In the Closing Note, it was clarified that (1) the types of data an organization is not required to port; and (2) the circumstances under which an organization is not required to port data, will be expressly set forth in a Schedule to the PDPA.[57]

---

[52] Public Consultation Paper issued by the Ministry of Communications and Information and the Personal Data Protection Commission on the Draft Personal Data Protection (Amendment) Bill, including related amendments to the Spam Control Act. https://www.mci.gov.sg/public-consultations/public-consultation-items/public-consultation-on-the-draft-personal-data-protection-amendment-bill.

[53] Consent is deemed to be given for disclosure to and use of personal data by third-party organizations where it is necessary for the performance of a contract; *id.* at para. 38(a).

[54] Consent is deemed be given after notifying the data subject of the intended secondary use and the individual does not opt out during the opt-out period; *id.* at para. 38(b).

[55] Which may include personal data of third-parties; *id.* para. 46.

[56] *Id.* para. 45.

[57] See, Closing Note to the Public Consultation on Draft Personal Data Protection (Amendment) Bill including related amendments to the Spam Control Act (5 October 2020), at para. 21. https://www.mci.gov.sg/public-consultations/public-consultation-items/closing-note-to-pc-on-draft-pdp-(amendment)-bill-including-related-amendments-to-spam-control-act.

5. Data Portability: A Comparative Study of Evolving Approaches

In this section, we embark on a comparative study of the different approaches toward data portability in Australia, the European Union, and Singapore. Australia approaches data portability as a cross-sectoral CDR; whereas the European Union and Singapore approach data portability as a personal data protection right. But even though the European Union and Singapore share this similar foundation, the Singapore approach is in fact closer to that of Australia due to its white-list approach, which involves specifying implementation details. The EU approach, in contrast, introduced data portability as part of the GDPR, leaving the market to sort out much of the implementing details. Another prefatory note is that while the European Union was first in the game with the introduction of data portability as part of the GDPR, which took effect in May 2018, Australia introduced data portability as part of its Competition and Consumer Act 2010 in August 2019, followed by the Consumer Data Right Rules for the banking sector in February 2020.[58] Australia has made significant progress in establishing the implementing standards and framework. Singapore introduced data portability vide the PDPA (Amendment) Bill, which was passed on November 2, 2020.

a. The Relationship between Access and Data Portability

The PDPA was amended to introduce a new data portability obligation.[59] It enables a data subject to make a data porting request to a data controller, who will have to transmit the data specified in the request to the receiving organization.[60] Where the data controller refuses to transmit data,[61] it has to notify the data subject and preserve the requested data for a duration, in the event that a review application is made.[62] The purpose of data portability is to provide individuals with greater autonomy and control over their personal data and to facilitate the innovative and more intensive use of personal data for the development, enhancement, and refinement of products and services provided *by other organizations*.[63]

By comparison, the EU GDPR's formulation of data portability specifies both the right for a data subject *to receive* as well as the right *to transmit* personal data directly from one data controller to another.[64] Data portability therefore complements the right of access.[65] The right to receive a copy of his or her personal data is part of the access obligation under the PDPA, and the data controller may meet a data subject access request "by providing the applicant a copy of the personal data and use and

---

[58] Commencement of CDR Rules. https://www.accc.gov.au/focus-areas/consumer-data-right-cdr-0/commencement-of-cdr-rules.

[59] Part VIB of the PDPA.

[60] Section 26H(1) & (2) of the PDPA.

[61] Section 26H(7) of the PDPA.

[62] Section 26J of the PDPA; for powers of review over a refusal to port or failure to port within reasonable time, see Section 48H(1)(c) of the PDPA.

[63] Section 26G, *supra*, note 26.

[64] Article 20 of the GDPR.

[65] *Supra*, note 29, at 5.

	Data right	EU GDPR	CC PA	SG PDPA
Access	Data subject has right of access & correction	Access	Access	Access
Copy	Data subject may request for a copy	Portability	Portability	
Transmit	Data subject may request for copy to be transmitted to a third-party		N/A	Portability

Figure 6.1 Comparison of data rights.

disclosure information in documentary form."[66] Thus, it is stated in the PDPC's advisory guidelines on key concepts that "the individual making the access request may ask for a copy of his personal data in documentary form . . . whether as physical or electronic copies."[67] Therefore, the way access and data portability complement each other in Singapore is different from that of the European Union, but the final result is the same for both jurisdictions.

In contrast, the implementation of data portability in the California Consumer Privacy Act of 2018 only requires the provision of personal data by the data controller to the data subject in "readily usable format that *allows the consumer to transmit* this information to another entity without hindrance" (emphasis added).[68] The same definition and approach are taken in the Philippines.[69] One drawback of this dependency on the data subject as the porting agent is that it does not create the impetus for the development of APIs and digital infrastructure to direct controller-to-controller porting of data.

Whereas the data portability implementations in the European Union, Singapore, and the United States are in data protection legislation, the Australian CDR implements data portability over customer data (businesses can be customers) and is thus not limited to personal data.[70] The Australian CDR is, therefore, potentially broader in scope than the data protection–based frameworks. Like the EU GDPR, Australia's CDR contemplates the disclosure of customer data either to the CDR customer for use as he, she, or it sees fit or to an accredited person.[71] Please see Figure 6.1 above.

---

[66] Regulation 4(2)(a) of the Personal Data Protection Regulations 2014. https://sso.agc.gov.sg/SL/PDPA2012-S362-2014?DocDate=20140519.

[67] *Supra*, note 29. See also, the individual participation principle in the OECD Guidelines which states that the individual should have the right "to have communicated to him, data relating to him within a reasonable time . . . and in a form that is readily intelligible to him," *supra*, note 20.

[68] Section 1798.100 of the California Consumer Privacy Act of 2018. https://leginfo.legislature.ca.gov/faces/codes_displayText.xhtml?lawCode=CIV&division=3.&title=1.81.5.&part=4.&chapter=&article=.

[69] The right to data portability is defined as the right "to obtain from the personal information controller a copy of data undergoing processing in an electronic or structured format, which is commonly used and allows for further use by the data subject"; Section 18 of the Philippines Data Privacy Act of 2012. https://www.privacy.gov.ph/data-privacy-act/#18.

[70] Section 56AI(1) of the Australian Competition and Consumer Act 2010. https://www.legislation.gov.au/Details/C2020C00079.

[71] Section 56BC(1) of the Australian Competition and Consumer Act 2010.

b. Objectives and Purposes of PDPA

The purpose clause for the new data portability obligation in the PDPA codifies the policy objectives, discussed in the preceding section, that had hitherto driven the development of data portability. First, it creates the consumer-driven impetus for movement of data across the economy by empowering data subjects with greater autonomy and control over their data. Second, the intended immediate beneficiaries are *other organizations* in order to support their use of data more intensively, through data-driven technologies like data analytics and machine learning, in order to support innovation.

These objectives are not dissimilar to the European Union, where the Article 29 Working Party had explained in its guidelines to data portability that "the purpose of this new right is to empower the data subject and give him/her more control over [his or her] personal data" and "it will facilitate switching between different service providers, and will therefore foster the development of new services in . . . the digital single market strategy."[72] But having said that, the *primary aim* is enhancing individual control over one's personal data and making sure that an individual plays an active role in the data ecosystem, since the GDPR regulates personal data and not competition.[73]

In comparison, the objective of the Australian CDR, given its implementation as a competition and consumer right, is simply stated as "to create more choice and competition, or to otherwise promote the public interest."[74]

The objectives and purposes of data portability in these regimes are similar, although their different emphases suggest the choice of regulatory regime and enforcement authority. The Australian CDR is a competition and consumer protection policy and is enforced via its competition and consumer protection law and regulator. Data portability in the European Union is enforced primarily as a data subject right via its data protection law and enforcement authorities. The Singapore approach straddles both: it is implemented in its data protection legislation, which recognizes both the rights of individuals to protect their personal data and the need of organizations to collect, use, or disclose personal data for reasonably appropriate purposes.[75] Thus, it is not surprising that the data portability policy objectives recognizes both a consumer-oriented right and a commercial benefit for receiving organizations.

c. Implementing Data Portability

Under the PDPA, a data porting request may be made by a data subject in his or her personal or domestic capacity,[76] and where there is an ongoing relationship between data controller and data subject.[77] The limitation to porting during an ongoing relationship is again consistent with the objective of managing compliance and implementation

---

[72] Article 29 Data Protection Working Party's Guidelines on the Right to Data Portability, at 3. https://ec.europa.eu/newsroom/article29/item-detail.cfm?item_id=611233.
[73] *Id.* fn. 1.
[74] Section 56AA of the Australian Competition and Consumer Act 2010.
[75] Section 3 of the PDPA.
[76] Section 26I(2)(a) of the PDPA.
[77] Section 26H(3)(b) of the PDPA.

costs, since data of past customers are frequently archived. However, in order to meet the objective of reducing friction in switching, the transmission of data when customers switch service providers should take place before the end of the relationship. Limiting data portability to personal or domestic capacity can be contrasted with the Australian CDR, which is framed as a customer right and, thus, covers CDR data relating to the supply of a customer good or service.[78]

Data portability is implemented in the European Union through the GDPR as part of its general data protection law. By contrast, the Australian CDR takes a sector-based *and* a white-listing approach, requiring only designated CDR data to be portable.[79] This sector-based, white-listing approach commenced with the banking sector[80] and will be followed by the energy sector.[81] Singapore contemplates a white-list approach which is intended to apply across all sectors, since one of the policy objectives for introducing data portability is to create a consumer-initiated impetus for data flows across its economy.[82]

d. What Types of Data May Be Ported

Under the PDPA, a data porting request is made for the transmission of applicable data, which is defined to be prescribed *personal data* in the possession or under the control of the porting organization. This sets the stage for the creation of white lists of personal data in order to provide regulatory clarity and certainty for data controllers and thereby assist in managing compliance and implementation costs.[83] In a nod to the fact that data is increasingly stored on the cloud, applicable data may be stored in or transmitted from Singapore or another country.[84] The categories of data that are excluded from the data portability obligation are *in pari materia* with those excluded from the access and correction obligation, such as derived data and commercial confidential information.[85]

Additionally, only data that exists in an electronic form when the data porting request is made need be transmitted.[86] Upcoming regulations may also limit the volume of data that such requests may cover by time period (e.g., past twelve months).[87] Alignments have also been made such that third-party data that form part of user activity data or user-provided data can be revealed by the data controller under, both access and data portability obligations.[88] This will reduce the compliance burden when porting

---

[78] Section 56AI, *supra*, note 24.

[79] Section 56BD of the Australian Competition and Consumer Act 2010.

[80] CDR Rules (Banking) (2 September 2019). https://www.accc.gov.au/focus-areas/consumer-data-right-cdr-0/cdr-rules-banking.

[81] "Consumer Data Right Widening from Banking to Energy Sector" (25 February 2019). https://www.accc.gov.au/media-release/consumer-data-right-widening-from-banking-to-energy-sector.

[82] *Supra*, note 42, and the discussion in the accompanying main text.

[83] Section 26H(2) of the PDPA.

[84] Section 26F(4) of the PDPA.

[85] See Schedule 6 and the new Schedule 12 of the PDPA, both of which enumerate common exclusions for the correction and data portability obligations; for the discussion relating to derived data and commercial confidential information; *supra*, notes 38 & 47, respectively, and the discussion in the accompanying main texts.

[86] Section 26F(2)(a) of the PDPA.

[87] Section 26F(2)(b) of the PDPA.

[88] Sections 21(3A) and 26I(2)(b) of the PDPA.

transactional data (e.g., electronic payment or funds transfers), which necessarily involves data of a third-party, outside the data subject–data controller relationship. These contribute to the objective of managing compliance and implementation costs.

The EU GDPR also contemplates that only personal data concerning the data subject or provided by the data subject are subject to data portability. The range of personal data that is covered by the EU GDPR data portability obligation is potentially wider than the PDPA, because the equivalent of user-provided and user-activity personal data are defined as subsets of the second limb (i.e., data provided by the data subject).[89] Conceptually, data falling within the first limb (i.e., data concerning the data subject) enlarges the combined set. However, the examples of data concerning the data subject that have been provided by the Article 29 Working Party are transactional records that would fall within the definition of user-activity data.[90] It therefore remains to be seen whether the conceptual differences in definitions will result in any practical difference in their real-world application.

With respect to third-party data, the Article 29 Working Party provides guidance that transactional records should be provided in response to a data porting request as they concern the data subject, notwithstanding the fact that they also contain third-party data.[91] The Article 29 Working Party guidelines go on to provide guidance on the processing of third-party data that are ported as part of transactional records. The receiving organization must identify a basis for processing third-party data in order to ensure that the rights and freedoms of third-parties are respected. Otherwise, the receiving organization may not process third-party data for its own purposes, but only for the provision of the service to the requesting user.[92] The position is similar to the PDPA where it is explicitly stated that the receiving organization must only use third-party data received from the porting organization for the purpose of providing goods or services to the requesting individual.[93]

Notably, the Australian CDR does not get into the details of user-provided, user-activity, or third-party data, since its analytical frame is competition and consumer protection, and not personal data protection. Further, while the EU GDPR and the PDPA exclude derived data from the ambit of data portability, the Australian Competition and Consumer Act 2010's definition of CDR data *includes* derived data.[94]

Similar to concerns of overprotecting confidential commercial information from abuse by fast followers and to preserve the lead time in the market for innovators,[95] the Article 29 Working Party has said that trade secrets and intellectual property are part of the rights and freedoms of others mentioned in Article 20(4) of the GDPR.[96] If there is any difference in approach, it is that the EU approach is focused on balancing the interests of the user in porting data against the intellectual property rights of the data

---

[89] Referred to in Article 29 as "observed data provided by the data subject by virtue of the use of the service or device"; *supra*, note 72, at p. 10.

[90] "As an example, telephone, interpersonal messaging or VoIP records may include (in the subscriber's account history) details of third parties involved in incoming and outgoing calls" *supra*, note 72, at p. 9.

[91] *Supra*, note 72.

[92] *Supra*, note 72, at pp. 11 & 12.

[93] Section 26I(3) of the PDPA.

[94] The definition of CDR data includes "directly or indirectly derived" data; see definition of CDR data in Section 56AI(2) of the Australian Competition and Consumer Act 2010.

[95] *Supra*, note 72 and the discussion in the accompanying main text.

[96] *Supra*, note 27, at p. 12.

controller, while the concern in Singapore is in balancing the interests of porting and receiving organizations. They are by no means mutually exclusive considerations, and we should expect that as data portability disputes are raised, both sets of interests will have to be considered.

e. Data Porting Technical Standards

Under the PDPA, data porting requests need to satisfy prescribed requirements.[97] While nothing has yet been prescribed, there are clear statements of intent to issue regulations covering, inter alia, white lists of data, the models (pull or push) for making and responding to data porting requests, technical and process details (e.g., porting time frame, data format, transmission and authentication protocols and security standards) to enable interoperability, and measures to protect consumers (e.g., cooling-off periods)[98] and to reduce market risks (e.g., blacklists).[99]

Under the EU GDPR, data portability between data controllers should be "without hindrance."[100] While the GDPR does not contemplate the establishment of subsidiary rules, it contemplates that data should be provided in a "structured, commonly used, machine-readable and interoperable format" and encourages data controllers "to develop interoperable formats that enable data portability."[101] The Article 29 Working Party explains that this does not create any obligation for data controllers to implement processing systems.[102] Because of the formulation of the EU GDPR data portability right as enabling the data subject to either receive personally or request for transmission to another data controller, the technical implementation could be either direct transmission or through an automated tool that allows extraction of the data to be ported.[103] The UK Information Commissioner's Office provides guidance on the meaning of "structured, commonly used and machine-readable and interoperable format," highlighting open data formats like Comma Separate Values (CSV), Extensible Markup Language (XML), and JavaScript Object Notation (JSON) as reasonable baseline formats that can be used in the absence of any industry standard.[104] Finally, the data controller is responsible for implementing security measures to ensure that data is securely transmitted and to the right destination.[105] The areas that are covered by the Article 29 Working Party are similar to the areas that have been identified for implementing regulations under the PDPA, although there are a number of points of departure.

---

[97] Section 26H(3)(a) of the PDPA.

[98] See also, Minister for Communication and Information (Mr. S. Iswaran) closing speech during the Second Reading (Nov. 2, 2020). https://sprs.parl.gov.sg/search/sprs3topic?reportid=bill-478.

[99] *Supra*, note 45, and the discussion in the accompanying main text.

[100] Article 20 of the GDPR, *supra*, note 27.

[101] Preamble 68 of the GDPR, *supra*, note 27.

[102] *Supra*, note 72, at p. 5.

[103] See also the recommendation of a self-service portal in the Section 999.313 of the draft California Consumer Privacy Regulations to be made under the California Consumer Privacy Act. https://oag.ca.gov/sites/all/files/agweb/pdfs/privacy/ccpa-text-of-second-set-clean-031120.pdf?.

[104] "Right to Data Portability." https://ico.org.uk/for-organisations/guide-to-data-protection/guide-to-the-general-data-protection-regulation-gdpr/individual-rights/right-to-data-portability/.

[105] *Supra*, note 72, at p.19.

Of the jurisdictions under review, Australia has made the furthest progress in the technical and operational details that are necessary for an effective data portability right. CSIRO's Data61 has developed very detailed binding Consumer Data Standards under the CDR rules,[106] which include APIs (admin, common, and banking) and data schemas. The level of technical and process details that are documented in the Consumer Data Standards portal is staggering, surpassing the (by comparison) rudimentary guidelines issued by the Article 29 Working Party and the UK ICO.

f. Data Porting Requests: Pull or Push Model

Singapore has stated the intention to specify the data porting request model—that is, pull or push model—for white-listed data sets. A pull model, for example, contemplates the receiving organization explaining to the data subject both the purposes that the ported data will be used for in the new service and what data is required to be ported, before the data porting request is made by the data subject through the receiving organization.[107] There is much to recommend it over a push model. However, this level of implementation detail is not found in the EU GDPR, except for the explanation by the Article 29 Working Party that the onus is on the receiving data controller to, first, state the purpose for the new processing clearly before any request for transmission is made, and thereafter to ensure that the data provided is relevant and not excessive with regard to its services.[108]

This latter requirement has caused concerns since, in the absence of a data porting request model, the receiving organization could receive an unspecified data set and a requirement to ensure relevance and proportionality for each transmission could create an unrealistic compliance burden.[109] This is a very real concern, and the Australian consumer data right includes a privacy safeguard that requires unsolicited consumer data, that is, data outside the scope of the consumer data request and which may also be outside the authorization given by the consumer, to be destroyed as soon as practicable.[110]

Although the Article 29 Working Party encourages data controllers to identify beforehand data in their systems subject to portability,[111] the lack of discussion of the data portability request model appears to have provided reason for concern. This may have led to suggestions that the Article 29 Working Party recognizes the possibility of using the "pull model" for transmission for the very same reason that this model provides "opportunities for individuals and receiving service to agree on appropriate processing of customer data before any data is transferred."[112]

---

[106] Part IVD, Division 6 of the Australian Competition and Consumer Act 2010; see also https://consumerdatastandardsaustralia.github.io/standards/#introduction.

[107] Supra, note 38 and the discussion in the accompanying main text.

[108] Supra, note 72, at 6.

[109] Supra, note 72, at 5.

[110] Section 56EG of the Australian Competition and Consumer Act 2010. https://www.legislation.gov.au/Details/C2020C00079; see also Office of the Australian Information Commissioner's Draft Chapter 4: Privacy Safeguard 4—Dealing with unsolicited CDR data from CDR participants (October 2019). https://www.oaic.gov.au/assets/engage-with-us/consultations/draft-cdr-privacy-safeguard-guidelines/Draft-Chapter-4-Dealing-with-unsolicited-CDR-data-from-CDR-participants.pdf.

[111] Supra, note 72, at 17.

[112] Comments by the Centre for Information Policy Leadership (CIPL) on the Article 29 Data Protection Working Party's Guidelines on the Right to Data Portability (15 February 2017), at 4; this should also overcome

In this area as well, the Australian CDR implementation has made significant progress. Consumer experience (CX) standards and guidelines have been developed as part of the Consumer Data Standards.[113] These are detailed documents that deal with the user experience and how information is provided to consumers and their consent obtained. Having delved into the details of user interface and consumer experience design, it is therefore not surprising that the CX guidelines contemplate a pull model as it is probably the more feasible one.[114]

g. Protecting Consumers and Preserving Ecosystem Integrity

Both the EU GDPR and Article 29 Working Party guidelines do not articulate measures to protect consumers or preserve the integrity of the data portability ecosystem. These are areas that Singapore has identified where measures that protect consumers (e.g., cooling-off periods) and reduce market risks (e.g., blacklists) will be included in the implementing regulations under the PDPA.

The model to emulate is (again) the Australian CDR, which has made significant progress in these areas. The Australian CDR has built consumer protection and ecosystem integrity into its CDR implementation by design. This should be unsurprising since the CDR is implemented as part of its competition and consumer protection legislation. Accreditation is a central feature of the Australian CDR implementation. The CDR provisions provide for an accreditation process,[115] such that (apart from the consumer himself or herself) only designated gateways[116] or accredited data recipients[117] can receive consumer CDR data. The requirement for accreditation establishes a high bar for entry but builds a holistic framework for preserving the integrity of the ecosystem by requiring every player that can receive CDR data to not only meet but maintain the accreditation standards. The drawback of this approach might be that the pool of accredited persons may not be large. Whether this, coupled with the sector-based approach, may collectively be too cautious an approach to take for achieving the desired outcomes of creating more choice and competition, only time will tell.

6. Conclusion: Open Data and Future Developments

The development of data portability policy and regulation in Singapore can be contextualized in its broader approach to data flows. From the micro to the macro level, there are clear policy developments that appear to promote the flow of data within an

one of the other issues raised by CIPL concerning the technical challenges in relation to the individual's ability to select data for porting, at p. 13. https://www.informationpolicycentre.com/uploads/5/7/1/0/57104281/cipl_comments_on_wp29_data_portability_guidelines_15_february_2017.pdf.

[113] https://consumerdatastandards.org.au/cx-standards/.
[114] CX Guidelines, slide 50. https://consumerdatastandards.org.au/wp-content/uploads/2020/04/CX-Guidelines-v1.3.0.pdf.
[115] Part IVD, Division 3 of the Australian Competition and Consumer Act 2010.
[116] Section 56AL of the Australian Competition and Consumer Act 2010.
[117] Section 56AK and 56BH of the Australian Competition and Consumer Act 2010.

organization, across the economy, and across borders. At the organization level, the policy discussions and amendments to the PDPA have included the introduction of policies to support data innovation, which finds articulation as a new exception to consent for business improvement. The PDPA amendments also introduce revisions to the existing research exception. These moves should provide clarity to organizations for the internal use of data for business improvement and research.[118]

The developments of competition policy and regulation and data portability have been discussed extensively in this chapter. These are only part of the policy and regulatory interventions that have been introduced to provide legal clarity and certainty for data flows across its domestic economy. The introduction in June 2019 of the Trusted Data Sharing Framework should also be seen as part of this set of developments.[119] Collectively, these developments operate together to provide a framework for voluntary data-sharing between organizations (i.e., Trusted Data Sharing Framework), consumer-initiated data-sharing between organizations (i.e., data portability), and access to data held by an organization (i.e., competition law). These are all measures to provide organizations with greater access to data and to maximize the benefits from the emergent and fast developing set of data-driven technologies like data analytics and machine learning.

Where there are willing commercial partners, the policy interventions have mainly been directed at promoting trust by establishing a set of baseline practices and providing a framework within which data-sharing discussions can take place. Hence, the introduction of the Trusted Data Sharing Framework in June 2019 to facilitate interorganization data-sharing. The establishment of a common framework provides the lingua franca to overcome misunderstanding, and other templates for data-sharing agreements, nondisclosure agreements, and data valuation also help reduce friction. The introduction of data portability has the benefit of promoting "the controlled and limited sharing by users of personal data between organisations and thus enrich services and customer experiences. Data portability may facilitate transmission and reuse of personal data concerning users among the various services they are interested in."[120] Data portability's role in promoting data flow across the domestic economy is by the creation of a consumer-initiated impetus coupled with a legal obligation for organizations to share data per the data porting request. These two initiatives should not be seen as mutually exclusive, but they can operate independently. And in those cases where market conduct requires it, competition levers can be brought to bear in the manner explained in the 2017 CCS-IPOS-PDPC joint study.[121]

---

[118] The "Public Consultation on Review of the Personal Data Protection Act 2012—Proposed Data Portability and Data Innovation Provisions" first proposed the introduction of provisions relating to data innovation, which have been introduced in the draft PDPA amendment bill as an exception to consent for use of personal data for business improvement purposes; revisions to the research exception were also proposed in the draft PDPA amendment bill. The rationale for the business improvement and research exceptions are provided in the "Public Consultation Paper issued by the Ministry of Communications and Information and the Personal Data Protection Commission on the Draft Personal Data Protection (Amendment) Bill"; *infra*, notes 40 & 48.

[119] https://www.imda.gov.sg/-/media/Imda/Files/Programme/AI-Data-Innovation/Trusted-Data-Sharing-Framework.pdf.

[120] *Supra*, note 66, at 5.

[121] *Supra*, note 34.

At the global level, Singapore has also been active in keeping the sea lanes open for cross-border data flows. Since the 2016 ASEAN Framework on Personal Data Protection[122] and its participation in the APEC Cross Border Privacy Rules and Privacy Recognition for Processors systems in 2019,[123] Singapore has worked tirelessly to establish bridges for trusted data flows between economies and regions. The recent amendment to its transfer regulations is another step in this steady march.[124] In 2020, a number of significant steps were taken. First, MAS and the US Treasury Department issued a joint statement recognizing the ability to aggregate, store, process, and transmit data across borders is critical to financial sector development.[125] Next, Singapore, Chile, and New Zealand also signed the first Digital Economy Agreement to establish new approaches and collaboration in digital trade issues, promote interoperability, and address new issues brought about by digitalization. One of the key features is to enable trusted data flows, covering a range of initiatives that includes cross-border data flows and personal data protection.[126] Similarly, the Singapore-Australia Digital Economy Agreement also covered cross-border data flows and personal data protection among other areas, including a new prohibition on data localization.[127] Further developments can be expected for data portability as another channel for cross-border data flows with the recent amendments, which contemplates that receiving organizations may be incorporated or resident in Singapore or *in an applicable country*. This implies an intention to extend data portability overseas, as was stated in the Public Consultation Paper.[128]

One can expect that upon the enactment of the PDPA amendments on data portability, implementation details, and adoption programs will soon follow. While the proposal of data portability regulations can be expected, there may be other areas of reform in the offing. Hearkening back to the 2017 Joint Study, there is an outstanding discussion about rights over data, which has since taken a slightly different path. A law reform paper published recently by the Singapore Academy of Law picked up that train of thought, and after reviewing the law on the protection of electronic databases and rights over individual records of data, the authors of the law reform paper advocated an introduction of a data portability right over nonpersonal data, in the mold of the Australian CDR.[129] This therefore suggests that the last word has not yet been heard on this topic, and the data portability conversation in Singapore looks set to continue.

---

[122] https://asean.org/storage/2012/05/10-ASEAN-Framework-on-PDP.pdf.

[123] "APEC Strengthens Trust with Data Protection System" (23 July 2019). https://www.apec.org/Press/News-Releases/2019/0723_IMDA.

[124] The Personal Data Protection (Amendment) Regulations 2020 inserted the new Regulation 10A of the Personal Data Protection Regulations 2014 that recognizes the APEC CBPR and PRP systems as legally enforceable obligations providing comparable protection as required by the transfer limitation obligation.

[125] https://www.mas.gov.sg/news/media-releases/2020/united-states-singapore-joint-statement-on-financial-services-data-connectivity.

[126] https://www.mti.gov.sg/Improving-Trade/Digital-Economy-Agreements/The-Digital-Economy-Partnership-Agreement.

[127] https://www.mti.gov.sg/Improving-Trade/Digital-Economy-Agreements/The-Singapore-Australia-Digital-Economy-Agreement.

[128] *Supra*, note 52 and the discussion in the accompanying main text.

[129] *Supra*, note 58.

7

Open Banking and the Economics of Data

*Yan Carrière-Swallow** and Vikram Haksar***

International Monetary Fund[1]

1. Introduction

Information sharing has always played an important role in finance. Information about borrowers is essential for banks to gauge the risks they take when offering a loan. Obtaining this information thus represents a key challenge for banks that lack it, and a key opportunity for banks that have it. The core information needed for conducting these assessments has traditionally been captured in data that records an individual's financial transactions, deposit account and loan balances, and loan repayment performance.

Since the late 1800s, information sharing in the financial sector has usually involved data being intermediated by credit bureaus[2] (Jappelli and Pagano, 2002). In some countries, credit bureaus arose as a market-based solution to alleviate information asymmetries, with operating costs borne by financial institutions. In others, laws or regulations require banks to share their clients' data with the credit bureau. Underpinning these approaches is the recognition of the value of data in finance and the importance of data-sharing to enable accurate risk assessment.

Over the past three years, open banking frameworks have been adopted in jurisdictions including Australia, Brazil, the European Union, the United Kingdom, India, Mexico, and Singapore, changing how data and information flow in the financial system: who has it, who doesn't, and who decides. While there are variations across jurisdictions, a common aspect is that open banking grants consumers the right to control who gets access to their financial data and provides an operational setting to exercise that right. In principle this means that a new financial intermediary in an open banking jurisdiction could approach individual clients of existing intermediaries and ask them to share their data to provide them services—and customers could require their current intermediaries to share all this data with new entrants. The stated

* Economist, Strategy, Policy and Review Department, IMF.
** Assistant Director, Monetary and Capital Markets Department, IMF.

[1] The views expressed in this chapter are those of the authors and do not necessarily represent the views of the IMF, its Executive Board, or IMF management. The authors thank Majid Bazarbash, Damien Capelle, Martin Cihak, Andrew Giddings, Emran Islam, Linda Jeng, Kathleen Kao, Inci Otker, David Rozumek, Marzie Taheri Sanjani, Chris Wilson, and Zhongxia Zhang for very constructive comments.
[2] Throughout the chapter, we use the term "credit bureau" generically to capture the main aspects of credit information sharing schemes, including privately held credit bureaus or publicly regulated credit registries.

Yan Carrière-Swallow and Vikram Haksar, *Open Banking and the Economics of Data* In: *Open Banking*. Edited by: Linda Jeng, Oxford University Press. © Oxford University Press 2022. DOI: 10.1093/oso/9780197582879.003.0008

objectives of these reforms are wider access, lower prices, and more innovative financial products and services.

The increasing relevance of data amid the general expansion of the digital economy has been driven by two technological trends. First, technological progress has drastically reduced the costs of collecting and storing data. Widespread digitalization leads to more data being produced as a byproduct of economic and social activities, including aspects of human interactions and experiences that used to be conceived as being entirely qualitative. Second, advances in analytic techniques have allowed for more advanced processing to extract greater value from available data. Multipurpose technologies including machine learning have pushed the use of data across sectors, with prediction algorithms deployed to develop self-driving cars, identify promising new drugs, deliver targeted advertising, and to improve the efficiency of business operations. For several of the world's most valuable publicly traded firms, data collection and processing are central to their highly profitable business models.[3]

The collection of personal data involves a trade-off between respecting the individual's desire for privacy—including from government—and reaping the commercial and social benefits that can be derived from its collection and dissemination. The sheer ubiquity of data generation—including very granular information on habits, relationships, locations, and tastes—has put into stark relief the issues of data privacy and security in the digital economy. In Carrière-Swallow and Haksar (2019), we discuss the many implications and trade-offs that arise due to data proliferation in the economy and call on governments to consider how data policies affect macroeconomic outcomes such as growth, equity, and stability. As Jones and Tonetti (2020) argue, giving the consumer the right to decide who gets access to their personal data leads to very different outcomes than if the data collector is allowed to make these decisions based on their private interests. These trends are also changing how consumers, companies, and policymakers measure and analyze the economy. Previous International Monetary Fund (IMF) work has studied the implications of big data and digitalization for the compilation of economic statistics (IMF, 2018a) and for real-time policymaking (IMF, 2017).

In the realm of financial services, open banking is motivated by the recognition that enabling access to data across incumbents and new competitors can facilitate entry, competition, and innovation through new and better products and services. Open banking involves many facets and approaches that vary across jurisdictions, from public mandates for reciprocal data-sharing among all regulated entities at the instigation of the consumer, to public encouragement by regulators, to private sector–led initiatives with public neutrality. Often, data-sharing is facilitated by the development of open application programming interfaces (APIs) that allow data to be transferred securely in standardized formats. This chapter will focus on open banking as a data access policy for the financial sector that allows for data-sharing subject to consumer consent, which changes the way in which information is obtained and shared in the financial system.

In economic terms, the data policy at the core of open banking involves two innovations with respect to information sharing that takes place through traditional

---

[3] In their October 2020 quarterly report filed with the US Securities and Exchange Commission, Alphabet (the parent company for Google Inc.) reported advertising revenues of USD 37.1 billion—generated by the company's data-driven ad targeting services—making up about 80% of total revenues.

credit bureaus. First, financial institutions can exchange data about customers with each other directly, rather than doing so through an intermediary. This allows them not only to obtain a preprocessed credit score but also to use the granular data to do proprietary analysis and offer more customized products. Second, open banking moves control over data access away from financial institutions and credit bureaus, and toward the individual customers. While credit bureaus tend to authorize data transfer when the customer engages in certain predetermined tasks—for instance, by submitting an application to rent an apartment or to finance a vehicle—open banking envisages the user being able to initiate a data transfer at will and for the user to be able to determine what is shared with whom. In short, open banking is a model of increased agency for consumers over their own financial data.

The chapter will be structured as follows: in section 2, we begin by reviewing some of the economic arguments for why data—and data access policies—are valuable and important in the broader digital economy.[4] We examine arguments in the literature about the source of the value of data, and discuss some of the novel economic properties of data. In section 3, we turn our attention to the use of data in the financial sector, and explain how data access can affect inclusion and discrimination in the provision of financial services. These discussions frame our exploration of the economics of open banking in section 4, which explores the main aspects of the policy's objectives and design features. Section 5 concludes with a discussion of challenges and opportunities facing open banking.

2. Starting Broad: The Value of Data

"Data is the new oil" has become a popular phrase in the financial media.[5] The metaphor alludes to the value that oil held as an input during the industrial revolution. But whereas oil's role in production processes is well understood and has been studied for decades, the role of data in the modern economy is perhaps less obvious. Data is pervasive, and particularly so in the highly profitable technology sector, but what exactly does it do in the economy?

It is useful to first ask where data comes from, by considering the conditions under which the decision will be made to record a piece of data. Data is often generated as a byproduct of economic activity, but a data collector will only decide to store data when the costs of doing so are smaller than the revenues they expect to derive from it. In the early phase of digitalization, many firms simply discarded most of the data generated by their operations and from their users' activity, assuming it was not of significant value and not worth the trouble to store and manage. Since then, the costs of collecting and storing data have fallen dramatically, while advances in analytics and computing power have multiplied the commercial uses of the data. The result has been a proliferation of data across all sectors of the economy.

---

[4] We offer a more comprehensive description of the economics and implications of data in Carrière-Swallow and Haksar (2019).

[5] See, for instance, *The Economist*, "The World's Most Valuable Resource Is No Longer Oil, But Data" (May 6, 2017), and *Financial Times*, "Data Is the New Oil . . . Who's Going to Own It?" (November 15, 2016).

How do economists think of the role of data in the modern economy? The vast literature has focused on two functions of data that lie at the source of its value. First, data is an input into the production of goods and services and into the process of innovation. Second, data creates and shifts information across economic agents, affecting the ways in which they interact and complete transactions. These two functions are often closely related—for instance, analysis of big data can be used to lower the cost of service provision (the efficiency effect), but it can also be used to conduct price discrimination (the information effect)—but discussing them separately allows us to describe the distinctive features of data in the economy. The proliferation of data has many macroeconomic implications, including for equity, since the value of data is not equally shared. A crucial aspect that determines the equitable and efficient functioning of data markets is the treatment of preferences for individual privacy, which gives rise to externalities when disregarded.

a. Data as a Factor of Production

The first function of data is as an input in the production of a good or service. Deriving value from data as an input requires costly processing and analysis, so that it can be used in combination with other factors of production such as labor or algorithms.[6] This is a salient way of thinking about the role of data used in artificial intelligence (AI) applications. In this function, data analysis is used as part of the innovation process, with new insights extracted from data leading to the development of new products or services.

The proliferation of big data and the development of more sophisticated and flexible machine learning algorithms have enabled data analysis to address increasingly complex problems. Data analysis is about using observations about the past to understand the present and predict the future. As Agrawal, Gans, and Goldfarb (2018) discuss, AI is being deployed as a general-purpose technology in an increasing number of fields to tackle very diverse problems. For instance, a car equipped with sensors may record the actions of a driver as she navigates city streets, building up a massive data set of human decisions in the face of various situations. Patterns in this data can then be analyzed using machine learning algorithms to predict and mimic human decision-making in complex road environments, which may then enable the production of a safe self-driving car.

Data has important characteristics that set it apart from other inputs, such as labor, capital, and oil. Jones and Tonetti (2020) emphasize that data is an input that is *nonrival*, in the sense that it can be used multiple times and by multiple agents simultaneously without being diminished. Most other economic inputs can be used once and are then exhausted. One important implication is that society will get more benefits from the data it generates when it is made widely available to many data processors. But will it be widely available? When a data processor has collected data that is valuable to their

---

[6] Estimating a production function including data—such as the function proposed in Jones and Tonetti (2020)—would require a quantification of data, which is a challenging subject due to data's intangible nature and the lack of market price signals for most types of data.

commercial interests, they have a strong private incentive to hoard the data and avoid granting access to their competitors. An important aspect of data policy is thus in setting the rules around who will have access to data, since this will have implications for competition, market structure, and equity in the digital economy.

The nonrival nature of data and its storage on interconnected systems means that limiting access to data imposes costs on the data collector. In economic terms, data is *partially excludable*, with the degree of cybersecurity proportional to the amount of resources dedicated to the task, but never absolute. An important recurring decision for the data collector is thus how much to spend protecting the data they have collected. From a policy perspective, it is important to assess whether the private incentives to secure data are aligned with public objectives, particularly when the data being handled is personal, sensitive, or even strategic with implications for national security.

b. Data Creates Information and Shifts It Across Agents

A second function of data in the economy is in creating and shifting information across agents. Consider the case of a company that collects data about its own operations; for instance, a big retailer that tracks goods as they move through the supply chain. Varian (2018) emphasizes that the firm's collection of data facilitates a process of learning by doing. Through data analysis, the firm becomes more self-aware, obtaining insights to identify inefficiencies and ways to improve its practices. The longer the firm operates and the bigger it gets, the more data it generates as a byproduct of its operations, and the more it can learn from its own past production decisions, allowing it to become still more efficient. This is a feature of the modeling approach taken by Farboodi and Veldkamp (2021), in which data provides information that reduces uncertainty about random variables that are relevant for production.

Personal and corporate data embeds information about economic agents—including consumers or firms—and access to it shifts information in the markets they participate in. When access to data serves to reduce information asymmetries between buyers and sellers, it can potentially lead to more efficient economic transactions. For instance, a company with access to data about the characteristics of potential consumers--such as their interests and buying habits--can use that information to offer a more personalized good or service, such as an advertisement for a product that they are more likely to find useful or desirable. This type of personalization can potentially make both the customer and the seller better off. Likewise, consumers with access to data on characteristics of available products can make more informed buying decisions, by more accurately assessing how products fit their needs. This can include data about product reliability based on the experiences of past customers and the ability to rapidly compare competing products using aggregation services.

c. Winners and Losers in a Data-Rich Economy

Unlike a commodity such as oil, data is highly heterogeneous in the sense that no two pieces of data are perfect substitutes and so usually will not hold the same value. The data collector's willingness to pay for obtaining access to data depends on many factors, including how much existing information asymmetry they face with their customers and competitors, their degree of market power, and the size of the market. Assessing how valuable personal data can be turns out to be quite difficult, even for the agents that have direct incentives to do so.[7] For instance, advertisers spend large sums on individual or pooled data about online users, on the premise that displaying a more targeted ad will make it more likely to generate sales. However, an incipient literature quantifying the effectiveness of this practice suggests that, while the gains from targeting ads may appear to be statistically significant, their impact on sales appears to be economically modest and inferior to what is spent on targeting (Marotta, Abhishek, and Acquisti, 2019), though Lewis and Rao (2015) have shown that estimates of the returns to advertising are necessarily imprecise.

While obtaining more information can increase economic efficiency, acquiring information that others do not have also confers a strategic advantage, potentially making some groups worse off. Acquiring data may thus generate considerable commercial (private) value for a data collector, but without necessarily increasing social welfare. If a firm enjoys market power, then gaining data about their customers' personal characteristics—say, their income or wealth—can allow them to implement price discrimination strategies that extract the consumer's surplus. For instance, an airline may observe the user's geographic location based on their IP address, and use this data to offer higher-priced fares to consumers residing in higher-income countries. These customers are likely to be richer and willing to pay a higher fare, allowing the airline to implement what microeconomists refer to as third-degree, or group-based, price discrimination.

The more specific data about income and wealth that can be observed by the retailer, the more granular price discrimination strategy can be implemented. For instance, a gardener or contractor may adjust the price they charge for services based on the value of the customer's home, which can be inferred from sales data about comparable homes or from publicly available tax appraisals. In the extreme, a monopolist seller with precise information on a customer's income and tastes might be able to implement first-degree price discrimination—offering each customer the product at the maximum price they are willing and able to pay—thus extracting all surplus from consumers. Ezrachi and Stucke (2016) go further, arguing that data-based "behavioral discrimination" can go beyond price discrimination strategies by using personalized emotional cues to influence consumer preferences.

Who will accrue the returns to data? A key question is to what extent the value of data comes from each individual data point or from its agglomeration and subsequent analysis. The answer is likely to differ according to the type of data and the context, but an important factor is the degree of substitutability between data and other factors of production. For instance, some types of data may require very advanced and proprietary

---

[7] The difficulty in measuring the value of data further complicates assessments of market dominance and consumer harms in data-intensive markets. While Furman (2019) describes how many of these markets feature one or two dominant firms, it is difficult to disentangle how practices such as data hoarding contribute to market concentration and contestability. Put simply, standard approaches to measuring concentration (sales or user concentration) or consumer harm (price-costs markups) may be harder to assess in data heavy businesses where services are offered to customers for free, but we do not observe the value of the data being given in exchange.

analytical tools to convert into useful information. In the case of big data sets used to train machine learning algorithms, most of the value likely comes from the analysis provided by the high-skilled labor required to process the data. In other cases, information may be extracted with less analysis, as when individual data is used to provide a targeted product. The value of such data may differ greatly depending on characteristics of the data subject. Being able to target an ad to a high-net-worth individual may offer a much higher return to an advertiser than targeting an unemployed worker. In such an application, the data collector who holds the individual's data may be able to extract most of the rents, while the processor offers more generic services.

Implications of data proliferation for economic inequality will depend on the market power enjoyed by data subjects, collectors, and processors. If a data collector enjoys market power, then obtaining granular information on their clients may enable them to extract considerable rents through the implementation of price discrimination strategies. Data may also represent a source of market power if a stockpiled data set acts as a barrier to entry that deters competition. This is quite relevant in finance, where banks have traditionally been able to hoard some of the data generated by their relationship with individuals and small businesses, even while sharing other types of data through credit bureaus. Since aspects of a small business's financial history may only be available to the bank it has done business with—particularly where the domestic credit bureau has narrow coverage of small to medium-size enterprise (SME) data—other lenders are rendered unable to accurately price the risk associated with extending a loan and are thus unable to compete with the incumbent.

While it may be tempting to infer the economic value of data based on transactions currently observed in the data economy, this is unlikely to provide an accurate or complete picture. The reason is that the data economy features externalities and market incompleteness that lead the price of data to differ from its true social value. The primary externalities emerge from the opacity of the market and a lack of recognition for individual privacy, which will be discussed extensively in section 4. For instance, if individual privacy rights over data are not defined in a particular jurisdiction, such that personal data can be collected and traded without an individual's knowledge or consent, then it may be quite inexpensive for a company to obtain an individual's personal data. The low price of this data, however, would not capture its full value.

d. The Meaning of Privacy in the Digital Economy

The ability to share data over networks and to make it public to a global audience has increased the saliency of privacy in modern markets. Economists have granted considerable attention to studying privacy, with Posner (1981) setting off a large literature that has recently been surveyed by Acquisti, Taylor, and Wagman (2016). Important benefits can accrue to the data subject from sharing their personal data, including the provision of innovative services and more customized products. But when the data subject is unaware, decisions made about their personal data can give rise to an externality: private decisions about whether to collect, process, or share personal data have a bearing on the economic well-being of the data subject, who may not be compensated. These externalities are often negative, with the use of individual data imposing disutility on data subjects. Sharing of data undermines the data subject's preference for maintaining their personal characteristics or actions private, and the data may be used strategically by economic agents that acquire it to extract rents from the data subject.[8]

There are many ways in which decisions surrounding data can lead to privacy externalities. Acemoglu et al. (2021) model a situation in which an individual reveals personal data about themselves to a data-collecting firm, but in doing so also reveals information about someone else. For instance, consider a social media user who reveals that they attended a high-value political luncheon with a friend. Doing so will provide valuable information about their friend to the social network. When the friend is not able to control access to this information, their privacy will tend to be undermined and too much data will circulate in the economy. Privacy externalities may emerge in other situations in the data economy. For instance, a data collector may sell access to individual data about one of their users to a third-party without the user's consent.

Nonrivalry means that society will derive the most benefits from data when it is made widely available. However, for the market to function efficiently, the benefits of revealing data must be weighed against the harm that can come from reducing privacy. As Acquisti, Taylor, and Wagman (2016) emphasize, privacy should not be understood as preventing the sharing of personal information, but rather as giving the data subject control over access to their data. To the extent that privacy is not internalized in the economic decisions of data collectors and processors, the market will tend toward the collection and resale of excessive personal data and insufficient protection of privacy. For the market for data to internalize this externality, data subjects need to be able to adequately control their data.

Jones and Tonetti (2020) model an economy where data is generated by economic activity and used by companies to produce goods and services. They compare outcomes when individuals are granted the right to control who has access to their individual data, versus a case in which those decisions are left up to the companies who collect the data. They find that giving individuals control over data access achieves higher levels of economic efficiency from wide data access, while also respecting individual preferences for privacy. When companies are given the right to govern data access, the result tends to be less competition, more data hoarding, and less privacy for consumers. This result reflects the insight that individuals are well placed to balance the benefits of data-sharing—including access to the better products and services that come from it— against their concerns about privacy.

How large are data privacy externalities? Reputation effects create private economic incentives for a firm to ensure their services are designed to respect and protect the privacy of its users. For a data-based company, the risk of being perceived as lax in their protection of user data––either from a data breach or by the revelation of misleading privacy policies––may lead users to limit sharing their data with the firm. On the other hand, the incentives to extract value from user data are strong, and reputational risks may be small if users are not made aware that their data is being processed or resold.

Valuing privacy is inherently difficult, even for one's self. A key empirical question is whether, given the substantial benefits to consumers and markets from revealing

---

[8] See Chapter 2 by Kaitlin Asrow for a more detailed description of the evolution of US data privacy rights and protections.

personal data, granting strict user control rights would lead them to stop sharing their data in most cases, which may make some services unviable and stifle future innovation. In discussing survey evidence on consumers' stated valuations of privacy, Winegar and Sunstein (2019) argue that information deficits and behavioral biases make these valuations uninformative about the true economic value of privacy.

Research in the literature on privacy has identified an apparent *privacy paradox*, whereby individuals place a much lower value on their privacy in their private actions than they do when asked to place a subjective value in surveys. A common example is the electronic disclosures ("I agree") that online platforms require their users to accept prior to using their services. While a large percentage of people tell surveyors they are very concerned by a company sharing their private information, almost all willingly grant their consent to do so in exchange for the most basic of "free" online services.[9] Indeed, Aridor, Che, and Salz (2020) study the implementation of the General Data Protection Regulation (GDPR) in the European Union, which mandated that websites offer their users the option of opting out of being tracked, and have found that only 12.5 percent of users of a particular website used the opt out despite it lowering the precision of the ads being displayed. This suggests that a significant share of users is privacy conscious, but also that the majority of users remain willing to engage in a standard data-for-service transaction even when given the option of opting out.

Even if consent is seen as a key mechanism for achieving customer control, difficulties exist surrounding how to make the consent process truly informed. It may be challenging to communicate clearly with customers the exact use of their personal data, particularly when this involves processing and cross-selling. And as the communications becomes more comprehensive, customers may see it as being too costly to fully engage with the complexity of the decision. There is an open question of the effectiveness of opt-out as a mechanism for giving users operationalizable agency over their data. In practice, opt-out options may be presented as a binary choice, with consenting to data-sharing cast against the option of being excluded from the service altogether.

In many instances, keeping data private will involve an efficiency cost. Posner (1981) emphasizes the efficiency costs of excessive privacy protection, because individuals that withhold material information can inflict substantial harm on their counterparts. He argues that there is a parallel between a firm concealing information about its product's defects to potential customers—a practice that is prevented by consumer protection laws—and an individual who conceals troubling past information before engaging in certain transactions. Posner cites the examples of a marriage undertaken when a partner has concealed his or her past misdeeds from the other, as well as a borrower who conceals his or her history of past defaults from a potential lender. In both cases, doing so imposes harm on the other party by having them take on greater risk than they are aware of.

---

[9] Some scholars argue that this is not a paradox at all, but rather reflects the difficulty of evaluating these types of trade-offs, which are inherently intertemporal and opaque. For instance, a user must decide if they are willing to sacrifice the tangible benefit of using a useful web page today, versus the potential cost of having their privacy compromised in unspecified ways at an unspecified time in the future.

3. Data and Discrimination in Financial Services

Data's function in shifting information across agents that participate in financial markets has been the subject of an extensive literature. This is a long-standing area of inquiry, since the provision of financial services relies upon data to record transactions and reduce information asymmetries. An important function of financial intermediaries is to channel idle savings to productive investment projects and consumption opportunities. To do so, lenders require data on potential borrowers to gauge their creditworthiness and to monitor their performance after a loan has been extended. Access to customer data is thus an important input into the business of financial intermediation, where lenders use it as a basis for determining the level of risk involved in extending a loan, and later as a means of monitoring the performance of their existing loans.[10]

Incomplete information sharing between agents prevents the efficient allocation of credit because of adverse selection. The idea is that agents with better information will seek to use it to their own advantage, and, fearing this, other agents that lack the information may avoid transacting with them altogether to avoid potentially large risks. Indeed, a borrower's willingness to accept a very high interest rate on a loan signals to the lender that they are unlikely to repay it. The higher the interest rate offered by the lender, the riskier the pool of borrowers willing to accept it. Stiglitz and Weiss (1981) show that, when lenders do not have full information about individual borrowers' ability and willingness to repay a loan, they are likely to ration credit—that is, some borrowers will not be offered a loan at any interest rate and will thus be excluded from the financial market. Adverse selection presents a particularly relevant friction in developing economies, where potential borrowers working in the informal sector or without previous access to financial services are often turned away by banks who cannot evaluate their ability to repay.

As discussed in the Bali Fintech Agenda (IMF, 2018b) and Sahay et al. (2020), the availability of more data about borrowers is a key part of the promise that technology offers to the provision of financial services. Delivering access to more granular user data can reduce information asymmetries and alleviate adverse selection problems that exclude disadvantaged populations from credit markets. The proliferation of data thus holds the promise of reducing lending costs and expanding the availability of credit. Indeed, there is empirical evidence that banning information sharing through regulation aggravates adverse selection problems and leads to more credit rationing.[11,12] One means of building histories of financial activity is to facilitate the sharing of individual financial data across financial service providers, which is a key aspect of open banking.

---

[10] The functions of data in finance are further discussed in Boissay et al. (2020) and Carletti et al. (2020). Other important uses of data by banks include in the provision of wealth management services, where access to data on the full range of a customer's financial assets and operations is crucial to providing a "whole of customer" service.

[11] He (2020) and Liberman et al. (2018) analyze the impact of a legal reform in Chile that required the national credit bureau to delete default information from the files of a segment of creditors. By reducing the information available to lenders about potential borrowers, the authors estimate that the measure had the effect of excluding vulnerable borrowers from obtaining future loans.

[12] See Chapter 4 by Matthew Adam Bruckner for a more detailed discussion of alternative data and consumer protection.

Data on borrowers' financial history has been collected, processed, and shared for decades through credit bureaus, and empirical evidence shows that doing so has led to more and cheaper credit.[13] A potential source of further reductions in information asymmetries is using nontraditional data to improve credit assessments. There is mounting evidence that the information collected in the context of online services—including social habits, payment of utility bills, and other traces of economic and social activity—form the basis for evaluating the creditworthiness of a borrower, including those who have not had previous interactions with a financial service provider.[14] For instance, Berg et al. (2020) find that a small number of individual data points related to an individual's technology usage can form a more accurate prediction of creditworthiness than a traditional credit score. Likewise, Frost et al. (2019) use data from an Argentine online retailer to estimate that BigTech lenders can use nontraditional data to outperform traditional credit bureaus in predicting a borrower's ability to repay. The use of alternative data may thus alleviate adverse selection effects, address collateral constraints, and broaden the number of clients able to obtain a loan.

The efficiency gains from improved data availability in finance may be unevenly shared across borrowing firms. Begenau et al. (2018) argue that the emergence of big data in the financial sector benefits larger incumbent firms more than smaller firms, who produce less data as a byproduct of their operations. A rich data vapor trail thus allows larger firms to lower their cost of finance, lowering their cost to finance expansion, which in turns generates more data. The implication for market structure is that data-based lending will tend to favor more concentration in production. On the other hand, Martinez Peria and Singh (2014) find evidence that the introduction and expansion of credit bureaus tended to benefit smaller, less experienced borrowing firms the most, since they are otherwise subject to the greatest information asymmetries and lack an established relationship with lenders.

The use of alternative data for credit decisions may also lead to the exclusion of those that exhibit traits associated with risky financial behavior. To understand why, consider the familiar example of a health insurance company that observes their customers' data. Just as knowledge of a preexisting medical condition may lead an insurer to charge higher premiums or deny coverage (Arrow, 1963), so too may data on risky or unhealthy behavior such as driving or heavy consumption of sugar-rich foods. It is conceivable that the unfettered availability of very granular data could undermine the risk-sharing function of insurance altogether. The proliferation of data potentially enables the insurance company to discriminate based on a wider range of criteria, such as the past demonstration of risky driving habits, or social connections to people that lead unhealthy lifestyles. Such discriminatory practices could involve the exclusion of vulnerable individuals from insurance markets. To avoid such an outcome, regulations would be needed to specify the types of data that may be used to make decisions, such as the common restriction of discriminating health insurance coverage based on a preexisting condition.

[13] This result is confirmed by Martinez Peria and Singh (2014) using firm-level data from 63 countries, and Djankov, McLiesh, and Shleifer (2007) for panel analysis of 129 countries.
[14] Bank for International Settlements (2019) discusses the use of data held by nonbank BigTech firms to provide financial services such as credit scoring and loan monitoring.

More broadly, data-based assessments raise concerns about introducing bias into credit decisions that may reflect average outcomes, but that are inconsistent with social norms and values. Consider a pattern of lending that effectively reduces access to individuals based on location or race. The use of AI algorithms—which produce accurate predictions but often lack a structural interpretation—may be perceived as a discriminatory black box that loan officers will not be able to explain to their customers or to regulators. Bazarbash (2019) points out that the opacity in interpreting decisions made using machine learning methods raises concerns about consumer protection. Using administrative data on US mortgage lending, Fuster et al. (forthcoming) compare different credit scoring methods for predicting default across genders and racial groups. They find that machine learning algorithms offer more accurate credit scoring than simpler linear methods, but that the benefits that could be derived from these methods—such as cheaper and more plentiful lending—are least likely to accrue to Black and Hispanic borrowers.

4. Open Banking: Toward a Complete and Competitive Data Market in Finance

As we have described so far, data plays a crucial role in the modern economy, and policies governing access to data will have a bearing on innovation, competition, and equity. Open banking has emerged as a new model for data-sharing within the financial sector. In Chapter 11 in this volume, Carrière-Swallow, Haksar, and Patnam (2021) offer a comparison of the main dimensions of selected open banking frameworks, which span advanced and emerging economies on multiple continents.

In this section, we explore four common objectives of open banking policies. First, perhaps the main innovation with respect to the traditional credit bureau model is the devolution of full control to customers over who gets access to their financial data. Second, open banking frameworks often have the explicit objective of increasing competition in the provision of financial services. Third, open banking has implications for cybersecurity risks in the financial system, and usually involves a framework for ensuring data security. Fourth, in view of the heterogeneity of data, open banking defines a perimeter of data types to be included, which presents important challenges.

a. Consumer Control over Access to Financial Data

Data markets are too often opaque. Consumers and companies exchange access to their data for services constantly, but the details and nature of the transactions are unclear. Consumers may be aware that the new app they downloaded will come to know their income, daily habits, and social network, and may use the information to customize their experience or show them more interesting advertisements. But what else can they do with this information? And with smart devices equipped with multiple sensors that can perceive every aspect of the environment around them, what data should be off limits, even if it might help the app further improve the customer's experience?

The current configuration of the data economy has delivered substantial profits to the leading companies—in large part on the basis of their commercialization of the insights obtained from user data—and the delivery of an impressive range of services to customers at little or no monetary cost.

A first step in achieving an equitable allocation of value from data is to complete the market by establishing and clarifying the rights of economic agents over the data they generate and exchange. Several jurisdictions have granted individuals a series of rights over access to their personal data, including limits on how the data can be used once it has been collected.[15] In the European Union, the GDPR came into effect in 2019 and granted citizens of EU countries with a series of newly defined rights over how their personal data can be collected, stored, and processed, including the obligation of processors to seek user consent prior to collecting or storing data, and the right to be forgotten. A similar approach has been implemented in Australia, where the authorities established the "Consumer Data Right" (CDR) in February 2020.

Given the importance of data to financial decision-making, the sector has long operated with a greater amount of clarity over data access rights than other sectors. The rules for what types of data are to be shared with credit bureaus are generally well established by law or regulation and are transparent and well understood. Customers are often able to obtain a copy of their credit file from the bureau upon request, and thus have access to a summarized version of the personal data made available to their lenders.

Open banking changes the traditional structure by moving to a devolved data-sharing system in which the customer has control over the decision of who gets access to any of the individual data that has been collected on them by the financial sector. Control over data access is likely to increase the returns consumers receive from the financial system, since it will subject banks to greater competition. It could be argued that the gains from granting individuals control rights may be smaller than those derived by Jones and Tonetti (2020) for other sectors of the data economy. This is because the starting point in finance is one that already features considerable data access through credit bureaus, reducing the scope for data hoarding by banks.

Once rights are established, individuals need to be able to meaningfully exert them in the data economy. The data-sharing in open banking is largely disintermediated—some jurisdictions allow for data intermediaries to emerge, but their participation is not required for data exchange to take place—and commonly contain three elements that operationalize user control over their data.[16] Data portability requirements mandate that a user be able to obtain all the data a data processor has stored about them. Data interoperability requirements mandate that data be stored and processed in standardized formats, ensuring that the data generated in one commercial relationship can readily

---

[15] Personal data denotes data that can be mapped to an individual person or (in some jurisdictions) business.

[16] In the Indian case, data aggregators act as intermediaries between the data subject and data processors (Carrière-Swallow, Haksar, and Patnam, 2021, and D'Silva et al., 2019). These regulated entities are charged with facilitating the transfer of data authorized by the individual in a way that is consistent with local laws and regulations and is stored and transferred in accordance with security standards. Importantly, regulations prevent these aggregators from engaging in data storage or processing of their own with the data they intermediate, thus restricting a potential source of externalities that could otherwise emerge.

be used in another. By creating an interoperable system of APIs, data-sharing can be automated across financial institutions once the individual has granted their consent to proceed with the transfer.

b. Promoting Competition in Financial Services

One important objective of open banking is to increase competition and innovation among financial institutions. By providing new entrants with access to the granular user data held by banks, open banking overturns the traditional information advantage held by incumbent banks based on their long-term relationships with their clients. This is meant to enable more robust competition from new entrants, including fintech and BigTech firms, who would otherwise face barriers to entry due to a lack of access to granular data about borrowers. In principle, greater competition could lower the cost of finance and promote innovation in the provision of financial services. The strength of this effect will depend on the size of the barriers entrants faced due to lack of data under the credit bureau model, which provided competing lenders with a customer's credit report but not the underlying granular data. One limit on these gains may stem from the scale of an incumbent's overall database, which has been accumulated over many years and over a large pool of customers. Open banking will only grant access to the individual data of those customers who grant their consent, not to the entire data set held by incumbents. Thus for new entrants into banking, accumulating enough customer data to produce advanced analytical tools may remain a challenge.[17]

Open banking could also have implications for the structure of the financial value chain. Data access under open banking may facilitate specialization in the provision of financial services, with intermediation separated from services that do not require a large balance sheet. For instance, an account aggregator service may seek authorization to obtain a client's full history of account balances and transactions from the multiple banks that serve them, thus providing a whole-of-customer monitoring service that may also include analysis and insights. Another example of specialization facilitated by data-sharing is the separation of funding loans and servicing loans in the case of mortgage-backed securities. This would be expected to lead to more innovation, better products, and lower costs to customers.

Forcing incumbents to share part of their data with new entrants without compensation could potentially lower the incentives to produce high-quality data in the first place. But in the case of the raw transaction and account balance data that has been the starting point for most open banking frameworks, this data is largely generated at near-zero cost as a byproduct of financial activities, such that altering the incentives surrounding their access is unlikely to affect their quantity or quality. But in the case of data that may be more costly or less standard to produce—for instance, data on SME operations—the loss of exclusivity over data may reduce banks' incentives to develop

---

[17] An alternative policy option to explore would be the establishment of a centralized data utility—similar to a credit bureau—that would allow for access to the universe of anonymized financial data held by regulated institutions for the purpose of developing analytical tools.

and monitor these relationships, since any insights earned through their risk taking must be shared with competitors.

Competition in open banking is facilitated by data portability and interoperability, which are common features of open banking frameworks but are not always mandated by regulators. Portability requirements expand the customer's right to obtain the individual data about them held by financial institutions. Whereas customers often have the right to request their credit report from a credit bureau—in some cases with the fee waved once per year—portability under open banking allows them to request *all* the underlying granular data at any time. But if the data is provided in nonstandard formats, it would be costly and difficult for a competitor to use this data, reducing but not eliminating the barrier to entry. Interoperability under open banking thus sets standards for data recording formats, ensuring that the data stored by one bank can be readily used by competitors who obtain it. The interoperable transfer of data from one institution to another is usually facilitated by an API.

c. Cyber Security in Finance

In section 2 we explained that data is nonrival and partially excludable, such that protecting data from misuse is costly for those who collect and process it. Kashyap and Wetherilt (2019) and Kopp, Kaffenburger, and Wilson (2017) argue that private incentives to secure data are subject to a systemic externality. Because a security breach at one entity can undermine public trust in the entire system, individual institutions do not have adequate incentives to invest in preventing these breaches from occurring. The implication is that an unregulated data-intensive financial system is likely to feature too much cyber risk and could be prone to instability when public trust is called into question following large data breaches.

Open banking frameworks feature disintermediated data flows between financial institutions, authorized by the individuals whose data is to be shared. This is thought to increase the amount of data flowing in the financial system and will likely mean that personal data is stored simultaneously by multiple financial institutions. By providing access to smaller fintech companies as well as large financial institutions, open banking also broadens the range of information security systems on which financial data is stored. There is a risk that this data will be misused by potential attackers, who can use the embedded information for targeted attacks on individuals and companies. The interconnected nature of the system creates a risk that an attack on one institution can allow the attackers to pivot internally through the API systems to threaten another institution.

Because the information flow under open banking is likely to increase the attack surface for cyber risks, an important aspect of these frameworks are the measures to ensure that the data flowing in the financial system remains secure. In order to ensure the security and interoperability of the system, read access to the open banking API is limited to regulated entities. In turn, the open banking regulator provides assurances to all parties that cybersecurity standards will be met and enforced throughout the system, which underpins public trust in the open data framework.

d. Setting the Data Perimeter: From Open Banking to Open Data

Open banking frameworks must define the perimeter of data classes that are subject to the interoperable data-sharing requirement. This is made challenging by the wide variety of data that is collected in the economy; as we discussed in section 2, data is far from homogeneous and features infinite varieties. In this respect, the sectoral approach of open banking allows for a more tractable perimeter than a whole of economy policy. The starting point for most frameworks involves all data on checking and saving account transactions and balances, with some including also credit card and mortgage balances and payments.

But the tidy definition of traditional financial data is being upended by the entry of technology firms into the financial sector, including both "BigTechs" such as Google and Amazon, and smaller "fintechs." As Berg et al. (2020) and Frost et al. (2019) demonstrate empirically, accurate predictions of creditworthiness can be achieved using data that is readily collected by a variety of online platforms, including mundane factors such as the model of a customer's smartphone, whether their email address contains their real name, or the pattern of their purchases from online retailers. As new financial service providers come to make credit decisions based on these types of alternative data, banks observe that open banking frameworks no longer offer a level playing field. While technology firms can request that their client authorize their access to all the financial data held by their banks, the banks are unable to obtain the valuable data held by the technology companies, since these belong to data classes that lie outside the open banking perimeter.

Open banking is an example of an open data policy focused on the financial sector, but it may hold the most promise by eventually expanding its scope to other types of data. As we discuss in Carrière-Swallow and Haksar (2019), other parts of the digital economy are plagued by opacity, with data-intensive sectors tending toward concentrated market structures with very high profits. A shift toward open banking's customer-centric approach to data access would represent a significant change in the functioning of data markets in sectors outside finance. Consider the creation of a secure API that would allow users to grant access to the granular data about their location history generated by their smartphone. Implementing such a system would not be without challenges, including the creation of new regulatory regimes for a highly diverse set of data processing firms. But these challenges can be viewed as incremental extensions to those that have already been overcome by open banking frameworks, which have safely and transparently expanded the perimeter of financial data exchange to previously unregulated non-bank competitors.

5. Conclusions

Data plays a crucial role in the modern economy. As a factor of production, firms require data in order to innovate and deliver their products and services. And as a source of information, data shifts advantages across economic actors. But how much data should we be sharing, and who should have access to it? Insufficient recognition of the privacy externalities involved in transactions involving data may lead to too much data circulating in the economy and could eventually undermine the public's willingness to participate in the data economy. For the data economy to deliver equitable and efficient outcomes, individuals must be granted some effective control over access to their data. In economic terms, "privacy" is achieved when the individual has a say in who can access their data—not when data access is denied.

Open banking has emerged as a data policy framework that promises to put the consumer of financial services in charge of who can access their financial histories. The objective of this disintermediated data exchange is to increase competition and innovation in the financial sector, while allowing individuals to control how much privacy they are willing to sacrifice in order to obtain more customized and superior services. Many economies—including both advanced and emerging markets—have already deployed open banking frameworks. While it is too soon to evaluate whether the policy is delivering on its objectives, new challenges have emerged that policymakers will need to address.

Open banking frameworks will face important challenges as they mature. First, open banking must ensure it creates a level playing field. Not all entrants enter the data economy with equal endowments: banks may have accumulated decades' worth of very granular data about their customers, through relationships that may originally have involved substantial risk. New fintechs and BigTech competitors enter the provision of financial services with a dearth of traditional financial data, but in some cases with a massive set of alternative data that banks are unable to observe in conducting their traditional activities. By defining a narrow perimeter of applicable data types limited to traditional financial data, some open banking frameworks could lead to very asymmetric sharing of data.

Second, open banking will also need to be mindful of the potential side effects when decisions on the granting of financial services become based on the application of AI to its big and widely shared data sets. Risks from algorithmic bias leading to financial exclusion of certain groups raise important policy challenges for the governance of the use of data in making decisions on service offerings.

If it is shown to be successful in achieving its objectives, authorities' experience with open banking may offer a steppingstone toward broader open data frameworks. In some jurisdictions, the consumer data right is being applied to financial data first, but authorities have publicly stated that they plan to expand the right to other classes of structured data in the future, including those related to the energy and telecommunications sectors. If open banking's clear rules focus on consumer rights, and tools for delivering effective control can be expanded to other classes of data, its legacy may end up being a nudge toward a more efficient and equitable digital economy. Going forward, an important challenge will be developing global policy frameworks for the management of data across sectors and borders, a topic which will be taken up in IMF.

References

Acquisti, Alessandro and Taylor, Curtis R. and Wagman, Liad, 2016. The Economics of Privacy (March 8, 2016). *Journal of Economic Literature*, Vol. 52, No. 2, Sloan Foundation Economics Research Paper No. 2580411, Available at SSRN: https://ssrn.com/abstract=2580411 or http://dx.doi.org/10.2139/ssrn.2580411

Acemoglu, Daron et al., 2021. "Too Much Data: Prices and Inefficiencies in Data Markets," *American Economic Journal: Microeconomics*, in press.

Agrawal, Ajay, Joshua Gans, and Avi Goldfarb, 2018. *Prediction Machines: The Simple Economics of Artificial Intelligence*. Cambridge, MA: Harvard Business Review Press.

Aridor, Guy, Yeon-Koo Che, and Tobias Salz, 2020. "The Economic Consequences of Data Privacy Regulation: Empirical Evidence from GDPR," Working Paper 26900, National Bureau of Economic Research.

Arrow, Kenneth. "Uncertainty and the Welfare Economics of Medical Care" The American Economic Review, Vol. 53, Issue 5 (Dec., 1963), 941–973. https://web.stanford.edu/~jay/health_class/Readings/Lecture01/arrow.pdf

Bank for International Settlements, 2019. "Big Tech in Finance: Opportunities and Risks," *BIS Annual Economic Report*. Basel, Switzerland: Bank for International Settlements.

Bazarbash, Majid, 2019. "Fintech in Financial Inclusion: Machine Learning Applications in Assessing Credit Risk," Working Paper 19/109, International Monetary Fund.

Begenau, Juliane, Maryam Farboodi, and Laura Veldkamp, 2018. "Big Data in Finance and the Growth of Large Firms," *Journal of Monetary Economics* 97: 71–87.

Berg, T. et al., 2020. "On the Rise of FinTechs—Credit Scoring Using Digital Footprints," *Review of Financial Studies* 33(7): 2845–97.

Boissay, F. et al., 2020. "BigTechs in Finance: On the New Nexus Between Data Privacy and Competition," forthcoming in B. Wardrop, R. Rau, and L. Zingales (eds.), *Handbook of Technological Finance*. Switzerland: Palgrave Macmillan.

Carletti, Elena et al., 2020. "The Bank Business Model in the Post-Covid-19 World," *The Future of Banking, vol. 2*. London, UK: Center for Economic Policy and Research.

Carrière-Swallow, Yan and Vikram Haksar, 2019. "The Economics and Implications of Data: An Integrated Perspective," Departmental Paper 19/16, International Monetary Fund.

Carrière-Swallow, Yan, Vikram Haksar, and Manasa Patnam, 2021. "India's Approach to Open Banking and Some Implications for Financial Inclusion," Chapter 11 in Linda Jeng (ed.), *Open Banking*. New York: Oxford University Press.

Djankov, Simeon, Caralee McLiesh, and Andrei Schleifer, 2007. "Private Credit in 129 Countries," *Journal of Financial Economics* 84(2): 299–329.

D'Silva, Derryl et al., 2019. "The Design of Digital Financial Infrastructure: Lessons from India," *BIS Papers* 106. Basel, Switzerland: Bank for International Settlements.

Ezrachi, Ariel and Maurice E. Stucke, 2016. "Virtual Competition," *Journal of European Competition Law & Practice* 7(9): 585–86.

Farboodi, Maryam and Laura Veldkamp, 2021. "A Growth Model of the Data Economy," Working Paper 28427, Cambridge, MA: National Bureau of Economic Research.

Frost, Jon et al., 2019. "BigTech and the Changing Structure of Financial Intermediation." *Economic Policy* 34(100): 761–99. https://doi.org/10.1093/epolic/eiaa003

Furman, Jason, 2019. "Unlocking Digital Competition," Report of the Digital Competition Expert Panel, H.M. Treasury, London, United Kingdom.

Fuster, Andreas et al., forthcoming. "Predictably Unequal? The Effects of Machine Learning on Credit Markets," *Journal of Finance*.

He, Zhiguo and Huang, Jing and Zhou, Jidong, Open Banking: Credit Market Competition When Borrowers Own the Data (November 13, 2020). University of Chicago, Becker Friedman Institute for Economics Working Paper No. 2020-168, Available at SSRN: https://ssrn.com/abstract=3736109 or http://dx.doi.org/10.2139/ssrn.3736109

International Monetary Fund, 2017. "Big Data: Potential, Challenges, and Statistical Implications," Staff Discussion Note 17/06, September.

International Monetary Fund, 2018a. "Measuring the Digital Economy," IMF Policy Paper, February.

International Monetary Fund, 2018b. "The Bali Fintech Agenda," IMF Policy Paper, International Monetary Fund, Washington, DC.

International Monetary Fund, Forthcoming. "Towards a Global Data Policy Framework," Staff Discussion Note, International Monetary Fund, Washington, DC.

Jappelli, Tullio and Marco Pagano, 2002. "Information Sharing, Lending and Defaults: Cross-country Evidence," *Journal of Banking & Finance* 26(10): 2017–45.

Jones, Charles I. and Christopher Tonetti, 2020. "Nonrivalry and the Economic of Data," *American Economic Review* 110(9): 2819–58.

Kashyap, Anil and Anne Wetherilt, 2019. "Some Principles for Regulating Cyber Risk," *AEA Papers and Proceedings* 109: 482–87.

Kopp, Emmanuel Albin, Lincoln Kaffenburger and Christopher Wilson, 2017. "Cyber Risk, Market Failures, and Financial Stability," Working Paper 17/185, International Monetary Fund.

Lewis, Randall and Justin Rao, 2015. "The Unfavorable Economics of Measuring the Returns to Advertising," *Quarterly Journal of Economics* 130(4): 1941–73.

Liberman, Andrés et al., 2018. "The Equilibrium Effects of Information Deletion: Evidence from Consumer Credit Markets," NBER Working Paper 25097, National Bureau of Economic Research, Cambridge, MA.

Marotta, Veronica, Vibhanshu Abhishek, and Alessandro Acquisti, 2019. "Online Tracking and Publishers' Revenues: An Empirical Analysis," unpublished mimeo, May.

Peria, Martinez, Maria Soledad, and Sandeep Singh, 2014. "The Impact of Credit Information Sharing Reforms on Firm Financing," Policy Research Working Paper 7013, World Bank.

Posner, Richard A., 1981. "The Economics of Privacy," *AEA Papers and Proceedings* 71(2): 405–09.

Sahay, Ratna et al., 2020. "The Promise of Fintech: Financial Inclusion in the Post COVID-19 Era," Departmental Paper 20/09, International Monetary Fund.

Stiglitz, Joseph E. and Andrew Weiss, 1981. "Credit Rationing in Markets with Imperfect Information," *American Economic Review* 71(3): 393–410.

Varian, Hal, 2018. "Artificial Intelligence, Economics, and Industrial Organization," in *The Economics of AI: An Agenda*. Cambridge, MA: National Bureau of Economic Research.

Winegar, A.G. and C.R. Sunstein, 2019. "How Much Is Data Privacy Worth? A Preliminary Investigation," *Journal of Consumer Policy* 42(3): 425–40.

8

Open Banking, Open Data, and Open Finance

Lessons from the European Union

Douglas W. Arner,* Ross P. Buckley,** and Dirk A. Zetzsche***

Europe's path to "open banking," "open data," and "open finance" rests upon four apparently unrelated pillars: (1) the facilitation of open banking to enhance competition in banking and particularly payments; (2) strict data protection rules reflecting European cultural concerns about dominant actors in the data processing field; (3) extensive reporting requirements imposed after the 2008 Global Financial Crisis to control systemic risk and change financial sector behavior; and (4) a legislative framework for digital identification imposed to further the European Single Market.

This chapter analyzes these four pillars and suggests that together they will underpin the future of digital finance in Europe and that together they effectively establish the basis for "open banking" and "open data" and also for "open finance." These European experiences provide profound insights for other societies facing choices as to the role of data in their future. In some, data will be controlled by a small number of massive firms and governments which use it for profit and suppression. In others, data will be under the control of individuals—democratized data—which should support a more open and innovative economy and society. In the evolution of these futures, legal and regulatory systems will play a central role.

1. Introduction

The next decade appears to be focused on questions of data in its role in finance, the economy, and society more generally. An increasing range of these discussions focuses on the idea of "open banking," an idea that is being expanded to ideas of "open finance"

* Kerry Holdings Professor in Law and Co-Founder, Asian Institute of International Financial Law, Faculty of Law, University of Hong Kong.

** Australian Research Council Laureate Fellow; KPMG Law and King & Wood Mallesons Chair of Disruptive Innovation; and Scientia Professor; UNSW Sydney.

*** Professor of Law, ADA Chair in Financial Law (Inclusive Finance), Faculty of Law, Economics and Finance, University of Luxembourg, and Director, Centre for Business and Corporate Law, Heinrich-Heine-University, Düsseldorf, Germany.

We would like to thank the Australian Research Council Laureate Fellowship, the Hong Kong Research Grants Council Research Impact Fund, and the Qatar National Research Fund for financial support. This work builds upon our analysis in D.A. Zetzsche, D.W. Arner, R.P. Buckley, and R.H. Weber," The Evolution and Future of Data-Driven Finance in the E.U.," *Common Market Law Review* 57 (2020), 331; and D.W. Arner, D.A. Zetzsche, R.P. Buckley, and R.H. Weber, "The Future of Data-Driven Finance and RegTech: Lessons from EU Big Bang II," *Stanford Journal of Law, Business & Finance* 25(2) (2020), 245.

Douglas W. Arner, Ross P. Buckley, and Dirk A. Zetzsche, *Open Banking, Open Data, and Open Finance* In: *Open Banking.* Edited by: Linda Jeng, Oxford University Press. © Oxford University Press 2022. DOI: 10.1093/oso/9780197582879.003.0009

and "open data" more broadly, in support of ideas of "open innovation."[1] The idea is that opening access to data will increase competition and innovation, thus benefiting both individuals and society more broadly. These ideas are taking on increasing importance as we see an increasing concentration of power in data industries, with related questions about the implications for innovation, prosperity, and inequality.

One can in some ways see a battle of visions of the future, from one where data are controlled by a small number of giant firms and governments which use their control for profit and suppression, to one where data are under the control of individuals—the "democratization" of data—supporting a more open and innovative economy and society. In the evolution of these futures, legal and regulatory systems will play a key role in determining the paths taken by different societies. The 2020 pandemic is strongly reinforcing these pre-crisis trends: COVID-19 has dramatically increased digitization generally, accelerated digitization of finance in particular through electronic payments and other transactions, and increased concentration of power in major data firms around the world.

Emerging from the COVID-19 pandemic, societies are faced with major questions about how to balance positive and negative aspects of digitization and datafication, in particular risks of concentration and dominance. "Open banking," "open finance," and "open data" are being presented as possible responses, both reducing the risks of concentration and dominance while at the same time maximizing the benefits of data for innovation and sustainable development.

If we look at approaches to "open banking," these are generally being characterized as mandatory (required by law, regulation, etc.), collaborative (involving industry and regulators working together), or voluntary (led by industry). The European Union has taken the leading role in the first of these approaches by being the first jurisdiction to implement mandatory open banking,[2] with its implementation in 2015 of the Second Payment Services Directive (PSD2).[3] It was thus the first jurisdiction to make data-sharing by banks mandatory, from 2018. As such, the European Union is central in all discussions of "open banking," as jurisdictions around the world are watching closely to see whether or not it is a success, something which is still too early to call.

However, any discussion of EU "open banking" cannot avoid looking at the broader context. In particular, the European Union is also the first jurisdiction to pursue a comprehensive approach to individual data sovereignty, also on a mandatory basis, with the General Data Protection Regulation (GDPR) of 2016, also effective in 2018. While not quite "open data," the GDPR provides for individual control over personal data, thereby relating to "open banking" provisions under PSD2.

Financial regulatory reforms, in parallel with and increasingly coupled to extensive reforms of data protection, the advent of open banking, and the development of digital identification regimes are forming a regulatory ecosystem in the European Union

---

[1] Henry Chesbrough, *Open Innovation: The New Imperative for Creating and Profiting from Technology* (Harvard Business School, 2003).

[2] The European Union was the first to implement "open banking" and the first to make it mandatory.

[3] Directive (EU) 2015/2366 of the European Parliament and of the Council of November 25, 2015, on Payment Services in the Internal Market, Amending Directives 2002/65/EC, 2009/110/EC and 2013/36/EU and Regulation (EU) No. 1093/2010, and Repealing Directive 2007/64/EC, 2015 O.J. (L 337) 35 (hereinafter "PSD2").

underpinning "open banking" and "open data" as well as "open finance." This chapter explores how these four areas of regulatory reforms, each introduced for their own discrete reasons, are interacting today in Europe.

One of the greatest challenges facing the financial industry globally today is at times conflicting requirements of data regulation and financial regulation. Major questions abound for societies around finance and the digital economy, including the role of data, technology, and regulation. This chapter demonstrates there is much to learn from a detailed analysis of the European Union's experience and its systems that govern finance and data in the European Union itself and extend extraterritorially to all those interacting with EU markets and citizens from around the world.

This chapter explores the relationship between financial regulation, data protection, regulatory technology (regtech), and the evolution of "open banking," "open data," and "open finance" in the European Union.

In Section 2, we consider briefly "open banking" and "open finance." In Sections 3 to 6, we analyze the four EU regulatory frameworks which are empowering "open finance" in the European Union.

While "open banking" is imposed on banks by PSD2 requiring incumbent intermediaries to share client data with new competitors (Section 3), it is PSD2's synergistic interaction with other policy measures which is proving transformative.

This is paralleled in a framework applying to data protection, privacy, and control more generally, which together form the basis of "open data": the rigorous data protection demanded by the GDPR[4] (Section 4), which has fundamentally altered how all firms—including financial services firms—deal with personal data.

However, much of the actual impetus for digital finance in Europe did not come from PSD2 or the GDPR but rather developed rapidly with the introduction of extensive, purely digital, reporting from intermediaries to regulators, pursuant to new financial legislation imposed after the Global Financial Crisis, including, inter alia, the Alternative Investment Fund Managers Directive (AIFMD 2011[5]) and the European Markets Infrastructure Regulation (EMIR 2012[6]), the fourth Capital Requirements Directive and the Capital Requirements Regulation (CRD IV[7]/CRR[8]) in 2013, and the reformed Markets in Financial Instruments Directives (MiFID II[9]) in 2014 (Section 5).

[4] Regulation (EU) 2016/679 of the European Parliament and of the Council of April 27, 2016, on the Protection of Natural Persons with Regard to the Processing of Personal Data and on the Free Movement of Such Data, and Repealing Directive 95/46/EC (General Data Protection Regulation), 2016 O.J. (L 119) 1.

[5] Directive 2011/61/EU of the European Parliament and of the Council of June 8, 2011, on Alternative Investment Fund Managers and Amending Directives 2003/41/EC and 2009/65/EC and Regulations (EC) No. 1060/2009 and (EU) No. 1095/2010, 2011 O.J. (L 174) 1.

[6] Regulation (EU) No. 648/2012 of the European Parliament and of the Council of July 4, 2012, on OTC Derivatives, Central Counterparties and Trade Repositories, 2012 O.J. (L 201) 1.

[7] Directive 2013/36/EU of the European Parliament and of the Council of June 26, 2013, on Access to the Activity of Credit Institutions and the Prudential Supervision of Credit Institutions and Investment Firms, Amending Directive 2002/87/EC and Repealing Directives 2006/48/EC and 2006/49/EC, 2013 O.J. (L 176) 338.

[8] Regulation (EU) No. 575/2013 of the European Parliament and of the Council of June 26, 2013, on Prudential Requirements for Credit Institutions and Investment Firms and Amending Regulation (EU) No. 648/2012, 2013 O.J. (L 176) 1.

[9] Directive 2014/65/EU of the European Parliament and of the Council of May 15, 2014, on Markets in Financial Instruments and Amending Directive 2002/92/EC and Directive 2011/61/EU, 2014 O.J. (L 173) 349.

But more was required to tie the pieces together: the fourth facilitative measure was cross-border digital identity pursuant to the eIDAS (electronic IDentification, Authentication and trust Services) framework,[10] which establishes a network of national identity providers which can be either public or private (Section 6).

We discuss the implications in Section 7, comparing these EU developments with other major jurisdictions, in particular the United States, China, and India. Section 8 concludes.

2. Open Banking and Open Finance

a. Open Banking and Open Finance and Their Role in Antitrust

Open banking is the regulatory response to the anticompetitive tendencies of the data economy where the size of the data pool determines competitive strength[11] and where technology firms like Amazon and Google have forgone profits for years to build dominant platforms. At the core are network effects, including economies of scope and scale, leading to the potential for industry concentration and dominance. At the extreme, data-driven industries are particularly subject to "winner takes all outcomes," with the potential for significant benefits followed by significant negative externalities. As the leading example, American tech and data markets have tended toward oligopoly or monopoly over time,[12] a process which has also occurred in China. Both jurisdictions have allowed commercial enterprises to acquire control of large consumer and other data pools. The core asset of those platforms is their pool of data from shoppers and merchants. Once this data pool is assembled it can be used for targeting advertising, undercutting prices, offering new tailored services faster to more clients, and/or data analysis in all markets where superior information benefits profits.

Legal competition/antitrust scholars argue that where investors reward growth over profit, predatory pricing becomes highly rational and striving for dominance, even where this is costly, is a worthwhile strategy since it ensures monopoly rents due to control over the essential infrastructure on which their rivals depend: "This dual role also enables a platform to exploit information collected on companies using its services to undermine them as competitors."[13] This has prompted the policy demand to treat data

[10] Regulation (EU) No. 910/2014 of the European Parliament and of the Council of July 23, 2014, on Electronic Identification and Trust Services for Electronic Transactions in the Internal Market and Repealing Directive 1999/93/EC, 2014 O.J. (L 257) 73.

[11] See Simonetta Vezzoso, "Fintech, Access to Data, and the Role of Competition Policy," in *Competition and Innovation* (Vicente Bagnoli ed., Scortecci, 2018).

[12] See Tim Wu, *The Master Switch: The Rise And Fall Of Information Empires* (Vintage, 2011) (arguing that American information industries tend to press toward monopolies); see also Ariel Ezrachi and Maurice E. Stucke, *Virtual Competition: The Promise and Perils of the Algorithm-Driven Economy* (Harvard University Press, 2006) (discussing the promise and perils of technology-driven competition).

[13] See Lina M. Khan, "Amazon's Antitrust Paradox," *Yale Law Journal* 126 (2017), 710; K. Sabeel Rahman and Lina Khan, "Restoring Competition in the U.S. Economy," in *Untamed: How to Check Corporate, Financial, and Monopoly Power* 18, 18 (Nell Abernathy, Mike Konczal, and Kathy Milani eds., Roosevelt Institute, 2016) (arguing that the potential harms from dominance of platform firms include lower income and wages for employees, lower rates of new business creation, lower rates of local ownership, and outsized political and economic control in the hands of a few); see also "Digital Platforms Inquiry: Preliminary Report," *Australian Competition & Consumer Comm'n* (2018). https://www.accc.gov.au/system/files/ACCC%20Digital%20Platfo rms%20Inquiry%20-%20Preliminary%20Report.pdf.

as a product, since information and data, although different from traditional goods and services, pose problems familiar to competition/antitrust law, such as monopolistic behavior and collusion.[14] Treating data as a product becomes a particular consideration in avoiding potential reductions in innovation and therefore in long-term growth and development. (The economics of data is explored in Chapter 7 by Yan Carrière-Swallow and Vikram Haksar.)

These debates are increasingly important in the European Union, the United States, and China, with global implications.

Open banking applies these insights to financial services where the controller of client data controls access to the client, and thus can impede or facilitate access of clients to new services.

In essence, open banking facilitates greatly increased levels of democratization of finance by enabling participants to simply, swiftly, and safely provide their raw financial data to competitors of their current financial services provider.[15] This should support the growth of many new competitors in financial services. Most financial ecosystems are dominated by a relatively small number of very large banks or, in the case of China, very large tech companies providing financial services. Open banking should result in a far greater range of product offerings and ecosystem participants. These new participants will not be burdened with legacy systems, and many will utilize more cost-efficient decentralized systems.

b. Countering Pro-Concentration Effects

Three data-related factors together may lead to friction in the market for financial services that prevents private ordering from leading to socially optimal outcomes, in the sense that market forces ensure competition among services providers. These factors are traditional economies of scale, data-driven economies of scale, and network effects.[16]

In this regard, Open Data (or Open Finance) is a two-edged sword. While the European Union (with the GDPR and PSD2) has required the financial industry to develop appropriate systems for data management and limited the use the industry can make of pooled data (thereby reducing the advantages of traditional financial institutions through their data pools), it has also driven the standardization of data processes outside of finance—potentially making for a larger data pool and enabling new entrants to potentially access more data of their individual customers. In other words, data are now more freely accessible and transferable than ever before. Large technology companies know well how to make use of the new rights to data transfer—much more so than do new entrants with access to customers limited by budgets and resources. This could prompt utterly unexpected results. While PSD2 and the GDPR

---

[14] See Mark R. Patterson, *Antitrust Law in the New Economy: Google, Yelp, LIBOR, and the Control of Information* (Harvard University Press, 2017) (arguing in favor of conceptualizing information and user data as a product, since information and data, although different from traditional goods and services, poses problems familiar to antitrust law, such as monopoly and collusion).

[15] See Christopher C. Nicholls, "Open Banking and the Rise of FinTech: Innovative Finance and Functional Regulation," *Banking & Financial Law Review* 35 (2019), 121, 123.

[16] D.A. Zetzsche et al., "From FinTech to TechFin: The Regulatory Challenges of Data-Driven Finance," *New York University Journal of Law & Business* 14(2) (2018), 393.

were originally designed to curtail the power of data behemoths, the eventual outcome of these two groundbreaking initiatives may well be less competition as there will be a greater concentration of data in the hands of the few.[17] As a result, it may be necessary for regulators to impose open data requirements only on firms with a potentially dominant position, regardless of whether they are financial institutions or tech firms.

c. The European Big Bang in Data-Driven Finance

Financial integration in Europe has evolved as a result of a series of major policy, legislative, and regulatory strategies and initiatives, developed and implemented since the 1980s.[18] These have included the 1986 Single European Act,[19] which established the key formative plan for integration in the context of the single market and which was also one of the triggers for the financial reforms in the United Kingdom known as "Big Bang";[20] the 1992 Maastricht Treaty[21] establishing the European Union as well as the structure of the single market and the single currency; the 1995 White Paper on enlargement;[22] European Economic and Monetary Union (EMU) in 1999 combined with the 1999 Financial Services Action Plan;[23] the 2001 Lamfalussy Report;[24] the 2009 de Larosière Report in the aftermath of the 2008 Global Financial Crisis;[25] and the Banking Union in the aftermath of the 2010 Eurozone Crisis.[26]

We suggest in this section that 2018 and the implementation of four separate legislative reforms should be seen as a new Big Bang in the European Union: one of data-driven finance and its regulation. We argue that the impact of the 2018 Big Bang will be transformative for European finance over the coming years and will be as important a milestone as those which have taken place before. However, unlike the list of developments in the preceding paragraph, Big Bang II has not been a carefully designed strategy to support further integration and evolution of finance in the European Union.

---

[17] See D.A. Zetzsche et al., "The Evolution and Future of Data-Driven Finance in the E.U.," *Common Market Law Review* 57 (2020), 331.

[18] For the evolution of the EU Single Financial Market, the role of financial regulation, and implications for global finance, see Emilios Avgouleas and Douglas W. Arner, "The Eurozone Debt Crisis and the European Banking Union: 'Hard Choices', 'Intolerable Dilemmas' and the Question of Sovereignty," *International Law* 50 (2017), 29; Douglas W. Arner and Ross P. Buckley, "Redesigning the Architecture of the Global Financial System," *Melbourne Journal of International Law* 11 (2010), 185; Rolf Weber and Douglas W. Arner, "Toward a New Design for International Financial Regulation," *University of Pennsylvania Journal of International Economic Law* 29 (2007), 391.

[19] 1987 O.J. (L 169).

[20] See Jamie Robertson, "How the Big Bang Changed the City of London For Ever," *BBC News* (Oct. 27, 2016). https://www.bbc.com/news/business-37751599[https://perma.cc/Q9B9-AUNH].

[21] Treaty on European Union, Feb. 7, 1992, 1992 O.J. (C 191).

[22] Commission White Paper on Preparation of the Associated Countries of Central and Eastern Europe for Integration into the Internal Market of the Union, COM (1995) 163 final (May 3, 1995).

[23] Implementing the Framework for Financial Markets: Action Plan, Financial Services Action Plan, at 16–27, COM (1999) 232 final (May 11, 1999).

[24] Final Report of the Committee of Wise Men on the Regulation of European Securities Markets (Feb. 15, 2001). https://www.esma.europa.eu/sites/default/files/library/2015/11/lamfalussy_report.pdf [https://perma.cc/27XB-M924].

[25] Report of the High-Level Group on Financial Supervision in the EU (Feb. 25, 2009). https://ec.europa.eu/economy_finance/publications/pages/publication14527_en.pdf [https://perma.cc/LMS3-NSP5].

[26] See Avgouleas and Arner, *supra* note 18.

Rather, the four legislative measures analyzed in this part were all implemented for separate reasons, but their combined effect has been to give an extraordinary, unanticipated impetus to the digital transformation of finance in the European Union. The measures are the digital regulatory reporting requirements particularly of AIFMD and MiFID II, the rigorous data protection of the GDPR, the open banking regime introduced by PSD2 (particularly combined with the data portability requirements in the GDPR), and the pan-European digital identity framework built pursuant to eIDAS. Each is considered in turn.

Reflecting this, the European Union's new Digital Finance Strategy 2020 uses this framework as the basis of a strategic approach going forward.

3. Open Banking: PSD2

The PSD2 mandates "open banking": that banks have to share customer data with third-parties—in many cases their new fintech and BigTech, as well as traditional, competitors—when directed to do so by their customers, reinforcing the requirements of the GDPR, discussed in Section 4.[27]

Besides extensive and purely digital reporting to regulators (further reinforcing the regtech cycle discussed below), PSD2 imposes to a certain degree "open banking" requirements, whereby incumbent financial intermediaries must share client data with third-parties, including potentially innovative new competitors.[28] By giving providers access to the clients' financial information, PSD2 opens the way for new banking products and services, and facilitates customers moving from one financial service provider to another. With the European Union functioning as first mover, other jurisdictions are considering whether and how to follow.[29] This renders the EU PSD2 experiment particularly valuable and significant not only in payments but also from the standpoint of the real impact of open banking and competition especially from nontraditional technology-focused competitors, including fintechs and BigTechs.

Such data will have been collected and digitized, repackaged for delivery to regulators and/or internal use and managed by new purpose-built systems, typically all at great expense and difficulty. PSD2 thereby sets the stage for the next level of the evolution of data-driven finance: broad competition among incumbent and new participants.

---

[27] Directive (EU) 2015/2366 of the European Parliament and of the Council of November 25, 2015, on Payment Services in the Internal Market, Amending Directives 2002/65/EC, 2009/110/EC and 2013/36/EU and Regulation (EU) No. 1093/2010 and Repealing Directive 2007/64/EC, 2015 O.J. (L 337) 35.

[28] See generally Markos Zachariadis and Pinar Ozcan, "The API Economy and Digital Transformation in Financial Services: The Case of Open Banking," SWIFT Institute Working Paper No. 2016-001 (2017). https://ssrn.com/abstract=2975199; Peggy Valcke, Niels Vandezande, and Nathan Van de Velde, "The Evolution of Third Party Payment Providers and Cryptocurrencies Under the EU's Upcoming PSD2 and AMLD4," SWIFT Institute Working Paper No. 2015-001 (2015). https://ssrn.com/abstract=2665973; Fernando Zunzunegui, "Digitalisation of Payment Services," Ibero-Am. Inst. L. & Fin. Working Paper No. 5/2018 (2018). https://ssrn.com/abstract=3256281; Oscar Borgogno and Giuseppe Colangelo, "Data, Innovation and Transatlantic Competition in Finance: The Case of the Access to Account Rule," *European Business Law Review* (forthcoming 2020). https://ssrn.com/abstract=3251584; Benjamin Geva, "Payment Transactions Under the E.U. Second Payment Services Directive (PSD2)—An Outsider's View," *Texas International Law Journal* 54 (2019), 211.

[29] See "Review into Open Banking in Australia: Final Report," *Australian Open Banking Initiative* (Dec. 2017). https://perma.cc/6QVD-U2R3.

a. PSD2's Open Banking Approach

PSD1[30] and its amending and complementary legislation adopted from 2007 through 2012[31] established the common European market in payment services with the Single Euro Payments Area (SEPA) framework. PSD1 was a success, in harmonizing payment transactions throughout the EU single market and in achieving significant market integration and related efficiencies in the commercial and consumer payment sector. When PSD2 was first discussed, the European payments sector was not in need of reform; but one recently completed successful reform project provided the background for advancing payments regulation, addressing the significant technical innovation since adoption of the PSD1 framework.[32] The reform was premised upon the notion that "[s]ignificant areas of the payments market, in particular card, internet and mobile payments, remain fragmented along national borders"[33] and that the existing framework suffered from legal uncertainty, security risks, and a lack of consumer protection. It was also difficult for payment service providers to launch innovative, safe, and easy-to-use digital payment services.[34]

The European legislation sought to "square the circle." PSD2 sought to enable

"new means of payment to reach a broader market, [while] ensuring a high level of consumer protection in the use of those payment services across the [EU]. This should generate efficiencies in the payment system as a whole and lead to more choice and more transparency of payment services while strengthening the trust of consumers in a harmonised payments market."[35]

PSD2 also set out to address the security risks relating to electronic payments[36] as well as extraterritorial payment transactions.[37]

In order to achieve equivalent rules for equivalent transactions, regardless of the technology used, legal form employed, or number of parties involved, and ensure equivalent protection for merchants and consumers,[38] PSD2 introduced a neutral definition

---

[30] See Directive 2007/64/EC of the European Parliament and of the Council of November 13, 2007, on Payment Services in the Internal Market Amending Directives 97/7/EC, 2002/65/EC, 2005/60/EC and 2006/48/EC and Repealing Directive 97/5/EC, 2007 O.J. (L 319) 1.

[31] See Regulation (EC) No. 924/2009 of the European Parliament and of the Council of September 16, 2009, on Cross-Border Payments in the Community and Repealing Regulation (EC) No. 2560/2001, 2009 O.J. (L 266) 11; Directive 2009/110/EC of the European Parliament and of the Council of September 16, 2009, on the Taking Up, Pursuit and Prudential Supervision of the Business of Electronic Money Institutions Amending Directives 2005/60/EC and 2006/48/EC and Repealing Directive 2000/46/EC 2009 O.J. (L 267) 7; Regulation (EU) No. 260/2012 of the European Parliament and of the Council of March 14, 2012, Establishing Technical and Business Requirements for Credit Transfers and Direct Debits in Euro and Amending Regulation (EC) No. 924/2009, 2012 O.J. (L 94) 22; Directive 2011/83/EU of the European Parliament and of the Council of October 25, 2011, on Consumer Rights, Amending Council Directive 93/13/EEC and Directive 1999/44/EC of the European Parliament and of the Council and Repealing Council Directive 85/577/EEC and Directive 97/7/EC of the European Parliament and of the Council, 2011 O.J. (L 304) 64.

[32] See PSD2, Recital 3.

[33] See European Comm'n, *Consultation on Green Paper—Towards an Integrated European Market for Card, Internet and Mobile Payments* (2012).

[34] See PSD2, Recital 4.

[35] See PSD2, Recital 6.

[36] See PSD2, Recital 7.

[37] See PSD2, Recital 8.

[38] See PSD2, Recital 10.

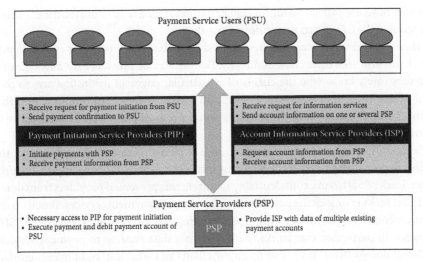

Figure 8.1 Service providers under PSD2.

of payment transactions.[39] Relating to that definition, the single license prudential framework for all "payment institutions," that is, providers of payment services unconnected to taking deposits or issuing electronic money, set out in PSD1 and refined and supplemented in PSD2, applies.

PSD2 responds, in particular, to new developments regarding internet payment services, such as payment initiation services[40] and account information services.[41] Both types of services "play a part in e-commerce payments by establishing a software bridge between the website of the merchant and the online banking platform of the payer's account in order to initiate internet payments on the basis of a credit transfer."[42] See Figure 8.1 for service providers under PSD2.

While both kinds of services are crucial in the modern payment services chain, each differs significantly from the other. In particular, "[w]hen exclusively providing payment initiation services, the payment initiation service provider does not at any stage of the payment chain hold the user's funds."[43] In turn, such a payment initiation services provider will not meet the definition and licensing requirement for payment institutions. However, "[w]hen a payment initiation service provider intends to provide payment services in relation to which it holds user funds, it should obtain full authorization [under PSD2] for those services."[44] The same applies to account information services—they rarely hold the funds; it is the additional use of information that provides the benefits to clients. Both payment initiation services and account information services require direct or indirect access to the payer's account, or the account data, respectively. For providing its services, and even demonstrating its benefits to clients, the service

---

[39] See PSD2, art. 2.
[40] See PSD2, art. 4(15). See also PSD2, Recital 29.
[41] See PSD2, art. 4(16) and Recital 28.
[42] See PSD2, Recital 27.
[43] See PSD2, Recital 31.
[44] See *id.*

provider must ask each client for consent first to access and then to use the data.[45] This is the result of the GDPR's consent rule laid out above.

There are two ways to contact new clients. First, the service provider could identify the clients and seek their consent directly. But the service providers are new entrants, and they rarely know who the clients of a particular payment institution are, so they cannot seek consent in the absence of support by the payment institutions. Given that client contact is one of the payment institutions' core assets, they have little incentive to let new providers contact their clients.

Second, the service provider may tap into the existing data pool and contact the clients for consent directly if the payment institution is unwilling to support the provider. Under PSD1, bank confidentiality requirements prevented providers from doing so. PSD2 seeks to unlock the potential for innovation in payment services. Based on the recommendations provided by the Open Banking Working Group (OBWG),[46] PSD2 requires, in particular, that banks share customer data relating to payment services with technology firms. It does so by giving clients an ownership right over their data and providing a specific use case for the data subject's data portability right granted by Article 20 of the GDPR, thereby linking PSD2 to the GDPR.[47] In this way, PSD2 aims to create a pro-innovative environment with a high level of customer service, while simultaneously upholding the principles of cybersecurity, data protection, *and* financial stability.

b. Transition to Data-Driven Finance

PSD2's central role in promoting "open banking" is triggering the transition to data-driven finance in Europe. On the one hand, PSD2 allows technology firms to enter the payment markets. In light of incumbents' control over client data, and due to the limitation that payment institutions must share client data with certain additional (tech-driven) service providers, only where a new entrant meets that definition can it hope to gain access to client data. This alone inspires innovative firms to focus on development of value-added services, accelerating the development of data-driven finance in Europe. Naturally, these entities will seek to keep their costs down and respond to regulatory responses like data-sharing and liability requirements by technical means.

On the other hand, in the context of "open banking," payment institutions must respond to PSD2 by providing data interfaces for third-party providers from which those providers can extract data of existing clients of the incumbents to provide value-added services. This will increase competitive pressures: banks' only rational response to defend what is increasingly becoming their most valuable asset as the evolution of data-driven finance moves forward—client data—will be to enhance service levels and so avoid their clients seeking those value-added services elsewhere.

---

[45] See PSD2, art. 64.

[46] See "B2B Data Sharing: Digital Consent Management as a Driver for Data Opportunities," *EBA Open Banking Working Group* (2018) 21. https://www.abe-eba.eu/media/azure/production/1979/eba_2018_obwg_b2b_data_sharing.pdf [https://perma.cc/7TNW-8J2K].

[47] See PSD2, arts. 66–67.

The costs for these additional value-added services will need to be kept as low as possible. The only way to do so will be to rely more heavily on technology, through advanced analytical tools and models, which form the core of the evolution toward data-driven finance. This process is then reinforced through the reporting obligations contained in PSD2 and elsewhere, thereby driving the consequential evolution.

While unintended, the outcome is nonetheless clear. Taking the process one step forward, however, is a system for making identification of customers easier, to enable them to more readily access financial services while also enhancing financial integrity through better customer identification and tracking. We analyze this in the next section. All of this enhances financial efficiency and benefits customers. It also makes it easier for new entrants to compete with established financial market participants and for customers to identify and transfer their data to innovative new entrants.

Nonetheless, we do not posit that the results of PSD2 will be all as expected. PSD2's objective is to enhance competition. Due to the data portability rights under PSD2, the door is open for large technology firms that know best how to use these data portability rights (which are not identical to the data portability right under the GDPR, which is designed to favor consumers) to enter financial services markets. While aiming at increased competition, the outcome may well be the opposite: the concentration of data-driven services in the hands of a few technology firms that provide financial services as one aspect of their data-driven business models.

4. Open Data: The GDPR

The European Union's GDPR is the most important change in data regulation since the first Data Protection Directive of 1995,[48] not only in the European Union but to a large extent globally. It has been—due to its exterritorial effect as stated in the Recitals and in Article 3(2) GDPR[49]—a game changer for data collection and processing in the European Union and worldwide.[50]

EU financial regulatory reporting requirements—discussed in Sections 3 and 5—have driven digitalization and datafication of finance and its regulation, causing an acceleration of the transition to data-driven finance in Europe's traditional financial services industry. The GDPR—while impacting all sectors of the economy—has triggered a similar process in the collection, use, storage, and protection of data in the financial sector. As financial regulation drove the digitalization of data, the GDPR has driven spending on systems designed to appropriately manage that ever-increasing volume of data. Such spending is supporting digitalization and datafication in the regulated financial industry and across the entire economy. We next consider the GDPR in light of its role as a key driver of data-driven finance.

---

[48] See Directive 95/46/EC of the European Parliament and of the Council of October 24, 1995, on the Protection of Individuals with Regard to the Processing of Personal Data and on the Free Movement of Such Data, 1995 O.J. (L 281) 31 [hereinafter GDPR].

[49] See GDPR, Recitals 24–25.

[50] The interpretation of the notion of extraterritorial effect has been clarified by the European Data Protection Board. *European Data Protection Board (EDPB), Guidelines 3/2018 on the Territorial Scope of the GDPR (Article 3)*—Version for public consultation (2018), adopted on Nov. 16, 2018.

a. Basic Principles of the GDPR

In the European Union, Article 8(1) of the European Convention on Human Rights (ECHR), Article 8(1) of the Charter of Fundamental Rights of the European Union (the Charter), and Article 16(1) of the Treaty on the Functioning of the European Union (TFEU) together provide as fundamental rights and freedoms that everyone has the right to have their personal data protected.[51] An extensive regulatory framework has developed around this over time, with the GDPR as the most important element. Specifically, the GDPR imposes rules that seek to protect natural persons in relation to the processing of their personal data.[52]

According to the GDPR:

[r]apid technological developments and globalisation have brought new challenges for the protection of personal data. The scale of the collection and sharing of personal data has increased significantly. Technology allows both private companies and public authorities to make use of personal data on an unprecedented scale in order to pursue their activities.[53]

The GDPR is thus a response to the substantial increase in cross-border flows of personal data between public and private actors across the European Union:[54]

[n]atural persons increasingly make personal information available publicly and globally. Technology has transformed both the economy and social life, and [is expected to] further facilitate the free flow of personal data within the [EU] and the transfer to [non-EU countries] and international organisations.[55]

In addition, EU law calls upon national authorities in the EU member states to cooperate and exchange personal data so as to be able to perform their duties or carry out tasks on behalf of an authority in another EU member state,[56] which is also a key focus of the GDPR.

In this environment, and based on the premise that the creation of trust is a crucial precondition for further developing the digital economy across the European internal market,[57] the GDPR seeks to ensure a high level of protection of personal data, through a "strong and more coherent data protection framework in the [EU], backed by strong enforcement."

The GDPR is designed to be technology neutral, that is, it does not depend on the techniques used for data collection and processing in order to prevent circumvention:[58]

---

[51] Svetlana Yakovleva, "Should Fundamental Rights to Privacy and Data Protection Be a Part of the EU's International Trade 'Deals'?," *World Trade Review* 17 (2018), 477, 478; Consolidated Version of the Treaty on the Functioning of the European Union art. 16, Oct. 26, 2012, 2012 O.J. (C 326).
[52] See GDPR, Recital 1.
[53] See GDPR, Recital 6.
[54] See GDPR, Recital 5.
[55] See GDPR, Recital 6.
[56] See GDPR, Recital 5.
[57] See GDPR, Recital 7.
[58] See GDPR, Recital 15.

The protection of natural persons should apply to [any] processing of personal data by automated means, as well as to manual processing, if the personal data are contained or are intended to be contained in a filing system.[59]

The GDPR is restricted to data processing of personal data in connection with a professional or commercial activity (in contrast to an individual's household activity).[60] However, the controllers or processers of social media or other providers of software for household activities are subject to the GDPR.[61]

b. Consent and Ownership

The most important building block of the GDPR is that natural persons should have control of their own personal data. This right does not apply to legal persons, however, given that legal persons do not benefit from the fundamental rights granted by the ECHR, the Charter, and the TFEU.[62] The key GDPR tool for control is the consent requirement stipulated by Article 6(1)(a) GDPR.[63] Natural persons must be clearly informed of the data collected as well as the purposes for which the personal data are used. According to Article 7(2) GDPR, the request for consent must be presented in an intelligible and easily accessible form, using clear and plain language. Even where consent has been given, the circumstances under which consent has been achieved will be reviewed to remedy coercive pressure to achieve consent:

In order to ensure that consent is freely given, consent should not provide a valid legal ground for the processing of personal data in a specific case where there is a clear imbalance between the data subject and the controller, in particular where the controller is a public authority and it is therefore unlikely that consent was freely given in all the circumstances of that specific situation. Consent is presumed not to be freely given if it does not allow separate consent to be given to different personal data processing operations despite it being appropriate in the individual case, or if the performance of a contract, including the provision of a service, is dependent on the consent despite such consent not being necessary for such performance.[64]

The GDPR further provides considerable detail on how consent must be achieved:

Consent should be given by a clear affirmative act establishing a freely given, specific, informed and unambiguous indication of the data subject's agreement to the processing of personal data relating to him or her, such as by a written statement, including by electronic means, or an oral statement. This could include ticking a box when visiting an internet website, choosing technical settings for information society

---

[59] See GDPR, Recital 15.
[60] See GDPR, Art. 2.
[61] See GDPR, Recital 18.
[62] See GDPR, art. 4(1).
[63] See GDPR, Recitals 40 and 42.
[64] See GDPR, Recital 43.

services or another statement or conduct which clearly indicates in this context the data subject's acceptance of the proposed processing of his or her personal data. Silence, pre-ticked boxes or inactivity should not therefore constitute consent. Consent should cover all processing activities carried out for the same purpose or purposes. When the processing has multiple purposes, consent should be given for all of them. If the data subject's consent is to be given following a request by electronic means, the request must be clear, concise and not unnecessarily disruptive to the use of the service for which it is provided.[65]

In addition, the data collected cannot be stored forever, but must be deleted in time frames that relate to the objective for which the data was collected.[66] Following the Google Spain decision of the Court of Justice,[67] the GDPR further establishes a right to be forgotten upon request of the natural person (understood as withdrawal of consent), where the data have been unlawfully processed or where the personal data are no longer necessary for the purposes for which they were collected or processed.[68] This in many ways is targeting both the potentially undesirable impact of network effects and economies of scope and scale in data, and their possible tendency toward undesirable natural monopolies.

The ownership approach embedded in the consent requirement is taken one step further with the data subject's right to data portability stipulated in Article 20 GDPR: any natural person can ask the current data controller to transfer the data gathered, stored, and processed to another controller in a structured, commonly used, and machine-readable format without hindrance from the current controller. The right to data portability is driven by antitrust law considerations but is applicable irrespective of the existence of a data controller's dominant market position.[69] This approach is reinforced further specifically for the banking industry in the context of PSD2's open banking provisions. However, in fact, the GDPR likewise imposes portability across the entire economy, not only in the context of payments, a subject we return to subsequently. (See Chapter 6 by Zee Kin Yeong and David Roi Hardoon for more reading on data portability and Singapore's approach.)

c. Data Management and Compliance Requirements

In addition to the mentioned fundamental principles, importantly in EU data protection law, the GDPR contains a number of specific data organization requirements. It furthers the use of pseudonymization of personal data as a measure to "reduce the risks to the data subjects and help controllers and processors to meet their data-protection obligations."[70] It also regulates the use of online identifiers[71] and imposes rules on

---

[65] See GDPR, Recital 32.
[66] See GDPR, art. 5(1)(c).
[67] See Case C-131/12, Google Spain SL v. Agencia Española de Protección de Datos, 2014 E.C.R 317; see also Rolf H. Weber, "On the Search for an Adequate Scope of the Right to Be Forgotten," *Journal of Intellectual Property, Information Technology and Electronic Commerce Law* 6 (2015), 2.
[68] See GDPR, art. 17(1).
[69] For further details, see Rolf H. Weber, "Data Portability and Big Data Analytics," *Concorrenza e Mercato* 23 (2016), 59, 66–70.
[70] See GDPR, Recital 28; see also GDPR, Recital 29.
[71] See GDPR, Recital 30.

tracing and profiling of users.[72] In particular, natural persons have the right to be subject to a decision by humans (in contrast to a decision based solely on automated processing, including profiling) where the decision produces legal effects, such as entering or termination of a contract or denial of rights.[73]

Article 25 GDPR also introduces the requirements of "privacy by design" and "privacy by default." These principles were originally developed and promoted by the Canadian Ontario Data Protection Commissioner, Ann Cavoukian.[74] Article 25(1) GDPR reads as follows:

> Taking into account the state of the art, the cost of implementation and the nature, scope, context and purposes of processing as well as the risks of varying likelihood and severity for rights and freedoms of natural persons posed by the processing, the controller shall, both at the time of the determination of the means for processing and at the time of the processing itself, implement appropriate technical measures, such as pseudonymisation, which are designed to implement data-protection principles, such as data minimisation, in an effective manner and to integrate the necessary safeguards into the processing in order to meet the requirements of this Regulation and protect the rights of the data subjects.

Consequently, the enterprises are obliged to implement privacy-friendly technologies into their technical systems.

Furthermore, in case of using new technologies causing substantive privacy risks, controllers of data are bound by the obligation to undertake data protection impact assessments (as prescribed in Article 35 GDPR). In addition, the security of data processing has become a key issue of the GDPR. According to Article 31, controllers and processors are obliged to implement specific data security (technical and organizational) measures that should help to identify and mitigate the respective risks.

Cross-border data transfer has been a hotly debated issue for many years.[75] In respect of private enterprises, the GDPR has now introduced a set of rules for transfers of personal data to third countries or international organizations—such transfers are legitimate in case of a positive adequacy decision, the existence of appropriate safeguards (in contractual relations), or the implementation of binding corporate rules (within corporate groups) pursuant to Articles 44–47 GDPR.

In addition, there are also new rules for the public sector: the GDPR addresses significant issues for regulators, particularly in the context of cross-border sharing of information—a core element of both pre- and post-2008 international regulatory initiatives.[76] Technically, the GDPR does not extend to public authorities such as those involved in public security and crime prevention,[77] tax and customs authorities,

---

[72] See GDPR, arts. 22–23

[73] See GDPR, art. 22(2).

[74] See Ann Cavoukian, "Privacy by Design, The 7 Foundational Principles" (Jan. 2011). https://www.privacybydesign.ca.

[75] See Rolf H. Weber and Dominic N. Staiger, *Transatlantic Data Protection in Practice* (Springer, 2017), 16–30; Erdem Büyüksagis, "Towards a Transatlantic Concept of Data Privacy," *Fordham Intellectual Property, Media & Entertainment Law Journal* 30 (2019), 139, 170 *et seq.*

[76] See GDPR, arts. 50, 60–62.

[77] See GDPR, Recital 19.

financial investigation units, or financial market authorities.[78] These public authorities are subject to more specific legal requirements the European Union has adopted for crime prevention.[79] If such specific sectoral legislation does not exist, general data protection requirements tailor-made for public institutions apply.[80] However, the GDPR is nonetheless significantly impacting the practices of financial regulators and their interactions with the financial industry—which is subject to the requirements of the GDPR—resulting in potential questions about the legality of submitting information to regulators about the activities of individual customers, such as in the context of anti-money laundering (AML) or other financial regulatory reporting requirements.[81] These arise in particular with the interactions between EU financial institutions and data about EU natural persons and the possible transfer to non-EU regulators (such as those in the United States).[82]

The detailed provisions of the GDPR are paired with severe enforcement mechanisms. On the liability side, any person who has suffered material or nonmaterial damage as a result of an infringement of the GDPR has a right to compensation from any controller or processor who was handling his or her personal data, even without contractual relationships between the person and controller/processor.[83] At the same time, the GDPR comes with heavy penalties: up to 4 percent of the total worldwide annual turnover of the corporate group to which the data controller or processor belongs.[84]

Initial implementation of the GDPR has left little doubt that the European data protection authorities are willing to impose sizable penalties.[85]

d. Driving the Next Stage of Open Banking and Data-Driven Finance: Open Data

In the context of European finance, the GDPR's initial impact comes from its requiring financial intermediaries to reorganize their data processing as well as client data policies to meet the requirements of the GDPR. The extensive details on personal data of individuals also require data categorization tools which allow for amendments and deletion after a given time frame or upon the natural person's request.

---

[78] See GDPR, Recital 31.

[79] Directive (EU) 2016/680 of the European Parliament and of the Council of April 27, 2016, on the Protection of Natural Persons with Regard to the Processing of Personal Data by Competent Authorities for the Purposes of Prevention, Investigation, Detection or Prosecution of Criminal Offences or the Execution of Criminal Penalties, and the Free Movement of Such Data and Repealing Council Framework Decision 2008/977/JHA, 2016 O.J. (L 119) 89.

[80] See GDPR art. 60; see also Regulation (EC) No. 45/2001 of the European Parliament and of the Council of December 18, 2000, on the Protection of Individuals with Regard to the Processing of Personal Data by the Community Institutions and Bodies and on the Free Movement of Such Data, 2001 O.J. (L 8) 1. In addition, EU law provides for many specific provisions of data processing by public authorities in sectoral legislation. For instance, see, with regard to financial legislation, CRD IV, MiFID II, AIFMD, and PSD2.

[81] See Iana Rezlauf, "EU Framework for Handling Big Datasets Mixed of Personal and Non-personal Data," CRi 7 21(1) (2020).

[82] Id.

[83] See GDPR, art. 82(1).

[84] See GDPR, art. 83.

[85] See Charlie Osborne, "Facebook Could Face $1.63bn Fine under GDPR over Latest Data Breach," Zero Day (Oct. 2, 2018). https://www.zdnet.com/article/facebook-could-face-billions-in-fines-under-gdpr-over-latest-data-breach/ [https://perma.cc/HU5D-AMWQ].

Financial intermediaries have often collected large amounts of data from and about their customers, over long periods of time. However, in many cases, these data have not been used effectively, because they have been restricted to certain business units, lines, products, or silos within individual firms.[86] Financial intermediaries are now obliged to build comprehensive systems for their data which address the collection, storage, use, and protection of the data according to the principles of the GDPR. The process of digitalization combined with systemization to meet the requirements of the GDPR has triggered a revolution in financial industry treatment of customer data, in the same way that MiFID II and its financial regulatory relatives have driven a revolution in financial industry collection and processing of business and regulatory data.

However, unlike the reforms which drive digitalization and datafication through the application of analytics to massive amounts of data—providing the impetus for data-driven finance in Europe's traditional financial industry—the GDPR instead creates barriers to centralization of individual customer data and its use, placing requirements on the financial industry to develop new systems of data management and also shifting control of many aspects of their data from financial and data intermediaries (which have collected it) to individual customers (who are its subject).

Arguably, this may impair fully data-driven business models. For instance, financial institutions cannot contact new clients for distribution or sales purposes after acquisition of data pools from third-parties unless the clients are legal persons only or the clients have consented ex ante, or the data pools were assembled through web-based gathering of user data.[87] Furthermore, data pools relating to the past become increasingly unreliable for data analysis or risk management purposes to the extent that the GDPR's deletion requirements apply, removing some upfront benefits from greater data-gathering activity. These deficiencies could be considered and remedied in the risk models, for instance, by adding further security margins to "old" or obviously deficient data pools, by mixing data from different sources, or by applying filters. But all of this requires further sophistication in data-gathering and processing methodology.

Another development is noteworthy. The GDPR's data processing rules also interfere in the internal organization of data intensive businesses, such as social media, health, or financial institutions. This has also driven the standardization of data processes outside of finance—potentially making for a larger data pool and enabling new entrants to potentially access more data of their individual customers. Large technology companies know well how to make use of the new rights to data transfer—much better than do new entrants with access to customers limited by budgets and resources: while originally

---

[86] See Remarks by Luiz Awazu Pereira da Silva and Goetz von Peter, "Financial Instability: Can Big Data Help Connect the Dots?" (Nov. 29, 2018). https://www.bis.org/speeches/sp181203.pdf.

[87] See Directive 2002/58/EC of the European Parliament and of the Council of July 12, 2002, Concerning the Processing of Personal Data and the Protection of Privacy in the Electronic Communications Sector, 2002 O.J. (L 201) 37 (introducing a specific data protection regime governing electronic communications). This Directive is expected to be replaced by a so-called E-Privacy Regulation, coordinated with and simultaneously with the implementation of the GDPR. See Proposal for a Regulation of the European Parliament and of the Council Concerning the Respect for Private Life and the Protection of Personal Data in Electronic Communications and Repealing Directive 2002/58/EC, COM (2017) 10 final (Jan. 10, 2017). However, political objections, particularly in respect of the proposed cookies rules, have caused a major delay, and it is not yet clear when this Directive will come into force; nevertheless, it might influence the financial intermediaries in the future.

designed to curtail the power of data behemoths, the result of the GDPR may be less competition from the greater concentration of data in the hands of the few.

5. Extensive, Digital Regulatory Reporting Obligations: Setting the Stage for a Move from Open Banking and Open Data to Open Finance

Since the 2008 Global Financial Crisis, in tandem with post-crisis international regulatory approaches, European regulators have imposed ever higher reporting obligations on financial intermediaries in an effort to combat systemic risk and address a range of integrity risks around money laundering, terrorism financing, and competition scandals (in particular about LIBOR and foreign exchange trading). The most important regulatory initiatives in this regard include those for: banking, CRR/CRD IV (finalized in 2013 and effective in 2014); asset management, AIFMD (2011/2013); financial markets, MiFID II/MiFIR (2014/2018); market infrastructure, EMIR (2012/ 2013); payment services, PSD2 (2015/2018); and money laundering, AMLD5 (Anti-Money Laundering Directive 2018/2020).

These frameworks share a common focus related to international financial regulatory standards in the European Union, and a common imposition of extensive reporting requirements upon the financial services industry. Regulators in the European Union, by requiring financial intermediaries to report far more data on their decisions, activities, and exposures, have triggered a revolution in Europe's regulated financial industry. Today, when faced with a proposed regulation, the financial services industry will demand sufficient time to build the necessary information technology (IT) systems to implement it. The necessity of technological implementation of regulatory reporting requirements has forced intermediaries and their service providers to continually invest in the development of their software and IT systems to ensure sufficient data are collected within their organization to meet reporting requirements, that these data are packaged and reported in the necessary structure and form, and that they flow from the supervised entities to the supervisors in the required manner.

This has also forced regulators and supervisors to develop data management systems capable of receiving and processing the volume of data being generated and delivered. This process of digitization of reporting and related compliance requirements across both intermediaries and regulators has led to a regtech "revolution" in the European financial services industry.

In addition, as the industry has digitized, and standardized data have been collected across the global operations of individual firms, it has begun to focus on better using the data being collected, to both reduce compliance costs and generate new opportunities. This is the process of datafication: the application of analytics tools to digital data, that is, the fundamental process of digital financial transformation and the evolution of data-driven finance in the traditional financial services industry.

In addition, as supervisors have been deluged with ever-increasing volumes of data, in digitized standard forms, supervisors have also had to enhance their data analytics tools. Once their analytics tools are enhanced, supervisors can handle even more data (and in turn, tend to ask supervised entities to collect and transmit even more of it, triggering another regtech cycle).

As an example, when fund managers were required by the AIFMD in 2011 to report extensive data on investment strategies in a purely digital manner,[88] there was an outcry from small and midsize firms arguing they would be disadvantaged relative to the large fund managers. Time has solved this problem. Seven years later the data stream from fund managers via national competent authorities to the European Securities and Markets Authority (ESMA) flows smoothly. We expect the same with regard to other regulatory initiatives if sufficient implementation time is granted, the latest example being the MiFID II implementation with its extensive reporting requirements and extraterritorial impact.

This development, examined elsewhere,[89] is central to the process of Europe's digital financial transformation because this regulatory evolution has forced the financial services industry (and its regulators) to digitize data collection and regulatory reporting comprehensively.

6. Digital Identity: Tying the Pieces Together

a. Toward Cross-Border ID

The eIDAS Regulation (eIDASR) was adopted in 2014 to provide mutually recognized digital identity for cross-border electronic interactions between European citizens, companies, and government institutions. Member states can notify the European Commission of their national form of eID. Other member states have been able to recognize these forms voluntarily since 2015 and have had to do so since 2018.[90] When an eID is ultimately recognized throughout the European Union, an individual can use it in any member state.[91] The eID is assigned a certain level of assurance based on its security specifications, and this allows states to determine the services in relation to which it may be used.[92]

This system does not make redundant individual sovereign forms of identity. However, it does allow national forms of digital identity to be recognized throughout the European Union, and thereby enables any EU citizen or entity so identified to enter into transactions digitally.

Rather than introducing a pan-European ID card system, which would have doubled the work for member states, the eIDASR has sought to ensure people and businesses can use their own national eIDs to access public services in other EU countries where eIDs

---

[88] See Dirk A. Zetzsche and David Eckner, "Investor Information and Reporting," in *The Alternative Investment Fund Directive* (Dirk A. Zetzsche ed., Wolters Kluwer, 2018).

[89] *See* Veerle Colaert, "RegTech as a Response to Regulatory Expansion in the Financial Sector" (June 2018) (unpublished manuscript). https://ssrn.com/abstract=2677116 [https://perma.cc/UM37-4GMS]; https://ssrn.com/abstract=2677116; Rodrigo Zepeda, "The 2018 Big Bang" (Aug. 30, 2017). https://ssrn.com/abstract=3029145 [https://perma.cc/E7SA-QZR6].

[90] See R. Bastin, I. Hedea, and I. Cisse, "A Big Step Toward the European Digital Single Market," *Deloitte* (2016), at 70–77. https://www2.deloitte.com/lu/en/pages/about-deloitte/articles/inside/inside-issue13.html [https://perma.cc/68LH-VS3B].

[91] *Id.*

[92] *Id.*

are available. The goal has been to create a European internal market for e-trust services by ensuring that eIDs work across borders and have the same legal status as traditional paper-based processes.[93] Use cases include submitting tax declarations, enrolling in a foreign university, remotely opening a bank account, setting up a business in another member state, and bidding for tenders.

Prior to eIDASR many different national standards for eIDs, independent from coordinated EU policy, were developed within EU member states. The eIDASR does not harmonize those standards, but focuses on their technical interoperability. By mandating that member states and eID providers meet certain identification obligations (including that the personal identification data uniquely represents the person to which it is attributed and that online authentication is available),[94] the eIDASR is designed to create trust.

b. eIDASR as an Open Standard

The eIDASR is a useful model for eID projects since it provides, in principle, an open standard not limited to EU jurisdictions.[95] Every national ID system that wants to connect to the eIDAS system can do so.[96] Connecting to the eIDASR does not require reform of national eID standards. Rather, by defining nodes (so-called "eIDAS connectors") that provide the cross-border links between other countries' systems and one's own system, any country could link to the eIDAS identification system in the European Union and European Economic Area, resulting—potentially—in a global eID network.[97]

While adopted in 2014, the implementation of eIDASR took some time, with public eID systems taking the lead.[98] However, in November 2017, the first private sector-run national eID scheme was notified to the European Commission by Italy, connecting all eIDs created by that private enterprise to the European eID network.[99] This enables Italian citizens and businesses to use their SPID (Italian eID) credentials to access public services in other member states.[100]

c. Toward an eID-Based Data Ecosystem

The eIDASR lays the foundation for a service-oriented ID base and for the establishment of electronic know-your-customer (eKYC) utilities in Europe. The European

---

[93] See Regulation (EU) 910/2014, of the European Parliament and of the Council of July 23, 2014, on Electronic Identification and Trust Services for Electronic Transactions in the Internal Market and Repealing Directive 1999/93/EC, 2014 O.J. (L 257/73) [hereinafter "eIDAS Regulation"].

[94] See *id.*, art. 7, at 87.

[95] Douglas W. Arner et al., "The Identity Challenge in Finance: From Analogue Identity to Digitized Identification to Digital KYC Utilities," *European Business Organization Law Review* 20 (2019), 55, 67.

[96] *Id.*

[97] *Id.*

[98] *Id.*

[99] *Id.*

[100] See "First Private Sector eID Scheme Pre-Notified by Italy Under eIDAS, Shaping Europe's Digital Future," *European Commission* (Dec. 7, 2017). http://bit.ly/2DmVQtV [https://perma.cc/N9XJ-Z4DM].

Commission's Consumer Financial Services Action Plan[101] aims to "work with the private sector to explore how they could use electronic identification and trust services for checking the identity of customers."[102] In particular, Action Item 11 states: "The Commission will facilitate the cross-border use of electronic identification and know-your-customer portability based on eIDAS to enable banks to identify customers digitally."[103] Such eKYC utilities are a major innovation that promise substantial reductions in customer onboarding costs for providers, and substantial increases in the integrity of onboarding processes as nefarious customers are limited in their capacity to shop around for a friendly and compliant, or perhaps inept, financial services provider. (The concept of digital identity is explored further in Chapter 12, by Greg Kidd.)

7. Evolving Approaches to Open Banking, Open Data, and Open Finance in the United States, China, and India

Individually and in combination, it is clear that these four separate EU initiatives—payments and open banking, data protection and open data, financial regulation, and digital ID—all independently drive forward the digitization and the datafication of finance in the EU Single Market, for both market participants and regulators. Together they also are driving the next stage of evolution of the European financial sector, particularly as outlined in the new 2020 EU Digital Finance Strategy. While the process is still evolving, based on the legal infrastructure now in place, the final outcomes are likely to see incumbent financial market participants, innovative fintechs, BigTechs, digital finance platform providers, and others increasingly competing with one another using ever-broader, and more highly analyzed, data sets. While client relationships were incumbents' core assets in the past, control over large volumes of data now replaces them.

In addition to their impact within the European Union, each of these discrete sets of regulatory reforms are also effective extraterritorially in many aspects, for firms and others engaging in financial services with EU customers or dealing with EU customer data. Thus, particularly, the impetus for development as a result of the combination of initiatives in the European Union is provoking global responses, and in many cases development of related strategies and significant expenditures in compliance and implementation of necessary IT and other systems.

---

[101] See "*Consumer Financial Services Action Plan: Better Products, More Choice*," European Commission (Mar. 23, 2017). *https://eur-lex.europa.eu/resource.html?uri=cellar:055353bd-0fba-11e7-8a35-01aa75ed7 1a1.0003.02/DOC_1&format=PDF* [https://perma.cc/M4FX-X28Q]. The Action Plan draws on previous work, such as a commissioned study asking for connection between eIDAS and the consumer financial services sector. See European Commission, Directorate-General for Financial Stability, Financial Services and Capital Markets Union, Study on the Role of Digitalization and Innovation in Creating a True Single Market for Retail Financial Services and Insurance (July 2016). https://ec.europa.eu/info/sites/info/files/study-digital isation-01072016_en.pdf [https://perma.cc/2KAN-VQJG] [hereinafter "European Commission, Digitization and Innovation"].

[102] Press Release, "European Comm'n, Consumer Financial Services Action Plan: Better Products and More Choice for European Consumers" (Mar. 23, 2017). https://ec.europa.eu/commission/presscorner/det ail/en/IP_17_609.

[103] See European Commission, Digitization and Innovation, *supra* note 101.

It is also clear that the policy concerns that have driven the development of these four EU pillars are driving an increasing range of other jurisdictions around the world to consider how best to approach the intersection of data, finance, and regulation, accelerated by the process of COVID-19 digitization globally. Beyond the European Union, the world is currently providing a laboratory of different environments in which data-driven finance can operate and evolve.

In the United States, a uniquely relaxed approach to privacy and data protection based on a market-based understanding of customer ownership coupled with an overriding distrust of state use of personal data has empowered a huge range of data applications that are increasingly raising concerns, particularly with the emergence of increasingly dominant data players such as Google, Facebook, and Amazon.[104]

In the European Union, we see the converse approach with the GDPR representing, so far, the global high point of data protection and rigorous information reporting requirements. This has meant the demand for regtech in the European Union is currently outstripping the capacity to generate the IT needed. However, when such systems designed to ensure individual control of data are combined with a distrust of public sector use of consumer data, particularly as is now being seen with US BigTech, a very different possible future emerges.

China has seen a similar pattern of BigTech emerging. In China, BigTech dominates daily activities including finance.[105] Somewhat ironically given China's history, the private sector, in the form of Tencent and Alibaba, have led the evolution of data amalgamation and use, including by establishing national identification systems to underpin their payments and other systems, and the burgeoning superstructure of other financial services applications being built upon them.[106]

India has adopted a comprehensive strategy around digital transformation and the development of data-driven finance through digitization and datafication, termed "India Stack,"[107] which is described in greater detail in Chapter 11 by Yan Carrière-Swallow, Vikram Haksar, and Manasa Patnam. As the foundational element, Aadhaar is a government-driven, national biometric database and identification system, which has empowered financial inclusion and provided the technological foundation for a whole range of innovations.[108] In many ways, India's top-down, state-led approach to designing digital infrastructure is the countermodel of the market-driven approaches of the United States and China.

India's strong centralized agenda to support digital financial transformation certainly demonstrates the potential of approaching data-driven finance strategically.[109] China's path to data-driven finance has been entirely different and emerged from the largely

---

[104] See David McLaughlin, "Why Were Facebook, Amazon, Apple, and Google Allowed to Get So Big?," *Fortune* (Mar. 16, 2019). http://fortune.com/2019/03/16/google-amazon-antitrust-laws/ [https://perma.cc/V2LC-R7KQ].

[105] See Louise Lucas, "The Chinese Communist Party Entangles Big Tech," *Financial Times* (July 19, 2018). https://www.ft.com/content/5d0af3c4-846c-11e8-a29d-73e3d454535d.

[106] See Gabriel Wildau, "China Unveils Digital ID Card Linked to Tencent's WeChat," *Financial Times* (Dec. 27, 2017).

[107] See "*What Is IndiaStack?*," IndiaStack. https://www.indiastack.org/%20about/.

[108] See "What Is Aadhaar?," Unique Identification Authority of India, Government of India. https://uidai.gov.in/my-aadhaar/about-your-aadhaar.html [https://perma.cc/X7YK-L5J6].

[109] See D.W. Arner, J. Barberis, and R.P. Buckley, "*FinTech, RegTech and the Reconceptualisation of Financial Regulation*," *Northwestern Journal of International Law & Business* 37 (2017), 371.

unfettered market activities of a small number of major tech firms, often with close state relations, but without any overriding national strategy prior to 2015–2016.[110]

In both the United States and China, free transferability of data has allowed acquisition of large pools of data, reflected in the emergence of a small number of very large firms based on network effects and economies of scope and scale for data. The outcome is both impressive and fearsome: for instance, while datafication of finance has outstripped other (seemingly more developed) countries, the market dominance of China's three digital finance superfirms, Baidu, Alibaba, and Tencent, have led to antitrust inquiries in both China and the United States (in the context of Google, Amazon, Facebook, and Apple).

a. Data Regulation vs. Financial Regulation

As mentioned, existing regulation will need to be reshaped to better accommodate the demands, and potential, of the rise of open finance, particularly through interactions with data protection regulation. Budgets for IT, cybersecurity, and IT risk will all need to grow substantially and even more rapidly than in the past, in the private sector and particularly for regulatory and supervisory bodies.

In addition, however, there is a more fundamental question regarding regulatory approaches to data-driven finance. To date, the impact of laissez-faire approaches to data regulation can be seen in the United States and China, both of which are now characterized by the dominance of their data sectors by small numbers of participants. In both cases, this has arguably been facilitated by few limits on individuals transferring ownership and control of data to BigTech firms, which in turn have benefited from network effects and economies of scope and scale in its amalgamation and use. In both cases, the concentration and dominance which have emerged are triggering both public and regulatory attention.

This affects financial law's objectives and hence the remits of supervisors. Where the power is in the data, we recommend financial regulators address the new systemic risk stemming from concentration of data in the hands of a few technology firms. This risk mirrors the traditional systemic risk represented by banks that are too big to fail or too connected to fail. In turn, we support market structure–related interventions which aim to maintain the independence of, and choice among, critical infrastructure providers as well as data portability rights in favor of financial customers. The measures that result may look similar to existing antitrust approaches, based on a financial law rationale: systemic risk.

---

[110] The very rapid growth in Ant Financial and other firms prompted the People's Bank of China to take steps to slow down developments and better manage potential risks in 2015–2016. See Weihuan Zhou, Douglas W. Arner, and Ross P. Buckley, "Regulation of Digital Financial Services in China: Last Mover Advantage," *Tsinghua China Law Review* 8 (2015), 25.

b. Toward Open Finance?

The EU experience highlights how, as financial systems digitize, it is necessary to carefully consider approaches to financial regulation, cybersecurity, data protection, digital identity, and competition. The approaches taken in different jurisdictions will be driving forces in financial and economic development and innovation in the twenty-first century.

While financial intermediaries have often collected large amounts of data, over long periods of time, these data were not used effectively.[111] Digitalization combined with systemization to meet the GDPR's data governance requirements has triggered a revolution in the treatment of customer data, in the same way that MiFID II and its financial regulatory relatives have driven a revolution in financial industry collection and processing of business and regulatory data.

Partly contradictory, the GDPR creates barriers to centralization of individual customer data and their use, placing requirements on the financial industry to develop new data governance standards and also shifting control, at least in name, of their data from intermediaries (which have collected it) to individual customers (who are the subject).

Finance has long been an information industry,[112] but financial regulation and data regulation evolved in distinctive noninteractive legal silos, based on very different underlying principles and policy objectives. How the financial sector and regulators come to terms with the interaction of these separate rulebooks will determine in many ways the future of data-driven finance in Europe and around the world.

Limitations on pooling and restrictions on cross-border storage and use of data are also encouraging significant research and spending on new systems of data aggregation and analysis which do not require individual data access, but rather are based on query-only or decentralized structures. These are driving innovation in data systems and analytics.

Thus, while regulation limits data-driven finance, it also drives the process forward in new ways through its focus on the use, collection, storage, transfer, and protection of data.

The transformative role of fintech around the world highlights how finance, data, and technology are now all tethered to each other.[113] As such, regulatory approaches in each area will interact with approaches taken in other areas. The European Union provides a vivid example of this through the interaction of key legislation such as MiFID2, GDPR, PSD2, and eIDAS. This combination of regulatory approaches and policies will continue to push forward data-driven finance both in the European Union and beyond.

As other jurisdictions around the world are increasingly forced to consider the interaction of financial regulation, data protection, and cybersecurity in the context of their

---

[111] See da Silva and von Peter, *supra* note 86.

[112] Finance is only now slowly evolving from an information into a data industry. Historically, information resided in parts of a bank and was not shared efficiently across the institution let alone analyzed and applied effectively.

[113] See generally European Banking Authority, *Report on the Prudential Risks and Opportunities Arising from FinTech* (2018); European Banking Authority, *Report on the Impact of Fintech on the Incumbent Credit Institutions' Business Model* (2018).

own cultural and political environments, the experience of the European Union will provide major lessons for policy and regulatory choices.

8. Takeaway: Three Lessons

In this chapter, we argue that a series of clearly motivated but uncoordinated projects played a crucial role in shaping Europe's financial ecosystem to make it more open to innovation by data-driven financial services providers of an increasing range of forms. However, what the European Union did without an overarching roadmap, other jurisdictions may—and we argue should—do so purposefully through careful development of coordinated legal and regulatory approaches to finance, data, and their interaction. In fact, with the 2020 Digital Finance Strategy, the European Union is now seeking to do exactly this: build its experiences into a strategy based around "open data" and "open finance." In this regard the European Union presents an interesting and still evolving case study, relevant to every other jurisdiction in the world. In the European Union, the road to data-driven finance has benefited from a robust rule of law environment (that ensures the viability of long-term investments), a strict approach to data privacy (that grants data portability rights to individuals rather than service providers), a willingness to use regulation to drive evolution of markets and societies, and an approach aiming at "controlled" rather than "cutthroat" capitalism.

In this respect the EU approach was enabled by a "traditional" cultural bias against data commercialization. This political and social environment was further supported by the European Commission and the European regulatory authorities (particularly ESMA and the European Banking Authority) playing a strong central role in developing regulatory frameworks to address key policy challenges around data and finance. Were it not for these new central EU financial regulators being able to extend their activities without long-standing bureaucratic legacy issues, few steps toward data-driven finance—outside of select jurisdictions such as the United Kingdom (an EU member for much of the historical evolution though not for its synthesis in the 2020 Digital Finance Strategy) and Luxembourg—may have been possible in the practice of financial supervision.

Europe's experience with its four separately designed policy and regulatory frameworks considered here will have a very important determinative impact on the structure of data-driven finance in Europe and in global financial markets, particularly as other jurisdictions consider how best to balance the objectives of data protection and financial regulation while supporting innovation, efficiency, and financial stability, and many of them look for role models. This will be driven by the familiarity of many institutions with the EU framework from having to implement its requirements for their European operations and because of its extraterritorial reach. The change from extending finance on the basis of what an institution knows directly about its customer to extending it on the basis of data analytics drawing upon huge pools of data is profound, with the potential for both highly positive as well as highly negative outcomes as this evolution plays out across Europe and the world.

In looking at these issues, based on experiences to date, we would suggest a number of central lessons. The first is that finance, data, and technology are now intertwined as a result of a long-term process of digitalization and datafication of finance in developed markets (a process that is likewise happening rapidly in emerging and developing markets). As a result, regtech, the use of technology for compliance, monitoring, enforcement, and system design in financial regulation, will continue to increase.

The second clear lesson is that each society must grapple with its own approach to data and its role in the society's future. These discussions will involve not only questions of finance and data regulation but also of social regulation and competition/antitrust regulation. As we have shown, different societies can have very different views on this issue and on the governance and economic systems they prefer in their futures. Everywhere, however, these issues will need to be addressed and the choices made, because otherwise globalization and network efforts will likely mean that decisions taken abroad will dictate the outcomes in markets around the world. While there appears to be a strong divergence in the use of data by governments, there appears to be an increasing consensus around the desirability of placing limits on the use of data by the private sector.

The third lesson is that because of the integration of data and finance, when designing financial regulatory systems and seeking to regulate data, it is necessary to consider the implications of the interaction of data and finance. As can be seen from the EU experience, conflicts between objectives and rules should be considered ex ante. One area where this is particularly important is in choices about whether to pursue open banking and digital ID strategies. At this point, the EU experience is at an early stage, but it will influence the approach taken in many other jurisdictions. European success or failure will echo around the world.

9

United Kingdom: The Butterfly Effect

Gavin Littlejohn,[*] Ghela Boskovich,[**] and Richard Prior[***]

1. Introduction

The United Kingdom's implementation of Open Banking has been under the global microscope from day one. While the journey has been fraught with challenges, the lessons coming from this grand experiment have been embraced the world over. The following history of the UK Open Banking journey underscores two components critical to success: an enshrined consumer data right and the important role standards play in promoting market scalability and interoperability.

The United Kingdom's journey to Open Banking has had a butterfly effect on the rest of the world: a particular approach in one small country, one flap of the proverbial wing, has resulted in a seismic shift in how other markets have undertaken opening up their own financial services markets. The United Kingdom's influence is evidenced in how Australia, Canada, Brazil, and multiple Asian markets are shaping their own Open Banking rules and implementation.

How these lessons came to light is shared in the following, but first a word on alphabet soup: this chapter is rife with acronyms. While full names and titles are provided, their acronyms are generously salted throughout; should the reader need a reminder, we have provided a glossary of terms at the end of the chapter for reference.

2. Being Open

a. Definition of Open Finance

"Open Finance" generally means that a consumer has full visibility of all her financial data and that the data itself is put into context, allowing her to make changes to her finances in order to improve her overall financial health and the economic value of her money. However, the definition is nuanced depending on the context and situation in which it is used. Open Finance is considered to be the next generation of "Open Banking," and the capitalized version of "Open Banking" used here references

[*] Chairman, Financial Data and Technology Association Global.
[**] Chapter Leader/Head of Europe at Financial Data and Technology Association.
[***] CEO, Financial Data and Technology Association.
The authors would like to recognize the following colleagues who, as well as being key players in the narrative itself, were kind enough to engage in discussion during the drafting process for this chapter: Ed Colley, Colin Garland, Imran Gulamhuseinwala, Ian Major, Philip Mind, Jason O'Shaughnessy, Dr. Bill Roberts, Gavin Starks, and James Whittle.

the government-mandated form of open banking. Similarly with Open Banking, there is no fixed definition of Open Finance, as the interpretation is influenced by the first exposure to the concept, as well as the market in which one operates.

The irony is that end customers do not use Open Banking[1] directly; rather it is the state of the market where all financial institutions must allow the end customer to direct their data via any regulated actor of their choosing. It describes the open movement of data in banking, in which the market actors cannot hoard that information. The end consumer benefits from the open market; the firms therein act as custodians of that financial information on behalf of the end consumer. Under Open Finance, the end consumer sees the full extent to which that information can be leveraged, offering additional choices on how their money is distributed across a wealth of financial products, offerings, and services based on efficient orchestration of that information. It encompasses the theory of the right product, at the right time, for the right price, for the right customer, scaled across all financial verticals. A number of the use cases that make the argument for harmonized Open Finance have already been in the market for nearly two decades. It is the culmination of these use cases, mandated by law, that now form the foundation for Open Finance.

Open Finance has at its core the role of the end customer, be they a consumer or business, choosing to share their[2] financial information hosted with one financial services provider with another provider. Data aggregation is the most familiar example of this domain of customer-permissioned data-sharing. Firms that provide the technology layer to extract the data from the host provider and forward it to the recipient provider are often referred to as data aggregators. Data aggregation represents the spirit of providing a holistic view of the consumer's financial situation, allowing for more insightful decisions on how that data is used to improve their financial outcomes. (For more reading, Chapter 1 describes the role of data aggregators, and Chapter 5 describes the common practice of screen-scraping, a methodology of data aggregation.)

b. The Particular Meaning of "Open"

How has data aggregation based on customer-permissioned data-sharing evolved into customer-permissioned data-sharing Open Finance?

Data aggregation developed in the US and UK markets without regulation and with no system-defined roles, rights, and responsibilities. The original host of that financial information had no technology or risk management role in the data extraction or sharing with another recipient party. The recipient party also had no right to be able to connect and receive the data. Why? Because until recently, there was no clearly defined data ownership structure. Who the data belonged to was not clear: did the end

---

[1] Open Banking is limited to the movement and sharing of payments data; it is generally understood that Open Banking is related only to what is covered by the European Union's Second Payments Services Directive; Open Finance is meant to include other financial services verticals information, like credit, savings, investment, and pensions.

[2] For the purposes of this chapter, pronouns "they, their, them" are used to refer to "end customer," given that the end customer can be an individual or a business.

consumer own their data, or was it the host financial institution? Until regulation stepped in to define ownership, the data aggregation market had no fixed parameters.

Enter regulation, specifically the European Union's Second Payment Services Directive (PSD2), which set those initial parameters. "Open" now describes an open market architecture, one in which firms' technology stacks enable data-sharing between regulated market actors via secure technical connections, under clear risk management requirements, when directed by the end customer to do so. Other regulation has sprung up across the globe, with some nuanced differences in other markets, but the underlying principle remains the same: an open market is one in which the market itself allows for an open and theoretically unfettered exchange of data among regulated actors.

Today, the definition of "Open" has evolved to encompass a wider array of ecosystem actors, all of whom execute this data exchange under new privacy laws[3] which ensure a customer data right and rely upon the customer's explicit consent in order to share that data. Open Finance also includes a liability framework and system of customer redress and a legal and regulatory framework to ensure vetting and authorization of participants, which enshrines certain rights and obligations in order to qualify for authorization. The technical architecture and system design, under a formal governance and funding plan, enables those rights to be exercised and obligations met; and ongoing compliance monitoring ensures this "open" system works.

3. The Egg—Factors that Shaped the Market

a. United Kingdom Importing Ideas and Technology from the United States and Australia

In the United States, data aggregation took hold inside banks first. In the United Kingdom, fintechs began as the primary users (and suppliers) of data aggregation. The difference in the origin of this first deployment of data aggregation has fundamentally determined the shape of, and the definition of "open" in, both markets. The stark contrast is reminiscent of the chicken-or-the-egg question: which came first matters, and has profoundly influenced the development of both regulation and market ecosystems. What follows is a brief history of the role of data aggregation in these markets, and how it has shaped the definition of Open Banking along the way.

Data aggregation in the United States saw two first movers in 1999—Yodlee and Cashedge—whose market model first evolved to provide whole market account aggregation as a service. Both firms cross-aggregated data from one firm to another. Other firms swiftly followed, including Plaid, Finicity, and MX Technologies. (See Chapter 5 for more details about data aggregation and the history of Yodlee.)

The large financial institutions in the United States have been and remain the primary customers of account aggregation services. Early on, big banks used aggregators because high net worth clients wanted to see all their account balances in a single web

---

[3] I.e., General Data Protection Regulation in Europe; California Consumer Protection Act in the United States; the Customer Data Right in Australia; the General Data Protection Law in Brazil; Personal Information Protection and Electronic Documents Act in Canada.

dashboard.[4] They used it to shape new offerings, and consumers became accustomed with such services precisely because big bank and brokerage adoption and consumption of aggregated data was de rigueur. The period 2005 to 2009 saw a rash of new fintech providers enter the market, using account aggregation to deliver market-neutral money management services: Wesabe, Geezeo, and Mint being prime examples. US consumers were already familiar with these types of services, and big institutions could not justifiably block these fintechs from engaging in similar activities, since the institutions were already offering such services.

As described in Chapter 5, data aggregation in this instance was executed by performing "screen-scraping." Screen-scraping is a process whereby the end customer grants permission to one brand to harvest data about the end customer held by another brand, by providing their confidential login credentials to the secure website. The recipient brand would pass these credentials, a password, through their digital real estate, typically without storing them, to the aggregation service they had chosen. The aggregator would, in most cases, enter the host account with the static password overnight, scrape the data from the browser, recompile it, and then upload it to the recipient account. A customer could log in to one brand's website and see, for example, their account balance with other firms. By and large, this was limited to information downloaded from large financial institutions. Screen-scraping technology has had a significant effect on the regulatory environment outside of the United States, primarily in the United Kingdom and across the European Union. (See Chapter 5 for more on screen-scraping and the evolution of data access standards.) It has not only allowed the value proof points to be established, but has created impetus from the banking sector to work with regulators toward a model where static passwords are not shared and where a regulated fintech has to identify itself during the connection.

In Australia, account aggregation took a different shape. In 2000, eWise Systems emerged to provide what was essentially client-side aggregation. eWise offered customers a service to privately and securely store, manage, and share their personal financial information. Rather than sharing a password with an aggregator, the password to access the financial account would be stored locally on the end customer's computer in a password safe, and the data would be downloaded to the customer's computer. Depending on the business model, the operation could then upload the data into another firm's database to be used to perform the service that was offered.

By 2001, both eWise and Yodlee had developed an initial strategy for market entry into the United Kingdom. Yodlee's entry strategy was underpinned by demand from Citigroup, already a significant customer for Yodlee in their US business, seeking to develop a UK proposition. eWise made an independent entry. Both firms sought to win business from a relatively new banking entrant, Egg, a digital banking proposition formed inside Prudential plc. Egg's Money Manager[5] proposition, announced in

---

[4] One of the first major account aggregation services was Citibank's My Accounts service, though this service ended in late 2005; Yodlee was Citibank's aggregator at that time. https://blog.starpointllp.com/?p=84; Yodlee also provided services in the 1990s to banks such as Bank of America, Citigroup Inc., and Wachovia; brokers such as Merrill Lynch & Co., Morgan Stanley Dean Witter & Co., and Charles Schwab & Co. https://www.americanbanker.com/news/screen-scraping-part-2.

[5] https://www.finextra.com/newsarticle/5684/egg-aggregates-finances-for-uk-consumers.

2002, selected eWise's approach to aggregate via secure password sharing. This decision set the UK market trajectory on a very different path than what had developed in the United States, as the credential sharing through screen-scraping technology supplied by Yodlee was never adopted at any scale by UK banks.

Another key difference between the US and UK markets was the rise of new UK fintech firms offering account aggregation. These new offerings, which became known as Personal Financial Management (PFM) tools, targeted end customers, not banks, as their primary clients. From 2005 to 2006, the UK market saw Money Dashboard, Love Money, and Kublax form—parallel to Wesabe, Mint, and Geezeo's development in the US market.

Despite Egg's initial partnership with eWise as a precedent, other UK PFM entrants all selected Yodlee as their data aggregation partner and had to do the heavy lifting of building products on their new aggregation connections and building their own categorization engines, since Yodlee had no transaction data to train their model. These firms had to do this while also marketing the opportunity to potential users and raising capital to maintain trajectory. Simultaneously, UK banks were educating customers not to share their passwords, arguing that the record of their customer's financial balances and transactions belonged to them and not the customer. In the United States, banks, being the primary consumers of account aggregation services,[6] did not discourage the sharing of passwords, as their customers were actively using bank-offered services, not a third-party outside of the bank network.

It is this particular argument—who owns the consumer's financial data—that resulted in the current disparity of usage of data aggregation in the two markets despite the offering arising at a similar time. It has also shaped the way Open Banking is defined in the different markets. At the moment, 2020 UK market penetration per capita of consumers sharing their financial data with third-parties is roughly a tenth of that in the United States. This disparity is not due to the relative recent success of application programming interface (API)-based technologies, nor to the quality of the end-customer propositions or the regulatory landscape, but almost entirely due to the fact that in the United States, the banks themselves were the early adopters and had been engaged with data aggregators for over twenty years. The US customer-facing fintechs did not have to educate the market about the aggregation process to the same extent. In the United Kingdom, and indeed throughout most of the European Union, banks have only really engaged in this practice since the Second Payment Services Directive (PSD2), which came into force in January 2018. (Chapter 8 describes PSD2 in more detail.) In the United Kingdom, consumer-side data aggregation growth came from propositions offered by firms without a banking license; for example, approximately one in every three UK businesses now uses a cloud-based accounting platform which connects to an open banking capability.[7]

---

[6] Many banks were using aggregators to tap into their own product siloed data; for customers with multiple accounts within an institution, this offered a single view of all their account balances at the bank, including credit cards that could be ported in, so clients could see both their payment accounts and lines of credit, as well as savings via a single dashboard.

[7] http://researchbriefings.files.parliament.uk/documents/POST-PN-0629/POST-PN-0629.pdf.

b. The Technology Landscape

It is worth mentioning the technology backdrop of this unfolding story. When the first customer-facing fintechs using data aggregation entered the US and UK markets, there were no social media giants, no cloud computing services, and no smartphone apps. While data science did clearly exist, new software tools, access to computing power, and practitioner enhanced skills sets have transformed the landscape. The United States has been typically more than two years ahead of the United Kingdom in transformational technology platform availability simply because the United States is the home market for these BigTechs, such as Facebook, Twitter, Apple, Amazon, and Microsoft. Conversely, continental Europe (and the United Kingdom) started later and built their own technology for aggregation, which slowed them down but also increased their business options as a technology supplier.

c. Learning to Execute

The first nonbank fintech firms in this domain had varying fortunes owing to the availability of technology, proposition execution, access to capital, and underlying market awareness of customers. In the United Kingdom, Kublax failed, ostensibly due to the loss of investor confidence. In the United States, Wesabe failed. Their proposition lead and CEO Marc Hedlund wrote an interesting blog[8] on their execution strategy and why it was not successful. Wesabe used the "download, upload" method, where the customer brought the data to their own computer, rather than sharing passwords. They had presumed that the customer wanted the best possible software solution and the strongest perceived security. The customer might even have told them that. However, the customer really wanted an easy and fast method to draw the data without multiple steps to get results; in short, no friction, maximum convenience. In the meantime, Mint, built on the Yodlee platform using screen-scraping, raised substantial capital, executed a convenient and useful product, rapidly acquired end-user customers and sold early to Intuit in 2009. Geezeo pivoted to providing their platform as a white label service to banks and credit unions, to much success, and was later acquired by Jack Henry & Associates in 2019.

Meanwhile in the United Kingdom, Money Dashboard and LoveMoney battled on, trying to build a user base and fund expansion in the face of stiff headwinds, the biggest of which was that the banks were not themselves adopters and therefore tried to block them. The banks' position negatively impacted fintech fundraising and customer acquisition alike.

---

[8] https://blog.precipice.org/why-wesabe-lost-to-mint/.

d. The 2008 Financial Crisis

The 2008 financial crisis had a profound effect on the rate of development of global fintech. On the one hand, access to capital was temporarily impeded. On the other, it catalyzed some changes to regulation and released some talent to the market that had been tied up in the incumbent banking sector.

While some hasty mergers had been arranged to help save the financial system from meltdown during the peak crisis, in the aftermath, financial regulators, policymakers, and competition supervisors became increasingly mindful that the concentration of product delivery in a few large actors was risky and unhealthy for consumers. Given the impact of an overheated mortgage market on the financial system, the investigating UK regulators, in the Mortgage Markets Review of 2009,[9] concluded that mortgages had been sold to people who could not reasonably afford them if subjected to minor changes in their situation or in market conditions. This resulted in proper affordability tests being required for mortgages and other lending products. Subsequent financial regulatory reforms have mandated better understanding of the customer's needs and financial position, selling products that are more suitable to the customer's situation, thereby treating the customer fairly.

e. The Contest for Data

Between 2009 and 2013, a range of new UK data aggregator fintech firms entered the market. To these entrepreneurs, it was clear that some form of account aggregation could help solve information asymmetry, allowing them to compete with incumbent players. It would also enable business propositions better focused on customer needs, reducing friction and workload on the customer, while simultaneously aligning with regulatory expectations and trends.

As development capital started to re-enter the market, attracted by increasingly innovative and farsighted UK fintechs, the banks in the United Kingdom, as elsewhere in the European Union, put up a concerted fight for control of the customer's data and, therefore, control of the customer's options in an effort to dampen the effects of this new competition. The result was additional friction in the customer experience of these new services, which reduced the likelihood of the customer using one of these services to facilitate switching to a better underlying product.

The battle for control of customer data was fought in the corridors of power in London and Brussels, and increasingly on Facebook and Twitter. The fintechs at the time were not organized and had no idea how to navigate political and regulatory channels, but they were early adopters of social channels and were effective at conducting open channel customer conversations. So the customer would ask their bank on a social channel whether it was "okay" to trust any particular fintech with their financial data, and the bank would invariably reply with various stock answers, along the lines of:

---

[9] https://www.fca.org.uk/publication/discussion/fsa-dp09-03.pdf.

"don't share the data as it belongs to the bank";[10]

"you will be in breach of your contract with us, if you share the data";

"we cannot validate the security of the fintech in question"; or

"don't share your secret passwords or we will not be able to compensate you if your bank account is hacked."

At face value, some of these may seem reasonable, but there was an expectation among fintech firms and customers that the bank would provide some rationale for these answers. For example, what if the bank account got hacked without any connection to the account aggregation process? Why should the customer be able to print off their accounts and share them offline but be prohibited from having their data shared digitally? Whose data was it anyway?

The extent to which the social media battle over data ownership cannot be underestimated. Whatever its reach, authorities and legislators in the United Kingdom and the European Union embraced the question. Data ownership is very much couched in the arguments pertaining to data privacy. Ultimately, in Europe, the General Data Protection Regulation (GDPR), which came into effect on May 25, 2018, affirms that "natural persons should have control over their own personal data."

Part of the context of ownership of data under the GDPR is framed under Article 20, which "aims to empower data subjects (i.e., the individual consumer) regarding their own personal data, as it facilitates their ability to move, copy, or transmit personal data easily from one IT environment to another"—personal identifiable information being considered property, and therefore consent to access or use that property indicates an original owner of said property, in this case the data subject. However, explicit ownership of data is still being debated under the GDPR, as data is not yet considered a commodity but information; that information, though, does not yet have explicit protections under intellectual property law.

For the United Kingdom and Europe, the debate has seemingly been settled: consumers own their data and grant explicit consent for other parties to access that data. There is a clear liability framework for the access and handling of that data, and a legal means of customer redress should something go wrong. This provided clarity to the banks on who actually owned customer data; they are custodians, not owners.

In the United States, a different tack has been taken: there is no single, large governing piece of legislation at the national level, but rather a hodgepodge of federal and state laws that cover data privacy.[11] At the moment individual states are taking the initiative to frame data protection legislation, like the California Consumer Protection Act and Maine's Act to Protect the Privacy of Online Consumer Information; in 2020, only three states have laws signed, the two aforementioned and Nevada. Twenty-four other states have proposed similar legislation, all in different stages of debate, and all

---

[10] https://twitter.com/davidjmaireles/status/714189251613749248?s=20.
James Eyres: "Data Wars: The Banks Awaken," *Financial Review* (Mar. 21, 2016). https://www.afr.com/technology/data-wars-the-banks-awaken-20160319-gnmfac?utm_content=bufferc1447&utm_medium=social&utm_source=twitter.com&utm_campaign=buffer.
[11] https://www.congress.gov/bill/116th-congress/senate-bill/3300?q=%7B%22search%22%3A%5B%22data+protection+act%22%5D%7D&r=1&s=1.

with distinct differences. There is growing support to have a single national standard, as evidenced by Senator Kirsten Gillibrand (D-NY) proposing creation of a new Data Protection Agency, under the S.3300 Data Protection Act of 2020.[12]

While there is still no legal framework to address data privacy and ownership in the United States, it is a fair assumption that the practice mirrors that in Europe. Other jurisdictions around the world follow similar suits, with some affirming in law a customer data right (ownership) with privacy protection.

4. The Caterpillar

a. Story of the UK Regulatory Journey to Open Banking

i. UK Competition: Office of Fair Trading, Competition Commission, and the Competition and Markets Authority

In 2012, the United Kingdom had two authorities involved in assessing and controlling fair competition in markets: the Office of Fair Trading (OFT) and the Competition Commission (CC). As a result of the concentration of particular banks in certain product lines due to mergers and the low rates of switching deposit accounts and ineffective pricing competition, the OFT commenced a Market Study of the UK banking market,[13] focusing on retail banking of consumers and small to medium-size enterprises.

In parallel, due to letters sent by HSBC warning their customers not to share data with a data aggregation service (that was not provided by them), Money Dashboard raised concerns with the OFT and engaged in explaining to the authorities about data asymmetry and better customer outcomes that might be delivered if applications built on data aggregation were not restricted from operating. It was pointed out that HSBC appeared to be offering account aggregation to their US customer base, while telling their UK customers that it was not safe. What was widely encouraged in one market was being suppressed in another.

In 2013, the CC, following suit, launched a more formal Market Investigation.[14] Early in the process they were thinking about options for making a meaningful difference: it was not just about the number of market participants but other factors that were inhibiting effective competition. The two authorities merged in late 2013, to establish a new Competition and Markets Authority (CMA). The CMA recognized early on the importance of data in effective competition; this was an early signal of the concept of a data economy.

ii. Her Majesty's Treasury, PSD2, and a Win for Fintechs

In early 2013, Her Majesty's Treasury (HMT) met with industry to discuss the role of account aggregation in improving customer outcomes. Part of the conversation covered

---

[12] https://www.congress.gov/bill/116th-congress/senate-bill/3300?q=%7B%22search%22%3A%5B%22d ata+protection+act%22%5D%7D&r=1&s=1.

[13] https://publications.parliament.uk/pa/jt201213/jtselect/jtpcbs/writev/banking/bs40.htm https://www.nao.org.uk/wp-content/uploads/2012/12/1213685.pdf.

[14] Investigation   Report.   https://www.oecd.org/officialdocuments/publicdisplaydocumentpdf/?cote= DAF/COMP/AR(2013)9&docLanguage = En.

the changing nature of the UK market landscape for the provision of professional financial advice.

Regulatory reforms had separated the product sale function from advisory services. The unintended consequence was that the general market lost access to financial
advisory services as the average consumer was usually not prepared to pay upfront. It
was also clear that the rapidly evolving age of applications and internet banking was
changing customer behavior and that the sort of informal advice provided in a bank
branch was becoming a thing of the past. Applications that were powered by an open
finance model could give the customer an opportunity to access a form of advice or
guidance at a low cost, using a channel that was becoming ubiquitous: internet and mobile banking.

Subsequent discussions considered whether a proposal for a policy to develop an
"Open Finance Policy" at a UK level would effectively enable all the financial data assets
to be enabled for access—a more difficult legislative accomplishment.

An idea floated by HMT was the possibility of adding data aggregation to the PSD2,
which was in a later stage of drafting at the European Commission. HMT thought it
might also align with some policy suggestions coming from Germany relating to how
to allow access to an account in a power of attorney situation, where a competent adult
may be given access and help supervise an account of a vulnerable account holder. The
key consideration for firms in this domain was that PSD2 was exclusively focused on
payment accounts, and not on data from loan, mortgage, saving, investment, pension,
and insurance accounts, many of which were already being connected via aggregation
to provide customer-facing solutions.

Was it better to hitch to a train that could make part of the market journey, or wait for
a train that may never arrive? HMT did not want to restrict their soundings on this critical issue to one fintech and asked Money Dashboard to help engage the small group of
firms active in this domain, suggesting that this cohort might wish to formally organize.
The result of this suggestion led to the formation of the Financial Data and Technology
Association (FDATA), a group firmly in favor of advocating for the inclusion of account
aggregation to PSD2, informally mid-2013, and formally established in 2014.

The firms in FDATA agreed that Open Finance was the long-term goal, but to cat-
alyze its development, using PSD2 as a first staging point on that journey made most
practical business and political sense. The assumption being that PSD2 would finally
bring data aggregation market propositions into the regulatory domain, provide data
access rights, and establish obligations to perform properly supervised standards, which
would build confidence with potential customers that this service was legitimate in the
eyes of the law. It was also assumed at the time that fintechs would be able to continue to
access other data assets outside the PDS2 regulatory domain (assets other than payment
data) via traditional screen-scraping technologies. The inaccuracy of this assessment
has been at the crux of some of the most hotly contested policy matters in the development of Open Finance and served as a marker of where prescriptive technology regulation has limited the ability to deliver new business models to market. This intersection
of technology and innovation has also shown the business model schism between firms
who were in the market before PSD2 and the rise of new firms built after the new regulatory framework was adopted.

iii. Second Payment Services Directive (PSD2)

Although PSD2 did not complete its legislative journey until 2015, there were no material changes from late 2013 when the Account Information Service Provider (AISP) role was added into PSD2, a confirmation that data aggregation would be formally included in the regulatory domain. This late addition to the regulation ultimately resulted in incongruity in the overall text, some earlier clauses conflicting with the rationale of the inclusion of account aggregation.

PSD2 policy objectives were designed to improve innovation, competition, and security in EU payments markets. In practice, this meant that firms holding the customer's payment account, such as banks, must allow the customer to choose another regulated party to:

- set up a payment (Payment Initiation Services Provider, or PISP); and
- share their payment and balance data (AISP).

These firms holding the customer's account (mostly banks) were called Account Servicing Payment Service Providers (ASPSPs). The AISP and PISP roles constituted new regulatory permissions. A firm wishing to perform in the market would, in the future, be able to apply for both or either permission, depending on their business model.

From 2014 it was clear that banks would soon be required to share the customer's payment data with a regulated actor of the customer's choosing and that when they did so, they would not be liable for what happened thereafter. The responsibility for safe custodianship was to be passed to the AISP when the new laws came into force.

On the whole, despite some anomalies, PSD2 was viewed by most market actors as a reasonably comprehensive piece of work, which commendably delivered on the required regulatory scope and liability framework. However, PSD2 was a product of its time, caught out by changing approaches to technology. PSD2 assumed credentials would be passed to enable the scraping of the data and that because fintechs, the "demand side," remained in control of the technology build, there was no required standardization. In 2013, when PSD2 was first drafted, through to its adoption in 2015, no substantive discussion focused on the technology that would be used to facilitate this new data exchange network. Although APIs had long been used in the market, and individual banks and fintechs were increasingly using APIs to move data between themselves, PSD2 did not consider that there would be an orchestrated shift to more fully adopt APIs, nor the need to standardize them for maximum harmonization of the ecosystem.

iv. UK Midata

In 2011, the UK government announced a new policy initiative called Midata,[15] aimed at digitally empowering the end customer by asking some large firms, on a voluntary basis, to make available customers' data by releasing it to customers in a portable electronic format. This was one of the first efforts to clarify and formalize digital customer

---

[15] https://www.gov.uk/government/news/the-midata-vision-of-consumer-empowerment.

data rights (the data subject being the absolute owner of their personal data), and a key steppingstone in developing this right.

Data-sharing under Midata was to be enabled via a Download CSV File through an agreement with the largest UK banks, signaling the eventual acceptance by the banks that customers could indeed control the sharing of their data. However, the banks had not capitulated to this consumer data right in full at the time, in 2014, and fintechs in the ecosystem were well aware that this "download-upload" data-sharing would hamper their ability to operate. Although Midata was unique to the United Kingdom, it mirrored some of what PSD2 would ultimately enable since account aggregation had been included in the legislation. If adopted, PSD2 would require data access that operated in the background with minimal friction. Insight into the need for frictionless data-sharing and access from the Midata initiative foreshadowed the spirited lobbying contest needed to smooth the data access wrinkle embodied in PSD2, which had yet to be ratified by the European Parliament at that point.

Midata ultimately failed. Failure was attributed to poor market coordination, low standardization, and, most importantly, an uneven user experience, where the customer would be made to constantly work for any useful outcome. One clear lesson from Midata, as well as the Wesabe failure, is that an overly repetitive "download-upload" experience does not make for a positive customer journey. Consent to access the data, once granted, necessitated that continual access to updated data be seamless and not involve the customer doing the heavy lifting. Midata, however, did help establish a general acceptance that the customer did, in fact, own their data; it allowed that idea to firmly take root for the authorities, the industry, and the consumer in 2011, a full year before the European Union began to work on its GDPR.

v. General Data Protection Regulation

Running on a near parallel timeline to PSD2, the GDPR was first proposed by the European Commission in late 2012. The GDPR was intended to harmonize data rules to reinforce the single market, provide consistent privacy and data rights for end customers, and clarify the legal requirements for data-sharing to which firms would have to comply.

In 2015, formal negotiations between the EU Council, EU Parliament, and EU Commission resulted in a joint proposal, which was ratified and adopted in 2016. The GDPR came into full force and effect in every EU member state in May 2018, four months after the ratification of PSD2.[16] The GDPR is an important piece of policy in the history of Open Finance, as it harmonized the legal right of the data subject (the individual) to choose to share financial (and other types of data) with some element of control over how that data is shared. While it created a framework for sanctions against firms that misused customer data, it did not provide a framework for compensating the customer for such activity. PSD2, on the other hand, provides a liability framework, where each regulated actor who holds the customer's payment data is responsible for

---

[16] PSD2 was adopted into law on November 25, 2015. https://eur-lex.europa.eu/legal-content/EN/TXT/HTML/?uri=CELEX:32015L2366&from=EN#d1e1854-35-1.
GDPR came into effect on May 25, 2018. https://eur-lex.europa.eu/eli/reg/2016/679/oj/eng.

its security and usage and is required to be in a position to compensate the customer if transactions go wrong.

This divergence between a liability framework when customers choose to share payments data versus the lack of a liability framework for sharing nonpayments financial data and other types of personal data is a considerable problem in the European Union, as well as the United Kingdom, that is yet to be solved. Despite the lack of a comprehensive liability framework and an absence of a customer redress model, the GDPR, for the first time in history, enshrined the right to privacy and spelled out in no uncertain terms that the consumer owns their data, not the institution that houses that data, and the consumer has a right to data portability and mobility—to share it with whom they chose, in an easily consumed format. Other governments and jurisdictions have been inspired to enshrine this right in law, and nearly 66 percent of nations worldwide have undertaken enacting privacy and data protection laws.[17]

vi. Data-Sharing and Open Data for the Banks Report

By 2014, when PSD2 was fully developed, HMT was keen to understand how to develop this new open banking ecosystem. HMT and the Cabinet Office commissioned a report on Data Sharing and Open Data for Banks[18] (the Banks Report). The Banks Report introduced the idea of an orchestrated market standard that would build on the PSD2 framework and require the banking sector to participate. The report explained to the UK government the potential of using APIs for customers, as well as bank services and products, data-sharing, as a means of further addressing the data asymmetry issue identified by the fintech firms. It delivered a solid body of evidence on the opportunity, providing initial ideas on the technical structure. The report's concluding recommendations noted that data access standards were critical, that they should be mandated, and that APIs based on OAuth 2[19] should be required.

This is the first foray into promoting technical standards as a necessary component for maximized harmonization and interoperability among ecosystem actors. For consumers to effectively share their data and for firms hosting and accepting that data share, at scale, across all market participants, can only be achieved via technology standardization. This lesson has been reinforced during the delivery of Open Banking in the United Kingdom, and this insight has been imported by other jurisdictions as they plot their own rollouts of Open Banking and Open Finance across the globe.

vii. Open Banking Working Group and Technology Standards

As PSD2 was being adopted by the European Parliament in the autumn of 2015, HMT requested the formation of an Open Banking Working Group (OBWG) to design how an API-focused response to PSD2 would function practically. OBWG included representation from across industry and government: trade associations, banks, fintechs, and regulatory authorities.

---

[17] United Nations Conference on Trade & Development, Privacy Tracker. https://unctad.org/en/Pages/DTL/STI_and_ICTs/ICT4D-Legislation/eCom-Data-Protection-Laws.aspx.

[18] https://assets.publishing.service.gov.uk/government/uploads/system/uploads/attachment_data/file/382273/141202_API_Report_FINAL.PDF.

[19] OAuth2 standards. https://oauth.net/2/.

In February 2016, HMT published their Open Banking Standard.[20] HMT's Open Banking Standard confirmed a joint industry approach to the security profile for data-sharing, aligning with work produced by the OpenID Foundation[21] using OAuth 2 and OpenID Connect (which are both described in more detail by Don Cardinal and Nick Thomas in Chapter 5). This early commitment to implementing standards to which all participants in the value chain should comply has proven to be accepted wisdom by other countries in planning their Open Banking roadmap. This lesson from the United Kingdom has become a best practice for creating an interoperable market architecture.

b. Aligning Financial and Competition Regulation: The Competition and Markets Authority

Throughout 2015–2016, the Competition and Markets Authority engaged with market participants, holding constructive talks with the Financial Conduct Authority (FCA), the Department of Business, Energy and Industrial Strategy (BEIS) (formed in July 2016), and HMT, as well as bank and fintech trade associations and consumer and business champions. In October 2015, at the same time as the OBWG was developing its work, the CMA provided a Potential Remedies List.[22] By April 2016, while HMT was satisfied with the Open Banking Standard produced by the OBWG, the CMA decided that its near-term focus would be on developing PSD2-related policies and that the CMA, not HMT, would implement these policies. The CMA published Provisional Findings[23] that included the intention to have Open Banking as a central component of their remedies package, sending a clear signal to industry on its policy direction.

i. CMA Final Report vs. PSD2 Requirements
In August 2016, the CMA published its Retail Banking Market Investigation: Final Report[24] (CMA Final Report, or CMA Final Order). The CMA Final Report made clear that the CMA was going to take decisive action to improve competition in the UK banking sector for demand deposit accounts (i.e., Personal Current Accounts (PCA) and Business Current Accounts (BCA)). The CMA would do this by imposing the standards outlined in the published HMT Open Banking Standard on the six largest

---

[20] Open Banking Standards. https://www.paymentsforum.uk/sites/default/files/documents/Backgro und%20Document%20No.%202%20-%20The%20Open%20Banking%20Standard%20-%20Full%20Rep ort.pdf.

[21] The OpenID Foundation is a nonprofit international standardization organization of individuals and companies committed to enabling, promoting, and protecting OpenID technologies. Formed in June 2007, the foundation serves as a public trust organization representing the open community of developers, vendors, and users. OIDF assists the community by providing needed infrastructure and help in promoting and supporting expanded adoption of OpenID. This entails managing intellectual property and brand marks as well as fostering viral growth and global participation in the proliferation of OpenID. OpenID allows a user to use an existing account to sign in to multiple websites, without needing to create new passwords.

[22] CMA Potential Remedies List, updated September 2015. https://www.fne.gob.cl/wp-content/uploads/ 2017/10/CMA3_Markets_Guidance_-_updated_September_2015.pdf.

[23] CMA Retail Banking Market Investigation—Provisional Decision on Remedies (May 17, 2016). https://assets.publishing.service.gov.uk/government/uploads/system/uploads/attachment_data/file/523755/ retail_banking_market_pdr.pdf.

[24] CMA Retail Banking Market Investigation Report, Final (2016). https://assets.publishing.service.gov. uk/media/57ac9667e5274a0f6c00007a/retail-banking-market-investigation-full-final-report.pdf.

UK: CMA Final Report	EU: PSD2
Nine firms in the UK, "CMA9"	All firms in the EU
Demand deposit accounts (PCA and BCA)	Demand deposit accounts (PCA and BCA)
	Credit Cards and other Payment types
	Corporate Payments
Open Data (bank products and services)	

Figure 9.1 Scope comparison between the CMA Final Report and PSD2.
Note: PCA (Personal Current Accounts) and BCA (Business Current Accounts).

banks in Great Britain (Barclays, HSBC, Lloyds, Nationwide, RBS, and Santander) and the three largest banks in Northern Ireland (Allied Irish Bank, Bank of Ireland, and Danske). These largest UK banks came to be known as the "CMA9" and were required to build and provide the capability to exchange data (including certain data on bank products and services referred to as "Open Data") and initiate payments, with authorized third-parties.

While there was much overlap between the scope of PSD2 requirements (which were due to come into force in January 2018) and the scope laid out in the CMA Final Report, it was clear that there would be a great deal of complexity in reconciling the differences. Central to this challenge was the fact that PSD2 was deliberately drafted to be technology neutral and did not require any technical standards. However, when it was assumed during the drafting of PSD2 that login credentials would pass through a static interface allowing for screen-scraping as the primary way to share data, PSD2 did not require nor anticipate APIs as a means to share those credentials.

In terms of actual product lines covered, the table in Figure 9.1 outlines differences in scope.

ii. Financial Conduct Authority

The European Union's adoption of PSD2 required each EU member state to transpose the new directive into national law. In the United Kingdom, this process was led by HMT, which transposed PSD2 in the United Kingdom's Payment Services Regulations of 2017. These new rules were then implemented by the United Kingdom's financial services regulator, the FCA, into its handbook, giving practical interpretive guidance to firms. However, the Payment Services Regulation 2017 did not exceed the implementation mandate of PSD2, which limited the financial regulator's authority in compelling the rest of the market to align with the approach required by the United Kingdom's competition authority.

iii. The Fundamental Problem of PSD2

The process of creating regulatory change through new law was made increasingly complicated by the speed of technology change. The ink was more or less dry on PSD2 by 2013, long before it was passed, but it did not come into force until 2018. The requirement to be technology neutral was supposed to be forward thinking, recognizing that law should not dictate technical choices. However, the technology shift from credential sharing and screen-scraping practices to API technology was accompanied by a shift in roles and responsibilities.

Before PSD2, fintechs had been primarily in charge of determining the technical specifications and building the technical connections for accessing data. Fintechs were designated "data recipients," meaning they request and receive the information. Because they were new firms in the market, they were unencumbered by legacy technology—unlike many banks, whose systems were already thirty to forty years old, including any inherited systems via merger or acquisition that depend on unique bridges in order to communicate. Unlike legacy banks, fintechs were free to choose the most modern and convenient means of accessing data; in this case, the choice was to build APIs, leveraging micro-services architecture. Best practices for building APIs tended to merge toward standardization, so although there are differences across APIs, the general market practice converged toward relatively similar standards for those builds.

PSD2 altered who determined the technical specs for the API build. Instead of the fintechs or "the data recipients," the banks, or the "data providers/donors" were now in charge of the technical standards, as they were the party being compelled to open up their tech stacks for third-party access. As mentioned, the complexity and uniqueness of each banks' architecture meant that there was virtually no common standard (nor specification) for these interfaces. In order for fintechs to connect to the banks, the fintechs would have to code to each bank's specific setup. Given the vast number of financial institutions across Europe and the United Kingdom, any data exchange between fintech and bank meant literally thousands of unique interface builds. PSD2 did not provide for any standard interface, and it did not require banks to conform to an interface standard that would allow the market to connect at scale. This left the market theoretically "open," but not accessible due to the thousands of costly bespoke interface builds fintechs would be required to do in order to access their customers' information locked inside the banks' tech stacks. The myriad of technical specifications, but no standards, failed to make the market interoperable and would have pushed fintechs out of the market due to the overwhelming cost of having to build literally thousands of unique interfaces in order to connect with even a fraction of the banks in the market. Authorities realized the mistake and returned to the drawing board to try to address the oversight.

iv. PSD2 Regulatory and Technical Standards

It was against this unenviable backdrop that the European Banking Authority (EBA) was required to draft the Regulatory and Technical Standards (RTS), providing technical guidance from the EU regulator to the national regulators or other national competent authorities on certain elements of PSD2. The EBA, in consultation with the European Commission, now had to consider the qualities, functionalities, and security requirements of an API technology, which had never been contemplated in the main text of PSD2. However, the EBA did not have the authority to compel anything by way of standardization or to fund a program to oversee delivery. The authority to compel the market to build to a specific standard remained in the hands of each member state's national competent authorities, which were often the national financial regulators, but in some cases, the national competition authority. The other challenge with ensuring that each national competent authority adopted and compelled a similar standard was that each member state had to adopt the RTS into its own on-shored legislation, which risked that each national competent authority would interpret the RTS differently, thereby letting subtle but significant differences slip in as to how the standards were implemented in each member state.

Given that many banks in the European Union and the United Kingdom had not been very supportive of PSD2, there was no incentive for them to deliver the capabilities that fintech firms had sought. The protracted negotiations meant that the RTS did not in fact come into force until after PSD2 had come into full force and effect. This has led to inconsistencies in interpreted standards across the EU member states. Standardization is essential to market harmonization: how data is exchanged efficiently and at scale depends on standards. It is something the European Union struggles with still today in its delivery of Open Banking.

Meanwhile in the United Kingdom, the FCA already had finalized its Approach Document[25] based on the UK Payment Services Regulation 2017 and opened the application process for firms to register under PSD2 in October 2017, before the EBA finalized its RTS at the end of the following month, on November 27, 2017.[26] Forging ahead before the EBA rules were fully formed created some additional complexity, inefficiency, and execution risk.

5. The Pupa

a. Formation of the Open Banking Implementation Entity

i. Payments UK
Following the CMA's Final Report in August 2016,[27] firms identified as having an "Adverse Effect on Competition"—the nine largest banks in the United Kingdom, the CMA9—were required to set up and fund an Open Banking Implementation Entity (OBIE) in order to deliver PSD2 in line with the United Kingdom's Open Banking Standard.

While the CMA9 were generally content that the use of APIs, as described in the Open Banking Standard, was the modern best practice from a security and performance perspective, these nine largest banks were keen to not waste time waiting for the official order. They consulted with their trade associations on how to proceed, and it was agreed that Payments UK, a trade association for financial institutions, technology providers, and payment processors, would help mobilize a program.[28]

By the end of September 2016, Payments UK had consulted with the CMA and the CMA9 on some choices for the leadership roles, including an Implementation Trustee

---

[25] https://www.fca.org.uk/publication/finalised-guidance/fca-approach-payment-services-electronic-money-2017.pdf.

[26] EU Required Technical Standards. https://eur-lex.europa.eu/legal-content/EN/TXT/?uri=uriserv:OJ.L_.2018.069.01.0023.01.ENG&toc=OJ:L:2018:069:TOC.

[27] https://assets.publishing.service.gov.uk/media/57ac9667e5274a0f6c00007a/retail-banking-market-investigation-full-final-report.pdf.

[28] Payments UK merged with other trade bodies in July 2017 to form UK Finance, a trade association for the UK banking and financial services sector, representing around 300 firms who provide credit, banking, markets, and payment-related services.

to oversee the delivery of Open Banking to the market. The CMA made clear that an order would be made to provide the Trustee with some delegated powers and that the CMA9 would fund the program. The CMA also said they would require the CMA9 to have representatives of other key stakeholders in the governance model. Although formal powers would not vest in the Trustee function until the publication of the CMA's Retail Banking Market Investigation Order 2017 in February 2017,[29] it was expected that the parties were to behave as though the appointment had been made.

ii. The Opening Period

The OBIE's early days were dedicated to setting up an appropriate governance structure, as well as working groups with representatives from each of the nine big banks and a collective of industry representatives from the fintechs, both bank and fintech trade associations, and consumer protection interest groups. The OBIE stood up an Implementation Entity Steering Group (IESG) to oversee the entirety of the work being done. The IESG was to be chaired by the Implementation Trustee reporting to the CMA and included a representative from each of the CMA9, five representatives responsible for convening advisory groups, two customer representatives for consumer and small businesses, and four observers from HMT, the Payment Systems Regulator, FCA, and Information Commissioner's Office.[30]

At the IESG's behest, the Trustee decided that the early breakneck speed at which the OBIE was tackling the delivery of PSD2 to the market would benefit from taking a more measured approach, one which would allow for more consensus and better alignment of market participants across the ecosystem. The focus was to develop a more responsive and agile approach that would allow for pivoting should concerns arise while executing on delivery. Coordinating the feedback from the various working groups, including the legal, consumer, and technical working groups, and reconciling some diverging interpretations for particular requirements proved challenging. As a result of the rapid hiring of the OBIE team, the amount of work produced by the various working groups in silos, and the ever-changing regulatory updates at an EU and UK level, concerns emerged about the trajectory of the UK Open Banking program.

iii. CMA's Retail Banking Market Investigation Order 2017

The CMA's Retail Banking Market Investigation Order of 2017 (the CMA Order) set out the framework for delivering Open Banking to the UK market, including establishing that the CMA9 funded the OBIE. The Implementation Trustee would propose the timetable and roadmap for delivery, and once approved by the CMA, the CMA9 would be required to comply with Trustee directions. The governance framework of the Order required wide market participation and consultation as an attempt to reach consensus at the IESG. In the event that no consensus was reached, it required the Trustee to make a decision and explain to the CMA.

---

[29] https://assets.publishing.service.gov.uk/government/uploads/system/uploads/attachment_data/file/600842/retail-banking-market-investigation-order-2017.pdf.
[30] See UK Gov. Implementation Entity Plan and Proposals. https://assets.publishing.service.gov.uk/media/5800ddf3e5274a67eb000000/Implementation_entity_plans_and_proposals.pdf.

While the CMA had put a lot of effort into the design of the governance and funding model, they did very little in commenting on technical design choices, other than to require that they be standardized and align with PSD2. The outcomes-based approach of the Order was of critical importance in the years ahead, where several times stakeholders did not agree on the approach, or where projects plans or technical choices had to be revised. This approach, rather than a highly prescriptive order, has been one of the most important contributions to the success of Open Banking in the United Kingdom. Parties were encouraged to align incentives and develop standards to which all actors were subject and—most importantly—able to meet. The Trustee's centralized coordination kept an eye on the health of the whole ecosystem of consumers, banks, and fintechs. This coordination also served as a risk mitigant, allowing all parties to provide feedback into potential risks in each stage of delivery, and as a forum for designing and collectively agreeing to the mitigants that would best reduce those risks. Rather than being told what to do, all parties in the market were able to contribute, making for a more orchestrated approach that could scale.

b. UK Open Banking Delivery

i. The Approach

In 2019, Dr. Bill Roberts, Head of Open Banking at the CMA, was asked to give his thoughts on an Open Banking delivery. He replied with the thought-provoking "we are planting a forest, not boiling the kettle." This philosophy underpins the reasoning why the Trustee has a clear mandate to make adjustments to deliver the best market-facing outcomes. These outcomes need to be sustainable and profound. Not every approach is successful, but the Trustee can and does develop policy and technical standards consultations, with a view to testing enhanced solutions.

The CMA9 were quite vocal about cost overrun: tension between scope creep and enabling further competition were often at the heart of their concerns. However, regulatory pressure and consumer protection often prevailed in those cases, and had the banks been less resistant, the process would have been less costly and more efficient.

But across the CMA9, some banks embraced Open Banking more than others, and this created tension within the cohort. To resolve this tension, a not-for-profit, member-only company was created to streamline costs, to develop standards and capabilities to support delivery to the wider PSD2 scope of products and enable the OBIE to engage more formally as a market solution with other banks in the ecosystem: Open Banking Limited (OBL).

OBL provided a developer portal, as well as a sandbox environment for firms to test and learn against API standards. It also provided a Trust Framework. At the core of this Trust Framework sat a Directory of regulated actors, which also hosted the banks' API end points. This enabled the bank to check the regulated permissions of the fintechs (also known as third-party providers, or TPPs) to make it easier for firms to securely connect with other regulated actors in the ecosystem.

In addition to the Developer Portal and Directory, OBL provided Testing Support capability and a Service Desk equipped with a central ticket system, enabling the OBIE to troubleshoot the qualities of the API performance and functionality. One key lesson from the Service Desk is that the more open and transparent the system, the better the overall health of the network.

Open Banking has been expensive; however, funding the OBIE has not been, in comparison to the real costs of large institutions having to upgrade their system to be PSD2 compliant. The upside of this, according to one CMA9 bank, is that the speed of new software releases has gone down from six to nine months to six to nine days, and that this particular firm had learned to consume their own APIs to better increase internal information flow.

This heralded a significant shift in attitude: CMA9 members and other UK banks gradually transitioned their thinking on Open Banking and PSD2 from compliance requirements to exploring opportunities to develop new innovative propositions. As they did so, the ecosystem, greatly encouraged by the OBIE leadership, started to become considerably more collaborative and less confrontational.

The OBIE also focused on other functional matters, like product quality, fraud reduction, and payment risk, and in turn built policy capabilities to manage these questions either via consultation or ecosystem collaboration in areas of mutual interest, as well as the interest of consumers and businesses.

Over the course of implementing PSD2 in the United Kingdom, the banks began to realize that if they embraced Open Banking, through partnerships and as becoming fintechs themselves operating as payment initiation providers and data aggregators, they could transform an existential threat that required costly compliance and competition risk into an investment and innovation opportunity. This perspective shift has contributed significantly to the success of UK Open Banking.

ii. Managed Rollout

In October 2017, the FCA began accepting regulatory applications from firms that wished to be considered for account information (AISP) and payment initiation (PISP) roles. The expectation was that firms with properly constructed applications would be authorized to operate three months following the application.

However, at this point, banks had not created a proper preproduction test environment, one which replicated their other product environments. Given that a number of fintechs were using screen-scraping to continue to serve hundreds of thousands of customers, there was significant concern that they could not migrate these customers over to an API service in time for a "go live" date of January 2018, when PSD2 officially went into effect. A lack of proper testing environment heightened the risk that these customers would be cut off from the fintech services. Banks, on the other hand, cited customer risk as a reason for not moving into full API production.[31]

To tackle the problem, the OBIE developed a plan for a "managed roll out," which orchestrated production testing by pairing up the banks and the fintechs to work together on a very small number of real API connections.

---

[31] Production here means making the service live and active.

In reality, in the first few months after PSD2 came into force on the January 14, 2018, only a small number of TPPs made it through the regulatory permissions process, most of whom had applied for AISP licenses. Because so few fintechs had been granted approval, it allowed for more controlled production environment testing: starting with low volumes of "real" customers. It also gave the banks time to build their own preproduction testing environments.

iii. The Importance of Standards

Specification and standardization were terms that had been used interchangeably during the lead up to PSD2 "going live," but the difference was critical and made crystal clear as firms prepared to launch their APIs. The CMA had required the nine banks to provide self-attested confirmation that they had designed their APIs to the agreed specifications. However, each of the banks had interpreted the specifications differently, so each TPP connection had to be built differently across those nine banks, requiring weeks of work to integrate. Banks could also run the API specifications over qualitatively different internal infrastructures. As more fintechs entered the ecosystem, and as banks introduced new versions of their APIs, it became clear that API uptime (actively working), connection success rates, and response speeds varied from bank to bank and were generally poor. Compounding the technical performance problems, the customer journey to connect to the fintech via the bank API was also poorly designed, some being impossible to navigate at all.

It became apparent that specifications were indeed not standards, and that by allowing each bank to interpret the build in their own way proved not only bad for API performance, it also adversely affected the customers' ability to avail themselves of the fintech services, with not just a bad enrollment experience but unreliable service, too. This challenge has continued to plague other markets, where banks have been left to build to their interpretation of specifications, rather than outcome-based standards. The United Kingdom, in stark contrast to PSD2 implementation in the rest of the European Union, course-corrected its delivery to embrace standards. It also explains why the UK model has been replicated by many other markets.

6. The Butterfly Spreads Its Wings

a. Shifting to Standards: Financial Grade API

To address this challenge, the Trustee issued the requirement for the CMA9 to implement the Financial Grade API (FAPI) Standard, created by the OpenID Foundation's FAPI working group. In order to assure this requirement was met, the OBIE commissioned and paid for a conformance test suite that measured the banks' API against the FAPI standard. This alignment to the FAPI standard improved first-time connection speed and ongoing uninterrupted access between the banks and fintechs. By implementing the standard, integration times were reduced from months to hours—it provided consistency, scalability, and interoperability for the whole market.

Operational guidelines were also introduced, providing expectations and benchmarks to ensure that the nine largest banks were maintaining and upgrading their API performance and capacity.

The OBIE also set forth official Customer Experience Guidelines (CEG), which explained in step-by-step detail for banks how the banks' user journey for Authentication and Authorization was to be designed. The CEG ensured an easy, seamless customer experience irrespective of the customer logging in via the web, an app, or a combination of both; it also improved consumer fintech adoption.

b. Outstanding Issues under PSD2

i. Liability Framework

The responsibilities of each actor in the value chain are clearly defined in PSD2's liability framework and prescribed customer redress system; however, the nuances of how this works in practice still require fine-tuning, especially in context of the ecosystem and technology choices of each jurisdiction. For example, some financial data can be shared with a single application through the PSD2 liability framework, yet other nonpayments financial data can be shared under just the GDPR, which offers no customer redress requirement. In some instances, data gathered under PSD2 is being shared with firms outside the perimeter of the regulation, where there is no clear liability assigned for this onward sharing of data.

Current PDS2 regulatory requirements are not closely aligned with the practical reality of how data is shared today. Issues such as data traceability, value of data, ease of demonstrating liability, and ecosystem-level training on what to do when things go wrong must still be resolved. There are signs of an appetite to address these issues in the United Kingdom in 2021.

ii. Strong Customer Authentication

The regulatory standards relating to PSD2 put the control of the authentication step in the hands of the banks and other ASPSPs. The bank can choose to apply a requirement to have the customer present for every session that exchanges data with a fintech, or, to require the customer to be present to reauthenticate at least once every ninety days. Many banks have chosen to put it in the beginning of the customer journey, which hinders fintechs' access to the data. Both of these Strong Customer Authentication (SCA) scenarios destroy most account aggregation business models, which operate frictionlessly in the background. Moreover, consumers are simply not in the practice of frequently working to reconnect applications, having grown accustomed to experiences provided by Apple, Google, Facebook, and the like.

By complying with PSD2 requirements to implement SCA, banks have blocked a pathway for the fintech to access these data assets on behalf of the customer. In other words, access to the customer's data is now blocked by a technology process, where there was never an intention in PSD2 to block access to nonpayments data. The issue is one of great concern to the market, but remains unresolved, although the UK authorities have encouraged the market to come up with proposed solutions.

7. First Downbeat of the Wing

a. Winning Business Models

Before PSD2, let alone the UK CMA Order, data aggregation–based business models were providing interesting services to the UK market. These businesses were attached to a regulated activity—financial services—but were not included inside the regulatory perimeter. However, few firms entered the market due to regulatory uncertainty. Authorities were convinced they should be, since these firms had reached significant scale because they reduced friction and generated value for their customers. Once it became clear these business models would be legitimized under the new regulations, the UK fintech market boomed.

Today, hundreds of new firms have enrolled into the Open Banking Sandbox environment, and a majority have been through regulatory applications to bring their new idea to market. Many of these propositions are starting to really scale: payment initiation services are catching on, offering a real alternative to card-based payments. Once SCA issues are resolved, the account aggregation business models will thrive. The reason for this growth is simple: financial services leaders, entrepreneurs, and investors believe that UK authorities are committed to making Open Banking work. They have proved this by designing governance and funding models that deliver a high-quality ecosystem, where rights of access are confirmed, actor obligations are clear, customer protections are ensured, technology works reliably, and customer journeys are frictionless.

b. Open Finance Back on the Agenda

In the summer of 2019, in response to the significant demand for Open Banking, the FCA formed the Advisory Group on Open Finance to provide a set of recommendations on harmonizing approaches across financial services, taking into account the regulatory perimeter, liability framework, role of explicit consent, trust framework, and ecosystem orchestration approach. In December 2019, the FCA published some initial findings of the Advisory Group. The Cohesion and Interoperability Working Group[32] said:

> The potential for open finance is to maximise federated open market innovation, competition and efficiency. Taking a user-centric design approach and ensuring common interoperability will drive up rates of adoption and inclusion while reducing friction and confusion for the end customer. Given the pace of change, now is the time to create foundational principles, practice and regulation.

They went on to list what cohesion and interoperability included and gave explicit advice that Open Finance "[e]nsure *openly licensed standards, shared* and *common processes, principles and practice are made compulsory around cohesion and interoperability across*

---

[32] Cohesion and Interoperability Advisory Group on Nopen Finance Advice Note. https://www.fca.org.uk/publication/documents/cohesion-interoperability-advisory-group-open-finance-advice-note.pdf.

the whole market." To further underscore how crucial standards are, the group advised the following:

> We note that any process must be adaptive to a rapidly changing landscape: there is no "endpoint" to innovation. The compulsion to adopt—and make accessible—standards should be on a continuous basis and to a predictable cadence (e.g. a six-month cycle).

The advice concludes that any fragmented approaches will lead to poor competitive outcomes, poor consumer value, increased risk and costs, and ultimately not meet the needs of a thriving digital economy. With findings so clearly articulated, the suggestion of HMT in 2013 to create a policy that brings all financial services into scope now has foundational principles generated from the experience of Open Banking.

c. Open Life

In September 2020, the United Kingdom's department for Business Energy and Industrial Strategy published a report called "Next Steps for Smart Data,"[33] which highlights terms of reference for a new working group set up across the UK government and its agencies to find a pathway to enable harmonized access for TPPs, with the customer's explicit consent for a wide range of data assets across industry.

There is a reasonable pathway from this initiative to build beyond Open Banking and Open Finance, toward Open Life. The keystone to this initiative is an explicit consumer data right enshrined in existing privacy legislation. Without a right to share and move one's data, and standards that harmonize interoperability of systems across different industries, Open Life would be a pipe dream. The experience of Open Banking has consistently reaffirmed this truth.

8. The Kaleidoscope

a. Impact on Other Markets

There has been global interest in the progress of UK Open Banking and what might happen thereafter. Did the experiment work? What went right? What went wrong? How does it compare with other markets? The use of the terms "Open Banking" and "Open Finance" is widespread throughout the world, although there is not a common understanding of its meaning. In Japan, the United States, and New Zealand, for example, there have been substantial efforts in the domain of API technology, running ahead of any changed regulatory context. There has been significant work in these markets to rebalance by instituting a broader underlying policy framework.

---

[33] https://assets.publishing.service.gov.uk/government/uploads/system/uploads/attachment_data/file/915973/smart-data-consultation-response.pdf.

In the United States, for example, in July, 2020, the Consumer Financial Protection Bureau announced its Advanced Notice of Proposed Rulemaking[34] with the intention to reform Dodd-Frank Section 1033, and provide some rights and obligations for participants when consumers authorize financial data-sharing.

The European Union has recognized the United Kingdom's success in delivering market-facing outcomes, but the European Union's lack of orchestration of standards has delivered low-quality technical implementations with missing functionality. There has been no EU Trustee equivalent to oversee that orchestration. Standards bodies do exist in Europe—the Berlin Group's Next Gen PSD2 Task Force and STET out of France are two examples—but on the whole, these groups have worked on specifications, not standards per se. These groups have all been bank-led, with no feedback from fintechs, customer representatives, or regulatory authorities until after those standards have been published. These published standards are a significant improvement to previous delivery approaches, but this fragmented approach still means inconsistent delivery and low interoperability across the whole of the EU financial services market.

The European Commission fully understands the difference between the generation of specifications and the orchestrated implementation of standards driven by performance monitoring. The EU Commission's problem has not been failure to recognize that the UK approach was delivering better market-facing outcomes, but that the wheels of legal and regulatory change move slowly, multiplied by the number of member states and their regulatory authorities, and so the Commission has only been able to encourage behaviors rather than mandate them, frustrating their good intentions.

The Australian authorities have a vision of a full suite of "Open" services underpinned by the Customer Data Right (CDR)[35] regime. They have chosen to emulate the orchestration process, but have recognized the incongruous impact and limited utility of allowing customers to share only some of their financial data and initiate payments without enabling all of their financial data to be used in this way. The CDR regime starts with Open Banking and moves through to Open Finance and Open Life as cardinal points in a clearly articulated journey. Australia, like the United Kingdom and the United States, has chosen to align behind the FAPI standard.

India has a new Data Protection Act[36] working through the legislative process, combined with a newly implemented Data Aggregators Regime.[37] Building on the success of Aadhaar and Unified Payment Interface, India needs no lessons on the importance of ecosystem coordination. Nevertheless, the iSPRT team, which has worked with ReBIT (Reserve Bank Information Technology) on the technical standards, has been regularly connected to developments in the United Kingdom to exchange lessons learned.

Canada, Brazil, and Russia are other large markets which have been influenced by the UK approach, but there is a clear vision to adopt a more comprehensive scope. The

---

[34] https://www.consumerfinance.gov/about-us/newsroom/cfpb-anpr-consumer-authorized-access-financial-data/.

[35] https://www.accc.gov.au/focus-areas/consumer-data-right-cdr-0.

[36] The Personal Data Protection Act 2019. http://164.100.47.4/BillsTexts/LSBillTexts/Asintroduced/373_2019_LS_Eng.pdf.

[37] https://www.cgap.org/sites/default/files/publications/2020_07_Working_Paper_India_New_Approach_Personal_Data_Sharing.pdf.

transition in Canada from "Open Banking" to the term "Customer Directed Finance"[38] sums up their intended positioning quite clearly.

The United Kingdom is clearly ahead of other markets in delivery terms but has now been overtaken by an increasing number of countries in policy development. While market-facing outcomes are the only thing that really matters, the UK authorities will want to ensure that the success they have seen with Open Banking gets translated into other market verticals under Open Finance, to ensure that the United Kingdom remains a leader in financial services innovation.

b. Global Open Finance Centre of Excellence

As PSD2 came into force in Europe, it became apparent that there were various capabilities that the marketplace urgently needed but for which there was no existing focal point or leadership to make these assets available. The Global Open Finance Centre of Excellence (GOFCoE), conceived to address these needs, is based at the University of Edinburgh, chosen for its internationally recognized strengths in super-computing and data science, Supported by a UK Research and Innovation grant seed fund in 2020, this major new international collaborative and convening body's research and development efforts are focused on coordinating a global approach to consistency in the design and delivery of open finance. GOFCoE offers a financial data sandpit to help banks fund managers, insurers, and fintechs to more rapidly develop hypothesize, prototype algorithms, test business models, and work with regulatory sandboxes to develop proof points.

It is also developing a Global Economic Observatory to engage in a longitudinal study of how humankind earns, spends, and saves through the lens of both consumers and businesses. Its Algorithmic Bias Test Laboratory is introducing a new capability to assist financial services practitioners in reducing discrimination and in providing assurance of compliance and ethical standards in their algorithmic distribution of products and services.

The Global Open Finance Technical Standards Working Group, in partnership with the OpenID Foundation, is focused on creating a digital library of international API standards, with the aim of harmonizing security standards for data-sharing, digital identity, conformance testing, and interoperability across markets. GOFCoE will also house an Economic Crime Unit, providing an international collaboration environment to enable enhanced pattern recognition research and development to reduce money laundering and fraud, as well as an Education and Training Programme to provide courses in machine learning in financial services, data ethics, and data governance.

GOFCoE embodies the key principle learned from the United Kingdom's implementation of Open Banking: standardization for maximum harmonization and scalability to allow the efficient movement of data to maximize the customer's economic value of their money.

---

[38] https://www.canada.ca/en/department-finance/programs/consultations/2019/open-banking/report.html.

9. Conclusion

While Open Banking in the United Kingdom has had its share of challenges, it remains the primary example of what good ecosystem orchestration looks like and is still relied upon to inform other Open Banking and Open Finance regimes across the globe. Myriad lessons have sprouted from this experiment, the most foundational of which are the United Kingdom's legacy and gift to consumers:

- the importance of an enshrined consumer data right;
- the importance of standards in promoting market scalability and interoperability;
- the need for an independent third-party to oversee market collaboration (Trustee);
- understanding that regulatory governance and policy framework are essential to market legitimacy and attracting investment; and
- understanding that the shift to a data economy requires thinking differently about regulation: it is more about data access than it is about a product or service.

These wingbeats from an island nation have turned into a hurricane of open data initiatives around the world: one shining example that provides a smoother, more efficient, and less costly map for other markets to follow.

Glossary of Terms

AISP	Account Information Service Provider
API	Application Program Interface: in layman's terms, an API allows pieces of software to communicate with each other. APIs give developers access to predefined functions so they don't have to be built from scratch every time. Following PSD2, all ASPSPs will have to provide a way for trusted third-parties to tap into a customer's financial information and even initiate payments. APIs are currently considered the most practical way to do this.
ASPSP	Account Servicing Payment Service Provider: in layman's terms, a bank or financial institution
BEIS	Department of Business, Energy and Industrial Strategy
CC	Competition Commission
CMA	Competition Market Authority
CMA9	UK's nine largest banks: HSBC Royal Bank of Scotland Lloyds Barclays Santander Nationwide Danske Bank Bank of Ireland Allied Irish Bank

FCA	Financial Conduct Authority
GDPR	General Data Protection Regulation
GOFCoE	Global Open Finance Centre of Excellence
IESG	Implementation Entity Steering Group, governed by the UK's OBIE
OBIE	Open Banking Implementation Entity, the Trustee in the UK
OFT	Office of Fair Trading
PFM	Personal Financial Management
PISP	Payment Initiation Services Provider
PSD2	Second Payment Services Directive
RTS	Regulatory and Technical Standards

10

The Australian Consumer Data Right:
The Promise of Open Data

Jamie Leach [*] *and Julie McKay* [**]

The introduction of the Australian version of Open Banking as part of an overarching Consumer Data Right is rapidly evolving (see the Introduction and Chapter 1 for more on "Open Banking"). At the time of writing this chapter, Open Banking appears divided into two stages: the introduction of data sharing (commonly referred to as "Read Access") as the first stage and the introduction of Action Initiation ("Write Access"), which is predicted but not guaranteed to soon follow. Also, Open Banking is launching in a phased and staggered manner with various participants such as banks, fintechs, and technology providers mandated to comply with shifting deadlines and ambiguity.

A pattern of a series of inquiries and reviews,[1] has emerged in Australia; it seems that as soon as an inquiry report is published, the Australian government seeks another yet further consultation,[2] shifting the already fluid goalposts. Delayed numerous times, with the finer aspects of rules and policy largely unfinished, the recommendation by review chair Scott Farrell is—at best—interpreted and echoed but not necessarily adopted by the Federal Regulator (the Australian Competition and Consumer Commission) and the Treasury Department. As the market attempts to comply and embrace Open Banking in its intended form, a failure to finalize the rules of engagement is drawing out the marketplace adoption and threatening to postpone the ultimate benefit for the consumer. What follows is an interpretation of the forthcoming Open Banking and Consumer Data Right regime as a snapshot in time.

1. Introduction of "Open Data"

Open data's evolution and the associated framework for data sharing within the Australian ecosystem have been slow to develop. Commencing with the publication of the government's own data sets in 2009,[3] the motivation to share private data would not

[*] Regional Director, Financial Data and Technology Association, Australia & New Zealand.
[**] Former Chapter Lead, Financial Data and Technology Association, Australia & New Zealand.

[1] See reviews, including: The Australian Government, Financial System Inquiry (Nov. 2014; the Murray Inquiry); The Australian Government Competition Policy Review (Mar. 2015; the Harper Report), the Parliament of the Commonwealth of Australia, Review of the Four Major Banks (Nov. 2016; the Coleman Report), The Australian Government, Productivity Commission, Data Availability and Use, Inquiry Report (Mar. 2017), and The Australian Government the Treasury, Review into Open Banking: giving customers choice, convenience and confidence (Dec. 2017, the First Farrell Review).

[2] The most recent being The Australian Government, Future Directions for the Consumer Data Right (Oct. 2020, the Second Farrell Review).

[3] https://data.gov.au.

Jamie Leach and Julie McKay, *The Australian Consumer Data Right: The Promise of Open Data* In: *Open Banking.* Edited by: Linda Jeng, Oxford University Press. © Oxford University Press 2022. DOI: 10.1093/oso/9780197582879.003.0011

gain momentum had it not been for a series of commissions, inquiries, and reviews held between 2014 and 2020.

While other jurisdictions were adopting various forms of open banking, Australia pursued a distinctive course in adopting an "open data" regime. In the global context, the Australian evolution of open banking is particular for three primary reasons: first, the government plans to apply the Consumer Data Right's (CDR's)[4] open data-sharing requirements economy-wide, beginning with the banking sector progressing to energy providers and telecommunication companies.[5] Second, unlike the UK and EU regimes, the Australian CDR provides for read-only capability initially, meaning the data recipient can only access data for information-gathering purposes.[6] More important, in conceiving a broader open data regime, the Australian government views the right to open data-sharing as an intangible property right (a *chose in action*). (To read more about the economics of data, see Chapter 7, by Yan Carrière-Swallow and Vikram Haksar; and for more on open data–related issues, see the Chapter 14, by Brad Carr.) The government proposed, accordingly, a consent right, which is a right to give instructions about how one's data is collected, stored, and used. This approach has flow-on impacts on other possible data rights, such as the right to privacy and the right to be forgotten. (For detailed discussion of data rights and protections, see Chapter 2, by Kaitlin Asrow.)

In 2014, the government's Financial Systems Inquiry (the Murray Inquiry)[7] recommended better data access. The 2015 Competition Policy Review (the Harper Report),[8] the 2016 Review of the Four Major Banks (the Coleman Report),[9] and the 2017 Productivity Commission's Data Availability and Use Report[10] made similar recommendations about a data-sharing economy. Each Review into financial services had a different scope and focus, but the conclusions were broadly consistent. As noted in the Coleman Report, "Australians should be able to trust that their bank will act in their best interests . . . [but] the major banks have significant market power."[11]

At the end of 2017, the Australian federal government announced the CDR's introduction to require sharing information in "a safe, efficient and convenient manner."[12] This announcement followed the Open Banking Review's final report, commissioned in 2017 by the Treasurer Hon. Scott Morrison MP and led by Scott Farrell (the Farrell Review).[13] Scott Farrell was instructed to make recommendations concerning the most suitable model of open banking for the country. The Farrell Review found:

---

[4] Competition and Consumer (Consumer Data Right) Rules 2020 pursuant to the Competition and Consumer Act 2010. https://www.accc.gov.au/system/files/CDR%20Rules%20-%20Final%20-%206%20February%202020.pdf.

[5] The government is considering applying CDR to private pension providers (specifically, superannuation funds) and other consumer services.

[6] There is no immediate plan to include a payments initiation capability, but the Australian government is assessing adding write-access capability, which would allow customers to give permission to data recipients to initiate financial services transactions, particularly payments.

[7] The Australian Government, Financial System Inquiry Final Report, Nov. 2014.

[8] The Australian Government Competition Policy Review, Final Report, Mar. 2015.

[9] Parliament of the Commonwealth of Australia, Review of the Four Major Banks: First Report, Nov. 2016.

[10] The Australian Government, Productivity Commission, Data Availability and Use, Inquiry Report, No. 82, Mar. 31, 2017.

[11] Coleman Report, *supra* note 3.

[12] Competition and Consumer Act 2010 (Cth) 56AA.

[13] Review into Open Banking in Australia—Final Report (Feb. 8, 2018). https://treasury.gov.au/consultation/c2018-t247313.

Open Banking is part of the Consumer Data Right in Australia, a more general right being created for consumers, to control their data—including who can have it and who can use it. – Mr. Scott Farrell, Chair of the "Open Banking Review"[14]

A timeline of two years between the Farrell Review's Final Report and legislative adoption at the end of 2019 is remarkably short for the passage of legislation intended to bring about significant change. However, the Farrell Review was the latest in a succession of public inquiries into financial services and competition.

In the same period, the Royal Commission into Misconduct in the Banking, Superannuation and Financial Services Industry (the Hayne Commission) was conducting work.[15] While its scope was broader, the Hayne Commission also noted the imbalance of power between financial institutions and consumers[16]—specifically, a lack of practical options for consumers in banking products and services.

Following these reviews' findings, the Australian government adopted a data-sharing right to empower consumers and promote banking services competition.

In the end, the First Farrell Review focused less on why to introduce open data-sharing and more on how to implement open data-sharing in banking. The First Farrell Review[17] made a total of fifty recommendations, including the regulatory framework. Other recommendations include keeping shared data secure and maintaining privacy, data types to share, and suitable data transfer mechanisms. The First Farrell Review also noted future issues to be considered, such as write access, digital identity, and the value of data transparency. Sections at the end of this chapter discuss these and other ongoing issues.

a. Objectives of the CDR

Four principles guide Australia's Consumer Data Right (CDR):

- The CDR should be consumer-focussed. It should be for the consumer, be about the consumer, and be seen from the consumer's perspective.
- The CDR should encourage competition. It should seek to increase competition for products and services available to consumers to make better choices.
- The CDR should create opportunities. It should provide a framework from which new ideas and business can emerge and grow, establishing a vibrant and creative data sector that supports better services enhanced by personalised data.

[14] https://treasury.gov.au/sites/default/files/2019-03/t286983_consumer-data-right-booklet.pdf.
[15] Royal Commission into Misconduct in the Banking, Superannuation and Financial Services Industry, Final Report, Feb. 2019.
[16] Royal Commission into Misconduct in the Banking, Superannuation and Financial Services Industry Final Report (Volume I), Feb. 2019.
[17] The first review chaired by Mr. Farrell is The Australian Government the Treasury, Review into Open Banking: giving customers choice, convenience, and confidence (Dec. 2017). The second review led by Mr. Farrell is The Australian Government, Future Directions for the Consumer Data Right (Oct. 2020).

- The CDR should be efficient and fair. It should be implemented with security and privacy in mind, so that it is sustainable and fair, without being more complex or costly than needed. [18]

Fostering competition in critical sectors of the consumer economy is the government's immediate policy objective. But the third principle above is another crucial indicator of the government's intention "[to lay] the tracks for Australia's future data economy."[19] Longer term, the government aims to seed a vibrant ecosystem for transformative innovation through data smart use.

The practical application of the CDR to the banking sector faces many similar issues also faced by other jurisdictions and described in the other chapters in this book. The distinctive framing of this permission right, existing privacy rules, and the regime's intended broad reach drives unique challenges and opportunities in Australia. The purpose of this chapter is to outline the CDR as it applies to banking in a way that highlights the challenges and choices made to deliver a unique and powerful transformation of Australia's data-driven economy.

After giving some background, this chapter describes the various roles and participants in the CDR ecosystem and then outlines the types of data subject to the CDR regime. Some readers may prefer to read the later Section 5 about CDR Data before reading about CDR participants.

2. Legislative Framework

The legislative framework for the CDR consists of five parts:

1. The enabling Federal (Commonwealth or Cth) legislation[20] adds to or amends existing laws, including:
   a. the Competition and Consumer Act of 2010 (Cth) (the CC Act);
   b. the Privacy Act of 1988 (Cth) (the Privacy Act); and
   c. the Australian Information Commission Act of 2010 (Cth).
   The enabling legislation broadly defines a set of powers, rights, and obligations to build a flexible framework and expand to cover various industries and data sets.
2. The Australian Competition and Consumer Commission (ACCC) was initially appointed as the designated regulator to develop and implement rules and regulations pursuant to the CDR (the ACCC Rules). The ACCC Rules set out detailed operating standards and requirements applicable to industry, subsector, or data set. For example, the ACCC Rules set out the principle of data minimization and the right to delete (discussed in Section 6d). As of February 2021, the policy

---

[18] The Australian Government the Treasury, Review into Open Banking: giving customers choice, convenience and confidence, Dec. 2017 (the First Farrell Review).
[19] Treasury Laws Amendment (Consumer Data Right) Bill 2019, Second Reading, Ministers Speech.
[20] Treasury Laws Amendment (Consumer Data Right) Bill 2019.

development's finalization and the rules framework transferred to the Treasury Department.

3. A government-appointed Data Standards Chair sets the Data Standards. The Data Standards include application programming interface (API) standards, information security standards, and interface design patterns and user experience guidelines. The government also appoints the Data Standards Body, currently Data61 (the data specialist division of the Australian national science research agency CSIRO). The role of the Data Standards Body is to assist the Data Standards Chair. Data61 leads the industry's technical discussions and makes final recommendations to the Chair about the relevant Data Standards. The Chair can appoint other advisers and has formed the Data Standards Banking Advisory Committee. The Committee consists of representatives from industry, consumer groups, and banks. For simplicity, this chapter will refer to the Data Standards Body to collectively mean the Chair, Data61, and the Advisory Committee. As of February 2021, this team and oversight of Data Standards and Technical Standards have also transferred to the Treasury Department.

4. Register of Accredited Participants (such as Accredited Data Recipients and Data Holders). The ACCC is currently responsible for building and maintaining the Register. The legislation envisages a separate Registrar, and the ACCC has indicated it will look to hand over this responsibility when a Registrar is appointed.

5. Legislative instruments issued by the responsible government minister (the Treasurer) (a Designating Instrument). By issuing a Designating Instrument, the minister makes a specific industry or sector and relevant data sets subject to the CDR. The first Designating Instrument issued by the minister made the banking sector (specifically Australian Deposit-Taking Institutions, or ADI[21]) subject to CDR obligations.[22]

Thus, the enabling legislation is essentially a framework for delegating broad powers to various bodies to make detailed rules about the CDR operation. Checks and balances on applying these delegated powers are primarily by ministerial and parliamentary oversight and a power to disallow the rules. The power to disallow a rule is generally exercised after the rule has been made, in contrast to a parliamentary debate, before a law change. Some have argued that a power to disallow gives the parliamentary weaker control over the consequences for the CDR.

This framework of delegating rulemaking powers builds in enormous flexibility and aims to be future-proof. But, by operating across different legislative acts, intersecting with and potentially overlapping with other areas of law, such as the Privacy Act

---

[21] An ADI is defined in the Banking Act (Cth) of 1959. Generally, it is a corporation that is licensed to carry on a banking business in Australia. This definition is somewhat circular, and a detailed explanation is beyond the scope of this chapter. But one defining characteristic of an ADI, as the name implies, is the ability to take money on deposit (other than in part payment for goods or services). Refer to the Section 4a on Data Holder *infra* for further comments on which financial service businesses are captured in the CDR.

[22] Consumer Data Right (Authorised Deposit-Taking Institutions) Designation 2019.

(discussed here and Section 6b) and other types of regulations (e.g., electronic payments rules for banks), enormous complexities and unintended consequences may arise in law and implementation.

While the technical Data Standards and ACCC Rules must be implemented together, there is no single independent governing body like the Open Banking Implementation Entity in the United Kingdom. This chapter will strive to highlight some critical areas of potential complexity. In the absence of live, in-market solutions and regulatory guidance, these complexities may make it difficult for early adopters to understand their rights and obligations and may result in unintended consequences.[23]

For example, the CDR sets out thirteen Privacy Safeguards that broadly mirror the long-standing Privacy Principles[24] in the Privacy Act. The Privacy Safeguards include several privacy-enhancing features, but some participants may find it difficult to distinguish when data is subject to the CDR Privacy Safeguards or the Privacy Principles. The blurry boundaries could lead to the unintended separation of data sets when the original aim of open data is to bring together disparate data sets to create new value and insights for promoting consumer-centered services.

3. Roles in CDR Ecosystem

There are six roles in the data-sharing ecosystem:

1. CDR Consumer—broadly, the persons or entities that have the right to request that their information is transferred from a Data Holder to an Accredited Data Recipient;[25]

2. Data Holder—broadly holds (or collects[26]) the original data about a CDR Consumer;[27]

3. Accredited Data Recipient (ADR)—an entity that is authorized to receive CDR Data. A Data Holder may become an ADR if it is accredited to receive CDR Data, which will be defined in the last section;[28]

4. Outsourced Service Provider—refer Section 4c for a discussion about intermediaries;[29]

5. Gateway—a Gateway may be necessary for some sectors to facilitate the transfer of certain CDR Data (e.g., some data about consumers' energy consumption is

---

[23] Maddocks, Consumer Data Right Regime Privacy Impact Assessment (PIA), Summary of Findings Nov. 29, 2019.

[24] The Privacy Act of 1988, Schedule 1—Australian Privacy Principles.

[25] Treasury Laws Amendment (Consumer Data Right) Bill 2019, Explanatory Memorandum.

[26] Broadly, Australian privacy laws and regulations, including the CDR, distinguish between various actions related to data including: collecting (or receiving), holding (or storing), using (or dealing with), correcting, and disclosing. A detailed explanation of each action is beyond the scope of this chapter. In this chapter, the terms will be used in a general sense unless it is necessary to highlight a specific point.

[27] Treasury Laws Amendment (Consumer Data Right) Bill 2019, Explanatory Memorandum.

[28] The Competition and Consumer Act 2010 (Cth) defines an "CDR Participant" as a Data Holder or an ADR (s56AL). An "Accredited Persons" includes ADRs and Data Holders if the Data Holder is granted accreditation to collect CDR Data.

[29] Defined in the ACCC Rules Section 1.10.

held by the Australian market operator rather than by each energy retailer who is a Data Holder);[30] and

6. Accreditation Register—a register of accredited persons who can request and collect CDR Data.

Broadly, a typical interaction between these actors could evolve as follows:

- A consumer opens a transaction account with a bank. In the ordinary course of providing banking services to the consumer, the bank collects data about the consumer and their transactions (the consumer's original data). In this case, the bank will be a Data Holder.
- An eligible CDR Consumer (refer Section 4 for a discussion about eligibility) gives consent to an ADR (e.g., a fintech offering a service to the consumer) to collect, hold, and use (and possibly disclose to another party) CDR Data held by the Data Holder.
- During the consumer interaction, the ADR sends a CDR Data request to the Data Holder. That request redirects the CDR Consumer to the Data Holder to be authenticated and authorizes the Data Holder to disclose the CDR Data to the ADR.

If the Data Holder authenticates the consumer, the Data Holder checks the Accreditation Register's ADR credentials. If the ADR credentials are validated, the Data Holder sends the requested CDR Data to the ADR. (If applicable, a Gateway may facilitate the interactions between Data Holder and ADR, for example, but disclosing CDR Data held by the Gateway to the ADR.)

The Australian CDR regime covers three types of data requests:

1. Product Data Request[31]—this request is for public information about products offered by the Data Holder. For example, standard fees and terms and conditions for a bank account. The data is not specific to a consumer, no consent is required, and the person making the request does not need to be accredited.[32] This request aims to make generic product data available in a standard form for services, including product comparisons.
2. Consumer Data Request made by an ADR[33]—the typical interaction outlined above is an example of this request and is consistent with other Open Data regimes.
3. Direct Request Service[34]—a consumer data request made directly by an eligible CDR Consumer. The aim is to allow consumers to request their own data directly from their bank and require the bank to disclose the data in human-readable

---

[30] Competition and Consumer Act 2010 (Cth); s56AJ; a Designating Instrument may define a Gateway for a specific industry. A Gateway is expected for the energy sector given the state-based nature of energy providers and existing data collection and sharing arrangements in that sector. No Gateway is expected for the banking sector.

[31] The ACCC Rules dated Feb. 4, 2020, Part 2.

[32] Competition and Consumer (Consumer Data Right) Rules 2020, Feb. 2020.

[33] The ACCC Rules dated Feb. 4, 2020, Part 4.

[34] The ACCC Rules dated Feb. 4, 2020, Part 3.

format.[35] At the time of writing, the ACCC Rules included this obligation, but the technical standards were still being developed.

4. CDR Consumers

The term "consumer" typically refers to a natural person, and rights under the Privacy Act are generally limited to such individuals. In contrast, rights under the CDR are not limited to natural persons. The definition of "consumer" under the CDR can encompass any legal person or entity (e.g., individual, joint holder, small business, partnership, companies, large enterprise, trust) capable of holding or using a designated banking product or service.

This approach follows the First Farrell Review recommendation to extend a right to request data to all economic actors. It also bypasses practical difficulties with distinguishing small, medium-size, and large businesses,[36] which have various thresholds across other laws such as taxation.[37]

A CDR Consumer is a person or entity about which there is CDR Data related to the supply of goods or services specified in the Designating Instrument.[38] For example, in the case of the banking sector, a person is a CDR Consumer because they have a bank account and use banking services. Similarly, a company that holds a bank account is the CDR Consumer. In that example, an individual authorized to act on behalf of the company grants consent to share data but is not the CDR Consumer.

Understanding who is a CDR Consumer and acting on behalf of a CDR Consumer can be critical when considering joint accounts or accounts with multiple authorized operators. For simplicity, this chapter will use the term "CDR Consumer" to mean any person or entity eligible to use the rights and tools provided under the CDR and will not distinguish between the subject of an account and the person giving consent.

The current ACCC Rules and Data Standards for banking impose certain limits on CDR Consumer eligibility. In the initial phase, only the following are eligible CDR Consumers:

- an individual over the age of eighteen or certain businesses (e.g., sole trader or proprietary company); and
- who holds an active open account with a bank; and
- who has access to their bank's internet system, will be an eligible CDR Consumer.[39]

The Farrell Review recommended that consumers have access to open and close accounts. The Review acknowledged the difficulties of making historical data available,

---

[35] Data Standard Body Technical Working Group, Decision Proposal 089—Direct Consumer Access, Nov. 2, 2019.

[36] Including small to medium-size businesses in the CDR is consistent with the policy objective of promoting greater competition within financial services. It is generally argued that larger businesses have sufficient market power relative to banks, do not need a data sharing right, and may introduce complexity given the unique nature of their banking products and services.

[37] Various legislation, for example, taxation, apply different criteria to classify a small versus large business.

[38] Competition and Consumer Act 2010 (Cth), s56AI(3).

[39] Maddocks, Consumer Data Right Regime Privacy Impact Assessment (PIA), 45.

particularly for a bank's inactive customers. The Review didn't expect that data to be available in the initial stages.[40] Accessing historical data on closed or inactive bank accounts remains in scope but is not currently scheduled.

This chapter does not discuss the authentication and security standards in detail. However, the decision to implement the OpenID Connect (OIDC) Hybrid Flow has implications for an eligible CDR Consumer and how consumers may perceive their relationship with an ADR or a Data Holder.[41]

The OIDC Hybrid-Flow is a browser redirect method in which the ADR redirects the consumer to the bank's (as Data Holder) authorization web page. The consumer enters his or her or its internet banking identifier, and the bank sends the consumer a One Time Password (OTP) (typically to their mobile phone) to complete authentication.

The Data Standard Body noted two advantages of a Hybrid/Redirect flow:

a. The user identifier, which is considered sensitive by many banks, is not shared with the data [recipient];

b. The device the customer uses to initiate [CDR] authorisation, which may differ from the device normally used for banking, is observable by the data provider. This assists in implementing fraud detection techniques that rely on the tracking and fingerprinting of devices used by customers. [42]

Using a bank's existing internet authentication credentials reduces the need to build separate processes to verify consumers' identities and authority to give instructions on the accounts. A Redirect flow is consistent with the First Farrell Review Recommendation 5.4, which was based on the UK approach at that time. The United Kingdom has since added a decoupled flow, which does not require redirecting the browser to the bank's authorization web page.

Aside from any technical consideration, any Redirect flow assumes the consumer has established internet access to the bank before the consumer can begin to use the services offered by an ADR. Further, the consumer must disclose an up-to-date mobile phone number to its bank to receive the OTP. Establishing this internet arrangement with the bank must occur before and outside the consumer's interaction with an ADR.

Needing to establish internet access to a bank is a potential point of friction during the ADR's interaction with potential users. Only consumers who can access internet banking (whether via mobile phone or computer) and can receive an OTP to their mobile phone can effectively take advantage of the CDR. Further, any difficulties during the authentication process, for example, if the bank has out-of-date mobile phone details, will need to be dealt with outside the consumer's interaction with the ADR.

Delays or frictions may result in consumers perceiving that the ADR service is not as reliable or is more cumbersome than their existing banking services. Frictions can

---

[40] The Australian Government the Treasury, Review into Open Banking: giving customers choice, convenience and confidence, Dec. 2017, Recommendation 3.2.

[41] Security Profile Standards as at March 2020.

[42] Decision Proposal 035—Customer Authentication Flow, Data Standards Body Technical Working Group, Oct. 21, 2019; 2.

inhibit a consumer's willingness or ability to switch banking providers and could undermine the government's policy objective of promoting competition.

a. Data Holders

Generally, there are potentially three types of Data Holders:

a. an entity of the type specified in the Designating Instrument that holds the type of data specified in the Designating Instrument (e.g., a bank that offers savings accounts to consumers);

b. an ADR that becomes subject to the obligations of a Data Holder through the principle of reciprocity (refer Section 4a ii for a discussion about reciprocity); and

c. an accredited entity specified in the ACCC Rules.[43]

i. Banks as Data Holders

Banking, more formally Authorised Deposit-taking Institutions (ADI),[44] is the first industry designated to share appropriately consented data under the CDR regime. The Australian Prudential Regulation Authority (APRA) is the regulator for banking, insurance, and superannuation, but is not the designated CDR regulator and cannot issue CDR-pursuant rules.

The list of institutions licensed as ADIs include:

- Australian-domiciled ADIs (including banks, credit unions, and mutual banks);
- Subsidiaries of foreign banks;
- Branches of foreign banks;
- Restricted ADIs (generally new ADIs or neo-banks that have a limited license and are in the early phase of their development); and
- Provider/purchaser payment facilities (e.g., PayPal).

Broadly, the four largest Australian-domiciled ADIs (aka, Tier 1 or the Big 4 banks) conduct approximately 80 percent of retail and small business banking activity in Australia. This business occurs through the banks' main brands, their subsidiary brands (e.g., Bankwest is part of the Commonwealth Bank of Australia group), and internet-only/digital brands (e.g., National Australia Bank and its internet brand UBank).

This brief overview of the Australian banking landscape helps understand the ACCC's phased rollout of the CDR.[45] Broadly, over the first year of the CDR, the obligation to share banking CDR Data applies as follows:

- Big 4 banks (own brand only)—the ACCC Rules refers to these banks as "Initial Data Holders."

---

43 Competition and Consumer Act 2010 (Cth); s56AJ.
44 As defined in the Banking Act 1959 (Cth).
45 Planned rollout as at February 2020.

- Big 4 banks (sub-brands and internet-only brands).
- Voluntarily-participating ADIs—the potential consequences for volunteering to participate early are discussed in Section 4a ii.
- Accredited ADIs—other ADIs not included above, such as Tier 2 banks, credit unions, and mutual banks not voluntarily participating. Foreign ADI or foreign branches of a domestic bank are expressly excluded.
- Other accredited non-ADIs are expected to capture other financial service providers that are not ADIs but offer facilities and accounts similar to those captured under the CDR (e.g., nonbank lenders and payment facility providers; note: "data aggregators" are not defined under the CDR). This may become more relevant when reciprocity is introduced (refer Section 4a ii for a discussion on reciprocity).

For simplicity, this chapter will refer to banks unless it is necessary to distinguish a licensed ADI.

The phased rollout demonstrates the interconnection between the legislation (which makes all banks subject to the CDR) and the flexibility of the ACCC's rulemaking powers to limit the law's broad application. Like the UK Open Banking regime, this approach aims to cover most consumer financial activity in the early phases. It also highlights the government's intention to create a level playing field by capturing as much of the financial services sector within the CDR remit as is practical.

At the time of writing, the Data Standards Body had commenced developing data standards for energy providers. This chapter does not go into a summary of operators in the Australian energy market. Unless otherwise specified, comments about the CDR currently proposed for energy market participants will focus on retail electricity and gas providers.

ii. Reciprocity—An Open Question

The First Farrell Review recommended:

> Entities participating in Open Banking as data recipients should be obliged to comply with a customer's direction to share any data provided to them under Open Banking, plus any data held by them that is transaction data or that is the equivalent of transaction data.[46]

The principle of reciprocity aims to balance obligations between participants (Data Holders and Data Recipients) and maintain a level playing field to promote consumer-centered competition. The First Farrell Review also recommended that the principle of reciprocity not "unduly extend the system's scope by stealth."[47]

Thus, the main obstacle to making reciprocity functional is to determine which data type an ADR might hold that is equivalent to Data Holder–held data (i.e., "banking" data) without overly broadening the CDR scope. As at the time of writing, this question has proved to be complicated. Many personal activities, unrelated to traditional

---

[46] Review into Open Banking, Dec. 2017, Recommendation 3.9, 44.
[47] Review into Open Banking, December 2017, Recommendation 3.9, 44.

banking concepts, create a digital trail that involves a financial exchange of some form. These transactions could come within the class of comparable banking data.

The principle of reciprocity is allowed under the legislation.[48] The ACCC Rules currently contemplate the phased introduction of an obligation on an "accredited non-ADI" (broadly a financial service business that is not a licensed bank but holds CDR Data, such as a payments gateway) to share comparable banking data from early 2021. However, the practical application of reciprocity to non-ADI data recipients remains an open question. (See Chapter 14, by Brad Carr, for a detailed discussion on reciprocity and open data.)

iii. Accredited Entities as Data Holders

ACCC Rules Section 7.2 sets out a final category of Data Holders. Broadly, a bank (being an ADI that is accredited to receive CDR Data) obtains a consumer's consent to collect and use CDR Data from another bank (the second bank being the Data Holder). The bank collecting the CDR Data can ask the consumer to agree to treat the receiving bank as a Data Holder instead of an ADR for that CDR Data. Treating the CDR Data recipient bank as a Data Holder potentially resolves many practical issues as banks look to compete by making it easier for consumers to switch account providers. (See Chapter 6 for a more detailed discussion on data portability.)

For example, a consumer has a deposit account with Bank T and a residential home loan with Bank M. In this case, both Bank T and Bank M are Data Holders of the consumer's banking data. Bank M convinces the consumer to move their transaction account from Bank T. Bank M obtains the consumer's consent to collect CDR Data from Bank T to make switching bank accounts easier.

Bank M is a Data Holder for the residential home loan and an ADR for CDR Data received from Bank T on the deposit account. This split in data sets gives rise to several different obligations. The data collected by Bank M as it processes activities on the residential home loan is subject to the Privacy Principles under the Privacy Act. On the other hand, the deposit account data collected from Bank T (plus data derived from that data, which might include all subsequent transactions and account balances) is subject to the CDR Privacy Safeguards and other ACCC Rules, including the consumer's right to delete.

Bank M can avoid this complication if it can convince the consumer to treat Bank M as a Data Holder across all data sets. However, if Bank M is classified as a Data Holder for all data sets collected, the consumer's right to delete will not apply to Bank M. The right to delete only applies to ADRs and not to Data Holders. This may be a competitive advantage for banks relative to other types of ADRs.

The government's privacy impact assessment (PIA)[49] also raised concerns about potential disadvantages for vulnerable consumers. Such consumers may feel compelled to agree to treat the recipient bank as a Data Holder. The PIA recommended that the ACCC Rules incorporate additional guidelines about how a bank may seek the consumer's agreement similar to the CDR consent principles.

---

[48] Treasury Laws Amendment (Consumer Data Right) Bill 2019; s56AJ(3).
[49] Consumer Data Right Regime: Privacy Impact Assessment Report, Nov. 2019.

b. Accredited Data Recipients

Generally, an Accredited Person is accredited to collect appropriately consented CDR Data and is listed on the Accreditation Register. An Accredited Person can be either an ADR (which may have or not yet received CDR Data) or a Data Holder (e.g., a bank accredited to collect CDR Data from other Data Holders).[50]

Some CDR obligations apply to the broader set of Accredited Persons, while some apply only to the narrower set of ADRs (e.g., the right to delete). A distinction may be necessary when considering practical differences between the role of a bank and other financial service providers (e.g., a fintech) within the CDR regime. It is outside the scope of this chapter to discuss how different obligations apply in different circumstances. Thus, this chapter uses the term ADR loosely to refer to any person who may or has collected appropriated consented CDR Data.

The Data Recipient Accreditor considers applications to become accredited to collect, hold, and use CDR Data. If an application is approved, the registrar adds the ADR to the Accreditation Register. The Accreditation Register is used during the consumer authentication flow to verify Data Holders and ADRs' status. During the initial phase, the ACCC will be the Data Recipient Accreditor, define accreditation rules, and build the Accreditation Register.

There are currently two registration types, Accredited and Active. Depending on the readiness of the ADR solution, initial accreditation receives the accredited title. The title will change to active when a working solution has passed all conformance testing and is ready to go live.

The CDR regime makes allowance for different tiers of accreditation. However, all ADR applicants must satisfy the highest, "unrestricted" accreditation level during the initial phase.

Generally, to achieve unrestricted accreditation, the ADR must demonstrate:

- That they are fit and proper persons to manage CDR Data. A fit and proper person test includes assessing: any conviction for any serious crime or dishonesty offence; whether the applicant is subject to any determination related to an individual's privacy (the Privacy Act only covers individuals, not businesses or other legal entities); and insolvency or bankruptcy;
- That they can protect the CDR Data from misuse, interference, and loss, and unauthorized access, modification, or disclosure. Schedule 2 of the ACCC Rules sets out the minimum information security controls required to meet Privacy Safeguard 12 (PS12, security of CDR Data held by ADR);
- That they have internal dispute resolution processes and are a member of a recognized external dispute resolution scheme for consumer complaints;
- That they have adequate insurance or a comparable guarantee; and
- That they have a local address for service (for foreign participants, this could be an agent).

---

[50] Refer to the previous section for how a bank, receiving CDR Data, may be treated as a Data Holder.

i. Insurance

The ACCC guidance states the purpose of insurance is to "reduce the risk of CDR Consumers not being appropriately compensated by reason of an accredited person's lack of financial resources."[51] The ACCC will not prescribe the insurance products an ADR must obtain, but it considers professional indemnity and cybersecurity insurance. (Chapter 3 explores insurance and other solutions for reducing customer liability risk.)

When assessing the adequacy of any insurance, the Accreditor will consider:

- Nature of the services or products provided to the consumer;
- Nature of the CDR Data likely to be collected and managed;
- Volume of CDR Data collected and held;
- Other financial resources of the ADR (thus a bank that is accredited to collect CDR Data may not need additional insurance because bank capital is well regulated and sufficient); and
- Scope, limit, and any exclusions of the policy (e.g., the policy should not exclude liability for the privacy and data-related claims).[52]

Safeguarding the financial resilience of all participants has benefits for consumers. Confidence in the robustness of the CDR regime ensures banks (as Data Holders) are not left to make consumers whole in the event of a data breach. However, attempting to provide consumers with an implied guarantee has its disadvantages.

In its guidance on adequate insurance, the ACCC states that it is:

> Mindful that the Australian insurance market is dynamic and that both the scope and amount of cover available in the market may change over time. [The ACCC] also acknowledges that Australia's cyber insurance market is relatively new and continuing to develop.[53]

The insured loss will need to include any loss incurred by the consumer who shared data with the ADR.

Insuring against loss by the consumer:

- could be outside the range of typical cybersecurity policies;
- the potential loss a consumer could experience as a result of misuse of their financial data could be disproportionate or unconnected to the nature of the ADR service;
- It could be challenging to trace a data breach (and thereby responsibility for the consumer's resulting financial loss) to a specific CDR participant.

These requirements for adequate insurance coverage or a comparable level of regulatory capital, coupled with the absence of an intermediary function (discussed in Section 4c iii), may limit who can participate during the initial phases of the CDR. In practice, only

---

[51] Consumer Data Right Supplementary accreditation guidelines: insurance, ACCC, May 25, 2020.
[52] Consumer Data Right Supplementary accreditation guidelines: insurance, ACCC, May 25, 2020.
[53] Consumer Data Right Supplementary accreditation guidelines: insurance, ACCC, May 25, 2020.

established businesses or incumbent banks may have sufficient resources. The outcome may be a higher caliber of CDR participants at the cost of higher entry barriers and lower competition or innovation.

ii. Direct Consumer Request

The CDR regime includes the right for a CDR Consumer to request his or her or its CDR Data from the Data Holder. The data must be in human-readable form and conform with the Data Standards. As of the time of writing, the standards for Direct Consumer Request were yet to be finalized.

Most online banking services offer a way for users to download raw data in some form. Providing access to standardized data across banks may have some benefit for consumers. But that benefit may come at an additional development cost for Data Holders. The First Farrell Review recommended that people who cannot usually access internet banking should still have a right to get their data. However, as discussed above, a CDR Consumer must have internet banking access to make a direct request to be eligible. In other words, the ACCC Rules and draft standards do not require a bank to offer a data request service in a branch.

It is also unclear how the ACCC Rules and standards can protect consumers from sharing their data with unaccredited parties. For example, a vulnerable borrower agrees to request and share their data on the promise of a more favorable credit decision from a nonbank lender. In part, the ACCC consultation on non-accredited data recipients (discussed in Section 4c iv) appears to deliver the benefit of direct consumer requests (e.g., the ability to share data with a trusted tax accountant). The Farrell Review recommendation was concerned with the broad-based inclusion of all consumers in the CDR regime. Debates about technical standards and prescriptive rules may have lost sight of this objective.

c. Outsourced Service Providers and Intermediaries

The First Farrell Review emphasized the importance of building trust through "safeguards to protect all participants[']" privacy, security, and accountability.[54] Further, the First Farrell Review recommended:

> A clear and comprehensive framework for the allocation of liability . . . should make it clear that participants [in the CDR] are liable for their own conduct, but not the conduct of other participants. To the extent possible, the liability framework should be consistent with existing legal frameworks.[55]

To this end, the legislation deems a contract to exist between the Data Holder, the ADR making an eligible request to the Data Holder, and, if applicable, a Gateway. The contract requires each party to observe the Data Standards and engage in conduct required by the Data Standards.[56] Thus, contractual liability to protect the CDR Data flows from

---

[54] First Farrell Review, ix.
[55] First Farrell Review, Recommendations 4.9, xvi.
[56] The ACCC Rules are a legislative instrument.

the Data Holder to, if applicable, the Gateway then onwards to the ADR, provided the Data Holder complies with the Data Standards.

i. Gateways

There is no designated Gateway in the banking sector, and this chapter will not go into Gateways in great detail. The draft Designating Instrument for the energy sector would appoint the Australian Energy Market Operator (AEMO) as a Gateway for the energy industry.[57] Generally, the enabling legislation included Gateways following early consultation on the energy sector. Energy providers are subject to a range of state-based laws, which complicates standardized data sharing.

The ACCC noted that the gateway model is the preferred data access model in the energy market because:

- [it] is the most suitable model to enable timely and effective implementation of the CDR for energy consumption data by leveraging AEMO's existing data transfer infrastructure and efficiencies in liaising with the ACCC Register of accredited data recipients;
- leverages AEMO's energy data and IT expertise, and its ability to facilitate industry readiness for and compliance with initiatives involving substantial IT components;
- [AEMO] is considered to most comprehensively address the assessment criteria. [58]

The AEMO is also a Data Holder for some data, for example, metering data.

ii. Outsourced Service Providers

The ACCC Rules defines an outsourced service provider. An accredited person (ADR or Data Holder) can disclose CDR Data to an outsourced service provider under a written CDR outsourcing arrangement.[59]

An outsourced service provider could include:

- data centers and backup providers;
- SaaS (software as a service) providers;
- PaaS (platform as a service) providers;
- cloud-based service providers, such as data storage.[60]

To protect the CDR Data, an outsourced service provider must meet the minimum information security controls set out in the ACCC Rules (Schedule 2). Otherwise, the outsourced service provider must comply with the terms of the contract with the accredited person. It is not required, for example, to join an external dispute resolution scheme.[61] Outsourced service providers are not recorded in the CDR Accreditation

---

[57] Consumer Data Right (Energy Sector) Designation 2020, s6(4); May 6, 2020.
[58] Consumer Data Right in Energy, Position paper: data access model for energy data, ACCC, Aug. 2019.
[59] ACCC Rules, Feb. 2020, s1.10.
[60] Consumer Data Right Supplementary accreditation guidelines: information security, ACCC, Sept. 23, 19.
[61] A bank is subject to regulations issued by APRA (the banking regulator), including regulations related to outsourcing arrangements.

Register. In practice, this means the fundamental limitation of outsourced service providers is that they cannot collect CDR Data on behalf of the ADR.

iii. Intermediaries

Notwithstanding the Farrell Review's recommendation,[62] the ACCC excluded intermediaries in the first phase of the CDR. The ACCC noted that the exclusion was the "position for the first version of the rules having regard to concerns raised by stakeholders regarding the risk of reduced consumer protections and the potential to undermine the CDR accreditation regime."[63]

In December 2019, the ACCC released a consultation paper on facilitating the participation of intermediaries. Generally, the fintech community argues that an intermediary will be essential for innovation and lower entry barriers for startups and new entrants. For example, an intermediary could maintain the highest level of data security, controls, and compliance procedures. Simultaneously, the startup using the intermediary could meet some lower tier of accreditation, depending on the CDR Data being used by the startup ADR.

Generally, few of the submissions to the ACCC consultation expressed any opposition to the inclusion of intermediaries. A consistent requirement was for intermediaries to be accredited, bringing it within the ambit of the CDR rules, standards, and privacy safeguards. Some submissions raised concerns about how accredited intermediaries (with all the relevant CDR obligations, including insurance, for example) and outsourced service providers (with the more limited contract-based liabilities) could both operate within the CDR framework.

Since that initial consultation, the ACCC has issued draft rules for the inclusion of an accredited collecting third-party (as discussed above, the main limitation of an outsourced service provider is that they are precluded from collecting CDR Data).[64] The proposed rules introduce the concept of a Combined Accredited Person (CAP) arrangement.

A CAP is an arrangement between a consumer-facing ADR (the Principal) and another accredited person (the Provider or data intermediary). The CAP arrangement appears to be modeled on the card payment network. Data aggregators are not contemplated in the CDR, but they could fit under this designation.

The draft rules require both the Principal and Provider to meet the unrestricted accreditation level and that the Principal is always liable to the consumer. At the time of writing, it is unclear how these draft rules will enable the economies of scale and lowered barriers to entry that could be achieved through data intermediation.

In subsequent releases of the proposed rules framework, several new levels of intermediary have been introduced. These range from a globally recognized Sponsor/Affiliate model that resembles the UK agency model to an amended "Insights Sharing" model that will allow non-accredited participants to receive insights/derived data from an ADR. Both of these models attempt to reduce the perceived risk and liability models

---

[62] First Farrell Review, Recommendation 5.8.

[63] Consultation on how best to facilitate participation of third-party service providers, ACCC, Dec. 2019.

[64] CDR Rules Consultation Draft Rules that allow for accredited collecting third-parties ("intermediaries"), ACCC, June 22, 2020.

while enabling customer choice. As the rules framework continues to evolve, the final appointment of these models remains unclear.

iv. Non-accredited Third-Parties

The ACCC consultation[65] also considered allowing the disclosure, with consumer consent, of CDR Data to non-accredited third-parties, such as personal tax accountants and lawyers.

Industry responses to this question were mixed but included the following points:

- When implemented, different accreditation tiers allowed under the CDR regime would enable other businesses and service providers to share and receive appropriately consented data. These lower levels of accreditation might be suitable for professional service providers, such as accountants and other trusted advisers;
- It is unclear how non-accredited third-parties would sit within the complaints and liability framework (e.g., the requirement for adequate insurance) and the consumer's right to delete; and
- The CDR regime includes a consumer's right to directly request from the Data Holder a human-readable version of the CDR Data (direct consumer requests discussed above). The consumer could then share the data with professional service providers, such as accountants.

5. CDR Data

Broadly, the types of banking data and products captured by the Australian CDR are similar to other open banking regimes. Participants often focus on CDR Data's specifics, but they need to be equally aware of what is not CDR Data and when CDR Data becomes non-CDR data. In practice, during the initial phases, an ADR might hold a combination of CDR Data and non-CDR data to deliver its services. CDR Data is subject to obligations, such as the consumer's right to deletion, where no similar obligation exists for non-CDR data. By mingling CDR and non-CDR data, a participant may impose obligations on parts of their business not usually captured by the CDR regulations. Further, it may be possible for data to switch from being CDR Data to being non-CDR data, giving rise to temporal complexities.

The Privacy Act generally distinguishes between the actions of collecting, holding (or handling), using (or dealing with), correcting, and disclosing data with various restrictions, rights, and obligations attaching to each activity. These actions may be further distinguished by whether the data is subject to consent or is unsolicited data. The CDR regime adds requesting data, resulting in data collection if the request is valid. For simplicity, this chapter will loosely refer to holding or using data as covering all data-related activities unless a distinction is necessary.

Defining CDR Data requires reference to three different sources:

---

[65] Consumer Data Right Consultation on how best to facilitate participation of third-party service providers, ACCC, Dec. 2019.

1. the definition in the enabling legislation;
2. the included data sets and any exclusions in the relevant Designating Instrument; and
3. the included data sets, any exclusions, and any phased implementation in the ACCC Rules.

The enabling legislation defines CDR Data as the class of information in the Designating Instrument or information wholly or partly derived from such information.[66] Broadly, an ADR might collect some CDR Data (following all the relevant consent and authorization protocols) and combine that with other data collected and held by the ADR. Subject to exclusions in the Designating Instrument and the ACCC Rules, a data set that combines CDR and non-CDR data becomes wholly CDR Data.

a. Banking Sector

The Designating Instrument for banking casts a broad scope for the sets of information included as CDR Data. It covers:

1. Goods or services offered to take money on deposit,
2. Make advances of money (loans),
3. Other banking-related financial activities, and
4. Purchase payment facilities.[67]

The Designating Instrument for banking makes two critical exclusions from CDR Data:

1. Certain credit information (as defined in the Privacy Act).[68]
2. Materially enhanced information.[69]

Materially enhanced information is an insight or analysis derived from CDR Data that is significantly more valuable than the source CDR Data. At the time of writing, there are no guidelines on what will meet the test of material enhancement. However, the ACCC Rules specify that a calculated account balance is not materially enhanced information. The CDR regime can share materially enhanced information by giving the Data Holder the right to charge for the insight or analysis.

Generally, the ACCC Rules divides CDR Data into the following (the Data Standards use a slightly different grouping):

- *Product Data* (some is required and some voluntary as at the time of writing). Product Data is general information, typically publicly available, about products and services offered by a bank. It includes product fees, interest rates, and features,

---

[66] Treasury Laws Amendment (Consumer Data Right) Bill 2019; s56AI.
[67] Consumer Data Right (Authorised Deposit-Taking Institutions) Designation 2019, s4(2).
[68] Consumer Data Right (Authorised Deposit-Taking Institutions) Designation 2019, s9.
[69] Consumer Data Right (Authorised Deposit-Taking Institutions) Designation 2019, s10.

for example. It is not specific to any consumer, no consumer consent is required to collect the data, and the data recipient does not need to be accredited.

- *Consumer Data* is data about a specific consumer's banking product or service and how they use that product or service. Other than the consumer (consumer requests are discussed above), only an ADR can request Consumer Data following the relevant consent and authorization protocols.

Consumer Data is further divided into:

- *Data about the consumer* (e.g., information about the consumer's identity or their associate; refer to joint accounts in Section 5c); the consumer's eligibility to use a product and contact details of the consumer or their associate.
- *Data about the consumer's account*, such as an account number balance and transactions.
- *Data about the features of the financial product* held by a consumer. For example, the applicable interest rate or fees may differ from the bank's generic product interest rates or fees.

The ACCC Rules and Data Standards include direct debit, payee, and scheduled payments information in account data. However, the Australian payments system is unique in that banks do not maintain data about customers' automatic debit payments. It is the retailer or merchant collecting the payment by debiting the consumer's account that keeps these records.

Consumers can build an address book of regular payees and a schedule of bill payments in most internet banking services. However, the consumer's direct debit authority to a retailer is a dominant bill payment mechanism for many Australians. Consumers often cite the arduous task of changing direct debit authorities with multiple retailers as the impediment to switching banks. The current CDR framework does not appear to offer an immediate solution to this friction.

The ACCC Rules sets up a phased introduction for sharing Consumer Data. As of the time of writing, Phase 1 (starting July 2020) includes primary banking products such as savings and transaction accounts, term deposits, and credit cards. Phase 2 is expected to start at the end of 2020 and includes more loan accounts, such as residential home loans. Data sharing for Phase 3 products are expected to start in early 2021 for the Big 4 banks and from mid-2021 for other Data Holders. Phase 3 products include business finance, overdrafts and lines of credit, leases, and other unique savings and transaction accounts.[70]

b. Retail Energy Sector

As of the time of writing, the proposed energy data set that may be subject to the CDR include:[71]

---

[70] Competition and Consumer (Consumer Data Right) Rules 2020, ACCC, Feb. 2020.
[71] Priority Energy Datasets Consultation, Aug. 29, 2019, Treasury; Decision Proposal 103—Electricity End Point URIs, Data Standards Body Technical Working Group, Feb. 28, 2020.

1. National Metering Identifier (NMI) standing data—this includes average daily load and metering installation type, which can help consumers manage their energy usage;
2. Consumer-provided data—for example, address and account holder name;
3. Metering Data—collected or estimated by the energy provider; and
4. Historical billing information—past billing statements.

Like the banking datasets, energy providers may also be required to share generic (non-consumer-specific) product data such as retail tariff rates and usage charges.

c. Joint Accounts

Joint accounts are the subject of an ongoing discussion between the Data Standards Body, the ACCC, and the industry.

These discussions highlight the trade-offs in designing an open data-sharing regime, including:

- explicit and informed consent of all parties associated with the account;
- convenient ease of use for consumers given their real-time, digital, mobile, and always available service expectations;
- offering solutions that work across the spectrum of potential consumers and not just digital and mobile natives or early adopters; and
- protection of vulnerable people, including those experiencing domestic violence (who may need additional protection against sharing identifying information), the elderly, and those needing support with services delivered electronically.

In Australia, joint banking accounts can take many forms depending on legal ownership, beneficial ownership, guarantors (in the case of loans), and authority to operate an account. For example, small businesses can operate under various legal structures. Different structures can result in various legal ownership of business assets, including bank accounts and managing finances. Residential home loans also have a few different legal structures that can change the nature of each borrower's financial obligation (typically spouses) and possibly guarantors.

In the initial stages, the CDR, as it applies to financial services and does not capture all joint accounts, and it is not practical to discuss how the ACCC Rules might apply in various cases. This section discusses the example of a bank account owned and operated by two adults for their benefit.[72]

As noted by the Data Standard Body, accounts are separate from consent.[73] At an account level, each account holder may have the authority to operate the account individually (known as "1-to-authorise"). Alternatively, an account may require both account

---

[72] Competition and Consumer (Consumer Data Right) Rules 2020, ACCC, Feb. 2020, Schedule 3 definition.
[73] Consultation Draft 5 Joint Account Election and Authorisation, Mar. 26, 2020, Data Standards Body Customer Experience Workstream.

holders to authorize activity (known as "2-to-authorise"). Banks may offer various dual operating authorities, for example, by allowing different types of authority depending on the type or amount of a transaction.

Suppose the CDR consent mirrors account-level operating authority then, in the case of "1-to-authorise." In that case, one account holder could consent to share information about the other account holder's identity (their associate). Sharing data without explicit consent contradicts the CDR regime's privacy-preserving objectives and may undermine trust in open data-sharing, particularly for vulnerable people.

As at the time of writing, the default data sharing status of a joint account (to the extent the CDR captures these accounts) is "2-to-authorise." Broadly, as a consumer moves through the authorization and consent flow, they will be presented with a list of accounts available for data sharing. Any joint accounts with "2-to-authorise" will be unavailable for data sharing and will not appear on the list. Data Holders are not permitted to show "unavailable" accounts or provide instructions for accessing those accounts.

As at the time of writing, the Data Standards Body is consulting on two alternative consent flows:

1. *Notification.* During the consent flow, the consumer is presented with a list of "unavailable" ("2-to-authorise") joint accounts. To change the account's data sharing status to "1-to-authorise," the consumer must contact their bank (the Data Holder) outside the CDR consent flow. Altering the data-sharing status requires agreement from the other account holder. Once the data-sharing status is switched from "2-to-authorise" to "1-to-authorise," the consumer restarts the consent and authorization process with the ADR.

2. *Election.* Similar to above, the consumer is presented with a list of "unavailable" joint accounts. Within the CDR consent flow, the consumer is given an election to update a joint account's data-sharing status. The request to switch the data-sharing status requires agreement from the other account holder.

Generally, Data Holders tend to prefer notification because it is easier to administer. An ADR may not prefer notification as it pushes consumers outside the consent workflow, creating another hurdle to onboarding a customer to the ADR's service. The alternative in-flow election process seems to solve the ADR's customer experience preferences. It introduces the dilemma of promptly getting the other account holder's consent to switch data-sharing status during the ADRs digital onboarding process.

The treatment of joint accounts is contentious for banks and energy providers. Retail energy providers note that joint account holders have different functions in their industry.[74] Energy account holders include:

- primary account holders;
- additional account holders with financial responsibility (e.g., a group of students renting a shared house);

[74] EnergyAustralia submission: Data Standards Body Technical Working Group—CX Consultation Draft 5: Joint Accounts #106.

- people with full authority on the account but who are not financially responsible (e.g., a carer or support person); and
- people with limited account authority and no financial obligation. For example, this person may register an energy account as life support critical due to medical machines used by an elderly family member living in a separate household.

d. Credit Information

Reducing information asymmetry between borrowers and lenders, refining creditworthiness forecasts, and meeting responsible lending obligations are primary use-cases for open sharing of banking data in Australia. Existing substantial restrictions on collecting and disclosing credit information set out in the Privacy Act aim to maintain fair access to credit for all consumers.[75] As a mechanism to freely share data, the CDR regime cannot mirror the same restrictions and relies on informed consent. Exclusions and overlaps between the two data-sharing schemes could result in some unintended consequences.

From June 2018, Australian banks started sharing and using comprehensive, or positive, credit information. Comprehensive credit information adds data about the type of account (e.g., a credit card or personal loan), the date the account was opened and closed, the credit limit, and the more contentious repayment history (has the borrower meet loan repayments on schedule).

The Designating Instrument for banks excludes certain credit information from CDR Data, such as:

- an inquiry (typically by a bank looking to offer a loan) about a consumer's credit arrangements with other lenders (the volume and frequency of such credit checks can be valuable predictive indicators of creditworthiness);
- insolvency and any court proceedings;
- the lender's opinion that the borrower has committed a serious credit infringement (broadly, a severe credit infringement is an interim step before a loan is in default; the lender's opinion could be materially enhanced information); and
- information about a variation to the loan terms and conditions as a result of a serious credit infringement. For example, a borrower experiencing temporary hardship might negotiate lower loan repayments rather than defaulting on the loan altogether.[76]

Similar exclusions for other industries, such as energy providers, were not available at the time of writing.

Potential overlaps between credit information collected via the CDR and the Privacy Act include:

---

[75] Privacy Act 1988 (Cth), Part IIIA.
[76] Privacy Act s6N(d),(i),(j) and (l) and s6S(2).

- information about the type of loan account and credit limit (consumer credit liability information);
- repayment history; and
- default information and any new loan arrangements as a result of a default.

Further, collecting bank transaction data via the CDR and using that CDR Data to assess creditworthiness might be sufficient to trigger the substantial Privacy Act restrictions on dealing with and disclosing credit information.

Generally, there are two arguments why credit information under the Privacy Act and CDR Data (to the extent it may be used to assess creditworthiness) can continue to coexist. The first is consent, and the second relates to data quality. The implied consent to share a borrower's credit information allowed under the Privacy Act is bundled into the loan terms and conditions and is evergreen. Suppose a bank discloses credit information to a regulated credit bureau, then under industry arrangements. In that case, the bank can request credit information about a consumer from the credit bureau without seeking the consumer's explicit consent for each request.

In contrast, CDR consent must be specific, unbundled, comprehensive, and current (CDR consent can expire). There is an ongoing debate about the effectiveness of informed CDR consent for vulnerable borrowers urgently looking to access essential credit. The primary argument for the efficacy of credit information obtained via traditional credit bureau arrangements allowed under the Privacy Act is its variety and veracity. Generally, all banks (as loan providers) must share credit information with a credit bureau, and the data is highly structured. This means the data covers broad segments of the Australian adult population (wide variety), and it has high veracity. Over time, the CDR Data standards should improve CDR Data veracity. The variety of CDR Data (the ability to represent Australian populations) may improve as more consumers consent to open data-sharing.

Thus, based on current credit scoring models, the critical distinction between the two data regimes is likely to turn on the exclusion of credit inquiries and changes to loan terms and conditions due to serious credit infringements. However, new lenders have begun to demonstrate the value of other data, such as recent spending activity, in assessing creditworthiness.

6. Consent, Consumer Experience, and Privacy

a. Consent

Clear, explicit, and informed consent is the cornerstone of the CDR. Consumer experience guidelines must balance precise control and simplicity to build confidence and trust in the system. The standards will invariably involve compromise. This section aims to highlight some of the compromises without outlining the end-to-end consent flow.

The Data Standard Body Consumer Experience (CX) working group has developed standards and guidelines for both ADR and Data Holders to implement a consumer interface that conforms to regulatory obligations. The CX Guidelines and Standards were developed following consumer research, industry consultation, and collaboration with various government agencies. The CX standards are mandatory, while the guidelines contain recommended CX flows and example wireframes.

Consent has five stages:

1. *Pre-Consent*: the CDR Consumer sees the ADR's product value proposition and learns about the CDR.
2. *Consent*: the CDR Consumer is presented with a list of Data Holders and CDR Data that may be shared with the ADR.
3. *Authentication*: the CDR Consumer is redirected to the Data Holder for authentication.
4. *Authorization*: the CDR Consumer selects the CDR Data to share and authorizes the Data Holder to share it with the ADR.
5. *Post-consent flow*: the CDR Consumer returns to ADR's space.

Both the ADR and Data Holder must offer, via the internet, a consent Dashboard to the CDR Consumer. The Dashboard must include information about the type of CDR Data, the duration of collecting or disclosing CDR Data, and the CDR Consumer's ability to manage and withdraw consent.

The guidelines recommend that the dashboards show all the consumer's data-sharing arrangements. However, as at the time of writing, there is no consent API in the data standards. Thus, there is no central point for the consumer to access all data-sharing consents. Each ADR and Data Holder can only show the consumer consents within their domain. Over time, as consumers add services, this could result in consumers having multiple dashboards.

At the time of writing, the information security standards specified only a single consent at one time. However, as noted by the Data Standards Body, single consent can result in cumbersome outcomes for consumers.[77] For example, a consumer might sign up for the basic service of the ADR. After using the ADR service, the consumer is convinced about its value proposition and decides to sign up for additional services. With single consent, the consumer would have to reauthorize all the services it wants to use. Conversely, single consent makes modification of existing consent clear and sets precise times when data become redundant (essential criteria in the consumer's right to delete, as discussed in Section 6d). The Data Standards Body is working to amend the standard to include concurrent consent.

b. Privacy Safeguards

The Privacy Act deals with information privacy rights and how businesses and agencies must handle personal information. The Privacy Act sets out thirteen Australian Privacy Principles (APP), generally:

---

[77] Data Standards Body Technical Working Group Decision 085—Concurrent Consents, Oct. 2019.

- general privacy principles (APPs 1 and 2);
- collecting data (APPs 3, 4, and 5);
- dealing with data (APPs 6, 7, 8, and 9);
- the integrity of data (APPs 10 and 11); and
- access to and correction of data (APPs 12 and 13).

The CDR Australian Privacy Safeguards (APS) generally mirror the APP. However, there are differences between the two privacy regimes.

The APP covers personal information about an individual. The APPs do not apply to data about a business (other than a sole trader) or other legal entities. Personal information may have a narrower scope than CDR Data. Personal information under the Privacy Act may exclude metadata, de-identified data, or, in some circumstances, derived data.

It is not practical to cover all aspects of the APS in this chapter. Generally, concerning CDR Data, an ADR must:

- comply with the Privacy Safeguards (APS); and
- does not need to comply with Privacy Principles (APP) concerning the CDR Data or any other personal information (non-CDR data) it holds about the consumer.

The obligations of Data Holders are more complicated. Generally, a Data Holder must comply with the APP when dealing with any personal information.

For CDR Data, the Data Holder must comply with:

- PS 11(1)—disclosure of CDR Data (quality of data), the related APP 10 will not apply;[78]
- PS 13—relating to the correction of CDR Data, the related APP 13 will not apply;[79] and
- PS 1—open and transparent management of CDR Data.

Outsourced service providers are not required to comply with the APS. Suppose the outsourced service provider is an APP entity under the Privacy Act. In that case, they must comply with the APPs regarding CDR Data, which is also personal information.[80]

The regulatory complexity and inconsistency of frameworks make it challenging to understand how the CDR will operate in practice. The approach of the Office of the Australian Information Commissioner (OAIC) and the ACCC to handling complaints under the CDR regime remains to be tested. Further, the treatment of personal information about other parties (e.g., the name of a person receiving money from a CDR consumer may appear in the transaction description on the CDR Consumer's bank account) disclosed due to the appropriately consented CDR Data is unclear.

It seems likely that Data Holders and ADRs will need to track what is and is not CDR, what is or is not personal information about a CDR consumer, and any overlaps between those data sets (which might give rise to different sets of obligations). A data set

---

[78] Competition and Consumer Act (Cth), s56EC(4)(a).
[79] Competition and Consumer Act (Cth), s56EC(4)(b).
[80] PIA, 53.

could change character over time (e.g., CDR Data that is subsequently de-identified) or as a result of some activity, such as mingling with other data (derived CDR Data, for example). This complexity suggests ADRs may, during the initial phases, find it challenging to offer sophisticated new services that involve multiple data sets.

c. Data Minimization Principle

Under the CDR legislation, Privacy Safeguard 3 (PS3) restricts an ADR from collecting CDR Data unless it responds to a "valid request" from the consumer.[81] A valid request must comply with the ACCC Rules and Data Standards, including consent. Under the ACCC Rules, the ADR must have regard to the data minimization principle.

Under the data minimization principle, when making a consumer data request on behalf of a consumer, the ADR must not seek to collect:

- more CDR Data than is reasonably needed, or
- CDR Data that relates to a longer date range than is reasonably necessary to provide the requested services.

The ADR must consider the data minimization principle when seeking the consumer's consent (PS3 includes attempting to collect data) and when ADR sends a data request to a Data Holder. The ADR's ability to meet this obligation in some part depends on the Data Standards and consent flows.

For example, transaction data APIs return both debit and credit transactions within the requested date range. Suppose the ADR's service only requires CDR Data sufficient to validate a consumer's income (by analyzing credit transactions on the consumer's account, for example). In that case, the current APIs will return more data (debit transactions) than reasonably needed.

Receiving unnecessary data triggers Privacy Safeguard 4 (PS4).[82] PS4 requires an ADR to destroy unsolicited CDR Data collected from a Data Holder. Privacy Safeguard 12 (PS12) addresses the security and destruction or de-identification of redundant CDR Data. Generally, where an ADR can meet the de-identification standards as per the Office of the Australian Information Commissioner[83], it appears the ADR may be able to retain de-identified data. Thus, following the example outlined above, it seems possible the ADR will need to delete the unsolicited debit transactions but may be able to retain de-identified credit transactions.

Whether the data request, which returned more data than necessary but conformed with the Data Standards, breaches the data minimization principle in the first instance will depend on the CDR regulator's compliance policies. This example demonstrates the potential practical complexity from overlaps between different legislation, the ACCC Rules and the Data Standards.

---

[81] CDR Privacy Safeguard Guidelines, Chapter 3, Office of the Australian Information Commissioner, Feb. 24, 2020.
[82] CDR Privacy Safeguard Guidelines, Chapter 3, Office of the Australian Information Commissioner, Feb. 24, 2020, 10.
[83] https://www.oaic.gov.au/privacy/guidance-and-advice/de-identification-decision-making-framework/

d. Right to Delete

The First Farrell Review stated:

> Given the many complexities involved in legislating for a right to deletion (including the range of legal obligations to retain records) and the fact that individuals currently have no right to instruct deletion of their personal information under the Privacy Act, it is beyond the scope of [the Review] to mandate a special right to deletion of information.[84]

Following this recommendation, the draft enabling legislation did not include a right to deletion.

However, when passing the legislation, the Senate made the following comment:

> The ACCC's recent digital platforms inquiry [unrelated to the CDR] supported a range of improvements to privacy protections. Amongst other things, it recommended giving consumers a "right to delete" across the economy—that is, allowing consumers to require data holders to erase their personal information.[85]

The government subsequently amended the law such that the ACCC Rules must include a requirement that an ADR deletes CDR Data in response to a valid request from a consumer (unless retention is required by law).[86] This obligation falls only on an ADR and is another reason why a bank that collects CDR Data will tend to ask the consumer to agree to treat the bank as a Data Holder for all data sets instead of an ADR for the collected CDR Data (refer to the Data Holder Section 4a).

The right to deletion means an ADR must distinguish when the consumer's CDR Data becomes redundant (generally when consent expires) and any CDR Data derived from the consumer's data. Retaining such distinctions appears straight forward, but the technical implementation of consent (discussed above), for example, could make it difficult for ADRs to draw bright, hard lines between different data sets.

As previously discussed, CDR Data includes the raw data the ADR collects from the Data Holder and any data derived from that raw data. An example of derived CDR Data might be a creditworthiness score calculated using a combination of the consumer's bank transaction data and other data held by the ADR.

Generally, if an ADR can adequately de-identify CDR Data and derived CDR Data, it may be possible to retain the de-identified data. If the ADR cannot meet the de-identification standard, then it must:

- delete the CDR Data and any copies;
- delete the derived CDR Data and any copies;
- direct any other person to which it has disclosed CDR Data to delete CDR Data;
- make a record to evidence the above steps; and
- notify the consumer who requested the deletion.[87]

---

[84] First Farrell Review, Recommendation 4.3.
[85] Treasury Laws Amendment (Consumer Data Right) Bill 2019, Second Reading Senator McAllister.
[86] Competition and Consumer Act 2010 (Cth), s56BA.
[87] ACCC Rules Feb. 4, 2020, s1.18.

The ACCC Rules incorporate the De-Identification Decision-Making Framework published by the Office of the Information Commissioner and Data61. That framework is a practical guide for data custodians to understand and operationalize de-identification. However, the ACCC Rules sets a broad scope for testing de-identification.

The ADR must have regard for the likelihood of any person becoming re-identified.[88] The reference to "any person" appears broader than just the CDR consumer who is the CDR Data subject. Further, the potential for re-identification must consider both the CDR Data and other information held by any person. The reference to "other information" appears to include any other data the ADR might legitimately collect or be able to access, for example, social media posts.

As outlined in the PIA,[89] CDR Data can include personal information about third-parties. For example, when a consumer transfers money to another person, the name and banking details of that person will likely appear in the consumer's bank transaction data. The CDR regime "represents a balancing of interests, between the privacy rights of the third-party individual against the utility for CDR Consumers to access and use their information, and the benefits of encouraging competition and innovation."[90]

In contrast, the de-identification standards appear to stretch to include de-identifying the third-party.

Strong privacy-by-design principles are essential for building trust in open data sharing. The counterbalance is creating a vibrant marketplace of new consumer services to be tested and flourish.

The economics of new business models may rest on retaining a deep set of de-identified data. Building a viable data set may be complicated under the current setting of the ACCC Rules' right to delete. Further, there is an inherent bias toward a bank that gets consumer agreement to be treated as a Data Holder instead of an ADR for any CDR Data the bank collects.

7. Future Considerations

In January 2020, the government announced an inquiry into future directions for the CDR. Among critical concepts, this inquiry focused on the second stage of the Open Banking framework development: Action Initiation. Mr. Scott Farrell also led this second and is slated to continue to chair subsequent reviews and inquiries. In March 2020, the second inquiry (the Second Farrell Review) of the same name released an issues paper[91] and sought comments on future possible use cases for the CDR, what future outcomes could the CDR regime help, and what is needed for this to happen and the following topics:

---

[88] ACCC Rules Feb. 4, 2020, s1.17(2)(d).
[89] Privacy Impact Assessment, Nov. 19, 2019.
[90] Privacy Impact Assessment, Nov. 19, 2019, Recommendation 7, 11.
[91] Inquiry into Future Directions for the Consumer Data Right—Issues Paper (Mar. 6–May 21, 2020). https://treasury.gov.au/consultation/c2020-62639.

- how the CDR can leverage international developments;
- switching; how the CDR could be used to overcome behavioral and regulatory barriers to safe, convenient, and efficient switching between products and providers;
- write access; the ability to initiate funds transfers;
- interoperability; potential benefits of linking other data portability regimes and accreditation frameworks;
- leveraging the CDR Infrastructure; and
- ethical, fair, and inclusive development of the CDR.[92]

Some of these topics are interconnected. For example, some industry commentators have argued that the switching will be more convenient if the consumer's chosen new bank can initiate funds transfers from the previous bank. However, as discussed above, switching bank accounts is also hampered by how the Australia payments system records direct debit arrangements.

Interoperability and leveraging international developments may be directed at the perceived divergence between the Australian Data Standards and international standards. Finally, a focus on ethical, fair, and inclusive future development may highlight ongoing community concerns about privacy and ethical or unbiased algorithms in decisions. One stark omission from both the first and second Farrell Review is a consideration of digital identity.

The authors argue that it seems premature to be conducting an inquiry into future considerations when the CDR's substantive functions are not yet operational. Scott Farrell has justified this exercise by explaining that creating future roadmaps for large-scale infrastructure or technology projects within the private sector before completing the initial stage is standard practice. He asks why this practice shouldn't be adopted by the public sector as well.

At the time of writing, there were no widespread consumer-directed use cases in the market for Open Banking. Conversely, one lesson learned during the early phases of the CDR, echoing Scott Farrell's sentiments, is that future planning is vital. The rollout of such a significant transformation must be phased. But participants and regulators need a shared understanding of the future direction of such a vital and innovative data-sharing framework.

8. Action Initiation

Mentioned at the beginning of the chapter, the future introduction of Action Initiation is considered a turning point for the expansion and catalog of use cases for the CDR. In the Final Report for the Inquiry into Future Directions for the Consumer Data Right,[93]

---

[92] *Id.*
[93] The Australian Government the Treasury, Inquiry into Future Directions for the Consumer Data Right—Final Report (Dec. 23, 2020, the Second Farrell Review). https://treasury.gov.au/publication/inquiry-future-directions-consumer-data-right-final-report.

led again by Scott Farrell (the Second Farrell Review), the definition of Action Initiation is given as:

> A third party with write access to a data holder sending instructions to the data holder. Instructions may include initiating payments from a customer's account, and actions, such as switching, opening or closing an account, or updating details.[94]

The report goes on the identify a series of elements that are required to complete an economy-wide system before the introduction of Action Initiation:

1. A secure communication channel is necessary for ensuring the integrity of any information sent or received;
2. A common set of standards is required to enable action initiation requests to be interpreted correctly by a service provider, allowing an interoperable and competitive system to develop;
3. An accreditation system is necessary to provide those receiving instructions with confidence about the legitimacy of the request's initiator and to ensure adequate protection for consumers;
4. Processes for enabling consumers to provide direction and authorization are needed to operate for the consumers' benefit; and
5. A transparent governance and liability framework would ensure, to the extent possible, that risks are appropriately assigned between participants in the system.

Not just focusing on data portability through Open Banking, the infrastructure created under the Consumer Data Right arrangements also provide the underlying elements needed to turn on Action Initiation.

These include:

- a secure process for sending encrypted data requests and information between participants;
- a process for standardizing the format of data requests and responses;
- an accreditation regime to regulate those who can send instructions to receive data;
- the foundational requirement for consumer consent and authorization for data sharing to occur; and
- a clear set of legislative boundaries as to what is and is not permissible, including security and privacy protections.

It would be preferential to extended existing digital CDR infrastructure rather than to create an entirely new system down the road. But this can only work by leveraging the consumer trust in any preexisting scheme. And for that to happen, the initial phase of Open Banking must be complete and launched successfully in the eyes of the consumer and participants alike.

---

[94] *Id.*

While additional risks may exist with the introduction of Action Initiation, there must be a balance between the customer's benefit and the accredited participants' obligations. The Second Farrell Review highlighted the need for existing processes to confirm the accuracy and correctness of customer's details before an instruction being carried out.

Given the sensitivity in updating personal information, Data Holders should take reasonable measures to mitigate perceived risks before acting on instructions and requests. Two examples, the updating passwords or mobile phone numbers, have been highlighted as posing significant risk and should not be updated, even with the consumer's consent:

> The expansion to write access may also raise new privacy and security implications, which will need to be appropriately addressed. In particular, as write access would allow third parties to modify a consumer's financial information, it may increase the motivation for unauthorised actors to target an accredited data recipient's information system. – OAIC[95]

a. Consent to Initiate Actions for Specific Purposes

As with data sharing ("Read Access") through the CDR, Action Initiation must also be enabled via a consumer consent model with accredited parties receiving consumer's active, informed consent to initiate on their behalf. The consent must include specific actions to be defined and their explicit agreements regarding the purposes for which these actions may be initiated. Action Initiation consents should be voluntary, express, informed, purpose-specific, time-limited, and quickly withdrawn.

The CDR will require both access consent and user consent for a consumer to engage an accredited party. The separation of these consents will grant consumers greater control over how the accredited party may act by adding additional usage consents if needed and the ability to revoke specific usage consents without terminating the entire arrangement. Aligned to the consent process for data sharing through the CDR, Action Initiation's consent process should be subject to the Data Standards Body's Consumer Experience Standards and Guidelines to ensure genuine consent is produced conveniently.

Consumers should provide enduring access and usage consents, allowing for Action Initiation to occur on their behalf for consent duration. It is considered that ongoing consent for Action Initiation may pose significantly more risk than the ongoing consent for data-sharing arrangement depending on the action's nature. In maintaining the current limitations of consent and authorization durations, Action Initiation should include the maximum twelve-month duration for consents and authorizations and the ninety-day notification requirement.

---

[95] Extract from The Office of the Australian Information Commissioner submission to The Australian Government the Treasury, Inquiry into Future Directions for the Consumer Data Right—Final Report (Dec. 23, 2020), 47.

The CDR was not designed to fulfill all legal requirements of entering a contract to provide consumer services. Ensuring this compliance is the accredited party's duty that is seeking to offer services to the consumer. The ability to enter into a contract with a third-party to act on their behalf already exists (i.e., an investment manager may buy or sell shares for a consumer with their ongoing participation in the process).

It may be possible for a consumer to enter into a contract with an accredited party outside of the CDR parameters to initiate a request within the regime then. For example, Katie agrees to Marketplace XYZ acting as her agent to enter into a new internet service provider (ISP) contract. This occurs outside the CDR. Katie then allows Marketplace XYZ to lodge product applications on her behalf through the CDR. She allows them to communicate as part of those applications that they are legally binding offers to enter into a service contract on her behalf. This occurs through the formal CDR channels. The prospective ISP may voluntarily choose to accept that assertion that Marketplace XYZ can enter into contracts on Katie's behalf. The CDR should support various products and services, such as more streamlined or automated switching, working together with existing legal frameworks.

9. Conclusion

In the three years that Open Banking and the CDR have been under consideration, development, and implementation, the following points have become apparent.

- The Australian CDR has the potential to become a world-leading, economic-wide, data-sharing and portability instrument.
- Starting with a single sector—banking—it has enabled the industry and the Federal Regulator to focus on and resolve some key challenges. Further, the data-sharing and action initiation phases can be introduced independently of each other, without contradicting existing regulation/legislative requirements.
- The CDR was intended to act as a digital power of attorney, allowing the customer to choose with whom they share their data.

The Australian government's recent decision to shift responsibility for developing and implementing the rules framework, technical standards, and data standards from the ACCC to another government department (the Treasury) has delayed the finalization and subsequent adoption of Open Banking in Australia. In conclusion, until the CDR rules framework is finalized, Open Banking's delivery is in limbo, and the vision of increasing innovation and competition remains in doubt.

11

India's Approach to Open Banking: Some Implications for Financial Inclusion

*Yan Carrière-Swallow, Vikram Haksar, and Manasa Patnam**

International Monetary Fund

1. Introduction

Over the past ten years, India has seen an ambitious overhaul of its digital infrastructure through the development of the so-called "India Stack."[1] The main objectives of this initiative have been to promote financial inclusion through increased access to financial services, improve the delivery of public services and benefits, and increase competition in the Indian financial sector. The Indian approach has had early success in promoting large increases in the number of individuals with bank accounts[2] and access to digital payment services among India's large previously unbanked population, earning praise for the speed with which financial inclusion has been increased (D'Silva et al., 2019). Moreover, these measures have set in motion a significant expansion of digital payments, with a more gradual progression in active use of new bank accounts. Based on the experience of other countries, this can support an expansion of broader financial services provision, with products offered that leverage data harvested from payments activity.

In this chapter, we argue that the Indian approach points to important synergies across the provision of three public goods. Its greatest promise lies in the trifecta of digital ID with a low entry cost, a system of open APIs facilitating interoperability in payments, albeit in a regulated space, and—perhaps most importantly—a mechanism to operationalize individuals' control over their personal data. This is a key step in operationalizing a data policy framework that grants individuals and companies rights to control access to their data. The introduction and regulation of data fiduciaries (referred to and regulated as "account aggregators" in India[3]) could reduce some of the

* The authors thank Linda Jeng, Elias Kazarian, Harish Natarajan, Kristel Poh, Damien Puy, Vishal Raina, Nilima Ramteke, David Rozumek, Tao Sun, Mario Tamez, and TengTeng Xu for insightful discussions and comments while remaining responsible for any errors or omissions. An earlier version of this chapter is published as an IMF Working Paper. The views herein are ours and do not necessarily represent the views of the IMF, its Executive Board, or IMF management.

[1] The India Stack corresponds to a set of application programming interfaces (APIs), open standards, and infrastructure components that allow Indian citizens to obtain a range of services digitally. See also Saroy et al. (2020) for further discussion.

[2] For instance, as we document later in the chapter, the use of bank accounts increased from a low 35% of adult population in 2011 to 80% in 2017.

[3] See "Non-Banking Financial Company—Account Aggregator (Reserve Bank) Directions, 2016." https://rbi.org.in.

Yan Carrière-Swallow, Vikram Haksar, and Manasa Patnam, *India's Approach to Open Banking: Some Implications for Financial Inclusion* In: *Open Banking*. Edited by: Linda Jeng, Oxford University Press. © Oxford University Press 2022. DOI: 10.1093/oso/9780197582879.003.0012

risks to privacy and identity theft that may in principle arise from the more widespread sharing of data envisaged in other open-banking applications.

What has set the Indian approach apart from many other open banking and broader data policy frameworks implemented around the world is its foundational approach based on the provision of extensive public infrastructures and standards. This has provided a platform for operationalizing user-authorized data portability and interoperability across the economy. The India Stack comprises four layers of infrastructure and standards: (1) digital identity; (2) an interoperable payments interface; (3) digitalization of documentation and verification; and (4) a consent layer—still under construction— for the management of individual data through regulated intermediaries.

This chapter begins with some context on the Indian financial landscape prior to the implementation of the India Stack reforms. It goes on to describe the reforms that have defined India's approach to open banking and open data. Finally, it discusses the main design choices in the India Stack and some potential implications, with some commentary about the applicability of elements of the Indian approach in other countries.

2. The Indian Financial Landscape

Until as recently as 2011, access to financial services remained low in India (Figure 11.1), with only 35 percent of adults in India possessing a bank account, well below the average of other emerging market economies (Demirgüç-Kunt et al., 2018). Even fewer

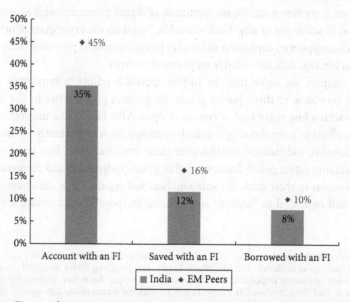

Figure 11.1 Financial service access and intermediation in India (% with bank account, 2011).

Source: Demirgüç-Kunt et al. (2018). *Note:* Compiled in 2011 using nationally representative surveys of more than 150,000 adults aged 15 and above in over 140 economies. In India, 3,000 people were surveyed. Emerging market peers are Argentina, Brazil, China, Indonesia, Kenya, Malaysia, Mexico, Peru, the Philippines, Romania, Russia, South Africa, Sri Lanka, Thailand, Turkey, Ukraine, and Vietnam.
Sources: IMF Financial Access Survey, Wold Bank, and BIS.

adults saved or borrowed with a financial institution, at 12 and 8 percent, respectively. The financial sector landscape was dominated by the public sector, with 61 percent of banking assets held by public sector banks (IMF, 2019).

The payments system, which plays an important role in promoting financial inclusion by facilitating the smooth operation and provision of financial services (BIS, 2016), was also gradually modernized through the establishment of the Real Time Gross Settlement system in 2004 and the passage of regulatory reform in 2007.[4] The reform empowered India's central bank, the Reserve Bank of India (RBI), to regulate and oversee all payment and settlement systems in the country and also to provide settlement finality together with a sound legal basis for netting (BIS, 2011). Despite these efforts, a low level of bank penetration went hand in hand with the population's high degree of dependence on cash, with currency in circulation amounting to approximately 12 percent of GDP (Chaudhari et al., 2019). Extensive use of cash took place despite several important constraints, including a high opportunity cost of holding cash and the limited availability of ATMs in India, at only 21 per 100,000 adults (IMF Financial Access Survey, 2018). A byproduct of reliance on cash for transactions is that they are often not recorded, thus generating no data for future use as a signal of company cash flow and consumer spending patterns.

Starting around 2010, several government initiatives set the stage for the expansion of financial access, laying a technological foundation for further improvements in financial inclusion.[5] To explain the evolution of financial access and intermediation in India over the past decade, we document in the following the chronology of reforms and public sector initiatives beginning with the large-scale provision of a national digital ID. This sequence of reforms provided the basis for several elements in the financial sector development process.

a. Launch of the Aadhaar Digital ID

The Aadhaar identification system, launched in 2010, is a digital identity infrastructure with a very low unit cost of operations, to which all residents of India are entitled.[6] Individuals may obtain an identification number that is unique and linked at the time of enrollment to their biometric identifiers—including a photograph, ten fingerprints, and two iris scans—as well as basic demographic data.[7] The twelve-digit number is randomly assigned at the time of enrollment, ensuring that no information about a person is contained in the number itself.[8] Crucially, for the goal of universality and promoting

[4] The Payment and Settlement Systems Act 2007.

[5] The RBI has also been actively involved in bringing about technological improvements in the payment systems, for example, through the triennial Payment System Vision document and dedicated committees to guide the use of ICT for the benefit of banking in general.

[6] While the universal ID system was announced and institutions created in 2009, the name Aadhaar was announced in March 2010, with the first number issued in September 2010. For details on the legal and institutional framework for the Aadhaar system that discusses how the Aadhaar ID is issued to residents, see World Bank (2017). It is important to note that the ID does not itself confer citizenship, rights, or entitlements.

[7] Only four demographic variables are mandatorily collected in Aadhaar, including name, address, gender, and date of birth. The biometric technology allows for bypassing fingerprint capture for manual laborers and the elderly and has enhancements allowing for retinal and potentially facial recognition.

[8] This contrasts with several other ID systems that have information encoded in the identity number itself (such as specific digits for gender, or a chronological order indicating the birthdate).

inclusion, registration for Aadhaar does not require previous physical identification, whether state-issued or otherwise, although the capture of biometric identifiers can be physically challenging in some groups (e.g., the elderly).

A motivating objective for introducing a national digital-identity system was to help improve the delivery of government services and reduce the leakages associated with its targeting (Sen, 2019). Aadhaar can be used to digitally authenticate individuals for a variety of public and private services, enabling biometric checks to reliably verify the identity of the holder, thus reducing the chances of false identities and fraudulent claims to state benefits. The Aadhaar number can be used across the country to authenticate an identity at any location, including online.

Interoperability is an important feature of the Aadhaar digital ID system that was not present by design in several other identity systems in India, such as tax cards, voting cards, and driver's licenses.[9] These legacy systems are more limited in scope and restricted to specific use cases, with a nonuniversal coverage, rendering them inadequate for identifying individuals across government services (Misra, 2019). Prior to Aadhaar, nearly half of India's 1.2 billion residents lacked a nationally accepted ID, often reflecting the absence of a birth certificate due to the incomplete coverage of the civil registry system. These limitations restricted the effective delivery of social welfare programs and banking services, which were often precluded by the complexity of verifying identity.

The Aadhaar database contains basic personal data on almost all Indian residents, and a key focus of its governance has been to adequately protect user privacy while enabling the provision of efficient identification services. The Unique Identification Authority of India (UIDAI) is a public agency, not reporting directly to any other Ministry, that facilitates the collection of demographic and biometric data during Aadhaar enrollment (often by third-party intermediaries), verifies its uniqueness, and stores the information on a central identity repository. The UIDAI is given a public mandate to provide identification services of Aadhaar holders and may charge a fee for doing so that is deposited in a government account. In turn, it is subject to extensive regulation requiring it to protect individuals' privacy, particularly by ensuring the security of their core biometric data.[10] Also, recent litigation in India has limited the scope of mandating use of Aadhaar data by the public sector and for financial service provision.

Figure 11.2 reports the cumulative number of unique Aadhaar numbers registered to Indian residents since its launch in 2010. Within three years, about 600 million Aadhaar digital ID numbers had been issued, equivalent to roughly half the Indian population. By 2017, over 90 percent of the Indian population possessed an Aadhaar number, and half of the identity holders had linked their bank accounts to their Aadhaar number.

It should be noted that India is not the only, nor the first, country to have adopted a digitally verifiable unique identity system, with similar digital ID schemes in place in countries such as Estonia and Uruguay.[11] According to the World Bank, eighty-three

---

[9] Indeed, to the best of our knowledge, most identity systems around the world do not build in interoperability by design.

[10] The UIDAI maintains that it stores data of all Aadhaar holders in a safe and secure manner, using advanced security technologies, in a centralized repository. A separate law on the protection of personal data (the Personal Data Protection Bill) is being currently considered by the Indian Parliament, which among other things proposes the setting up of a Data Protection Authority.

[11] Find a discussion of comparative country approaches to digital ID systems in OECD (2019).

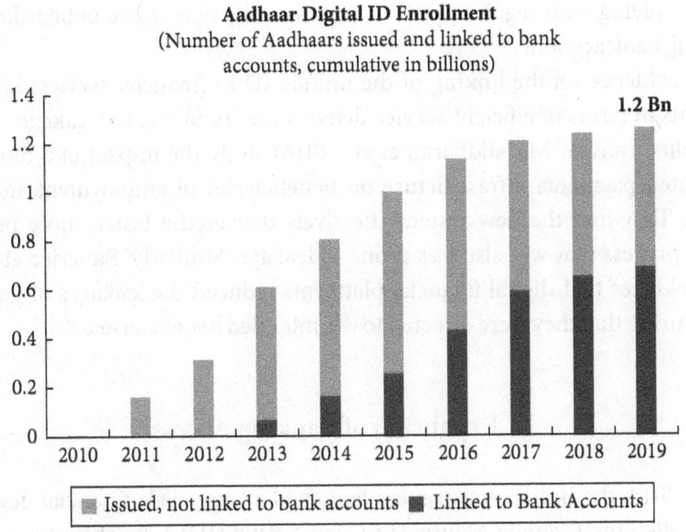

Aadhaar Digital ID Enrollment
(Number of Aadhaars issued and linked to bank
accounts, cumulative in billions)

Figure 11.2 Aadhaar Digital ID Enrollment.
(Number of Aadhaars issued and linked to bank accounts, cumulative in billions.)
Source: UIDAI.

countries collect fingerprints or biometrics for issuing a digitized ID (World Bank ID4D Global Dataset, 2017). What sets the Indian experience apart is the large scale and low unit costs of operating the program, which aimed to create a digital ecosystem around the identity. These aspects enabled a large population of over a billion people to enroll in the program and quickly acquire a national identity that could be used in all aspects of economic life.

The technology that enabled Aadhaar as a foundational identity for a digital ecosystem involved several application programming interfaces (APIs). These APIs allow public and private service providers to authenticate identity using the underlying data biometrics, demographics, and links to individual phones registered with Aadhaar to facilitate authentication by means of a one-time password (World Bank, 2017). Using these technologies, the launch of the digital ID was immediately followed by its linking with several public sector services, including banking services. For instance, to facilitate access to the banking system, the RBI enabled the holder of the Aadhaar ID to authorize a bank to obtain an electronic verification of her identity through the UIDAI in 2013.[12] This new authorization procedure provided an electronic substitute for the know-your-customer (KYC) procedure required for any bank onboarding process and was called e-KYC (for "electronic KYC"). The eKYC service adheres to the principle of data minimization, sharing only relevant demographic data and the photograph of the identity holder with the service provider, after the identity holder provides consent. According to one industry-linked think tank, this system has drastically reduced the

---

[12] Essentially, the bank can obtain a copy of the letter issued by the UIDAI that contains the Aadhaar holder's name and address almost instantaneously via a secure internet query to the central Aadhaar ID database.

cost of complying with regulatory KYC requirements during the onboarding process for opening bank accounts.[13]

Recent evidence on the linking of the unique ID to financial services shows positive benefits in terms of efficient service delivery and reducing the leakages associated with benefits transfer. Muralidharan et al. (2016) study the impact of a biometrically authenticated payments infrastructure on beneficiaries of employment and pension programs. They find the new system effectively delivered a faster, more predictable, payments process that was also less prone to leakage. Similarly, Banerjee et al. (2020) provide evidence that digital financial platforms reduced the leakages of government funds, ensuring that they were directed to the intended beneficiaries.

b. Expansion of Banking Access

In August 2014, the Indian government launched a large-scale financial development program called the *Pradhan Mantri Jan Dhan Yojana* (JDY). Its objective was to provide access to banking services for all unbanked households in India together with convenient access to saving accounts through a debit card and mobile banking. A variety of features distinguished this financial inclusion program from previous similar programs,[14] including the provision of a no-frills, zero-balance account with a debit card and access to mobile banking for funds transfer, overdraft facilities, and provision of basic life insurance coverage (approximately USD 440) to all account holders (Agarwal et al., 2019).

Within a year of its inception, the program opened 166 million accounts, and has expanded since then with almost 384 million accounts in operation in 2019. Eighty percent of the accounts opened reside in public sector banks, and half of these accounts have been opened in rural areas (RBI, 2018). An important feature of the JDY was that bank accounts under this scheme could be opened using the Aadhaar ID and subsequently linked to it for the transfer of government benefits.

As shown in Figure 11.3, the introduction and expansion of the JDY coincided with a period of rapid increase in financial access, in which the percentage of adults with a bank account increased from 35 percent in 2011 to 80 percent in 2017. This effect is also documented by Agarwal et al. (2019) using Indian administrative microdata, who find that the number of accounts steadily increased at a rate of 14 percent per month since the start of the program, with 77 percent of the accounts maintaining a positive but low balance (approximately USD 7 in 2017, which is about 60 percent of the rural poverty line in India). As D'Silva et al. (2019) underscore based on cross-country experience, this represented an impressive leapfrogging with respect to traditional financial development processes, with India increasing access to bank accounts by what has taken countries at the same level of development forty-seven years to achieve.

However, despite this surge in the number of new accounts, it is not clear that there has been a similar increase in the usage of financial services. Agarwal et al. (2019) find

---

[13] See statements by the Indian Software Product Industry Roundtable, available at https://ispirt.in.

[14] The RBI launched a similar simple account scheme in 2005, though this does not seem to have led to much financial activity among those who opened the accounts.

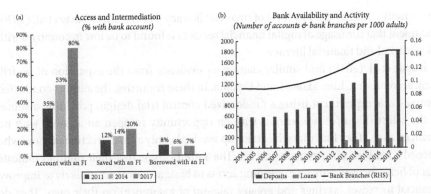

Figure 11.3 Indicators of access to financial services in India.
Sources: Demirgüç-Kunt et al. (2018) and IMF Financial Access Survey.

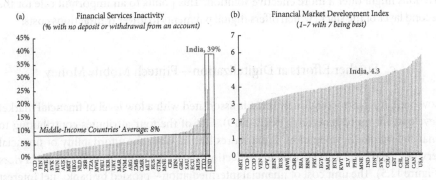

Figure 11.4 International comparators of financial market development.
Sources: Demirgüç-Kunt et al. (2018) and World Economic Forum.

that 81 percent of new consumers do not deposit any money into their new accounts,[15] and 87 percent do not withdraw any cash after opening the account. Based on analysis of the data reported in Demirgüç-Kunt et al. (2018), the effective use of financial services remains low despite increased access to finance in India (Figure 11.4). From 2011 to 2017, the share of adults in India who save with a financial institution increased only slightly from 12 to 20 percent, and the percent of adults who borrow in fact decreased from 8 to 7 percent. In 2017, only about 39 percent of the survey respondents reported sending or receiving domestic remittances using a financial institution. The bulk of remittance transfers are conducted with cash, in person, or using a network of relatives and friends. Even among the population possessing a bank account, nearly half (48.5 percent) of the accounts remain inactive, making India the country with the highest inactivity rate in the world.[16] It should be noted that one of the reasons for the

---

[15] As these were zero-balance accounts, the cost to the user of opening an account and not using it is minimal.

[16] Inactive accounts are defined as not making any deposit or withdrawal within a year. The rate of inactivity was 23% in 2014. Sahay et al. (2020) also show that financial inclusion in payments in India—both traditional and digital—is lower than the Asian average. Moreover, gender gaps in digital financial inclusion are high in India: for instance, men are 20 percentage points more likely than women to own a mobile phone.

low activity could be the low level of financial literacy. For instance, Sahay et al. (2020) document that the usage of digital financial services is found to be low in countries with lower digital and financial literacy.

Dupas et al. (2018) find similar cautionary evidence from the expansion of no-frill bank accounts in Chile, Malawi, and Uganda. In these countries, the authors conducted a small-scale experiment using a randomized control trial design, providing a subset of the selected sample households with an opportunity to open an account with no financial costs. They find that while take-up was high, only a small fraction of those who opened a bank account actually used it. The authors argue that their findings indicate that policies focused only on expanding access to basic accounts are unlikely to improve financial increases (savings and greater take-up of insurance) on their own. They do find some suggestive evidence that barriers such as transaction costs may be responsible for limited usage, suggesting that financial products that are tailored to overcome such frictions might offer a more effective solution. This points to an important role for the second layer of the stack, which offers digital payments to lower transactions costs.

c. Further Efforts at Digitalization—Fintech Mobile Money

Low banking intermediation in India is associated with a low level of financial market development more generally (WEF, 2019). Out of the four attributes contributing to financial market development, India scores low on both the affordability of financial services[17] and ease of access to loans, reflecting in part the high cost of financial services (Figure 11.5). The unit cost of financial intermediation—proxied by banks' net interest margin—has hovered about 3 percentage points in India during the past decade, above levels in advanced economies albeit lower than the average for emerging economies (World Bank, 2019).

One factor that has been shown to reduce the frictions confronting financial intermediation is the existence of a system that facilitates information sharing across financial institutions. Such systems, commonly known as credit bureaus or loan registries, can allow financial institutions to price, target, and monitor loans and enhance competition in the credit market, and have been associated with deeper financial markets and a reduced cost of credit (Djankov, McLiesh, and Schleifer, 2007). In India, the Credit Information Bureau India Ltd. was established in 2000, and three other Credit Information Companies (CICs) were set up since the enactment of the Credit Information Companies (Regulation) Act in 2005. However, as recently as 2014, the coverage of CICs accounted for only 19.8 percent of the adult population, and they did not collect individual- or firm-level data relating to income, personal financial information, including ownership of a business, tax statements, utility payment records/telecom data, check bouncing, bankruptcies, and court judgments (RBI, 2014). As part of its modernization efforts, from 2015 onward, the RBI expanded the coverage of information collected and stipulated that all credit institutions are required to submit data on

---

[17] The affordability of financial services is measured in the index by asking the survey respondent, "to what extent does the cost of financial services (e.g. insurance, loans, trade finance) impede business activity?" (see WEF, 2019, for further details on the methodology).

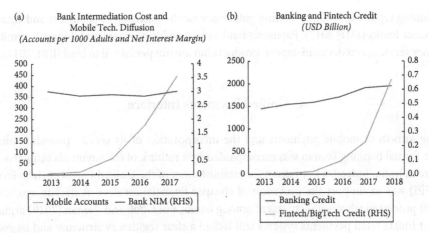

Figure 11.5 Financial cost of intermediation and fintech expansion.
Sources: IMF Financial Access Survey, Wold Bank, and BIS

individuals and firms in the formal sector to credit registries. Currently, India's credit information companies cover approximately 56 percent of the population (World Bank Doing Business, 2019). Yet a large portion of businesses operating in the informal sector and lower-income households are excluded from these credit registries, as they often lack the necessary information financial institutions require to assess their creditworthiness. This reduces their chances of getting financed and raises the cost of the loan when they do.

The advent and rapid growth of new financial technologies such as mobile money and digital wallets offer an innovative technological solution to fill the financial infrastructure gap and alleviate frictions related to the limited use of formal financial services. This is because the use of mobile money allows consumers to perform financial transactions in a relatively inexpensive and reliable way (Jack and Suri, 2014), eliminating geographic barriers, and can be used as a mechanism to hold savings by both the banked and unbanked (Morawczynski et al., 2009). As Figure 11.5 (left panel) shows, the number of mobile money accounts in India has grown rapidly, and these now serve over half the population (GSMA, 2018). For instance, Paytm, one of the largest mobile money service providers in India, serves over 400 million users and over 14 million businesses as of 2019 (Business World, 2019). At these initial stages of expansion, already, mobile payments are estimated to account for 0.3 to 0.6 percent of GDP in India (BIS 2019, FAS 2019). For India, the large-scale expansion of mobile money is found to be associated with favorable economic outcomes, such as increased resilience to shocks for households and improved sales for firms operating in the informal sector (see Patnam and Yao, 2020). The expansion of mobile money was also accompanied by a rapid increase in fintech and BigTech lending (right panel), whose growth far exceeded the growth of domestic credit by the traditional financial sector (see Cornelli et al., 2020). Despite its rapid growth, it is important to note that fintech/BigTech lending remains a very small share (about 0.1 percent) of overall lending.

Recognizing the rapid growth of private sector–led mobile-banking and credit growth, and its role in improving financial inclusion, the RBI established a differentiated banking regime in India by issuing guidelines for the licensing of payments and small finance banks (IMF, 2017). Payments banks can provide payment and domestic remittance services and demand deposit products but are not permitted to lend (RBI, 2014).

d. Unified Payments Interface

The growth of mobile payments and the incorporation of its service providers into the formal banking system was accompanied by a rethink of the payments infrastructure in India. Indeed, a key reason for establishment of the Unified Payments Interface (UPI) was to support the provision of cheaper financial services. A decade ago, the RBI processed wholesale settlement among banks, but Cook and Raman (2019) argue that India's retail payments systems still lacked a clear regulatory structure and lagged behind especially for low-value transactions.[18] In 2007, the Payment and Settlement Systems (PSS) Act authorized the RBI to create a separate nongovernmental institution to operate retail payment systems.[19] This led to the inception of an independent not-for-profit organization, the National Payments Corporation of India (NPCI), overseen by the RBI in its role as a regulator of the national payments system (see Saroy et al., 2020, for additional details on the regulatory timeline of payment systems).[20] By 2018, the NPCI processed 48 percent (by value) of all electronic payment transactions in India (RBI, 2018).

Upon creation, the RBI transferred the operation of ATM operations to the NPCI whose role in debit/credit card transactions has since then increased. Taking advantage of the Aadhaar ID, the NPCI began to offer the choice of linking a person's debit card to their Aadhaar identity. Prior to this, the use of credit and debit cards in India was very low, with approximately twenty million credit cards in the country and only two million digital payment acceptance points, such that in effect, many features of card-based payment systems were inaccessible to the larger population (Raghavan, Jain, and Varma, 2019).

This innovation was also central to India's ambitious financial inclusion initiative, the JDY, where each of the new accounts created was accompanied by an Aadhaar-linked "Rupay" debit card. By 2011, the NPCI) launched the Aadhaar Payments Bridge (APB) and the Aadhaar Enabled Payments System (AEPS), which use the Aadhaar number as a central key for channeling government benefits and subsidies electronically to the intended beneficiary's bank account.[21] These payment services were in part created to

---

[18] See Cook and Raman (2019) for a detailed description of the payments infrastructure that existed before 2009 and a variety of partly unsuccessful and decentralized attempts to modernize the retail payments sectors.

[19] The PSS Act designated the RBI as the authority for regulation and supervision of payments systems and as the authority to issue authorization to entities desirous of operating a payment system, including nonbank entities. The setting up of an umbrella organization for payment systems was also part of the RBI vision document 2005–2008 (see https://rbidocs.rbi.org.in/rdocs/PublicationReport/Pdfs/62764.pdf).

[20] The organization's fifteen-member board included representatives from each of the ten shareholder banks (public and private) and five independent representatives, which included one RBI nominee, but there was no direct regulator representation (Cook and Raman, 2019).

[21] The AEPS is a bank-led model that allows online interoperable transactions at point of sale through the business correspondent of any bank using Aadhaar authentication. The APB is used to channel government benefits to beneficiary bank accounts.

help achieve the government's vision of linking the JDY bank accounts, Aadhaar numbers, and mobile phone numbers—the so-called JAM initiative (JDY bank accounts, Aadhaar ID, and mobile payments)—to solve frictions and increase access to finance in India.

However, the growth of private nonbank fintech providers added new dimensions as the payments systems in place were not interoperable outside of the public-sector financial landscape, which limited the ability of nonbank fintechs to provide payments services. An existing system established by the NPCI, the immediate payment service (IMPS), allowed for an instant 24/7 interbank electronic fund transfer payments but was interoperable mainly within the banking sector, and thus typically available only to the segment of the population holding a bank account.

To encourage broader interoperability and to provide an easy-to-use product over the existing IMPS, the NPCI introduced the UPI in 2016, a standardized protocol within the payment infrastructure that enabled banks and nonbanks to operate with each other.[22] This design was created with the main objective of expanding the perimeter of interoperability, simplifying the transfer of funds between any stored-value accounts held at banks or nonbanks.[23] It also covered peer-to-peer (P2P) transactions made at request between users of either banks or nonbanks. What enabled such an architecture were the existence of APIs able to provide instantaneous authentication and authorization of both the payment service provider (banks or nonbanks) and the identity holder.[24]

While using UPI does not require an Aadhaar ID, use of the Aadhaar has greatly facilitated eKYC compliance for opening bank accounts needed to access the UPI system. Another useful feature in the UPI architecture is that a user can use any application to send or receive money directly from their bank account and, thus, is not restricted to the interface provided by their banking service provider. This increases the competition for user acquisition and innovation in the design and performance of banking service apps.[25]

It is important to note the presence also of alternate architectures, such as AEPS, that do not require the use of a smartphone for conducting a digital payment. Aadhaar-based authentication can be enabled via biometrics through the payment-accepting merchant's terminal or point-of-sale machine. In effect, this means an individual can pay for items at a point of sale, with Aadhaar biometrics, with payments settled in the background over the AEPS.

This novel payment interface provides an alternative by which the unbanked informal-sector population could access digital payment services. Figure 11.6 shows,

---

[22] Nonbank participation through nonbank PPIs has been allowed since October 2018.

[23] More details on the objectives of the UPI can be found at https://www.npci.org.in/what-we-do/upi/product-overview. The NPCI also provides an alternative payments service for more bulk payments—National Automated Clearing House—to facilitate interbank, high volume, electronic transactions for banks, financial institutions, Corporations, and government.

[24] Raghavan, Jain, and Varma (2019) document a growing list of India Stack APIs and their impact factors, including services to prove identity, completing KYC, making digital payments, signing documents digitally, and sharing of data.

[25] See Raghavan, Jain, and Varma (2019) for further technical details on this and other operational aspects of the UPI.

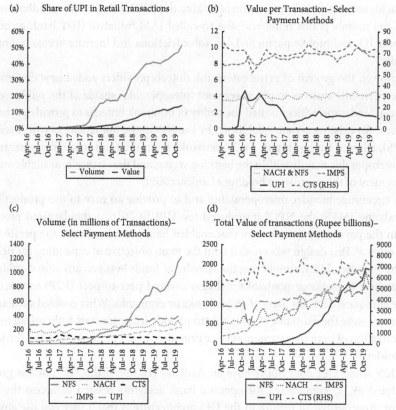

Figure 11.6 Indicators of retail financial transactions in India.
Source: Data from a subset of retail transactions at the National Payment Corporation of India (NPCI). NACH is automated clearing house; NFS refers to Inter-bank ATM cash withdrawal; CTS is cheque clearing; IMPS is instant money payment system and UPI is Unified Payments Interface.

for instance, the evolution of different payment systems within the retail sector in India; while check payment remained the dominant mode of transacting, digital payments (including P2P transactions) have increased rapidly. As D'Silva et al. (2019) emphasize, the UPI has expanded rapidly since its inception in early 2016, particularly in terms of the volume of transactions. At the same time, we find that the narrower interoperable payment system—the IMPS—operated by banks for their account holders—also grew rapidly in terms of gross values transacted, while its volume growth remains low relative to the UPI. This suggests that the UPI may responds to different use cases, bringing in specific segments of the unbanked population whose transactions may have fallen outside the formal financial system.

Notes: Data from National Payments Corporation of India for a subset of retail transactions. NACH is National Automated Clearing House; NFS refers to interbank ATM cash withdrawal; CTS is check clearing; IMPS is immediate payment service; and UPI is Unified Payments Interface.

3. The India Stack: Key Features

As discussed in the introduction to this chapter, the India Stack contains four layers of digital infrastructure that have been introduced gradually over the last decade. The first is the "presenceless layer," featuring the Aadhaar digital ID system that allows for identity verification and for the mapping of information across data sets. The second is the "cashless layer," built on the UPI's interoperable payments system. The third is the "paperless layer," which allows for the verification of digital documents that can replace traditional paper analogs. The fourth is the "consent layer"—which is on the cusp of becoming fully operational—that will involve the operation of data fiduciaries that act as intermediaries between individuals and financial companies. These fiduciaries will be charged with facilitating the aggregation of individuals' financial data across their accounts at multiple financial institutions and sharing that data with interested third-parties subject to the individual's consent.

The first two layers of the India Stack—which have been in operation together since 2016—make up the interoperable payments system that characterizes the core of open banking systems in other jurisdictions. The fourth layer will introduce the sharing of customer data that is held by each financial institution and financial service provider. Later in this chapter we will argue that this final layer may be particularly transformative given the synergies it will gain from the success of the other layers.

How does the Indian approach to open banking compare to the designs that have been implemented in other countries? Table 11.1 offers a comparison to several jurisdictions that have implemented or are in the final stages of preparing their open banking frameworks, including Australia, the European Union, and the United Kingdom. Regulated data-sharing subject to user consent exists in several of these jurisdictions. There is considerable variation across countries in terms of the data classes that must be shared, with some countries including a very narrow set of traditional bank account data, whereas others have added information about other products, such as mortgage loans and credit cards. In the case of Australia, the Competition Authority is directing the open banking initiative plans to expand the perimeter of data classes to include energy and telecommunications accounts.

While no single aspect of the India Stack is entirely unique, it strikes us that the key differences of the Indian approach are (1) comprehensiveness, in the sense of the stack seeking synergies across multiple infrastructure layers; (2) introduction of a centralized digital ID that has helped millions of people get an ID for the first time and that allows for eKYC verification; (3) introduction by the public sector of standards and open APIs facilitating (but not mandating) interoperability of payments; and (4) operationalization of consent for user data-sharing by data fiduciaries in finance and, eventually, in other sectors.

It is worth remarking that the perimeter of the ecosystem in the Indian design is broad, encompassing existing financial intermediaries and new tech entrants, including smaller fintechs and large BigTechs. However, to participate fully in the stack, entrants must accept to be regulated as financial entities by the financial regulator[26] or to have

---

[26] See the following Section 4 for further details on the payments bank license.

Table 11.1 Open Banking Design Choices: India and Selected Other Jurisdictions

Jurisdiction	Launch	National Digital ID	Perimeter of Participants	Interoperable Payment Initiation ("Write Access")	Data-Sharing ("Read Access")		
					Mandate	Data Classes	Features
Australia	2020	Yes	Accredited data recipients (ADRs), including banks and nonbanks	Not included in initial design	Regulated	Business and individual bank/credit card account balances and transactions; mortgages; retirement savings accounts. Future: energy and telecom account data	Fully reciprocal for all ADRs
China	–	Yes	Banks and regulated fintechs	Yes; no mandate	Market-driven	Account information	n/a
European Union (PSD2 & GDPR)	2019	None across the EU; strong customer identification; national schemes exist in some member countries	Banks, regulated fintechs, payment service providers	Yes; mandate	Regulated	Payment account data	Asymmetric; banks required to share. Others subject to GDPR portability requirement with 30-day delay
India (UPI)	2016	Yes	Licensed banks (UPI)	Yes; no mandate	Mix of market-driven and regulated	Digital payments; later other sectors	Reciprocal
New Zealand	2017	No	Banks, regulated fintechs	Yes; no mandate	Market-driven	Payment accounts data	
United Kingdom	2018	No	Banks and regulated fintechs	Yes; mandate	Regulated	Account balances; transactions	Banks; nonbanks may participate voluntarily

Source: Authors' compilation based on information from BCBS (2019), Ehrentraud et al. (2020), and national authorities.

payments services they provide linked to regulated banks. To facilitate the former, India innovated by introducing new types of bank licenses, including a more restricted "payments bank" license, which has lower thresholds of regulatory requirements but are more limited in the financial services they can offer. This is a difference compared to other open banking models that allow fintechs and third-parties to provide financial services without being subject to the same degree of regulation as traditional banks, but instead subject to a more focused regulation, for example by specially designated open-banking authorities, that may be more focused on data and consumer protection practices. Arguably, the approach in India could raise the threshold of entry into the system for smaller tech providers, though further analysis is required of the trade-offs involved.

That said, the Indian design spans data shared by consumers and by small to medium-size enterprises (SMEs), such that the impact on provision of finance including credit, in principle, may be closer to that seen in closed-loop systems in China.[27] Moreover, it is possible that an entrant could obtain user data through the consent layer and offer services without participating in the payments layer of the stack, and hence in principle avoiding the need to be regulated, though it is hard to see how this would work in practice. Last, by contrast with some approaches like the Second Payment Services Directive (PSD2), data-sharing is by design symmetric (as in other countries like Australia): to get data, participants must also be willing to allow others access to their customers' data.

We discuss some of these design choices and their implications for open banking models more broadly in the next section.

4. Discussion of the Indian Open Banking Model

a. Digital ID (Aadhaar)

The introduction of low-cost digital ID has facilitated a large expansion in the user base, and this has been crucial for the success of open banking in India. The ubiquity and low cost arising from both technology and the fact that a self-declaration is all that is required to establish an identity could be appealing to other developing jurisdictions. The combination with biometrics and the fact that the UPI does not require access to a smartphone may also be appealing to many jurisdictions, as technological exclusion across income and age characteristics is common around the world (e.g., older populations may not be comfortable using smartphones to access mobile banking).

Aadhaar has been an important part of delivering more efficient KYC. While a physical meeting is typically required to open an account at a financial institution, the process can be greatly expedited, and subsequent verification of transactions is easy and quick with Aadhaar. Thus, in principle it seems that a system of digital ID can go a long way to reducing the costs of complying with KYC requirements and, given the strength

---

[27] China's Alipay and WeChatPay are celebrated for their ability to leverage SME payments data to provide a full suite of financial services to SMEs. That said, the constraint remains that all intermediaries in the India Stack must be regulated, and hence to take advantage of data-driven analytics to provide financial services up the value chain requires also that these tech intermediaries comply with financial regulation and obtain full bank licenses.

of the unique biometric ID, is a more robust solution to establishing identity than other more traditional means. However, even with digital ID, the establishment of beneficial ownership in a money-laundering tax-fraud (ML/TF) and tax base–shifting context remains a challenge.[28]

Around the world there has been concern with the scale of digital ID provision under the auspices of the central government and the potential for its use in applications that infringe on individual rights for privacy. An interesting feature of Aadhaar's governance is that the UIDAI is a separate body under the government of India. Could the establishment of an independent government agency with a mandate to manage identity separate from the other interests of the state be a way forward? This has been the subject of litigation in India, and the Supreme Court has established limits on the mandatory use of digital ID and affirmed the individual right to privacy, which is reflected in the development of modern data privacy legislation currently before parliament. This suggests that to successfully implement such a stack-based approach, there is a need to have a modernized privacy framework.[29]

b. Payments (UPI)

In order to participate in the UPI system, fintech firms are required to operate, either through an institution with a banking license or by obtaining a special payment bank license that would bring them within the financial regulatory perimeter. The key difference between a payments bank and a full bank license is that the former's activities are restricted mainly to acceptance of demand deposits and provision of payments and remittance services. Keeping all participants in the payments system within the regulatory perimeter allowed the RBI to promote financial inclusion while fulfilling its objective of ensuring the system's stability and resilience.[30]

The design has proven sufficiently flexible to facilitate entry of a large number of new tech-based payment service providers into the UPI, increasing competition and user choice. A question that arises is whether the compliance costs associated with being regulated as a type of financial intermediary acts as a barrier to entry for smaller service providers, thereby reducing competition in favor of existing intermediaries, many of whom are state-owned banks or BigTech competitors. Arguably, this is a matter of balance between financial stability and efficiency. In principle the payments landscape in India should be poised for greater competition, supported also by a commitment that participants in UPI not charge consumers for use of the system in the first few years

---

[28] The Financial Action Task Force (FATF) acknowledges that non-face-to-face onboarding and transactions conducted using trustworthy digital ID are not necessarily high risk and can be standard or even lower risk. See FATF published guidance on Digital ID, which clarifies how and the extent to which a digital ID is appropriate for use for KYC purposes (FATF, 2020).

[29] This is a key conclusion also in the Basel Committee on Banking Supervision report on open banking (BCBS, 2019).

[30] As noted in the circular establishing the payments bank license, the RBI notes that the primary objective of setting up payments banks is to further financial inclusion, among other things, by enabling high volume–low value transactions in deposits and payments/remittance services in a secured technology-driven environment (RBI, 2014). Arguably the Indian approach built in upfront steps to maintain stability that were subsequently adopted in part by countries with large closed-loop operators, such as the People's Bank of China's steps in 2018 to regulate mobile payments settlement.

(Google Payments, 2019). However, there are some concerns that while interoperability has increased contestability and facilitated entry by diverse actors into UPI, the inherent network scale advantages of BigTech providers could allow them to acquire a dominant position in the market.[31]

A crucial feature of the payments system layer of the India Stack is the RBI's support for interoperability, which in principle sets the stage for a more competitive payments landscape. The public sector (through the NPCI) developed an open API standard, and UPI defined a payments markup language that standardized instructions for sending and receiving money within the system. Entrants were invited—but not mandated—to utilize the public infrastructure drawing on this standard. To facilitate P2P payments, the RBI also helped to develop payment aliases and helped banks agree to a common authentication system. The RBI facilitated the provision of extensive technical support to merchants and the design aspects of the UPI to include third-party technology players.

Interoperability of the payments system has been operationalized through open APIs, available to banks and to fintechs that set up payments banks or leverage links to existing banks. This has set the stage for greater competition in the provision of a broad range of financial services that leverage data collected via the payments interface.[32] While other jurisdictions have accommodated a range of fintech payment providers, not all are fully interoperable, which limits the scale of activity that can be achieved and creating an advantage for data-rich BigTechs, which leverage large existing platforms and networks. By contrast in India, it is possible for a user to transfer funds across accounts at different providers—from a wallet issued by one provider to another user's wallet issued by another provider—instantaneously. The combination of licensing and open systems has therefore in principle set the stage for a more competitive financial services landscape than might have otherwise arisen given the strong economies of scale inherent in payment networks, though as noted earlier, the jury is still out on how the relative effects of interoperability and network scale will play out and whether further policy action will be needed to support competition.[33] Furthermore, risks of open-API architectures for cybersecurity highlight the need to consider policies to ensure adequate investments by regulated entities in protecting data security and individual privacy.

c. Data-Sharing

A key challenge of data policy is to ensure that access to personal data is handled according to the preferences of the individuals it affects. Some jurisdictions have taken a rights-based approach to individuals' control of personal data. In the European Union, the General Data Protection Regulation (GDPR) is a prime example establishing the obligations of the data controller and processor to ensure that the rights of the data subject are respected as data is transferred for analysis and value extraction. In practice,

---

[31] See a discussion in Frost (2021) who find that big techs process the bulk of transactions on UPI.

[32] See BIS (2020) for a discussion of how data generated by digital payments systems can be utilized in the provision of other financial services.

[33] See BIS (2020) for a discussion of how network effects in payment systems can generate high concentration that threatens competition.

the approach has involved the controllers issuing GDPR-compliant checklists for data subjects to complete in order to gain access to services.

The India Stack's approach to the control of data is more operational. The "fiduciary"—in the current state of the stack a "financial data aggregator"[34]— has the responsibility to manage the subject's data and rights and seek consent for data processing. In doing so the fiduciary may not access or store the data being shared but will be allowed to charge fees to offer the service. This limit on access to the subject's data by the fiduciary marks a very different approach than in other jurisdictions, where aggregators offer their services in exchange for access to the data that can be used to offer other financial services. In principle, the Indian approach should better align the interests of the fiduciary with that of the subject. Moreover, this limited data aggregation role should facilitate operational compliance with India's incipient privacy framework while allowing a wide class of service providers to gain access to the financial data of consumers and businesses.

In addition to being a consent manager, the fiduciary can also be thought of as a trust engine that is powered by the multiple layers of the India Stack. This is accomplished by completing several links. First, the fiduciary can authenticate the subject using their digital ID. Second, the digital ID offers a mechanism for generating trust that the data is indeed that of the subject. Then, the fiduciary uses digital ID to link to the third layer of the stack, mapping individual identity to the veracity of digital documents laying out the data subject's financial assets, liabilities, and cash flows. This allows the fiduciary, combining these layers, to essentially assure third-parties of the provenance of the data subject's identity, data, and documents underpinning their balance sheet. This is a powerful basis for establishing trust, reducing the key friction of asymmetric information that impedes the offering of financial services. If successful, it should offer a package solution to third-parties wishing to offer financial services to data subjects, encompassing a model of management of data usage of households and small businesses within the regulatory perimeter.

The rationale for ensuring that open banking involves interoperability is that the network externalities in payments and data can then accrue to all users regardless of their provider, precluding these being appropriated by individual institutions.[35] A level playing field can be provided by making data-sharing reciprocal across financial service providers. This avoids the concerns expressed in the European Union, where PSD2 mandates that banks share extensive user financial data with fintechs, which are not required to reciprocate by sharing their user data with the banks.

The extent to which open banking frameworks can ensure a level playing field is determined by the data classes that are included in data-sharing schemes. In India, data-sharing extends to more classes of data than in many other jurisdictions, such as the European Union and the United Kingdom. While it will initially remain limited to data

---

[34] The regulatory framework for these aggregators is laid out in RBI (2019). In principle this concept will be extended to health and insurance data, though there does not appear to be an expectation of extending the notion to data managed by controllers and processors such as search and social media businesses among other nonfinancial/health/insurance providers.

[35] An interesting issue also is the potential for sharing of information generated within the open banking ecosystem with other existing information aggregators such as credit registries. The scope for this, including in India, is a topic for further examination.

concerning financial services, it is intended to expand to insurance and health data. However, there remain level-playing-field concerns with BigTechs, which will be able to obtain financial data from incumbent banks/fintechs but will not have to surrender nontraditional data such as social media or web-browsing behavior, or location data. These classes of data are outside the open banking data-sharing perimeter but can nonetheless inform financial decisions such as credit assessments.[36]

A final noteworthy feature of the Indian approach to open banking is that the perimeter of data subjects is broader than in most other jurisdictions. Many open banking approaches are focused on consumer data and their access to financial services. The Indian approach extends this to include also small businesses, which can participate in the payments and data layers of the stack and gain access to improved financial services and access to funding.

Currently, a series of data aggregators have received regulatory approval from the RBI, but the take-up of these services remains limited. It is worth noting that there are practical limits to even fiduciary-based data-sharing, as cross-country attitudes to data-sharing with financial intermediaries are quite variable (Ernst and Young, 2019). In the development of the system, it will be crucial that aggregators operate in a way that builds and preserves the public's trust in their data management practices.

5. Conclusion

The India Stack has implemented open banking principles of competition and contestability through interoperability and data-sharing in the financial sector. By bringing in a diverse range of banks and nonbanks together under a common infrastructure, this architecture has potentially facilitated financial inclusion, as evidenced by the increase in high volume–low value payment transactions. The overall structure of this publicly provided digital infrastructure has the scope to support the provision of many financial services and to further deepen financial inclusion.

The entry of new and efficient payments providers could in principle increase competition for existing financial intermediaries, given that fees derived from payments can be an important source of income for existing banks. Future research will need to consider the implications of these technological developments for competition, market structure, and financial stability and efficiency trade-offs in financial sectors around the world, including in India.

The potential of the infrastructure provided by the India Stack could extend far beyond finance. As a broader data policy framework, the confluence of the four layers described in this chapter form the basis for a competitive and inclusive digital economy in which individuals exercise meaningful control over their data. The data fiduciary model is of general interest as an approach that could operationalize control of personal data by the data subject, facilitating data-sharing while preserving privacy. The operations of the recently approved account aggregator fiduciaries will be interesting to

---

[36] See Berg et al. (2020) for analysis of how such nontraditional data can improve credit scoring.

watch as the scope of data classes is expanded to nonfinancial data, including in health services.

References

Agarwal, Sumit et al. 2019. "Banking the Unbanked: What Do 255 Million New Bank Accounts Reveal about Financial Access?" Research Paper No. 2906523, Georgetown McDonough School of Business.

Banerjee, Abhijit, Esther Duflo, Clement Imbert, Santhosh Mathew, and Rohini Pande, 2020. "E-governance, accountability, and leakage in public programs: Experimental evidence from a financial management reform in India." American Economic Journal: Applied Economics 12, no. 4 (2020): 39–72.

Bank for International Settlements (BIS), 2011. "Payment, clearing and settlement systems in the CPSS countries." Basel, Switzerland.

Bank for International Settlements (BIS), 2019. "Big Tech in Finance: Opportunities and Risks." Basel, Switzerland.

Bank for International Settlements (BIS), 2020. "Central Banks and Payments in the Digital Era," Chapter 3 in BIS Annual Economic Report. Basel, Switzerland.

Basel Committee on Banking Supervision (BCBS), 2019. "Report on Open Banking and Application Programming Interfaces," Basel, Switzerland: Bank for International Settlements.

Berg, Tobias et al., 2020. "On the Rise of FinTechs—Credit Scoring Using Digital Footprints," Review of Financial Studies 33(7): 2845–97.

Chaudhari, Dipak, Sarat Dhal, and Sonali Adki, 2019. "Payment Systems Innovation and Currency Demand in India: Some Applied Perspectives," Reserve Bank of India Occasional Papers Vol. 40, No. 2.

Cook, William and Anand Raman, 2019. "National Payments Corporation of India and the Remaking of Payments in India," Working Paper, Consultative Group to Assist the Poor.

Cornelli, Giulio et al., 2020. "Fintech and Big Tech Credit: A New Database," Working Paper 887. Basel, Switzerland: Bank for International Payments.

Demirgüç-Kunt, Asli et al., 2018. "The Global Findex Database 2017: Measuring Financial Inclusion and the Fintech Revolution," World Bank Group.

Djankov, Simeon, Caralee McLiesh, and Andrei Schleifer, 2007. "Private Credit in 129 Countries," Journal of Financial Economics 84(2): 299–329.

D'Silva, Derryl et al., 2019. "The Design of Digital Financial Infrastructure: Lessons from India," BIS Papers No. 106. Basel, Switzerland: Bank for International Settlements.

Dupas, Pascaline et al., 2018. "Banking the Unbanked? Evidence from Three Countries," American Economic Journal: Applied Economics 10(2): 257–97.

Ehrentraud, Johannes et al., 2020. "Policy Responses to Fintech: A Cross-Country Overview," FSI Insights 23. Basel, Switzerland: Bank for International Settlements.

Ernst and Young, 2019. Global FinTech Adoption Index, https://www.ey.com/en_gl/ey-global-fintech-adoption-index.

FATF, 2020. FATF Guidance on Digital ID, Briefing Note, Financial Action Task Force.

Frost, Jon. et al. 2021. Presentation to Luohan Academy Symposium. Basel: Bank for International Settlements.

Google Payments, 2019. Real-Time Payments Systems & Third Party Access, https://static.googleusercontent.com/media/pay.google.com/en//about/business/static/data/gpay-rtp-2019-whitepaper.pdf.

IMF, 2017. "India—Financial System Stability Assessment," IMF Country Report No. 17/390, Washington DC.

IMF, 2018. "2018 Article IV Consultation," IMF Country Report No. 18/254, Washington DC.

IMF, 2019. "2019 Article IV Consultation," IMF Country Report No. 19/385, Washington DC.

Jack, William and Tavneet Suri, 2014. "Risk Sharing and Transactions Costs: Evidence from Kenya's Mobile Money Revolution," *American Economic Review* 104(1): 183–223.

Misra, P., 2019. "Lesson from Aadhaar: Analog Aspects of Digital Governance Shouldn't Be Overlooked," Pathways for Prosperity Commission Background Paper Series; No. 19. Oxford, United Kingdom.

Morawczynski, Olga and Mark Pickens, 2009. "Poor People Using Mobile Financial Services: Observations on Customer Usage and Impact from M-PESA," CGAP Brief, World Bank, Washington, DC.

Muralidharan, Karthik, Paul Niehaus, and Sandip Sukhtankar, 2016. "Building State Capacity: Evidence from Biometric Smartcards in India," *American Economic Review* 106(10): 2895–929.

Organisation of Economic Cooperation and Development (OECD), 2019. "Digital Government in Chile—Digital Identity," OECD Digital Government Studies. OECD Publishing, Paris.

Patnam, Manasa and Weijia Yao, 2020. "The Real Effects of Mobile Money: Evidence from a Large-Scale Fintech Expansion," Working Paper 20/138, International Monetary Fund, Washington, DC.

Raghavan, Vivek, Sanjay Jain, and Pramod Varma, 2019. "India Stack—Digital Infrastructure as Public Good," *Communications of the ACM* 62(11): 76–81.

Reserve Bank of India (RBI), 2014. "Guidelines for Licensing of Payments Banks," November 2014.

Reserve Bank of India (RBI), 2016. "Master Direction: Non-Banking Financial Company— Account Aggregator (Reserve Bank) Directions" (updated on November 22, 2019).

Sahay, Ratna et al., 2020. "The Promise of Fintech; Financial Inclusion in the Post COVID-19 Era," Departmental Paper 20/09. International Monetary Fund, Washington, DC.

Saroy, Rajas, Ramesh Kumar Gupta, and Sarat Dhal, 2020. "FinTech: The Force of Creative Disruption," RBI Bulletin, November.

Sen, Srijoni, 2019. "A Decade of Aardhaar: Lessons in Implementing a Foundational ID System," Issue Brief No. 292, Observer Research Foundation.

World Bank, 2017. "Privacy by Design: Current Practices in Estonia, India and Austria," Identification for Development, World Bank Group.

World Bank, 2019. "Global Financial Development Database," World Bank Group.

World Economic Forum, 2019. "Global Competitiveness Report."

12

Digital Identity

Exploring a Consumer-Centric Identity for Open Banking

Greg Kidd[*]

1. Introduction

Today's banks create accounts for customers and attach a form of the customer's identity to each bank account. The definition of "digital identity" from a bank's point of view is whatever the bank needs to compliantly identify, authenticate, and authorize the customer (and not an imposter) before undertaking particular services. To put it more simply, a digital identity is a means for people to electronically prove who they are. While a traditional definition of "identity" is "who or what a person is," the definition of "digital identity" extends to a computer-readable representation of the same notion. Each bank maintains its own digital ledger, creates its own digital accounts, and has its own segregated store of digital identity credentials necessary for carrying out its offering, typically in accord with laws and regulations.

Currently, there is no existing form of universal digital identity that can work across these bank silos, let alone national boundaries. And certainly no notion of a portable "self-sovereign identity" (SSI) exists other than as a theoretical construct. There is no formal definition of SSI, but there is some agreement on what should be its common features.[1] According to Wikipedia, an SSI is one in which individuals can fully create and control their digital identities without needing to request permission from an intermediary or centralized authority.[2] In 2016, Christopher Allen and the Sovrin Foundation proposed three categories of requirements for an SSI system: security, controllability, and portability.[3] Following their proposal, in 2018 Alexander Muele et al. proposed four necessary components of an SSI system: identification, authentication, verifiable claims, and attribute storage.[4] To date, the concept of prescriptive, top-down

---

[*] Greg Kidd is currently CEO of GlobaliD, the creator of a global namespace for unique identities for all individuals and entities. Previously he served as the Chief Risk Officer for Ripple, and as an early adviser/investor for Marqeta, Square, and Twitter. He previously worked as a Director for the Promontory Financial Group and as a Senior Analyst for the Board of Governors of the Federal Reserve in the Payments Group. He leads the venture group Hard Yaka, which has invested in scores of global identity, payment, and marketplace startups.

[1] Grüner Mühle and Meinel Gayvoronskaya, "A Survey on Essential Components of a Self-Sovereign Identity," *Computer Science Review* 30 (2018), 80–86. https://arxiv.org/pdf/1807.06346.pdf .

[2] From Wikipedia. https://en.wikipedia.org/wiki/Self-sovereign_identity.

[3] C. Allen, "The Path to Self-Sovereign Identity" (2016). http://www.lifewithalacrity.com/2016/04/the-path-toself-soverereign-identity.html. A. Tobin and D. Reed, "The Inevitable Rise of Self-Sovereign Identity," *Sovrin Found.* (2016) https://sovrin.org/wp-content/uploads/2018/03/The-Inevitable-Rise-of-Self-Sovere ign-Identity.pdf.

[4] Mühle and Gayvoronskaya, *supra* note 2.

Greg Kidd, *Digital Identity* In: *Open Banking*. Edited by: Linda Jeng, Oxford University Press. © Oxford University Press 2022.
DOI: 10.1093/oso/9780197582879.003.0013

constructs of digital identity issued by authorities or institutions such as banks could not be more diametrically opposed to the bottom-up concept of a user-centric and user-controlled digital identity.

Present assumptions of open banking do not explicitly challenge the existing "account-owned identity" construct that prevails today, in which banks and other firms assign some form of identification to the customer, often on an account-by-account basis. If anything, it reinforces the existing framework by purporting to grease the wheels of bank data portability between different siloed banking entities. At question in this chapter is whether such a status quo mechanism for constructing and verifying identity is desirable or workable for open banking as well as for any forward-looking framework of data rights in modern society as discussed in Chapter 2 by Kaitlin Asrow.

a. Compliance and Digital Identity

It is worth noting that the current top-down construct of identity, whereby individual companies and countries delegate identities to individuals and entities in a siloed manner, has performed poorly on a number of metrics. When it comes to dealing with challenges such as terrorist financing, money laundering, rogue regimes, financial exclusion, privacy breaches, ad targeting via spam, and more recently, tracking and surveillance of COVID-19, current constructions of digital identity have proven to be speed bumps at best and absolute barriers at worst to the achievement of pragmatic outcomes. Academic studies[5] and a UN study[6] have assessed the effectiveness of a standard box-checking approach to fighting money laundering at a fail rate of 99 percent—a stunning indictment of the status quo orthodox thinking around anti–money laundering and know-your-customer (AML/KYC) regime in the financial sector.[7]

The ad hoc approach of having different top-down government or corporate entities propagating a patchwork of solutions for creating, authenticating, and authorizing the actions of various identities has proved woefully inadequate in coverage as well as from a security, privacy, and trust point of view. On top of that, the friction from placing the burden on users to remember countless numbers of passwords ensures a suboptimal user interface/user experience (UI/UX) experience, overlaying inconvenience and inefficiency on top of ineffectiveness. The result is to foster phishable attack vectors that play to the strengths of malevolent actors rather than to the potential contributions to the public good.

---

[5] Lanier Saperstein, Geoffrey Sant, and Michelle Ng, "The Failure of Anti-Money Laundering Regulation: Where Is the Cost-Benefit Analysis?," *Notre Dame Law Review Online* 91(1) (2015). http://scholarship.law.nd.edu/ndlr_online/vol91/iss1/4.

[6] United Nations Office on Drugs and Crime, Independent Evaluation Unit 2011. United Nations Global Programme against Money Laundering, Proceeds of Crime and the Financing of Terrorism (GPLM).

[7] Ronald F. Pol, "Anti-money Laundering: The World's Least Effective Policy Experiment? Together, We Can Fix It," *Policy Design and Practice* 3(1) (Feb. 25, 2020, 73–94. Quote: "Likewise, FATF blames governments for 'taking a tick-box approach to regulatory compliance, and focusing on process rather than outcomes' (Lewis 2019), seemingly oblivious to public policy issues such as whether the design or implementation of its policy model contributes to (or causes) such behaviors. Unasked, for instance, is whether FATF's model is itself a 'tick-box' regulatory framework. . . . whether FATF's idiosyncratic assessment methodology forces governments to measure processes rather than outcomes, of which it now complains."

Banks or the fintechs that individually dare to implement alternative risk-based controls for digital identity face the greatest risk of all—regulatory and reputational punishment under the "tall poppies" philosophy when one stands out too much from the pack. While the 2020 Financial Action Task Force (FATF) Guidance on Digital Identity[8] mentions risk-based principles twenty-two times, little to nothing is mentioned about the freedom for institutions to explore how privacy, security, and inclusion innovations can be leveraged without incurring the negative scrutiny of regulators or reticence of legacy bank compliance officers. In addition, FATF did not discuss the notion that competition and innovation through open banking could potentially help accelerate more creative and inclusive approaches to digital identity.

2. Background: Lessons from the World Wide Web

Examples of true protocol solutions for digital identity can be found in the historical evolution of the internet—most notably, in the creation and adoption of the "domain name system" (DNS). Prior to DNS in the 1990s, the internet was in the provenance of universities and governments with little personal or business adoption. It was left to compartmentalized operators of non-internet services, like France's Minitel or US-based CompuServe, Prodigy, or AOL, to get people and businesses online. Like account-owned identity practices of banks today, each of these internet offerings were a world unto themselves that locked their users into segregated silos that eschewed interoperability.

The insight behind DNS was a linguistic construct: that a global namespace to address and differentiate every computer site could enable an interoperable "World Wide Web" (WWW). Every person and business no longer needed to navigate within the silos of countries and corporations because the "web" served as an interoperable protocol *across* those boundaries. In short order after the appearance of DNS and the WWW, the dominant corporate players of the 1990s became footnotes in history, and the world has not looked back since. The triumph of a truly interoperable construct has proved to be the tipping point for making the internet the foundation for modern societal and commercial interaction rather than an esoteric scientific sideshow.

It has been only relatively recent that the notion of a single global internet where users can travel and authenticate worldwide has begun to splinter. First, China erected a combination of legislative and technical barriers dubbed the Great Wall to stop apps like Twitter and Facebook (and their attendant identity schemes) from taking root in their country of one-plus billion people. And of late, the United States has looked to "return the favor" by threatening to ban first TikTok and then the even more popular WeChat from the United States along with possibly similar bans from other US-friendly (or fearful) jurisdictions. But despite those headwinds, the WWW has been a splendid example of a protocol that made possible an "Open Internet" that is miles ahead on interoperability than any open banking arrangement and supporting digital identity system for authentication and authorization.

---

8 "2020 Guidance on Digital Identity," *Financial Action Task Force*. http://www.fatf-gafi.org/media/fatf/documents/recommendations/Guidance-on-Digital-Identity.pdf.

The question then is what does the equivalent to a WWW for computer sites look like for digital identity. Whereas there was a domain naming system that revolutionized the adoption of the internet, what is the equivalent "identity naming system" (INS) and resulting ecosystem that would solve our trust issues around identity in modern society, including those necessary for making open banking a de facto reality. Just as DNS toppled the interoperability challenges posed by Minitel and AOL and provided the building blocks for the WWW, so too might an INS provide the foundation for solving the portability challenge discussed in Chapter 6 around user identity that no single country or corporation could achieve alone.

3. Identity 101: What Does "Identity" Mean?

According to the *Oxford English Dictionary*, the term "identity" is defined as the following:

- quality or condition of being the same (*a*1310; 1756 in sense "individuality, personality", 1801 in sense "distinct impression of a single person or thing presented to or perceived by others") . . . ,
- condition or fact that a person or thing is itself and not something else (8th cent. in a British source),
- fact of being the same (from 12th cent. in British sources),
- continual sameness, lack of variety, monotony (from 12th cent. in British sources; 14th cent. in a continental source) . . .[9]

These definitions for the term "identity" do not translate easily into practical constructs useful for answering "how should identity be constructed to facilitate open banking?" While each of these meanings do not appear inconsistent upon first glance, the devil is in the details in designing an identity regime that makes both economic and ethical sense for societies adopting open banking and open data. (See Chapter 8 for how the European Union, for example, is approaching digital identity and open banking.)

Given that banking is a regulated KYC industry for AML and Bank Secrecy Act (BSA) purposes, there is a presumption that banks must know the ultimate beneficial owner of the customer—that is, the real person behind a personal or business identity. For example, Superman or Mother Teresa may be the identity known to the public, but Clark Kent and Anjezë Gonxhe Bojaxhiu are the true identities behind those personas when it comes to opening and maintaining something as mundane but as regulated as a checking account.

For a customer to view, transact, open, or move a bank account under open banking, the real identity behind the name used must also be trusted by the data controlling party that is being asked by its customers to share their data. A corollary question is whether a society should allow persons to have more than one identity (especially as a privacy preserving mechanism) and that each identity should be able to open independent

---

[9] *Oxford English Dictionary*. https://www-oed-com.proxygt-law.wrlc.org/view/Entry/91004?redirectedFrom=identity&Dictionary.com.

accounts. In China, there is the notion of persons having only one real identity (i.e., in WeChat) rather than the countless avatar-based identities in the US-centric ecosystem (i.e., Twitter, Facebook) for which the true underlying person is abstracted away from both the general public as well as the social media company itself. For example, the actual Tennessee Republican Twitter account "TNGOP" has about 20,000 followers, but the "Ten_GOP" version backed by a Russian troll farm claiming the same status had more than six times as many followers and provided spicier (albeit fake) postings. The reader can guess which account was more popular as a source of retweets by President Donald Trump and his campaign team. But while the US public has turned mostly a blind eye to allowing synthetic identities to exercise free but fake speech, such a permissive construct for identity is unworkable for the banking sector. It is one thing to allow fake identities to engage in fake news, but quite another to allow those imposters to move money within an open banking ecosystem—for both fraud and compliance reasons.

a. Three Primary Functions of a Digital Identity

Ultimately, the key issue is that the financial services industry needs to have its own context-specific working definition of "identity" that can enable users to hold, send, convert, load, move, and spend money. Regardless of whether one is a capitalist, socialist, communist, or some other "-ist," we live in an exchange economy where monies pass between two hands—increasingly electronically rather than via private cash transactions. For this to happen, and happen correctly, the payment system needs to conduct three functions:

1. *Identification* of the parties to an exchange so that the correct parties and underlying accounts are selected for effecting transactions. If Superman wants to send funds to Mother Teresa under traditional or open banking, then the two accounts concerned (i.e., the underlying identities of the sender and recipient plus their account numbers) must be known to the enabling financial institutions.

2. *Authentication* of the parties means ensuring that the party making the request is who they say they are. Someone can look very much like Superman (likeness) and even be able to identify the accounts that are controlled by Superman, but that does not mean that they *are* Superman. Or to put this in crypto terminology, *only* the real Satoshi (or his or her agent) can authenticate themselves by signing in with certain public keys associated with early blocks of mined bitcoins. When the Australian tech entrepreneur Craig Wright claimed to be Satoshi and identified 145 accounts he said he controlled, the actual owner(s) authenticated themselves by signing a message (which only they could do) stating, "Craig Wright is a liar and a fraud," thus debunking his claim. Something you know about identity (i.e., an account number, mother's maiden name, or Social Security number) is not the same as something you, and presumably you alone, have. Authentication is ideally about the latter, while mere identification is about the former.

3. *Authorization* is what you are allowed to do with your identified account after you have authenticated that you are the person who has permission to act with

the identified account. Your authorization may be higher or lower depending on the trust that the enabling party places on the correctness of your identification details (this is the correct account rather than a typo) and authentication (I believe you are who you say you are).

For open banking to work, these three functions, identification, authentication, and authorization, have to operate across banks rather than just within each siloed entity. If each bank has different standards for identification, authentication, and authorization, then friction for sharing data, processing transactions, as well as moving accounts is maximized rather than minimized. Payment systems like ACH/SEPA, FedWire, and card processing are protocols for easing the burden of transferring money between the silos. But without open banking, there are no such protocols for transferring bank account data, or the actual accounts themselves. Most open banking initiatives today are still struggling with how to have enough proof of identity to achieve the bare minimum act of sharing data (i.e., read access)—which is far short of the more ambitious tasks of permitting user-approved third-parties to initiate actual transactions, open accounts, or transfer existing account relationships from one institution to another (i.e., write access), complete with balances.

Bank account data and the accounts themselves currently belong to banks, just as phone numbers used to belong to phone companies. It used to be that when you changed phone companies you had to give up your old phone number and start over with a new one. That meant telling everyone to update their directories with your new phone number. The Federal Communication Commission in the United States and its equivalent international regulators finally forced phone companies to give up their ownership of telephone numbers, allowing people to own their own phone numbers and shop for the best service without fear of losing their long-established association with a given number.

The portability enjoyed in the phone industry has not yet materialized in the financial industry—where account numbers are still owned by banks rather than by customers/end users. When you change banks, you get a new account number and have to update all your direct deposit and bill pay details or else havoc ensues. Each bank has its own respective system of identification, authentication, and authorization that works with the bank's internal account numbering system. There is also no model for a universal directory of all valid bank account numbers and corresponding owners as there is with phone numbers (the white and yellow pages) or with domain names (the WWW). Open banking could break down these silos but to date has yet to develop the kinds of interoperable protocols enjoyed in the mobile phone and internet industries.

Even without the full portability of account numbers, the banking industry could still agree to common protocols for third-parties to access account data and initiate transactions on behalf of the users via application programming interfaces (APIs)—but by and large, banks have failed to provide such on and off ramps of their own free will. Most banks have failed to provide any APIs, let alone standardized APIs. The absence of bank-based APIs created a gap for third-parties like Yodlee, Plaid, and Salt Edge to scrape the data through building bots that imitate the behavior of humans logging into their own accounts as described in Chapter 5 by Don Cardinal and Nick Thomas. The gray area of scraping relies on users delegating their bank authentication credentials (username and password) to third-parties, which tokenize these credentials for security and then act on behalf of the user.

The challenge is that once the bot is essentially authenticated as the user, it is unclear what authorization, if any, should be granted by the bank to the third-party for any access to account data and funds. In short, once the bot has identified an account (benevolently with the help of the account owner, or malevolently with credentials purchased on the Dark Web) and authenticated, what limits apply under either traditional or open banking (not just for add/editing/deleting data, but also for sending, converting, loading, moving, and spending funds). After all, as discussed by Steven Boms and Sam Taussig in Chapter 3, the services running these bots are not the regulated entities shouldering the responsibility for making the customer whole over errors and fraud associated with shortfalls of identification, authentication, and authorization.

Many banks have argued that they are protecting their customers by not opening up their accounts to the risks of screen-scraping. Their argument is that open access entails too much risk—especially fraud, when user details are collected by a third-party to access the desired data. Banks have traditionally shouldered the burden of customer losses due to both fraudulent and erroneous transactions conducted via open banking. Banks now want to know who will be liable for the inevitable losses their customers will incur when they unwittingly delegate identification and authentication credentials to an untrustworthy third-party. When that unwitting bank customer later claims that actions taken upon their account were "unauthorized" even though they willingly identified their own account and granted authentication details to the malevolent party, regulation often lays responsibility upon the bank to reimburse the customer for losses (see Chapter 3 on customer liability). For banks that carry potential liability, open banking can look like an open invitation for abuse at their expense, not to mention a grave competitive threat as switching costs between banks and even nonbanks are reduced and banks are increasingly forced to compete to gain or retain deposits. (See Chapter 1 for a description of the open banking landscape.)

What has played out in the market is that banks have generally paid lip service to open banking while foot dragging on its implementation. When implementation has moved forward, it has done so in a manner that looks very little like a unified protocol-based approach for accessing the data. Regulators in countries like Singapore and especially Australia have been more thoughtful and forceful in getting their handful of banks to play along with standardized and *mandated* approaches to API access. But what about the rest of the world where regulators and/or industry self-regulation and standard setting are lagging?

Given that there are tens of thousands of banks in the world and no open banking equivalent of WWW protocols in communication (TCP/IP), email delivery (SMTP), or domain names (DNS), there is little possibility that interoperability between banks and third-parties will be effective and efficient in the short to medium term. Exploiting the paucity of standardized APIs between banks and fintechs has been the bread-and-butter business of data aggregators, such as Plaid, and is the rationale for Visa's USD 5.3 billion acquisition of this less than ten-year-old startup.[10] Plaid's magic has been to

---

[10] On November 5, 2020, the Justice Department (DOJ) sued to block Visa's acquisition of Plaid as anticompetitive and a threat to the types of innovation that open banking could bring. The DOJ stated: "The complaint alleges that Visa's CEO viewed the acquisition as an 'insurance policy' to protect against a 'threat

take advantage of and bypass how identification of bank accounts, authentication, and authorization have been traditionally conducted in a closed-loop system of traditional banking, using bot-driven logic and scraping (supplemented more recently by ad hoc API pay-to-play deals with banks that have taken more of a "if you can't beat them, join them" perspective on their customers' access to and use of their banking data), giving bank customers easier access to fintech services and products. The Plaid-like solutions are still clumsy and slow compared to the level of interoperability already enabled in the telecom and internet sectors. Don Cardinal and Nick Thomas describe the current evolution of screen-scraping to APIs in Chapter 5.

4. Short Survey of Digital Identity Systems

Many countries, nonetheless, are attempting to adopt and implement digital identity systems. This section briefly describes a few programs of note.

a. Singapore

Many have pointed to smaller countries with state-based digital identity solutions that have worked optimally at a local level ("local optimum") when mandated by the government and strictly enforced. There is no better example of a top-down nationally mandated identity solution than that of Singapore's. The National Digital Identity (NDI) program[11] functions as a mobile crypto-based identity that allows residents to use a centralized set of credentials to carry out transactions in both the private and public sectors. Originally started in 2003, the program has evolved into a cornerstone of Singapore's Smart Nation project to support citizens' "digitally-enabled life" in both the digital and physical realms, leveraging the authentication program Singpass and identity data sources like MyInfo and the Immigration and Checkpoints Authority's national registry. Interestingly, Singaporeans were already familiar with the notion of a national identity system through prior national ID systems implemented by the British during colonial times. (This is ironic given the British themselves have steadfastly resisted the notion of such schemes for themselves on privacy grounds, but have recently announced plans for their own digital identity program.[12] See the following

---

to our important US debit business.' This acquisition is the second-largest in Visa's history, with an extraordinary price tag of $5.3 billion. Visa's CEO justified the deal to Visa's Board of Directors as a 'strategic, not financial' move, and noted that in part because 'our US debit business i[s] critical and we must always do what it takes to protect this business.' Unless acquired, Visa feared that Plaid 'on their own or owned by a competitor [was] going to create some threat' with a 'potential downside risk of $300–500M in our US debit business' by 2024. If Plaid remained free to develop its competing payment platform, then 'Visa may be forced to accept lower margins or not have a competitive offering.'" See the Department of Justice press release (Nov. 5, 2020). https://www.justice.gov/opa/pr/justice-department-sues-block-visas-proposed-acquisition-plaid.

[11] GovTech Singapore, "Giving Every Citizen A Unique Digital Identity." (Sept. 24, 2018). https://www.tech.gov.sg/media/technews/giving-every-citizen-a-unique-digital-identity?utm_medium=recommender_0&utm_source=aHR0cHM6Ly93d3cudGVjaC5nb3Yuc2cvc2Nld2MyMDE5L25kaQ==&utm_content=aHR0cHM6Ly93d3cudGVjaC5nb3Yuc2cvbWVkaWEvdGVjaG5ld3MvZ2l2aW5nLWV2ZXJ5LWNpdGl6Z W4tYS11bmlxdWUtZGlnaXRhbC1pZGVudGl0eQ==.

[12] https://www.gov.uk/government/news/next-steps-outlined-for-uks-use-of-digital-identity.

section.) By all reports the Singapore system works well, but possibly because there is more cultural acceptance by Singaporeans of a nationally dictated solution. Their success in this and many other areas may not be easily replicated elsewhere. Within a smaller nation-state, open banking may be easier to roll out with a ubiquitous and portable standard for identity authentication.

b. United Kingdom

When the British have attempted their own digital identity solution, they took on a more modest scope of focusing only on public sector integrations—leaving out the banking sector altogether. The effort ran over budget and four years behind schedule before getting to market in 2016. At the time of writing, the sign-up rate for GOV.UK Verify was only 43 percent.[13] GOV.UK Verify has been deemed an "onerous system not fit for purpose" by the United Kingdom's own Public Account Committee.[14] The scope and scale of the project, which was relatively modest to begin with, have been reduced further rather than expanded into something more ambitious or useful. There is now little prospect that this identity initiative could enhance the speed or scope of adoption of the UK Open Banking regime nor replicate the success of Singapore's NDI program.

c. Sweden

The Nordic countries have a successful history with digital identities. Take Sweden, for example, which has managed to build its own bank-led national identity system. BankID was first issued in 2003 and is currently used by eight million people on a regular basis for a wide variety of private and public services.[15] It is based on a federated electronic identification (eID) model, which requires collaboration between banks and identity service providers. The credential is used both for identification as well as signing of documents in a legally binding manner in compliance with Swedish law. The offering is available on smart cards, computers, mobile phones, and tablet devices. BankID is a proprietary, near-monopoly offering that is often the only means by which a person can access many services in Sweden. However, the closed nature of the offering makes competition, permissionless innovation, and access by non-Swedes a practical impossibility.

d. Estonia

In contrast to Sweden, the Estonian e-residency (which the author has) is an entirely open protocol that could be potentially interoperable with other like systems across Europe or other parts of the world. While the word "e-residency" would imply many

---

[13] Dashboard—Gov.UK Verify. https://www.gov.uk/performance/govuk-verify.

[14] Public Accounts Committee Parliament UK, "Accessing Public Services Through the Government's U.K. Verify System" (May 8, 2019). https://publications.parliament.uk/pa/cm201719/cmselect/cmpubacc/1748/1748.pdf.

[15] https://www.bankid.com/en/om-bankid/detta-ar-bankid.

legal privileges, the reality is that the holder garners no right to Estonian residency, travel privileges, voting, medical, or any other benefits. The real reason for getting this credential is the theoretically greater ease of being banked in Estonia. But as a non-Estonian who has attempted to make good on even this thin strand of benefit, the author can assure you that unless you actually live and work in Estonia, your e-residency is more useful as a wall plaque than as an actual conduit to banking in the country. The slim hope of a practical application for a foreigner to access bank services in Estonia has shrunk[16] even more since the Danske Bank branch in the country is alleged to be the conduit for the largest money-laundering scandal in the history of the world with fines projected in the USD 2 billion range.

e. India

Another novel and perhaps the best known nation-state approach to digital identity is India's biometric-based, universal digital identity system: Aadhaar[17] (for a description of the foundational role Aadhaar plays in India's open banking approach, see Chapter 11, and see Chapter 2 on data protections). With over one billion users in its centralized database, Aadhaar is arguably the largest identity database in the world (biometric or otherwise). First launched in 2009 and implemented by 2012, Aadhaar created a unique numerical identifier tied to biometric details (fingerprints and iris scans) to facilitate administrative efficiency for both public (e.g., voting and social service benefits) and private (e.g., banking) services throughout India.[18]

The top-down nature of the system has garnered heated concerns over the privacy issues engendered by tying a twelve-digit number to each person's biometric credentials and storing all that data in a monolithic central server. While it is not a legal requirement to obtain an Aadhaar ID, early trends suggested that Aadhaar ID might become so ubiquitous that it would become mandatory in practice for opening bank accounts or mobile phone accounts in India. Nonetheless, the Indian Supreme Court set limits on institutions' ability to require Aadhaar IDs for opening government benefits and business services accounts and, more importantly, that Indians have a fundamental right to privacy under the Indian Constitution.[19]

Assessing this system as a global model, given that the only requirement to get an Aadhaar number is the ability to provide a biometric fingerprint or iris scan, there is no reason why the system would not work beyond Indian borders. In fact, there is no way to tell whether a recipient of a new Aadhaar identity is, in fact, an Indian or a foreign citizen. That means there is no practical prohibition on the use of the existing Aadhaar system by persons outside of India. In theory, Aadhaar could be the foundation for a

---

[16] "Estonia's Digital Residency Programme Faces First Headwind," *ComputerWeekly.com*. (Apr. 23, 2018). https://www.computerweekly.com/news/252439704/Estonias-digital-residency-programme-faces-first-headwind.

[17] https://uidai.gov.in/what-is-aadhaar.html.

[18] Billy Perrigo, "India Has Been Collecting Eye Scans and Fingerprint Records from Every Citizen. Here's What to Know," *Time* (Sept. 28, 2018). https://time.com/5409604/india-aadhaar-supreme-court/.

[19] Stacey Kiran, "India Supreme Court Deals Blow to Biometric ID System," *Financial Times* (Aug. 24, 2017). https://www.ft.com/content/473c8532-888f-11e7-bf50-e1c239b45787.

global rather than national identity system, but there is no indication that any such expansion is or has been considered by current or past Indian leadership. Granted that serving one-plus billion Indian residents is a prodigious task, the raw technical capacity of Aadhaar and the team backing it begs the question of why the infrastructure isn't extended to the world at large. Upon speaking with founding members and current leadership, we have learned there is no current capacity for Aadhaar to expand beyond India—and especially not to Western countries where privacy concerns would prevail about the centralized vulnerability of a single database storing all, biometrically confirmable, user identities.

f. Pakistan

Not to be outdone by India's biometric identity program, Pakistan has implemented its own biometric-based Computerized National Identity Card.[20] Like other Balkanized national payments systems, the Pakistani and Indian offerings are not interoperable. Similar to how US state driver's licenses have failed to be standardized and centralized[21] at the federal level, nation states have generally failed to make their own offerings interoperable.

Singapore, the United Kingdom, Sweden, Estonia, India, and Pakistan all serve as examples of the limits of nation-state-based identity schemes. Without a global identity "protocol," identity offerings remain mired in what one might call "local optimizations," which is doing the best possible with geographically limited country-based schemes that either do not or cannot scale across borders.

g. Corporate Identity Schemes

An alternative to government-sponsored identity programs are corporate-led initiatives that have potential for more organic adoption. Facebook is an obvious potential scheme—but its lack of any sort of verification regime ensures the number of fake accounts number in the billions of accounts per year.[22] Mastercard and Visa also have merchant account memberships in the tens of millions and cardholder accounts in the billions, but they fail to organize those accounts into a cohesive identity platform that could be accessed by third-parties or end-user customers as a self-sovereign resource. Both of the card networks speak to the principles of digital identity and authentication in white papers,[23] but, significantly, they both ban the practical application of such methods when it comes to their issuing platforms. Any third-party that wishes to issue

---

[20] https://www.justice.gov/eoir/page/file/1130671/download.
[21] American Civil Liberties website (ACLU). "The broad and diverse opposition to a standardized driver's license plan reflects the reality that this scheme is nothing less than a national ID," said Katie Corrigan, an ACLU Legislative Counsel. "The proposal would be ineffective, expensive and would represent a serious threat to core American liberties." https://www.aclu.org/press-releases/criticism-growing-nation-wide-standardized-drivers-license-plan.
[22] "CNN Business Facebook Has Shut Down 5.4 billion Accounts This Year," *CNN* (Nov. 13, 2019). https://www.cnn.com/2019/11/13/tech/facebook-fake-accounts/index.html.
[23] "Digital Identity Restoring Trust in a Digital World," *Mastercard* (Mar. 2019). https://www.mastercard.us/content/dam/mccom/en-us/issuers/digital-identity/digital-identity-restoring-trust-in-a-digital-world-final-share-corrected.pdf; and Visa Digital Authentication, "New Opportunities to Enhance the Customer

cards to a global population of users is forced to serve its members through national or regional bank channel partners. Global fintech companies like Coinbase or Blockchain. com, each with over thirty million accounts worldwide, are forbidden from leveraging the card networks for issuing universal payment cards to these preverified users. These blockages are not regulatory, but rather a reflection of private incentives to preserve the local fiefdoms of the card networks' local banking partners at the expense of practical, universal, and/or self-sovereign-based identity solutions at a global level. Even with Mastercard and Visa, the global reach of the card issuance in financial services does not necessarily lead to global identity standards and access.

Another example of Mastercard and Visa blocking innovation around identity relates to how the card networks bundle three value-added offerings in a manner that stymies the potential for lower costs and faster offerings. The Mastercard and Visa networks bundle the following three functions:

1. *identifying and verifying* the cardholder and merchant at the time of a transaction;
2. *clearing* payments and fees between all issuing and acquiring partners through a centralized exchange; and
3. *settling* funds from the issuing banks and to the acquiring banks over ACH, wire, SEPA, or an equivalent system in each country.

In situations where a consumer and a merchant both have digital wallets with the same nonbank, such as Square Cash, Venmo, or PayPal, funds could be cleared and settled directly as on-platform digital transfers without touching the bank rails of Mastercard's and Visa's bank partners. Only the identities of the payor and payee need to be authenticated by the respective card and point-of-sale terminal. These cheaper and faster digital wallets complete transactions bypassing banks in much the same way Alipay and WeChat optimize clearing and settlement in China. These nonbank players would gladly pay the smaller portion of interchange fees related to the direct cost of authenticating the payor and payee, rather than paying oligopoly-priced interchange fees to the issuing and acquiring banks. Such a practice bypassing banks could catapult Mastercard and Visa into true identity providers but would cannibalize their core interchange business. Discover Card was hungry enough as a losing competitor in the marketplace to support PayPal in pursuing a similar tactic with Home Depot in 2012, but execution in the brick and mortar business was subpar and failed to ignite the market or incite Mastercard and Visa to follow suit. To this day, Mastercard and Visa block the sharing of their networks of billions of cards and fifty million merchants as identity platforms with third-parties. One must join their closed networks and agree to use their costly, slow, and rigid clearing and settlement bundle. The mechanisms to achieve innovation and competition are already at hand, but the will (or regulatory mandate) to forcibly allow their use is lacking in the United States, Europe, and worldwide for the most part. Just as locking in customers has been a profitable strategy for banks, so too has locking in cross-sold interchange fees has been a profitable strategy to the benefit of banks as well as a barrier to more open markets and consumer options.

Journey." https://www.visa.co.ao/dam/VCOM/global/visa-everywhere/documents/visa-aite-digital-authent ication-infographic.pdf.

5. Who Should Own Customer's Digital Identity and Data?

The ownership question and answer is often presumptively assumed by policymakers to be "the government owns the individual's identity and data" or by the private sector to be "incumbent financial and tech companies own the individual's identity and data." Both assumptions are wrapped in a paternalistic rationale that these institutions do so on behalf of, and for the good of, the customer. The paternalistic, guardian view is that the demands for privacy and security are so complex and overwhelming that only institutions can be trusted to handle the responsibility of the task at hand. Regardless of whether one is more trusting of governments or corporations, both views make (and open banking does not contradict) a parochial and institutional presumption that top-down control is the presumptive solution to how privacy, security, and trust in society can and must operate.

The alternative proposition is that customers themselves should and can own their own identity and dictate who has access to, and use of, the data associated with their identity. The proposition presumes that agency can effectively be vested in the customers themselves, with only limited grants to governments and corporations to service those customers. Just as consumers can now own domain names and phone numbers and designate web-hosting firms and phone companies to service their domains and phone numbers, so too could consumers own their financial identities and delegate roles to banks and other financial institutions to compete for servicing the consumers' financial activities. The extension of this alternative proposition is that owning one's identity and data is in fact an actual human right with a reciprocal responsibility of all persons and organizations to maintain one's identity rather than only a subset of a population that shows up on the radar of a particular government, financial, or other organization. (See Chapter 2 for more reading on data rights.)

a. Designing an Inclusion-Based Identity

When one thinks of digital identity, it is assumed that it is something everyone possesses independent of it being granted by a government or a private sector company. This perspective is quite at odds with how one thinks about digital identity in an open banking ecosystem. If everyone has an identity from birth, then one could ask whether individuals would benefit from having other identifiers from birth—that is, a phone number for life, a tax ID for life, and yes, even financial account(s) for life. Which phone company, government, or bank *serves* those respective identities is very different from saying that phone companies, governments, or banks *create* those identities. As long as the identifiers are standardized and ubiquitous, then the notion of portability could become practical reality. Just as there is a global SMS standard for phone companies and TCP/IP/HTML standard for the WWW, so too could there be common identity protocols that would grease the wheels for a significant acceleration in open banking activities.

An interesting thought experiment we had when I worked at the Board of Governors of the Federal Reserve was over the implications of what would happen if the United States (and other countries) adopted a one-tier rather than two-tier financial ledger system that rooted individual identity in a universal rather than in multiple bank ledgers. (How this could work also has been the topic of discussions around how a digital dollar could work.) The Federal Reserve could run a single ledger based on identity (either for every American resident—or, more imaginatively, for every person or entity in the world). Any identified person or entity could hold digital dollars directly on the ledger. This does not mean banks would become obsolete any more than if a single registry of all web domain names or phone numbers managed by one entity would mean the disintermediation of multiple internet or phone companies. Banks would still be entities that serviced those accounts for intermediation—paying interest on those deposits in exchange for being able to create credit by lending out those deposits and earning a margin—just as they do today. The difference is that everyone would be banked by default, and there would likely be one or more institutions of last resort (i.e., the postal system,[24] money transmitter, or other nongovernmental organization) that would provide services for even low-value accounts that banks find too unprofitable to service. The bottom line, though, is that everyone would be electronically banked by default, from birth to death, as a right and responsibility of digital identity. Open banking could transform financial inclusion in such a scenario.

The arguments for this scenario are not social agenda arguments *per se* (as one might use in extolling the virtues of universal public education or healthcare) but rather a more pragmatic economic argument that it is simply more efficient and effective to have everyone in an electronic money system rather than have some people or entities fall outside of it. It does not mean that one cannot still have cash or other forms of money, but with everyone having at least a seat at the economic table there is a big payoff in enabling everyone to pay and be paid electronically. In contrast to the current world where a payor or sender always has to figure out a way to get cash to a party that has no electronic identity and, therefore, no electronic account, the payor/sender would have the simplicity of systems that can always route a payment to anyone because everyone, by default, has a digital identity that incorporates the capacity to receive and hold funds electronically. In contrast to the current reality in which the payee/recipient must choose to be paid outside the banking system (e.g., the unbanked cashing checks for high fees), the world moves to a reality whereby the payor/sender determines the method of payment with a fully built-in, electronic option. Such a foundation would be rocket fuel for a deep adoption of open banking.

If the notion of a universal account sounds futuristic or far-fetched—think again, as it already exists. Tax ID systems or government benefits systems (be it the US Social Security number or its equivalent elsewhere) are already in use throughout the world. Of course this is a paternalistic top-down system, but the point is that every resident (and even nonresidents) in the United States has access to a Social Security or tax number, which is already associated with a ledger of value. Granted, the store of value is a future promise (typically post-retirement), but the entire supporting ledger system for a current account is already in place. It would simply be a matter of political will to apply these numbers to current accounts rather than just retirement accounts—for Americans, but also for any person. As the Indian biometric identity system could be

---

[24] *See* Mehrsa Baradaran, *How the Other Half Banks* (First Harvard University Press, 2018).

used for the world's seven-plus billion people rather than just India's one-plus billion, so too could any tax ID numbering or phone numbering system be used as a foundation for a global financial inclusion-based identity, authentication, and authorization system. And with that ubiquitous foundation and standardization, open banking is transformed from an exercise in cat herding, to a practical and sweeping achievable global mandate.

Now granted, the question is whether tax IDs and phone numbers are the best identifiers when used in conjunction with authentication and authorization. And the clear answer is that no, these are not the best for a myriad of reasons that revolve around the nation-state's segregated systems of tax and phone number schemes. But there is another example of a working foundation that is not based on tax IDs and phone numbers. And that is the example of Domain Name System (DNS), which ensures a mutually exclusive and collectively exhaustive list of all the worldwide websites in existence. Unlike the number-based constructs of tax IDs and phone numbers, DNS is a linguistic construct that has none of the limitations of cobbling together national tax ID schemes. One merely types in a domain name and one is transported to a unique website anywhere in the world. There is no Chinese or Brazilian web addressing—there is only the WWW. Granted the Chinese or Iranians may try to wall off particular IP addresses outside of their geographical footprint, but they are not running their own intranets with segregated versions of TCP/IP or DNS. It remains one global protocol at least as far as identifying websites for routing purposes.

The DNS overlay is arguably the most proven, scalable, and effective in the history of mankind. Its conception was to create survivability of networks in the event of a nuclear attack that might decapitate a more centralized (and efficient) network protocol. And it has worked—not because it is the most efficient (sending everything in duplicative packets to be reassembled in full at the point of arrival is anything but efficient), but because it is sustainable *and* simple and standardizable. It scales and dominates in spite of its lack of efficiency because it is good enough on the efficiency front and overwhelmingly superior on the effectiveness front as an easy to execute standard across corporate and nation-state silos. Stacked up against the Gutenberg printing press for books, SMS for text messaging, and SMTP for email, the DNS has the prodigious standing as the most powerful protocol in the world as it leverages the network of the WWW that dominates our society today.

6. Identity Naming System: A Global "Namespace" for Digital Identity

The concept of a "namespace" (be it represented in words, numbers, or a combination of both) could be either universal or federated. In a universal system, there is one overall naming/numbering system to which everyone adheres. Alternatively, in a federated system, there can be any number of namespaces or numbering systems that each operate as "mutually exclusive and collectively exhaustive" within their own subdomain, but would be potentially duplicative of names and numbers in other subdomains. Examples of universal namespaces are Twitter and Skype—where your handle is globally unique, and there is no tiered naming or account numbering system. Alternatively, the WWW is universal at the ".com" level, but federated to the extent that individual countries can have various identifying suffixes, as well as the existence of ".net," ".org," and many other federated flavors.

a. Universal vs. Federated

To find an address in a federated system, you need to first know which subdomain you are searching in. In the current realm of banking, each bank effectively operates its own identity subdomain, and there is no universal identifier for users of banking services. Each customer has both a bank account number and an identifying bank (subdomain) number in the form of an ABA or SWIFT routing number. Compare this with the universal numbering system used by telecommunication companies where there is one overall identifying system containing all the phone numbers, which in turn are serviced by individual telecoms. In practical terms, this means that you do not need to know which phone company someone subscribes to in order to call them, but you do need to know which bank they have an account with in order to send them money. The point being is that banking, and especially open banking, could be more universal—like telecoms—if the public policy to support this as a conduit to open banking were more explicit.

In seeking an aspirational foundation and roadmap in the case of digital identity, one might do well to understand why a universal linguistic approach to identity trumps a federated and/or numerical approach, especially those underpinning other competing protocols in history.[25] For an INS, names are unique "handles" rather than being actual names of real people or entities. While no two people or entities can have the same name, it is possible for an individual user to have multiple names, each for a different purpose. For example, one name may represent the user's business identity, while another represents his or her personal identity.

In a universal INS, each of a user's names is distinct. That is, the attestations (i.e., evidence or proof) associated with a name are unique to that particular name: for each name, the user's personally identifiable information (PII) can be used to generate attestations for that name, but if the user has multiple names, they will have to generate attestations for each of their names in turn. One of the key tenets of INS is that there is no way of knowing that two or more names are owned by the same person. Because only the public attestations are revealed and not the underlying PII, it is impossible for an outsider (or even an intruder into the INS system) to discover that two names belong to the same individual. This is vital when it comes to maintaining the user's privacy and can even have safety implications in societies or domestic situations where a second, "secret" identity can be used as a means to earn freedoms that would otherwise be taken away.

---

[25] The prior protocol of TCP/IP was not replaced but rather overlaid. TCP and IP are addresses for machines to find other machines and as such are not very human-friendly. Other federated protocols for identity were silo solutions like America Online, where one had an identity and a name that worked just within AOL but would not be recognized or interoperable with CompuServe.

b. Zero-Knowledge Proofs

Once a person or an entity has a name, they can proceed to collect attestations about their name from third-parties—ideally in a manner that can be cryptographically signed to ensure that such verifications can be trusted to have happened at a particular point in time, about a particular named identity, and by an identified (and hopefully trusted) third-party. Such attestations can be simple things like "round-tripping" a phone number under one's control (with a signature by Twilio). Or the attestations can be more complex, such as verification of a driver's license by an Onfido, or bank credentials by Plaid. Attestations can also be about proving that one can log in to a social media account, pass a captcha challenge, or show that another named identity has "vouched" for you. In each of these cases, the collection of PII has two components:

1. the type of information that has been verified, along with who verified it and when it was verified; and
2. the actual underlying data itself (such as the actual phone number, date of birth, bank account number, age, citizenship).

In some cases, once an identity has been authenticated, it may be enough to know that certain attestations are in place and sufficient to authorize a particular permission. But in other cases, it is not enough to know that the data is on hand and verified, but also that some particular criteria are met about the data. The discipline of zero-knowledge proofs is the ability to answer with probabilistic certitude a question such as "is this person over 21" without having to reveal or share the underlying data (i.e., a birthdate). Such proofs preclude the privacy and security risk of having to expose or share more data than is necessary to meet a particular compliance or risk parameter in a given set of circumstances.

Once a person or entity has a name and the attestations for verifying the identity and reputation associated with this name, zero-knowledge proofs can be used so that the person or entity can provide permission to act without giving up PII. This would require the data to be organized in such a way that can be interrogated with zero-knowledge proofs. If banks operating under the dictates of open banking felt comfortable trusting such proofs, there would be no longer the requirement for banks to collect PII from users as long as they could access that information in the off chance that they needed to meet a compliance obligation, such as filing a Suspicious Activity Report. Today, there's not a single bank that takes advantage of zero-knowledge-proof-based tools, bypassing the need to collect and retain copious amounts of PII. In the alternative reality of using zero-knowledge proofs, banks would only need to authenticate your name and then authorize your requests based on the proofs you had—all without you revealing your underlying PII on the blockchain. But such a reality is far from the mindset of banks' standing operating procedures and the mindset of being the controlling entity of their customers' PII.

c. Ownership of INS Names

Similar to website domain names, INS names can be transferred from one owner to another. Ownership of a name would usually be lifelong. But for role-based names, ownership can change with circumstances—for example, the name "POTUS" (President of the United States) may be transferred to a new owner after a presidential election. A name also may be transferred when a business is sold, or in any other situation where the current owner agrees to give the name to someone else. When a name is transferred, all the public attestations about that name are also transferred to the new owner. Most crucially, the underlying PII is not transferred. In this way, the name has a trail of provenance that stays forever with that name. Since the attestations are preserved with the change in ownership, an understanding of why authorizations were granted (for actions such as transferring funds between parties, firing missiles, etc.) can be maintained in a world of rules and laws.

While it is a matter of public record that a name was transferred to a new owner, this may or may not affect the name's reputation. For names representing branded entities, the reputation of the name may have an enduring provenance that is stronger and more persistent than the ownership of that name by one particular individual. As well as transferring names to a new owner, a name's owner may choose to release a name they no longer want. When a name is released, the name goes back into the pool of names that others may claim as their own. Taken together, the three processes of claiming, transferring, and releasing names allows a user to set up the identity or identities that they want to control and keep relevant over time.

Finally, since names and biometrics are tokenized and stored on mobile devices, the loss of a device could potentially mean that the user had lost control over the name stored on the device. As soon as a device is lost, stolen, or compromised, the user can immediately revoke the name(s) held on that device. That renders the name or names unusable, preventing anyone who has the device from using those names, even if the built-in biometric and other checks on the device were bypassed. Once the user has a new device (or regains control of the initial existing device), they can then choose to restore their name(s) on the new device. As well as mitigating security concerns, these revoke and restore actions allow users to keep their INS names when upgrading to a newer phone.

The "right to be forgotten" included in the European Union's General Data Protection Regulation implies that a user may request that their PII be hidden or removed at their discretion. While INS allows for this, the fact that a particular attestation was generated at a specific point in time is immutably recorded into a blockchain, allowing third-parties to determine whether or not the public history for a name had not been altered, even if the PII associated with the attestations had been removed. The only exception to this "right to be forgotten" is the regulatory-mandated recordkeeping requirements of information of "legitimate interest" needed to meet AML/BSA/KYC reporting requirements.

For INS to serve as a better alternative, one has only to look back at the pre-DNS world to understand the consequences of continuing down our current fragmented identity path. Prior to a global namespace for domain names there was no WWW, and society made do with fractured, closed-loop communication networks like AOL and

French-based Minitel. Had people been satisfied with these locally optimized (and thus locally constrained) solutions, there likely would not be the ubiquitous and inclusive internet that we enjoy today. In terms of digital identity, the equivalent of AOL and Minitel would be present-day corporate and governmental silos, such as Facebook, WeChat, and India's Aadhaar system. While these systems may work well locally, they actually impede the path to a global and inclusive identity protocol, one that is privacy-preserving, secure, and ultimately trusted.

INS could provide a better path. By using unique names and associated attestations, the reputation of actors can be understood and actions allowed or blocked accordingly. This is a real rather than a window-dressing defense against bad actors, who otherwise could play havoc with fake news, fraud, money laundering, terrorist funding, and other coercive and abusive behavior. The inappropriate use and leaking of data, as exposed by cases such as Facebook and the Panama Papers, becomes exponentially harder when INS-verified names and attestations are required for particular actions that pose a risk to people's privacy and security. Furthermore, the use of long-lived names with a rich history of attestations helps to build trust that not only is someone who they claim to be but that they will continue to behave in a reputation-enhancing way in the future. In this way, privacy, security, and trust are grown rather than traded off.

d. Ubiquity

One of the key concepts behind INS is that it is ubiquitous. Rather than only covering a particular subset of people and entities that happen to want to use a particular system, or who reside in a particular country, an INS name is available to anyone. This includes the poor and those from countries or in circumstances where they would ordinarily be excluded from traditional identity systems. This allows everyone to experience the freedoms and responsibilities associated with having an identity. By selecting a name and anchoring attestations to that name, anyone in the world is able to build a reputation that can allow or prevent that person from performing various actions.

An identity ecosystem is enhanced not by excluding problematic actors but by deliberately including all—and in particular, bad actors. Named bad actors are meant to be in a system that limits bad actions by restricting their permissions. To achieve this, the bad actors' named identities must be confidently known so their permissions can be limited in matching with their reputation. The concept of good and bad actors depends on context. This means that the INS protocol itself does not attempt to classify actors as good or bad. Because attestations are inherently neutral, they can be used by different countries and regimes to identify the group of individuals and entities that fall under their jurisdiction, while ignoring those names that do not meet their requirements. It does not matter whether a particular regime is privacy-preserving or privacy-shredding, libertarian or totalitarian—either a given name has the attestations required for a particular permissioned activity in that jurisdiction, or it does not. This allows corporate and government rules to be respected, with permissions granted or denied accordingly. This is a fundamental lubricant and accelerant for open banking to work and spread not just within national jurisdictions—but across them as well.

Another key difference with INS is that named identities are both persistent and portable, allowing them to be used across all legal and corporate regimes without having to be reconstructed from scratch. The attestations built up over time form a "bundle of sticks" that the user can bring to any table. If those sticks are sufficient to allow a permissioned activity, then permission is granted. If not, then the user can either seek out additional attestations to meet the regime's requirements, or decide that the permissioned activity isn't worth the effort and abandon the request. Either way, both parties have exercised their free will in deciding whether or not to go ahead with the activity. This applies in particular to open banking, where there will be a default to the lowest common denominator between two parties negotiating access to particular user data, transactional initiation privileges, and the ability to open and move user accounts.

In today's world, however, people interact and do business all over the globe. Just as DNS operates in a simple but universal manner, INS also could operate in a global sphere where interactions across boundaries are the norm rather than the exception. Paternalistic companies and even national-based approaches should not be speed bumps, let alone barriers, to cross-border transactions and interactions. Unlike these segregated systems, a global INS protocol would be a transformative solution that sees privacy, security, and trust as mutually complementary rather than as competing values. The simple aim of INS is to ensure that it is easier to build and maintain a good name instead of starting anew after debasing a prior name. While making it more desirable to maintain a good reputation in a name rather than rebuilding from scratch may seem like a fairly humble goal, the success of DNS in promoting the trust and adoption of a ubiquitous namespace for websites is instructive and compelling as a model for what INS could achieve.

7. Conclusion

Currently, most banks view themselves as guardians of their customers' identities through creating and controlling the identities correspondingly attached to their customers' bank accounts. Not surprisingly, banks are account-driven (rather than identity-driven). The banks are like the sun, and their customers are like planets that revolve around the sun's gravity force. The bank's pull on its depositors and their data the way the sun pulls on its orbiting planets. Open banking proposes a model in which multiple suns, such as other banks and fintechs, could also pull on these planets. Such a scenario would be messy from a physics point of view, but also would be potentially disruptive to the oligopolistic status quo that has historically dominated the financial services industry.

Clearly, advocates for open banking believe that the competitive and innovative benefits of easier data-sharing between (with appropriate customer consent) banks and other fintechs would be beneficial to consumers and businesses. That in itself is a disruptive and progressive proposition. But there is a more radical concept behind the open banking proposition that is based on interoperability as well as data portability, as explored by Zee Kin Yeong and David Roi Hardoon in Chapter 6.

The truly radical proposition behind open banking is the concept of self-sovereign powered forms of open banking whereby the end user, rather than the bank or fintech, is at the center of the solar system, owning and controlling access and use of their bank account data in the same way users now control their phone numbers. In this construction of open banking, banks service user-controlled accounts, just as the telecoms service self-sovereign phone numbers. It is a model predicated on the user initiating and maintaining data-sharing through consent. No more Dickens-like "please sir, may I have some more" moments whereby the consumer has to politely ask/beg for access to their own data. (Kaitlin Asrow proposes a consumer-centric data rights framework in Chapter 2.)

A user-centric notion of data ownership, access, and directed use differs significantly from current open banking discussions happening in various countries today—not even in more open banking–friendly jurisdictions like Singapore or Australia. But it could be, if there is a willingness to think of open banking in the out-of-the box way that internet innovators conceived of the DNS for the WWW which transformed a previously less accessible internet used primarily by governments and universities into a ubiquitous internet for universal use. Crossing that chasm is unlikely, though, as long as digital identity (and all the authentication and authorization that goes with identity) is mired in fragmented silos at the national government and individual corporate levels. When access protocols are developed to be optimal only on a local or national level, the result is a halting and closed-loop innovation on the scale of an AOL or Minitel. Not exactly useless, but far short of the Holy Grail of what open banking—and open data—could be if consumers, rather than banks, were the centers of their solar systems. Copernicus be damned.

13

Decentralized Finance: The Future of Crypto and Open Finance?

Nic Carter[*][**][***]

1. Introduction

In parallel to the open banking and growing open finance phenomena described in this book, a related but distinct movement is taking place: the rise of decentralized finance built atop crypto-financial infrastructure. By this, we refer to the provision of a subset of financial services through smart contracts[1] and tokens circulating on public blockchains. Unlike open banking, which seeks to link disparate bank ledgers, through bridging technology either by market forces or government mandate, decentralized finance aims to unite a global, jurisdiction-independent userbase on shared, public ledgers. Attempting to substitute standard legal protections with *lex cryptographia*,[2] decentralized finance entrepreneurs envision an open-source set of financial experiences in which end users can audit and verify the very software code they are entrusting their assets to.

While decentralized finance (DeFi) is distinct from open finance, it shares many of its key traits and surpasses them in certain respects:

- developers can build and deploy value-bearing contracts to public blockchains without permission and without a traditional contractual relationship with end users;
- end users can freely move from one smart contract-based product to another, as keypairs are substituted for identity; and
- the interlinking smart contracts that mediate these experiences are open source and auditable. Chiefly these products are on platforms that aim to be permissionless (to

---

[*] Disclaimer: The author's firm has an active position in Bitcoin. All mentions of protocols, tokens, and digital assets in this chapter are merely exemplary and do not constitute endorsements.

[**] The author would like to thank Alex Treece and David Hoffman for their feedback and contributions to this chapter.

[***] Partner at Castle Island Ventures.

[1] "Smart contracts" refers to programmatically codified relationships over property, with automated enforcement of terms. They can cover a subset of cases that are highly codifiable—for instance, a financial derivative. For more nebulous contracts like, for instance, a SAFE note, they obviously wouldn't substitute. See Nick Szabo, "Smart Contracts: Building Blocks for Digital Markets" (unpublished manuscript, 1996). https://www.fon.hum.uva.nl/rob/Courses/InformationInSpeech/CDROM/Literature/LOTwinterschool2006/szabo.best.vwh.net/smart_contracts_2.html.

[2] It is still to be seen how legal courts would view blockchain transactions serving as a form of law. For more on how public blockchains can be understood as an alternative legal regime, see Aaron Wright and Primavera De Filippi, "Decentralized Blockchain Technology and the Rise Of Lex Cryptographia." Available at SSRN 2580664 (2015).

Nic Carter, *Decentralized Finance: The Future of Crypto and Open Finance?* In: *Open Banking.* Edited by: Linda Jeng, Oxford University Press. © Oxford University Press 2022. DOI: 10.1093/oso/9780197582879.003.0014

both develop on and get access to), interoperable, auditable, and trust-minimized,[3] satisfying these qualities to various degrees.

Fundamentally, the DeFi sector aspires to flatten the topology of finance and return margins that might be captured by financial institutions to end users as a consumer surplus. The sector is premised on an ideology of disintermediation, with apolitical protocols and clearly stipulated rules (defined in code) deemed preferable to traditional financial intermediaries. Its popularity can be understood as a reaction to restrictions on various classes of financial activity, imposed either by risk-averse bank sectors, or to government-imposed restrictions on capital formation and flows.

The DeFi sector is still incipient but is growing rapidly and has caught the attention of policymakers. Its highly open and permissionless approach is both the core value proposition and a potential catalyst for regulatory attention. But the scope and nature of financial activity taking place in this permissionless, open-source context should command attention. DeFi promotes a far less constrained, far more interoperable, and directly auditable version of financial services from which open banking enthusiasts can take lessons. Already, the DeFi sector has begun converging with the traditional, regulated financial sector, presaging a possible world in which public blockchains are seamlessly incorporated into established financial networks as alternative payments and settlement rails. This transition might however compromise the features of decentralized finance that its adherents find so valuable—a lack of transactional encumbrances, the absence of identity from the system, and the permissionless deployment of certain financial contracts.

As an industry premised on digital bearer[4] assets, DeFi introduces novel classes of risk, many of which are still poorly understood. Additionally, the specter of both reintermediation and the desire for points of centralization by financial regulators grappling with the sector threatens to derail DeFi industry objectives. This chapter also explores some of these systemic risks and trends that will impact open finance.

2. Defining "DeFi"

While the term "DeFi" can be used to generally refer to all permissionless financial applications relying on public blockchains, the cryptocurrency industry views "DeFi" as a term of art that refers more specifically to derivative contracts deployed on smart contract blockchains that facilitate asset swaps, programmatic leverage, and risk transformation. Arguably, however, to the extent that facilitating the conveyance of value on public platforms—which exist on thousands of nodes globally and rely on a distributed base of industrial validators—can be understood as finance, even the most basic features of a blockchain like Bitcoin,[5] which is largely single-purpose, can fall under

---

[3] "Trust minimization" refers to reducing the amount of trust that a user must place in specific entities to feel secure using a financial system, product, or service.

[4] I view these digital assets as bearer-like even though—unlike with cash—ownership can be recorded on blockchain. I call them "digital bearer assets" because, instead of ownership through title registration, knowledge of the digital assets' keys is tantamount to ownership of the digital assets.

[5] We capitalize the term "Bitcoin" when referring to the network and protocol, and lowercase "bitcoin" when referring to the asset.

the decentralized finance moniker. Under this broader definition, "decentralized finance" captures all financial activity occurring on public blockchains; the narrower definition would limit the scope, perhaps too narrowly, to trust-minimized "high finance" facilitated by contracts on-chain, including the on-chain creation of derivatives, asset swaps, leverage, insurance, and other forms of risk transformation. I focus on the narrower definition in this chapter, but expect the definition will be better reflected by the broader version, which will also inevitably converge with aspects of open finance.

a. Decentralized Exchanges of "Pseudo-Equity"

Due to the growth of third-party financial assets (initially "utility tokens"[6] but increasingly "pseudo-equity"[7]) alongside fiat-pegged tokens (which are more suitable as a medium of exchange), smart contract-optimized blockchains like Ethereum have been able to cultivate a rich environment of exchanges "on-chain." These on-chain exchanges refer to exchange products that enable users to find counterparties and settle without depositing assets with a third-party exchange. Instead, users engage in trades through smart contracts, which settle directly on the blockchain without ever surrendering custody.

While these products are referred to as "decentralized exchanges" (DEXs), it is simpler to understand these not as exchange venues but rather as a form of bilateral or multilateral trade, facilitated by software, between mutually consenting parties. As Coin Center's Peter Van Valkenburgh describes it:[8]

Calling those tools "a DEX" and referring to "DEXs" as a category of things that exist in the world (rather than actions) does the entire technology a disservice: it wrongly portrays software tools as persons or businesses with agency and legal obligations. Corporations and persons—legal or natural—definitely have agency and obligations; software tools do not. Corporations and persons can be held responsible for their actions, software tools cannot.

Under this interpretation, users do not use a DEX product the same way they use a centralized securities exchange; instead, they use public software tools to find acceptable terms for an asset swap with contracts deployed on the blockchain itself to handle execution and settlement. The DEX phenomenon is further explained below in Section 4(c).

---

[6] "Utility tokens" are effectively digital arcade tokens that are presumed to accrue value due to their required usage in a product or marketplace, the theory being that sufficient utility will manifest in stable financial value.

[7] By "pseudo-equity," we refer to tokens that entitle token holders to control rights over economically valuable property (typically a smart contract), and in some cases, cash flows deriving from that property. These tokens are not issued as registered securities offerings, but are rather issued directly to a global audience of investors through public blockchain infrastructure.

[8] See Peter Van Valkenburgh, "There's No Such Thing as a Decentralized Exchange," The Block (Oct. 3 2020). https://publications.parliament.uk/pa/cm201719/cmselect/cmpubacc/1748/1748.pdf .

3. Overview: Comparing Blockchain-Based DeFi with Open Finance

Before describing DeFi in more detail, I want to provide an overview of how the DeFi movement and open finance are motivated by similar goals of improving the competitive landscape, including a desire to improve financial inclusion by reducing switching costs and making user data (or assets, in the case of DeFi) more portable. They accomplish this in disparate ways. Open finance involves either mandating financial institutions to unencumber user-permissioned data in order to enhance competition; or alternatively, building interoperation between incumbent firms and fintech entrants that is enhanced by private sector solutions. DeFi, by contrast, does not seek to link multiple financial databases through either private sector agreement or state mandate, but instead envisions an entirely novel financial system where a global userbase is united on one database—the ledger maintained by the blockchain. Additionally, the core service providers are not financial institutions, but rather contracts deployed to these blockchains. In theory, since duplicating and iterating on open-source code is trivial and switching from one liquidity pool to the next is seamless,[9] users are empowered to decide where to conduct activities and rents are difficult to collect.

a. Crypto Interoperability

In practice, the crypto-financial industry remains somewhat fragmented as there are multiple popular blockchains that do not cleanly interoperate. Partial solutions like "wrapping" Bitcoin, mainly through intermediaries, and tokenizing it on Ethereum have sprung up, but these interoperability solutions are, for the most part, not trust-minimized.[10] Additionally, it is not clear whether, under current trust assumptions, a single blockchain can scale to a global userbase of retail transactors.[11] As the default choice for DeFi applications, Ethereum is at capacity and experienced a surge of fees in 2020 that priced out smaller users, rendering only larger transactions in value viable.

---

[9] One infamous example would be the hostile fork (or clone) of Uniswap, the popular DEX by its competitor Sushiswap. Within a week of launching, Sushiswap had attracted USD 1.4 billion worth of liquidity, much of it siphoned from Uniswap (Sushiswap offered temporarily better terms to liquidity providers). This provoked outcry, but fundamentally these smart contracts are simply code deployed on blockchains and can be trivially replicated and modified. This means that successful products are aggressively forked and iterated upon by competitors without restriction.

[10] For definition of "trust-minimization," see *supra* note 6.

[11] Since the standard trust assumptions of public blockchains require that an individual be able to replay the entire history of transactions and stay current with new transactions as they are added to the chain tip, merely increasing the data throughput of the system in order to scale to a global userbase is infeasible; it would rapidly eliminate the ability of transactors to verify the validity of inbound transactions. Thus, scaling approaches generally involve creating subledgers, deferring settlement, or bundling transactions off-chain and periodically settling on-chain.

b. Clear Settlement vs. Scaling

Numerous proposals exist to increase the throughput of these systems, but a fundamental tension remains in trying to scale DeFi. Scaling blockchains by deferring settlement would preclude the convenient DeFi features associated with settling on the blockchain. Alternatively, scaling by producing numerous distinct ledgers would lead to fragmentation, inhibiting the core idea that powers DeFi: the notion of uniting transactors on a single ledger. This tension gets to the heart of an embedded paradox troubling the DeFi phenomenon: the touted benefits of uniting transactors on a single ledger would become meaningless if scaling public blockchains meant only a network of distinct ledgers that have to periodically communicate and settle with each other. Already interoperability challenges are emerging, as Ethereum groans under the weight of its own transactional usage, and users look to alternative smart contract protocols.

c. Open Access

Despite these tensions, it is worth pointing out the domains in which DeFi shines when evaluated from an open finance lens. First, due to the general lack of identity within public blockchain systems, DeFi solutions are not opinionated in terms of who can access and use them. This open access can be understood as generally positive for financial inclusion (for individuals in countries with poor access to the financial system and seeking to earn USD-denominated yield, for instance). But open access is also a key risk factor as it opens up the DeFi system to illicit usage. Importantly, inasmuch as DeFi solutions are simply smart contracts that users can freely interact with, accounts are inherently portable. Withdrawing funds from an interest-bearing pool and moving them to another pool is seamless. The commitment to neutral financial *protocols* rather than financial service providers promises to inculcate a competitive dynamic whereby entrepreneurs compete to provide popular interfaces based on shared underlying blockchain infrastructure.

d. Composability

Additionally, the combination of strong settlement finality[12] and the concentration of activity onto a single ledger enables the highly desirable quality of composability. As stated, a highly composable system is one in which distinct components can build upon and reference each other, allowing for complexity and more sophisticated products to emerge. With composability, certain DeFi applications might refer to or rely on a half

---

[12] Final transactions are those which are not reversible. Physical cash transactions, for instance, settle immediately, whereas credit card transactions are not final for the period in which they can be contested. Public blockchains offer "probabilistic" finality, which means that transactions are presumed to be final once the ledger has accumulated sufficient computational work, such that a reversal would be implausible or expensive. For additional explanation on finality, see Elaine Ou, "Cryptocurrency Deals Can Always Be Erased, for a Price," *Bloomberg* (Jan. 16, 2019). https://www.bloomberg.com/opinion/articles/2019-01-16/bitcoin-and-other-cryptocurrencies-are-open-about-being-at-risk.

dozen other systems within a relatively short period. While this has the potential to introduce systemic risk, and cascading failures if individual components or modules fail, it also allows for the creation of abstractions and novel financial products.

We will sketch out an example[13] to demonstrate the level of composability currently exhibited on DeFi. The yEarn protocol is an on-chain asset manager, which pools users' funds and deploys them against a variety of strategies in order to obtain a return. The yETH vault is one of the products offered by yEarn in which users deposit Ether (ETH) and the system endeavors to seek a return with those funds. yEarn works by taking Ether deposits from users, bundling them together, and depositing them into the Maker contract, using this Ether collateral to produce Dai, a dollar-denominated stablecoin. At this point, the Dai (effectively a loan granted by the Maker system against risky Ether collateral) is then deposited into the Curve.fi liquidity pool as a source of liquidity, and yEarn thus becomes a liquidity provider. Curve is a decentralized exchange optimized for stablecoins. Liquidity providers putatively earn a return for making markets—and are also rewarded with the local pseudo-equity token in the Curve system, CRV, which is subsequently sold for ETH by yEarn.

To summarize, this process entails an asset manager transparently pooling user funds, depositing these pooled funds into an overcollateralized[14] lending system to create a dollar-denominated token (Dai), which is then subsequently deposited into a decentralized exchange to provide liquidity for automated market making, a compensated activity (assuming the market-making is profitable). These tokens then (optimistically) earn a return, and the individuals depositing into the initial pool collect a yield. This process combines a number of entirely distinct modules, each expressed as code deployed on the network Ethereum. Developers of one module do not need to be aware of third-parties using their protocol. Permission is neither sought nor required.

e. Auditability

Another touted advantage of DeFi from an open finance perspective is its auditability. Due to the innate transparency of public blockchains, data from these systems can be queried by any third-party running a node. This allows for risks, especially with regard to collateral quality, to be evaluated in real time. Using publicly accessible blockchain data, service providers are now developing automated risk-scoring protocols[15] to assess collateral quality and system solvency in various lending products. Of course, this also means that end users have a lack of privacy when transacting on DeFi, indelibly so if their identity can be connected to their blockchain address.

---

[13] The inclusion of this example does not reflect the author's views on the viability of these products. For more details on the processes described in this section, see Andre Cronje, "yETH Vault Explained," *Medium* (Sept. 4, 2020). https://medium.com/iearn/yeth-vault-explained-c29d6b93a371; and Yearn.Finance, "yETH Vault Mechanics" https://docs.yearn.finance/products/yvaults#yeth-vault-mechanics. At its peak, yearn.finance managed USD 967 million in user deposits in strategies like these (see https://defipulse.com/yearn.finance).

[14] The minimum collateral ratio is 150%.

[15] See, for example, Gauntlet's real-time risk management product, discussed by John Morrow, "Risk Scores for DeFi—Alpha Release," *Medium* (Oct. 13, 2020). https://medium.com/gauntlet-networks/understanding-risk-in-defi-f64574593979.

f. "Bearer-like"

DeFi protocols are generally built with user self-custody in mind, and cryptoassets are intended to be "bearer-like" and fungible. Analogous to the physical possession of cash, the mere knowledge of the cryptoasset's private key entitles the individual the ability to spend the cryptoassets, thus making the individual the genuine owner of the cryptoassets in the eyes of the blockchain protocol. However, cryptoassets differ in significant ways from typical bearer instruments, such as cash,[16] which maintains no ownership record and for which physical possession entitles the bearer ownership or title. Unlike cash, cryptoassets are linked to a form of identity and can therefore maintain a record of ownership.

These blockchain protocols generally presume that the assets are fungible and "bearer-like." However, these core assumptions break down once identity link via private keys is introduced and individuals or parties are associated with their addresses. For example, liquidity pools in MKR or Compound require collateral fungibility. In other words, they cannot tolerate different classes of risk based on who is providing liquidity. Many DeFi enthusiasts hope that eventually privacy tools will enable genuine fungibility for the collateral flowing around the DeFi system.

g. Portability

While depository relationships with banks or brokers tend to be long-term and "sticky," users in the blockchain context can take physical receipt of their cryptoassets and move them with little difficulty. This ease of portability is generally challenging or not possible with other types of asset classes, particularly securities. Blockchain's portability feature has the emergent consequence of enabling collateral to flow rapidly between DeFi protocols. A typical end user might retain ownership of their keys and interact with contracts registered to the blockchain through a software or hardware interface that enables the user to sign transactions safely—instead of consigning the user's assets to a third-party and granting control to an agent.

4. Public Blockchains and Decentralized Finance

After the preceding introductory comparative overview, this section explores certain key aspects of DeFi in more detail but does not dwell on the technical features of the public blockchains that power DeFi. (For introductory works covering how blockchains function, see Narayanan, Antonopoulos, or Rosenbaum.[17]) Nevertheless, there are some important features of blockchains worth revisiting in this context, to help us

---

[16] For example, cash, bearer's bonds, negotiable instruments made payable to "bearer," and so forth.

[17] See Arvind Narayanan et al., *Bitcoin and Cryptocurrency Technologies: A Comprehensive Introduction* (Princeton University Press, 2016); Andreas M. Antonopoulos, *Mastering Bitcoin: Unlocking Digital Cryptocurrencies* (O'Reilly Media, Inc., 2014); and Andreas M. Antonopoulos and Gavin Wood, *Mastering Ethereum: Building Smart Contracts and Dapps* (O'Reilly Media, 2018).

identify the differences between modes of user engagement with public blockchains and with traditional banking systems and, ultimately, with open finance.

a. Bitcoin

A blockchain using Proof-of-Work, such as Bitcoin, is a protocol that cultivates a shared, continually updated global ledger upon which participants converge. This type of blockchain stipulates which addresses can spend which coins and under which conditions as well as facilitate transactional finality when updates occur. Identity is deliberately absent from the system, with pseudonymous public-key addresses serving as a substitute. Users do not need to register with a third-party to use Bitcoin; they must simply generate sufficient randomness to construct a unique secret in order to devise a pair of public and private keys. If the randomness is sufficiently unique, the user can plausibly assert that they alone are the sole proprietor of that data and hence of the coins, which are encumbered and linked to their address. Knowledge of the private key with a corresponding public key, which contains value in an output on the Bitcoin ledger, entitles you to spend those coins.

Private keys do not "store" units of bitcoin; the units of bitcoin can be said to exist on the virtualized ledger replicated across thousands of nodes globally, which reach periodic synchrony.[18] Keys are merely an entitlement to unlock coins and assign them to a new address. In this manner, bitcoin is "bearer-like" as discussed earlier. Units of bitcoin are not redeemable (as, for instance, a banknote used to be redeemable for gold), but knowledge of a private key is the sole determinant of a valid spend on the blockchain even if that knowledge was obtained illicitly. There is no recourse on Bitcoin, and transactions are final after sufficient block confirmations. In this respect, Bitcoin resembles cash in an online context; it is somewhat (albeit not perfectly) private, settlement is rapidly final, and transactors have full autonomy with whom they transact.

In blockchain transactions, it is the receiving party's responsibility to verify the integrity of the transaction. Verifying that an inbound Bitcoin transaction is legitimate entails downloading the history of the ledger from the peer-to-peer (P2P) network,[19] double-checking that all bitcoin transactions or "spends" are valid to prevent double-spending, and confirming that all new bitcoins were created fairly under network rules. By operating a node on consumer hardware, a user could cheaply determine that a payment they are receiving is final (according to their self-directed standard of probabilistic settlement finality) and not counterfeit. More importantly, they can conduct this validation for themselves without relying on any trusted third-party, and without trusting their transactional counterparty. This grants Bitcoin the quality of being able to

---

[18] Bitcoin's trust model requires that nodes agree on a single, unified state of the world, such that transactors cannot spend the same coins with multiple parties at the same time. Thus, nodes in the network collectively update their state every ten minutes, on average.

[19] As of October 2020 at the time of writing, the bitcoin network was about 304 GB in size. A transaction that you are the recipient of party A submits a transaction to the blockchain, reassigning coins to party B. It's B's responsibility to verify the integrity of the transaction (by running a full node which trustlessly consults the blockchain).

settle payments rapidly on a cross-jurisdictional basis between parties that do not trust each other and may not even have knowledge of each other, much less a relationship.

Transactions are broadcast to miners who arrange them in blocks and register them to the final blockchain, in exchange for conducting economically costly computational work. Mining is a competitive, free market activity in which industrial entities compete for the privilege of bundling and registering transactions to the blockchain. Miners are compensated with a bitcoin-denominated reward consisting of a protocol-defined subsidy as well as transaction fees, which are set by a first-price auction. They are economically incentivized to include user transactions that they receive from nodes because these transactions are fee-bearing. Miners have full discretion over the transactions they choose to include in blocks, and individual miners can censor specific addresses should they choose or even mine fully empty blocks; but the free market nature of mining suggests that another miner would eventually select the excluded transaction in exchange for the fee.

That said, a miner with an overwhelming share of hashpower, which is the combined computational power of the Bitcoin network, could arbitrarily censor transactions and otherwise interfere with the network. A competitive and distributed mining environment is a core assumption that must hold for the network to function in an orderly manner. So far, no individual miner or entity has obtained sufficient market share to interfere with the network, nor would they be economically incentivized to because they have exposure to the Bitcoin network through their single-purpose mining hardware, which depreciates over a period of years. Thus, any damage to the bitcoin unit price on account of malicious behavior would punish them economically, since miners hold on their balance sheet synthetic future units of bitcoin instantiated in mining hardware.[20]

For end users to have the confidence that they will have access to the network and will be able to transact, they must believe that the free market competition for transaction registration is sufficient to enforce a heterogeneity and noncartelized set of entities. If real-world user identities can be linked with their addresses and transactions, and the validator network becomes cartelized, the network assurances become impaired as miners at this point can censor end users. This quality of excludability might be a desirable feature of a financial network in the eyes of regulators, but Bitcoin's core value proposition is a censorship-resistant network for conveying and storing value without the aegis of any legal system,[21] and this is fundamentally why it is valued by end users. Thus, compromising on those features by, for instance, adding know-your-customer (KYC) procedures at the address level, or regulating the transactions that miners are permitted to register to the blockchain, is incompatible with the network's established goals.

Bitcoin is both a monetary and financial phenomenon, by its creator's intention[22] and its revealed trajectory since launch. Bitcoin is a financial technology inasmuch as it

---

[20] See James Prestwich Hasu and Brandon Curtis, "A Model for Bitcoin's Security and the Declining Block Subsidy" (2019). https://medium.com/@hasufly/research-paper-a-model-for-bitcoins-security-and-the-declining-block-subsidy-11a21f600e33.

[21] See Yassine Elmandjra, "Bitcoin: A Novel Economic Institution," *Ark Invest* (2020), and Eric Chason, "How Bitcoin Functions as Property Law," *Seton Hall Law Review* 49 (2018): 129.

[22] In announcing Bitcoin to the cryptography mailing list, Bitcoin creator Satoshi Nakamoto characterized it as a monetary network, emphasizing the fixed supply characteristics (see "Bitcoin v0.1 Released." https://satoshi.nakamotoinstitute.org/emails/cryptography/16/). Satoshi also compared Bitcoin to gold, stating that "it's more typical of a precious metal" on the P2P foundation website (see "Bitcoin Open Source Implementation of P2P Currency." https://satoshi.nakamotoinstitute.org/posts/p2pfoundation/3/#selection-9.0-12.0).

facilitates final settlement of value between mutually untrusting counterparties through a communications medium. It is monetary in that it is opinionated about monetary policy and boasts clearly defined monetary rules, which are presumed to be sound and immutable. Nonmonetary use cases of Bitcoin have been the source of controversy[23] and are generally deprioritized by developers and protocol design. The Bitcoin protocol is chiefly interested in cultivating its own UTXO[24] set—the set of virtual bills that hold value. After about twelve years of operation, there are 68 million UTXOs summing up to 18.5 million BTC—the units of digital currency represented on the ledger—held in 31.8 million unique nonzero addresses, of which about a million are active on a typical day.

Bitcoin also includes a rudimentary scripting language, which enables the inclusion of more specialized spending conditions in transactions; users can, for instance, specify that an output must be a certain age to be spent, or require a quorum from a certain number of keys to be spendable, or require that a spender must have knowledge of some specific data to spend the coins.

Bitcoin's native script, called Bitcoin Script, is a variant of the stack-based Forth programming language. It is deliberately limited and not Turing-complete,[25] which means that it cannot perform arbitrary computation. This is done out of prudence, as more expressivity could introduce bugs and because the Bitcoin protocol is focused on mediating the transfer of units of bitcoin, rather than anything else. Bitcoin's scripting abilities constitute primitives—basic programming building blocks—which allow for the construction of more creative financial instruments like derivatives or transactions, which encode specific conditions. Currently, conditions expressed in these scripts define the spending conditions for a large fraction of outstanding coins.

At present, 5.85 million BTC (equivalent to USD 66.6 billion at the time of writing) are encumbered in "pay to script hash" outputs, meaning that these coins have specific spending conditions attached to them. By inspecting the blockchain, it is possible to know that, for instance, at least 211,000 BTC are publicly revealed to be held in outputs, which require the presence of at least two out of three predetermined signatures to be spent.[26] Such multisignature transactions are one basic building block of decentralized finance as they permit more complex transactional and trust arrangements to be developed.

However, since Bitcoin Script is challenging to interpret and program with, and not Turing-complete, more expressive protocols like Ethereum were developed. It is Ethereum's blockchain that hosts most of the popular decentralized finance applications, alongside a handful of other similarly expressive protocols more optimized for smart contracts.

---

[23] See "OP_RETURN," *Bitcoin Wiki*. https://en.bitcoin.it/wiki/OP_RETURN#:~:text = OP_RETURN%20 is%20a%20script%20opcode,be%20used%20to%20burn%20bitcoins.

[24] UTXO stands for Unspent Transaction Output. Bitcoin transactions contain bundles of valid UTXOs. Think of these like virtual bills holding variable amounts of value. Bitcoin is a token-based, not an account-based, system. The protocol manages the conveyance of these outputs.

[25] "Turing completeness" means that a computer or language can be used to conduct arbitrary computation

[26] See "P2SH Statistics" at TxStats. https://txstats.com/dashboard/db/p2sh-statistics.

b. Ethereum

In many respects, Ethereum is similar to Bitcoin as described above: identity is largely expunged from the system, and knowledge of a private key is tantamount to ownership. Like Bitcoin, it is currently a Proof-of-Work network, and settlement is probabilistic (yet generally considered final within a few minutes). Miners have a slightly greater ability to interfere with end users because in some cases they can extract economic value from reordering transactions,[27] but this is not a significant hindrance to the network at present. Like Bitcoin, Ethereum transactions are generally final (with some high-profile exceptions[28]), a property that enables desirable features like composability and atomicity.[29]

Unlike Bitcoin, Ethereum is Turing-complete, which means the system can be programmed to solve any reasonable computational problem assuming sufficient memory and resources are available.[30] The trade-off for this richer and more expressive feature is costlier validation[31] and greater potential for significant bugs or loss of funds. Ethereum's programmability has made it the default destination for capital formation (i.e., the 2015-17 ICO phenomenon), third-party tokens like stablecoins, and more recently, a vibrant ecosystem of derivatives and swap products.

c. Decentralized Exchanges

Ethereum, as with Bitcoin, is permissionless and does not require identity verification to make transactions. Only knowledge of a private key corresponding to an account bearing a balance on-chain[32] is necessary. As a consequence, the usage of these DEX tools, which exist primarily as publicly visible contracts on-chain, is largely permissionless—at least at the blockchain layer itself.[33] While there are many other DeFi value propositions that we will cover in this chapter, the notion of a DEX typifies the DeFi phenomenon. DEXes combine a reliance on third-party assets inserted on-chain, the permissionless nature of public blockchain transactions, and an insouciant attitude to financial regulations. For instance, DEXes, existing as contracts enabling users to pool liquidity and engage in bilateral trades, do not enforce KYC restrictions or identity verification.

---

[27] For a discussion of how miners can extract value from reordering transactions, see Philip Daian et al., "Flash Boys 2.0: Frontrunning, Transaction Reordering, and Consensus Instability in Decentralized Exchanges," *arXiv preprint arXiv:1904.05234* (2019).

[28] See Matthew Leising, "The $55m Hack that Almost Brought Ethereum Down," *Coindesk* (Sept. 17, 2020). https://www.coindesk.com/55m-hack-ethereum-down.

[29] "Composability" refers to the property in contracts that allow them to reference each other and enable the construction of complex interlinking systems. "Atomicity" refers to a property of chained transactions whereby either all are completed or none are.

[30] For a more complete comparison between Bitcoin and Ethereum, see EthHub, "EthHub CFTC Response" (Feb. 15, 2019). https://unlock-protocol.github.io/ethhub/other/ethhub-cftc-response/.

[31] It is more challenging for an end user to run a node and audit the validity of an inbound transaction. Since the ability of any user to replay the history of the network is at the core of the public blockchain trust model, introducing richer computation would complicate this process of validating transactions from other parties.

[32] As compared with Bitcoin, which employs a token-based or UTXO model, Ethereum employs an account-based model.

[33] Permissions could be inserted, for instance, at centralized on-ramps, such as exchanges, where users might seek to exchange fiat currency for cryptocurrency in order to transact within the DeFi ecosystem.

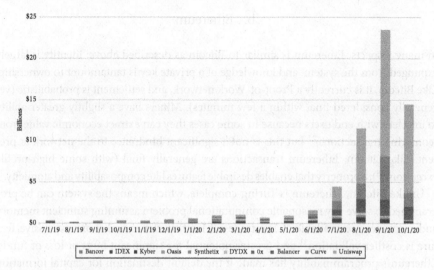

Figure 13.1 Decentralized exchange volume, USD.
Source: Dune Analytics. Note: October 2020 data extrapolated from partial data.

Due to the noncustodial nature of DEX trades (as compared with deposit-taking centralized trading exchanges) and the complete lack of an obligation to share one's personal data with the network, these decentralized exchange products are extremely popular. Indeed, in August 2020, the most popular DEX, Uniswap,[34] surpassed the daily exchange volume of Coinbase,[35] the largest regulated centralized cryptoasset exchange and brokerage in the United States. This is particularly noteworthy because Uniswap exists solely as a set of interlocking smart contracts deployed on Ethereum, depends on a decentralized network of independent liquidity providers, and boasts no infrastructure of its own aside from the Ethereum blockchain. The Uniswap contracts had been primarily written by a single individual, whereas Coinbase has hundreds of employees and has raised hundreds of millions of dollars in venture financing.

In August 2020, Ethereum-based DEXs mediated approximately USD 24 billion worth of transactions, each settling on-chain, with Uniswap and Curve being the most popular venues (see Figure 13.1).

With this background, we can summarize the extent of the decentralized finance phenomenon as it pertains to public blockchains. The core qualities offered by the DeFi sector (under the narrower conception as defined above) are as follows:

1. DeFi products are built on public blockchains like Ethereum, which grants them a robustness and resistance to shutdown that standard banking applications do not possess or aspire to. This feature, together with open-source and publicly auditable contract code, enables *trust minimization*—the notion that an end user can theoretically audit and verify the system in its entirety.

---

[34] For more background on Uniswap, see Olga Kharif, "DeFi Boom Makes Uniswap Most Sought-After Crypto Exchange," *Bloomberg* (Oct. 16, 2020). https://www.bloomberg.com/news/articles/2020-10-16/defi-boom-makes-uniswap-most-sought-after-crypto-exchange.

[35] Mathew Di Salvo, "Trading Volume on Ethereum-Based DEX Uniswap Beats Coinbase Pro," *Decrypt* (Sept. 10, 2020). https://www.decrypt.co/40201/uniswap-24-hour-trading-volume-beats-coinbase.

2. DeFi products are *programmable*, which is to say any developer can permissionlessly deploy a set of smart contracts to the blockchain. End users can take advantage of these deployed smart contracts by making base-layer transactions (which requires only knowledge of keys pertaining to the tokens or native cryptoassets to act as owner of the digital assets) and an interface through which to engage with the deployed smart contracts.

3. DeFi products that exist on the same blockchain are *interoperable*, which means that they work seamlessly together. Rather than having multiple databases communicate with each other (as is the case with banks and fintechs communicating via APIs), networks like Ethereum are large, unitary databases that host a large number of users[36] and a vibrant ecosystem of financial assets. As such, communication between various financial protocols within a given blockchain is seamless. The combination of settlement qualities of public blockchain assets "on top" of tokens circulating underneath means that these contracts can interlock cleanly with no counterparty risk that might result from unexpected settlement reversals. This feature is often referred to as *composability*.

4. DeFi products are, with some exceptions, *permissionless* to access—so end users can use them without KYC restrictions or other forms of identity verification. This permits more efficient applications without the burden of compliance—but remains the source of potential regulatory concern.

5. Existing as deployed contracts on public blockchains, DeFi products are transparent by design. As replicated, shared databases, transactions on blockchains like Bitcoin and Ethereum can be scrutinized by anyone with access to the data on the replicated ledger (commonly referred to as a full node). This means that individual positions can be assessed, and risk in collateralized systems can be ascertained in real time. While additional privacy remains a feature that developers are seeking to add to blockchains, the transparency enables *auditability* and makes querying data on these financial products trivial.

It is worth noting that blockchain-based DeFi, which runs on single-threaded computers[37] with limited data throughput, is still crucially limited in a number of ways. Lacking a notion of on-chain identity or credit, the sector cannot replicate many of the essential features of finance or banking, like credit or underwriting.[38] Thus, while DeFi users can engage in interest rate swaps, asset pooling, and risk transformation, there is no notion of maturity transformation—converting liquid deposits into illiquid, productive capital—in the space as of yet. It is therefore critical to interpret "finance" in decentralized finance in the context of what public blockchain-based systems are capable of. In this instance, it chiefly refers to the exchange of value and the transformation of risk, rather than core banking activities.

---

[36] At the time of writing (October 2020), there were 48 million addresses on Ethereum with a nonzero Ether balance—although one address does not necessarily correspond to one individual.

[37] Currently, the established security model that underlies Ethereum and other blockchains requires that full nodes validate the entire history of transactions. Thus, transactions cannot be parallelized; every node in the network must be aware of and process each transaction in order to have a complete, global view.

[38] For more on this, see Jake Chervinsky, "DeFi Lending Doesn't Exist Yet," *Bankless* (Sept. 3, 2020). https://bankless.substack.com/p/defi-lending-doesnt-exist-yet.

Additionally, a full conception of blockchain-based DeFi requires philosophical context. It is a movement deeply impregnated with ideology. Public blockchains are premised on a notion of disintermediation of payments and the elimination of discretion stemming from monetary systems,[39] while generally seeking to minimize state oversight and control over payments. DeFi adherents take this teleology one step further, envisioning not only novel payments systems but a rich set of financial services that a global user base can access without restriction—one in which margins are eliminated and returned to end users as efficiencies. As Zetzsche, Arner, and Buckley describe it:[40]

> DeFi enthusiasts go beyond technical decentralization. For them, DeFi offers governance structures they perceive as the "democratization" of finance, while incumbents might well view such structures as "anarchy". At the core of this claim lies a positive connotation of disintermediation (understood as disrupting incumbent financial institutions, particularly those that are very large: the "too-big-to-fail" problem at the heart of the 2008 financial crisis) and of decreasing state influence and control of the financial system.

The openness facilitated by DeFi—in which a global user base, united only by their usage of public blockchain assets, can engage with complex financial contracts without restriction—is only possible absent state regulation. Thus, the core qualities listed above must be caveated in that they only pertain to the more limited functions that DeFi can plausibly claim to satisfy, and these qualities may only obtain temporarily, as regulators begin to grapple with the industry.

5. An Alternative, Permissionless Financial System

Despite the shortcomings mentioned above, in 2020, DeFi products and ancillary business models have seen a dramatic uptick in usage, which can be directly ascertained by inspecting the blockchains themselves. The usage modes that have gained meaningful adoption thus far can be grouped into a handful of broad categories:

1. *Noncustodial exchange*: These are products that allow traders to exchange assets (typically tokens circulating on Ethereum or Ether itself) without relying on a third-party for custody. Trades settle "on-chain" and are hence final. Generally, these exchanges do not require KYC, as they simply constitute software running on blockchains, allowing users to pool liquidity and define rules for exchange. Examples include Uniswap, Curve, and Balancer.
2. *Risk transformation*: This is a broad category encompassing a variety of methods to pool liquidity and transform risk. Through these products, users can borrow

---

[39] For insight into Satoshi's objectives when creating Bitcoin, one ought look no further than the first post on the P2P foundation forum: "The root problem with conventional currency is all the trust that's required to make it work. The central bank must be trusted not to debase the currency, but the history of fiat currencies is full of breaches of that trust." https://satoshi.nakamotoinstitute.org/posts/p2pfoundation/threads/1/.

[40] Dirk A. Zetzsche, Douglas W. Arner, and Ross P. Buckley, "Decentralized Finance (DeFi)," *IIEL Issue Brief 2* (2020).

tokens against liquid collateral and lend out their own tokens to collect interest. Popular projects involve locking up an excess of risky crypto collateral in order to produce stable outputs, like a USD-linked stablecoin. Some of these systems use programmatic risk management and constant overcollateralization to maintain system solvency. Examples include Maker, Compound, and Aave.

3. *Asset management*: These include active or passive strategies enabling users to pool funds and target a return or a specific portfolio, employing the token-swapping products available on Ethereum. Examples include Melonport, Tokensets, and YFI.

4. *Programmatic derivatives*: Taking advantage of the relative simplicity of expressing derivative contracts in code form, these products enable users to trade specific flavors of risk like options or bespoke derivatives, such as swaps. Examples include UMA, dy/dx, and Synthetix.

5. *Insurance*: These are products that enable users to pool risk and buy and sell insurance coverage, chiefly as protection against the failure of DeFi contracts. Examples include NexusMutual and Opyn.

6. Categories of Cryptoassets in DeFi

The most popular of these protocols by usage numbers[41] are decentralized/noncustodial exchange products, as well as autonomous interest rate protocols. Additionally, while the above types of protocols represent enabling infrastructure that permit a variety of financial engagements, the assets themselves circulating on these platforms have expanded—both in terms of their aggregate value and their transactional usage. The relevant assets can be demarcated as follows.

a. Stablecoins and DeFi

The term "stablecoins" has no official definition and generally refers to a second generation of "cryptoassets that "seek to stabilise the price of the 'coin' by linking its value to that of an asset or pool of assets."[42] Some of these stablecoins reference baskets of currencies centrally managed to maintain price stability. Certain other stablecoins— sometimes referred to as "cryptodollars"[43]—are tokens tracking the return of the US dollar and are more cash-like. For the most part, these cryptodollars are tokenized representations of bank liabilities and are redeemable for actual USD. A smaller subset of stablecoins are issued programmatically against risky crypto-native collateral or

---

[41] Usage numbers visible on-chain at Dune Analytics. https://explore.duneanalytics.com/dashboard/defi-users-over-time.

[42] Note that "stablecoins" can be used to refer to tokens which derive their value from their convertibility for reserves of sovereign currency held in a commercial bank, as well as nonconvertible tokens whose value derives from collateral backing the asset and other stabilizing mechanisms like interest rates. For more, see G7 Working Group on Stablecoins, "Investigating the Impact of Global Stablecoins," *Bank for International Settlements* (Oct. 2019). https://www.bis.org/cpmi/publ/d187.pdf.

[43] For a discussion of "cryptodollars" versus "stablecoins," see Castle Island Ventures, "Cryptodollars: The Story So Far" (June 2020). https://www.castleisland.vc/cryptodollars.

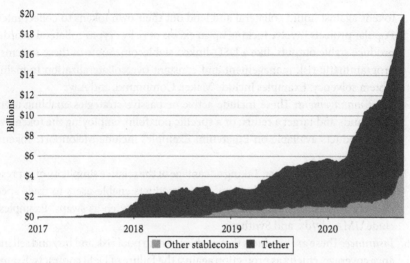

Figure 13.2 Stablecoin free-floating market cap.
Source: Coin Metrics.

employ other algorithmic schemes for stability. The largest fiat-convertible stablecoins include Tether, USD Coin, TrueUSD, Binance dollar, and Paxos dollar. By contrast, the most popular synthetic stablecoins[44] issued against crypto collateral include Dai (issued against Ethereum and a basket of other tokens) and sUSD (issued against Synthetix).

The supply of stablecoins circulating on public blockchains has grown from almost zero in 2017 to over USD 20 billion today. Tether, issued against deposits in offshore banks maintains dominance, but US-based stablecoins are gaining prominence. In particular, USD Coin (USDC) issued by the Centre Consortium with reserves custodied in US banks, has grown from USD 520 million in January 2020 to USD 2.84 billion in current supply at the time of writing (see Figure 13.2).

Increasingly, stablecoins are displacing "native" units of these blockchains (i.e., Bitcoin and Ether) as the preferred form of collateral for these financial applications because stablecoins minimize volatility and are, thus, more suitable as media of exchange (see Figure 13.3).

At the time of writing, stablecoins account for USD 4 billion worth of settled value per day, on a trailing thirty-day basis, surpassing the combined value settled by Bitcoin and Ether. In relatively short order, these dollar-pegged tokens have become the primary transactional medium for crypto-financial applications. Fundamentally, certain stablecoins offer privacy and settlement assurances which approximate (but do not match) those of physical cash, in a digital context. They are "bearer"-like in the blockchain sense (i.e., knowledge of the keys is tantamount to ownership) and offer individuals worldwide access to dollar IOUs representing US dollars held in commercial banks. For individuals with no access to dollar-denominated savings products, stablecoins offer the prospect of diversification from their local currency.[45]

---

[44] For a taxonomy, see Jeremy Clark, Didem Demirag, and Seyedehmahsa Moosavi, "SoK: Demystifying Stablecoins." Available at SSRN 3466371 (2019).

[45] Although, it's worth noting that the legal entitlements of the owners of stablecoins differ by issuer and generally do not include FDIC deposit insurance, unlike domestic commercial bank deposits.

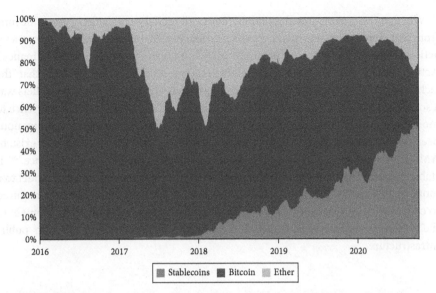

Figure 13.3 Relative share of on-chain transaction value in USD terms (select cryptoassets).
Source: Coin Metrics.
Note: Covers BTC, ETH, and select stablecoins (USDT, USDC, TUSD, GUSD, BUSD, HUSD, and DAI).

Furthermore, using interest rate swap products, users can get access to interest rates indexed to the demand for crypto-native capital, which frequently drives rates well above the risk-free rate.[46] Effectively, stablecoins, in conjunction with a liquid and accessible money market on DeFi, grant users access to dollar-denominated finance, regardless of the nature of their local banking sector.

Unlike the "native" units of currency on these blockchains, fiat-convertible stablecoins are more accountable to the traditional banking system and to regulators. The issuers behind stablecoins like Tether and USDC reserve the right to blacklist addresses should they get a request from law enforcement or in the case of a hack, and they actively take advantage of this functionality.[47]

To create or redeem a fiat-convertible stablecoin, an entity must have a direct relationship with the issuer and pass sufficient KYC. However, most stablecoin transactions are P2P directly on the blockchain, taking place between end users who have no obligation to furnish any identity information, so stablecoin issuers have limited sight into P2P transactions on-chain. This particular model, whereby creations and redemptions occur with known counterparties, but the majority of transactions are opaque to stablecoin administrators, has been dubbed "permissioned pseudonymity."[48]

---

[46] Real-time cryptocurrency interest rates for both centralized and decentralized lending facilities visible at Defirate. https://defirate.com/lend/.

[47] The blacklisted addresses on Tether can be tracked in real-time at Dune Analytics. https://explore.duneanalytics.com/public/dashboards/3zhIaRUCFgmZMKqHG0pguvSvw1aOGL8gxFtZ2ujf. USDC has also begun freezing addresses at the behest of law enforcement.

[48] For more on permissioned pseudonymity, see J.P. Koning, "From Unknown Wallet to Unknown Wallet," *Moneyness blog* (Nov. 6, 2019). https://jpkoning.blogspot.com/2019/11/from-unknown-wallet-to-unknown-wallet.html; and Antony Lewis, "KYC in Stablecoins," *Bits on Blocks* (visited Sept. 27, 2021). https://bitsonblocks.net/2019/10/30/kyc-in-stablecoins/.

Whether this permissioned pseudonymous risk model—which departs significantly from that employed by payments companies, like PayPal, that are aware of every transaction on their networks—can persist in perpetuity is an open question. The Financial Action Task Force (FATF) noted pointedly in their recent "12 Month Review" that "the lack of explicit coverage of peer-to peer transactions via private/unhosted wallets was a source of concern for a number of jurisdictions,"[49] adding, seemingly in reference to more decentralized stablecoins like Dai, "there are residual risks relating to anonymous peer-to-peer transactions via unhosted wallets, jurisdictions with weak or non-existent AML/CFT regulation and so-called stablecoins with decentralised governance."[50] If stablecoin administrators must progress from the very occasional blacklist model to a more aggressive blacklist policy, or even a whitelist approach where they are required to collect identity data on every token transfer, stablecoins will lose a core element of their value proposition—less encumbered digital cash-like transactions on public infrastructure.

b. Liability-Free Cryptoassets

"Native" cryptoassets constitute the base of DeFi. Initially employed as the sole media of exchange, these cryptoassets have become widely employed as collateral. Ether is the default asset on Ethereum, but over USD 1 billion of wrapped Bitcoin also circulates within DeFi applications on Ethereum. Currently, 8.6 million Ether and 158,000 BTC are held as collateral in DeFi applications, equivalent to USD 3.2 billion and USD 1.7 billion, respectively, at the time of writing.[51] When employed as collateral in DeFi systems, users in some cases surrender immediate control of their coins—for instance, if they use their coins to provide liquidity to an automated market maker exchange in exchange for a return—but they retain ownership and can withdraw their coins at their discretion. Given that native cryptocurrencies like Bitcoin and Ether are not guaranteed or backstopped by any third-party, but instead have a solely market-determined value, they make suitable collateral for these systems. Since these protocols are credibly decentralized, users can transact freely and engage with decentralized finance products in a relatively unconstrained manner without fear of censorship.

c. Pseudo-Equity

A final class of tokens circulating within the DeFi ecosystem can be understood as ersatz or primitive equity products. These are assets which derive their value from control rights and underlying cash flows accruing to DeFi protocols. For the most part, these are not issued under established securities law processes, do not involve traditional disclosure norms that public markets investors might expect, and are not formally attached

---

[49] Financial Action Task Force, "12 Month Review of the Revised FATF Standards on Virtual Assets and Virtual Asset Service Providers" (June 2020). https://www.fatf-gafi.org/media/fatf/documents/recommen dations/12-Month-Review-Revised-FATF-Standards-Virtual-Assets-VASPS.pdf.

[50] *Id.* at 17.

[51] Data courtesy of DefiPulse. https://defipulse.com.

to a corporate entity. However, many of these tokens confer some of the rights associated with conventional equity securities, giving rise to the pseudo-equity appellation.

Issuance and liquidity for pseudo-equity is facilitated by the presence of decentralized exchange products, providing a global audience of investors access to these products without reliance on centralized, regulated exchanges. The issuance and exchange of pseudo-equity motivate end users to engage with DeFi products (in particular, DEX products), which in turn contributes to their popularity (because pseudo-equity can be contractually associated with DeFi projects and, thus, derive fees and cash flow from the contractual arrangements).

7. Systemic Risk: Is Genuine Openness a Poisoned Chalice?

The features that render DeFi more fundamentally "open" than traditional financial networks involve considerable trade-offs. There are a number of issues present in DeFi that established financial institutions face to a lesser degree. Chiefly, these include pitfalls involved in transacting with digital bearer assets, the possibility of systemic failures due to interconnectedness, and the constant specter of enforcement due to a general rejection of identity-based compliance processes.

Incorporating digital bearer assets can be extremely costly to users who lose keys. By design, there is no recourse for key loss. The flipside of composability is potential cascading failures if a key lynchpin fails. Convertible fiat-backed tokens are a clear potential point of compromise here, since they account for a significant fraction of the collateral backing DeFi products. At the time of writing, USD 422 million worth of USDC is being employed as collateral in Maker,[52] against which Dai is issued. However, as Dai is largely unregulated and Maker is more decentralized in nature, no freezing function exists, as is the case with USDC and Tether. Thus, if Centre were ever pressured to eliminate the USDC from the asset pool backing Dai and to freeze the USDC collateral, the system could become insolvent or otherwise impaired. Since Dai is considered to be a credible, censor-resistant, low-volatility asset, it is widely employed in other DeFi protocols. Thus, a compromise of its underlying collateral (which could spark a rapid devaluation) would have knock-on effects on other DeFi protocols. The nature of such extreme interconnectedness is such that the failure of a single popular component can be systemic.

Another issue with the permissionless and unrestricted pooling of assets that is common within DeFi is the potential for systemic "taint" if coins associated with illicit activity enter a pool. This raises difficult questions for participants in the pool, counterparties in transactions, and the developers maintaining the pooling software. This question has yet to be seriously explored within the DeFi sector.

Additionally, open questions linger around the legal treatment of stablecoins and the quality of their settlement assurances, and the rights of token holders in a situation of liquidation, collateral impairment, or distress. Unlike deposits at commercial banks, stablecoin balances are not federally insured. Since stablecoins have become the most

---

[52] Data found at Dune Analytics. "Maker DAO MCD," Dashboard by Fredrik Haga. https://explore.dunean alytics.com/dashboard/maker-dao---mcd.

widely used medium of settlement within DeFi, the sector is now more vulnerable to pressure, especially through the centralized administrators and banks holding the reserves backing the DeFi system.

Financial crimes enforcement agencies have taken notice of the DeFi phenomenon and have made it clear that they plan to grapple with it. The US Department of Justice, in their recent *Cryptocurrency Enforcement Framework*, mentioned the sector specifically as a topic of interest, noting that "decentralized platforms, peer-to-peer exchangers, and anonymity-enhanced cryptocurrencies that use non-public or private blockchains all can further obscure financial transactions from legitimate scrutiny."[53] Indeed, precedent stemming from the EtherDelta settlement[54] with the US Securities and Exchange Commission (SEC) suggests that securities regulators consider decentralized exchange administration to be a covered activity, in particular if these contracts are facilitating the exchange of unregulated securities.

While public blockchains do not require user identities to operate, opting instead for a pseudonymous model, they also explicitly reject KYC as part of an ideological commitment to privacy and digital cash. Nonetheless, identity is gradually being reinserted into these systems. Centralized exchanges are the primary points where users initially acquire the cryptoassets, and these centralized exchanges represent the best opportunity for regulators to tie blockchain addresses to individuals. The FATF's Travel Rule[55] stipulates that user data must travel with withdrawals from Virtual Asset Service Providers (VASPs) and is gradually coming into effect on a jurisdiction-by-jurisdiction basis. The question for the industry is whether these novel requirements require disclosing one's own blockchain address when withdrawing from a VASP, as is the case in Switzerland.[56] As public blockchains remain largely traceable, disclosing one's on-chain identity is tantamount to surrendering financial privacy. If this model were to become the default, and VASPs (and the governments regulating them) were able to characterize most on-chain addresses and tie them to user identities, the permissionless nature of DeFi would be significantly eroded, and so would its core value proposition.

Chainalysis estimates[57] that 60 percent of bitcoins that are not lost are held by licensed exchanges. With offshore and largely unregulated exchanges like BitMEX being targeted by the Department of Justice and the Commodity Futures Trading Commission

[53] "Cryptocurrency Enforcement Framework," Report of the Attorney General's Cyber Digital Task Force, U.S. Department of Justice (Oct. 2020). https://www.justice.gov/ag/page/file/1326061/download.

[54] "SEC Charges EtherDelta Founder with Operating an Unregistered Exchange," *Securities and Exchange Commission* (Aug. 25, 2018). https://www.sec.gov/news/press-release/2018-258.

[55] See Recommendation 16. Financial Action Task Force, "Guidance for a Risk-Based Approach to Virtual Assets and Virtual Asset Service Providers" (June 2019). https://www.fatf-gafi.org/publications/fatfrecommendations/documents/guidance-rba-virtual-assets.html.

[56] Ciphertrace CEO Dan Jevans explains the Swiss interpretation of the Travel Rule on the Unchained podcast, stating, "[The Swiss government] is extending it to self-custodial wallets where you have to make declarations about who you are. So they've taken it beyond VASP to VASP. They're stretching the boundary [and] extending it to more self-custodial wallets." See "Why the Travel Rule Is One of the Most Significant Regulations in Crypto," *Unchained Podcast* (Aug. 4, 2020). https://unchainedpodcast.com/why-the-travel-rule-is-one-of-the-most-significant-regulations-in-crypto/.

[57] "60% Of Bitcoin Is Held Long Term as Digital Gold. What About the Rest?," *Chainalysis Blog* (June 18, 2020). https://blog.chainalysis.com/reports/bitcoin-market-data-exchanges-trading.

(CFTC),[58] the fraction of exchanges—and hence users of cryptocurrency—that is accountable to engaged regulators is growing.

If financial regulators are able to tie individuals to blockchain transactions, they will eventually seek to regulate DeFi processes to the extent that they touch their mandates. Given that DeFi protocols reject KYC and other forms of authentication and require only ownership of digital assets, more regulatory attention appears inevitable. Thus, the longevity of the current regime of radical openness and low compliance barriers in the blockchain-based DeFi space remains questionable.

8. Prospects for the Convergence of Decentralized and Traditional Finance

As the scope and intensity of blockchain-based transactional activity grew, its collision with the traditional financial sector was inevitable. Early on in Bitcoin's history, US banks refused to do business with digital currency exchanges, but as attitudes moderated and the core technology became better understood, Tier I banks began to service these entities.[59] The prospects for integration brightened in the United States with two letters from the Office of the Comptroller of the Currency, one clarifying that federally chartered banks could provide custody services for cryptoassets,[60] the other ratifying a status quo whereby banks were holding dollar reserves for stablecoin issuers.[61] This guidance provides strong clarity for banks to begin to incorporate public blockchains as an additional settlement network.

Additionally, crypto exchanges have begun to pursue bank charters under Wyoming legislation creating Special Purpose Depository Institutions (SPDI).[62] Kraken Financial, a subsidiary of Kraken, a long-running cryptoasset exchange, was the first entity to receive the SPDI charter and may apply for access to the federal payment system at the local regional branch of the Federal Reserve System.[63] Either through crypto-native institutions leveraging the Wyoming legislation for access to base money or via established banks building crypto-custody products, the emergence of a novel class of financial institutions which engage with cryptocurrency while maintaining direct access to the Federal Reserve System is a genuine prospect.

---

[58] "CFTC Charges BitMEX Owners with Illegally Operating a Cryptocurrency Derivatives Trading Platform and Anti-Money Laundering Violations," *CFTC* (Oct. 1, 2020). https://www.cftc.gov/PressRoom/PressReleases/8270-20.

[59] In 2020, JPMorgan announced that they would provide banking services to crypto exchanges and custodians Coinbase and Gemini. See Paul Vigna. "JPMorgan Extends Banking Services to Bitcoin Exchanges," *Wall Street Journal* (May 12, 2020). https://www.wsj.com/articles/jpmorgan-extends-banking-services-to-bitcoin-exchanges-11589281201.

[60] "Federally Chartered Banks and Thrifts May Provide Custody Services for Crypto Assets," *Office of the Comptroller of the Currency* (July 22, 2020). https://www.occ.gov/news-issuances/news-releases/2020/nr-occ-2020-98.html.

[61] "Federally Chartered Banks and Thrifts May Engage in Certain Stablecoin Activities," *Office of the Comptroller of the Currency* (Sept. 21, 2020) https://www.occ.gov/news-issuances/news-releases/2020/nr-occ-2020-125.html.

[62] For more detail on the Wyoming SPDI, see "Special Purpose Depository Institutions," *Wyoming Division of Banking*. http://wyomingbankingdivision.wyo.gov/home/areas-of-regulation/laws-and-regulation/special-purpose-depository-institution.

[63] For more on Kraken's SPDI approval, see "The First Cryptocurrency Bank," *The National Law Review* (Sept. 22, 2020). https://www.natlawreview.com/article/first-cryptocurrency-bank.

One novel dimension of blockchain-based assets is their portability. Users can take self-custody of their assets without relying on a third-party. In this paradigm, exchanges and brokers are relegated to mere interfaces, as opposed to the sole and fundamental means of engagement with one's assets. The ease of withdrawing one's funds—compare this with withdrawing gold from a vault or securities from a broker—means that service providers covering cryptoassets face the continual prospect of asset flight, which acts as a disciplinary force. After a series of aggressive liquidations on the Bitcoin derivatives exchange BitMEX in March 2020, traders withdrew 103,000 BTC from the exchange in under a month, worth over USD 1 billion. These dramatic asset flows are facilitated by the ease of undertaking physical settlement and portend a competitive and mercurial environment for custodians and brokers.

Additionally, as ambitions to create central bank digital currency (CBDC) expand, the installed base of fiat-convertible tokens circulating on-chain could be leveraged for a hybrid model. While the eventual nature of a US CBDC is still in question, domestic stablecoin issuers could advocate for a public-private partnership in which they continue to maintain relationships with their userbase and facilitate P2P, cash-like transactions, while backing the fiat IOUs circulating on-chain with high-quality base money. This would be an improvement from a reserve quality perspective from the current model based on commercial bank liabilities.

Already, major fintechs have embraced public blockchain assets,[64] albeit with varying levels of functionality. While Square's Cash App permits Bitcoin deposits and withdrawals, Robinhood, PayPal, and Revolut offer financial exposure but not direct access to the underlying assets. Increasingly, fintechs are taking notice of the presence of blockchain-based assets in the portfolios of their users and have begun to incorporate blockchain accounts—both directly on-chain, and at custodial exchanges—into financial tracking. Account aggregation is trivial for on-chain addresses, as the entire history of activity is present on the public ledger; sharing a blockchain address is typically sufficient to draw in a user's transactional history. Fintechs or neobanks offering high-yield savings products may also be enticed by the structurally high yields available in the cryptodollar lending space. Already, uninsured money market accounts offering users access to DeFi yields in a familiar interface have emerged.

Lastly, securities offer a final point of incipient integration between decentralized and traditional finance. Developments like Ethereum's ERC-1404 standard[65] permit the whitelisted trading of assets, allowing users to transfer security claims on a public blockchain without risking their distribution to unauthorized parties. Already, the SEC has permitted the issuance of securities on Ethereum through this standard,[66] indicating their openness to the presence of securities on public blockchains, provided the existence of certain constraints. These tokens could plausibly be employed in existing DeFi

[64] Major fintechs offering crypto products include Robinhood, PayPal, eToro, Square's Cash App, Mogo, Hype, SoFi, and TradeStation.

[65] For more on ERC-1404, see Tokensoft's Erc1404.org. https://erc1404.org/.

[66] The securities in question are ArCoin (for more on ArCoin, see Danny Nelson, "605 Days Later: How ArCoins Got the SEC Go-Ahead as an Ethereum-Traded Treasurys Fund," *CoinDesk* (July 29, 2020). https://www.coindesk.com/arcoins-blockchain-traded-fund-arca-tokensoft); and INX (see SEC Form F-1, "Registration Statement," *INX Limited* (Aug. 19, 2020). https://www.sec.gov/Archives/edgar/data/1725882/000121390019016285/ff12019_inxlimited.htm).

infrastructure, mirroring the existing securities-backed lending industry, this time in an on-chain and automated context.

Fundamentally, public blockchains and the emerging suite of financial products built atop them aspire to be decentralized and disconnected from the established financial system. However, user demands for intermediated services like custody, alongside the growing importance of the industry, have caused a natural convergence with the financial sector to take place. As mentioned, however, the permissionless and unencumbered nature of blockchain-based DeFi can make for an uneasy marriage with regulated institutions. Nonetheless, blockchain-based DeFi can serve as the foundation for rich ecosystems of ever-evolving services and products.

9. Conclusion

As we have shown, public blockchain-based DeFi is motivated by many of the same ideals that underscore the open finance movement: interoperability, granting better outcomes for users of financial services by stimulating competition service providers, and providing the ability to freely move between providers. These objectives are implemented in different ways. Open finance is concerned with linking established financial firms and fintechs and creating protocols to share user-permissioned data; decentralized finance envisions an entirely novel and distinct financial system built atop public blockchains, in which users primarily self-custody their assets and interact with autonomous, clearly specified open-source financial applications.

At its current stage, public blockchains like Ethereum conjoin tens of millions of users worldwide on a single replicated database. This enables seamless composability between different financial applications which reference each other freely. Open finance and open data by contrast must reckon with installed financial plumbing and involves finding communication bridges between bank databases. DeFi may face a paradox if liquidity becomes more fragmented across blockchains, or Ethereum scales by distributing transactions to multiple subledgers which periodically reconcile—it risks losing the composability advantages which are its selling point, especially with regard to more complex financial applications.

In my view, the products offered by decentralized finance have reached a level of maturity where they are challenging established financial infrastructure. Much of the enthusiasm for DeFi is predicated on its repudiation of identity-based compliance, as well as the strong portability of assets between distinct financial products and the ability of end users to retain custody of their assets. The promise of permissionless innovation in financial services for a global audience, without requiring bank charters or onerous regulatory oversight, has driven a wave of activity in the sector. Whether the open qualities of DeFi can endure is the sector's existential question. Its genuine permissionless quality—its key value proposition—may have to be dialed back, as regulators turn their gaze to DeFi, and it becomes further integrated with the established financial system.

14

From Open Banking to Open Data and Beyond: Competition and the Future of Banking

Brad Carr[*]

1. Introduction

Technological innovation has quickly outpaced rules required under mandatory Open Banking[1] models, which were designed in a different economy for a different financial services industry. Meanwhile, consumers are also becoming aware of the value of their personal data. Such is the dynamism of the current financial sector and the depth of opportunities presented in the modern use of data that Open Banking needs further renewal, even as it is still taking hold.

In the first chapter, Andres Wolberg-Stok argued for open banking to evolve into open data, which would involve the sharing of customer-permissioned data across industry sectors rather than being limited to one sector. Open data trends amplified by the COVID-19 pandemic are speeding up changes to current market structures in our financial and economic system. The emerging structural changes have overtaken the original design and goals for industry-specific Open Banking initiatives, impacting competition in ways that could counter the original intent of the Open Banking movement—namely, improving competition for consumers. For instance, current Open Banking requirements may lead to new concentration effects of valuable data stored in certain sectors of an economy. As traditional sectoral boundaries have blurred and new business models based on data-sharing have emerged, we can no longer contemplate financial services in isolation, but rather consider personal data held by banks along with data sets from all other realms of a consumer's life: health, telecommunications, social media, energy usage, and much more.

Significant increases in the adoption of digital services driven by the pandemic[2] have dramatically raised customers' expectations of these services, as many of them work

---

[*] Managing Director, Digital Finance at the Institute of International Finance.

[1] Lower-case "open banking" refers to nongovernment-mandated sharing of customer-permissioned data by banks with third-parties. Capitalized "Open Banking" refers to the government-mandated form of open banking. See the introduction to this book, by Linda Jeng.

[2] For example, 91% of Americans banked online or via mobile app in July 2020, while only 52% are visiting physical bank branches during the pandemic. See DepositAccounts Survey (Aug. 27, 2020). https://www.depositaccounts.com/blog/online-banking-spikes-amid-pandemic.html.
Meanwhile, Europe saw an 72% increase in the use of fintech apps since the coronavirus. See Simon Chandler, "Coronavirus Drives 72% Rise in Use of Fintech Apps," *Forbes* (Mar. 30, 2020). https://www.forbes.com/sites/simonchandler/2020/03/30/coronavirus-drives-72-rise-in-use-of-fintech-apps/?sh=6dcb763166ed.

Brad Carr, *From Open Banking to Open Data and Beyond: Competition and the Future of Banking* In: *Open Banking*. Edited by: Linda Jeng, Oxford University Press. © Oxford University Press 2022. DOI: 10.1093/oso/9780197582879.003.0015

from home[3] with live visual connectivity, shop from home via enhanced e-commerce platforms, and entertain at home with sophisticated live video streaming and gaming experiences. As customers' expectations of digital services have risen, so have their demands for immediacy and customization in these services. In turn, as consumers use more digital services, they create more and richer data flows, which enable even more customized delivery, better targeting consumers and meeting their expectations. All of this is self-reinforcing and further increases the digitalization of our economy. The richness of data flows is being leveraged to enable personalized delivery. Digitalization and these environmental changes are also driving a nascent consumer awareness of the value of the data they personally generate, and a desire for greater control of their data. Consumers are finding that their user experiences are improving and becoming more customized. For example, social media and personal e-commerce behavior could be useful for credit underwriting. Online businesses use a customer's browsing history to quickly identify interesting products for the shopper, and consumers, in turn, appreciate decreased friction in their user experience. However, data personally generated by consumers is monetarily valuable as described in Chapter 7, and having access to their data provides significant competitive advantages.

The combination of this digitalization trend and the blurring of traditional sectoral boundaries presents challenges for policymakers and market participants alike: how to adapt and redefine business models and regulation as we move beyond Open Banking to Open Data. This evolution will be critical to maintaining the aspirations of an open data economy, decentralized finance, and greater consumer empowerment—in the face of technological and commercial trends that are instead increasingly pointing to a new form of recentralization. This is essentially the task to modernizing Open Banking to be fit for purpose in a cross-sectoral platform economy.

2. Competition: The Historical Context

Both notions of competition and consumer empowerment have been at the heart of the open banking policy debate. These two primary objectives help ensure that consumers have a greater range of available offerings and greater control over their data. These objectives remain both noble and relevant. But the frenetic pace of change in the digital economy has itself disrupted the trajectory of open banking, giving rise to new risks as well as opportunities. It prompts a rethink on how open banking needs to further evolve in pursuit of these notions.

After the global financial crisis of 2008, some have postulated that mandatory Open Banking was originally intended as part of a deliberate punishment for big banks as part of the public backlash to the last financial crisis, particularly in those markets where taxpayer funds were deployed to help stabilize particular banks. When publishing the United Kingdom's Independent Commission on Banking report in 2011, Sir John Vickers highlighted insufficient and misdirected competition, bank switching, and the

---

[3] In the United States, remote work of 5 plus days experienced a 44% increase in workers post-coronavirus. https://www.statista.com/statistics/1122987/change-in-remote-work-trends-after-covid-in-usa/.

need for an added Financial Conduct Authority mandate on competition, alongside the higher profile findings on ring-fencing and added capital requirements.[4] Oliver Wyman expert Doug Elliott later reflected:

> A key motivator for the UK government to push Open Banking, for example, is be-cause they frankly have growing concern that there is as they see it an oligopoly of retail banks in the UK, and they have become frustrated about other things, they have tried to break that up, so one of their thoughts is "hey, maybe if we allow FinTechs and others to come in more freely, that will help with the competition issues."[5]

Even looking past the speculative notion of "punishment" and the prevailing anti-bank public sentiments at that time, the effort to promote competition against large incumbent banks does fit with the prudential notion of reducing interconnections with sys-temically important banks and addressing the "Too-Big-to-Fail" problem that held such a prominent policy focus.

However, while the competition motivation for Open Banking was framed a decade ago in terms of supporting challenger banks and new entrant fintech firms to expand the range of market participants, the broader market dynamics across finance and tech-nology have shifted dramatically since. In the new information age where data is power and an essential input, there is now the risk that the beneficiaries might in fact be a small group of dominant tech giants (or "BigTech"). Thus, the data-sharing heralded by Open Banking could in fact be used to drive a new kind of market concentration.

Notwithstanding the intent of enabling challenger banks to compete more readily against larger incumbents, there so far has been little traction in most markets. A year after the European Union's Second Payments Service Directive (PSD2) launched, only 22 percent of consumers had heard of Open Banking, and only one-fifth of those knew what it meant.[6] Part of that slow uptake may be a factor of the parties involved: that the smaller and newer firms faced challenges in operationalizing open banking in an environment lacking standard application programming interfaces (APIs) for sharing data (see Chapter 5 for a discussion of API standards). It also takes time to build brand recognition and trust with customers—for handling both their data and their money. Concurrently, large banks have quickly accepted this, accepting competition from new, smaller players, occasionally expressing frustration at the implementation and reputa-tion costs, but largely viewing the competitive threat from challenger banks as an im-petus for themselves to innovate.[7]

---

[4] Sir John Vickers, Independent Commission on Banking, Final Report Publication: Opening Remarks (Sept. 12, 2011). https://webarchive.nationalarchives.gov.uk/20120827143059/http://bankingcommission. independent.gov.uk/.

[5] IIF, FRT Podcast, "Episode 74: Consumer Data Rights." (May 13, 2019) https://www.iif.com/Publicati ons/ID/3346/FRT-Episode-34-Consumer-Data-Rights.

[6] MoneyLive, "Future of Retail Banking, 2020." https://marketforcelive.com/money-live/post/future-ret ail-banking-report-2020/.

[7] Jon Rees, "UK Banks See Open Banking as 'Inconvenience' Not Opportunity, Says Challenger," S&P Global Market Intelligence (Aug. 28, 2018). https://www.spglobal.com/marketintelligence/en/news-insights/ trending/0e_vnvkf3hoojw0uvrzd_g2.

3. Inflection Point: BigTechs and the Platformization of Financial Services

If slow uptake and minimal impacts on competition dynamics have been the story to this point, we now enter a pivotal stage—an inflection point, perhaps—where the dynamics themselves are beginning to change, presenting potential for other commercial beneficiaries.

This phenomenon is not specific to Open Banking but is also reflected in the evolution of how new entrants and new offerings have manifested themselves in the market for financial services more broadly. Financial technology or "fintech" was initially heralded as ushering in new entrants, fintech startups, that would target specific niches in the value chain, driving an "unbundling" of financial services. However, the propensity for unbundling has been quickly superseded by a trend of "rebundling," led by the digital platforms of BigTech firms. Whereas the newer, dedicated "fintech" firms typically operate just within the realm of financial services, BigTech companies can offer financial products as an extension to a much wider set of business lines.[8]

The business model of BigTech firms is primarily founded on the development of an interconnected ecosystem of products and services, across e-commerce, social media, operating systems, and search engines.[9] Their forays into financial services involve penetrating a specific "unbundled" service, and "rebundling" it with their nonfinancial offerings, leveraging their existing network effects. Unlike new entrants to an unfamiliar business line, BigTech firms can quickly achieve scale, using their existing digital ecosystems of millions of active users. The ability to further build on their networks and to expand their suite of user data can be valuable for reinforcing the strength of their ecosystems, in addition to whatever direct revenue may be generated.[10] Both armed and incentivized with these existing network capacities, the expansion of BigTechs into a new product market can be extremely rapid, as has been the case in China, and beyond the scope of what traditional supervisory monitoring and regulatory tools might keep pace with.[11]

The advent of rebundling presents new policy considerations, and a new challenge for regulatory frameworks to keep pace with. This concern has also been recognized within the regulatory community, with European Central Bank supervisory board member Pentti Hakkarainen observing:

> As the trend towards unbundling is accelerated by innovation and digitalization, the current framework may need to be reviewed to ensure a level playing field and to maintain the principle of "same activity, same risks, same supervision and regulation."[12]

---

[8] Lucia Pacheco and Pablo Urbiola, "From FinTech to BigTech: An Evolving Regulatory Response," *BBVA Research Working Paper 20/09* (2020). https://www.bbvaresearch.com/en/publicaciones/global-from-fint ech-to-bigtech-an-evolving-regulatory-response/.

[9] Santiago Fernández de Lis and Pablo Urbiola, "Digital Transformation and Competition in the Financial Sector," *BBVA Research Working Paper 19/02* (2019). https://www.bbvaresearch.com/en/publicaciones/digi tal-transformation-and-competition-in-the-financial-sector/.

[10] *Id.*

[11] IIF, "FinTech and Market Structure in Financial Services," Letter to Financial Stability Board (Mar. 19, 2019). https://www.iif.com/Portals/0/Files/32370132_iif_fsb_fintech_report.pdf.

[12] Pentti Hakkarainen, remarks in *IIF Digital Interchange* (Sept. 13, 2020); IIF video at https://www.yout ube.com/watch?v=5Wew_q0moQE&list=PLJDiecAPqXi3fKoF-u3IxKOa2zt_BLL44&index=10; transcript

In considering the competitive anomalies in this sector, the increasing trend toward partnerships between banks and tech firms of varying sizes is apparent. Many of these partnerships are highly cooperative and can serve to reduce risk, improve operational efficiency, and deliver innovation to a wider group of customers. But the form of some of these partnerships may also have a pronounced impact on the outlook for competition, with some economists warning that BigTech companies could dominate the origination and distribution of loans to consumers and small to medium-size enterprises (SMEs), leaving the banks to become the mere "low-cost manufacturers," supplying and funding the loans that are instead intermediated by the BigTechs.[13]

In some places, this is already happening. While PayPal operates under different regulatory structures in different jurisdictions—in the United States, it has quickly become one of the largest SME lenders while operating as a regulated money transfer business (rather than as a bank). In China, disclosures for the aborted Ant Financial Initial Public Offering in 2020 revealed that the funding for 98 percent of their consumer loans were provided by its partner banks and other financial institutions.[14] Peterson Institute analyst Martin Chorzempa described the Ant scenario as "[i]t's the western bankers' worst nightmare of what would happen under an open banking system . . . Essentially, the banks lose their direct relationship with the customer and all of it is mediated by the platform."[15]

As a global trend, the growth in BigTech credit provision has continued to accelerate significantly since 2015, while credit provision by smaller fintechs has been receding since 2017, as shown in Figure 14.1.

A key question then is the level of market power that a BigTech platform may potentially hold, and whether we may in fact be giving way to a new oligopoly comprised of a handful of large platforms. Other concerns about the impacts of BigTech firms for competition include whether customers might be "steered" from within a platform toward the BigTech's own proprietary services and whether a platform could exploit data to apply a form of primary price differentiation, adjusting prices for customers found to be insensitive to price or unwilling to switch.[16] Perhaps with Chorzempa's "nightmare" scenario in mind, some banks have sought to proactively adjust, choosing to build platforms of their own, rather than waiting to become a mere product provider to a tech firm's platform.

Itau CEO Candido Bracher described how banks are facing a "defund or duck" dilemma, presenting them a choice on whether to focus on product or distribution in the advent of the platform economy. While it is not an absolute "black or white" equation, Itau has chosen to emphasize distribution, building a platform in order to maintain a sense of primacy with the customer relationship. Bracher explains:

of speech at https://www.bankingsupervision.europa.eu/press/speeches/date/2020/html/ssm.sp200916~e52 c53cd6b.en.html.

[13] Miguel de la Mano and Jorge Padilla, "The Pros and Cons of Big Tech Banking," *Compass Lexecon* (July 2019). https://www.compasslexecon.com/wp-content/uploads/2019/07/CL_Expert_Opinion_Big_Tech_B anking_July-2019.pdf.

[14] Ryan McMorrow, Nian Lu, and Sherry Fei Ju, "The Transformation of Ant Financial," *Financial Times* (Aug. 26, 2020). https://www.ft.com/content/c636a22e-dd3f-403e-a72d-c3ffb375459c.

[15] *Id.*

[16] de la Mano & Padilla, *supra* note 14.

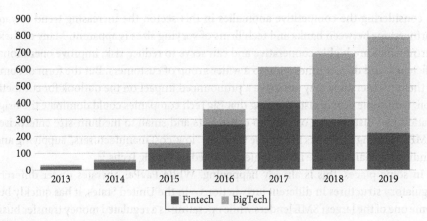

Figure 14.1 Fintech and BigTech Credit (USD billions).

Source: BIS.

. BIS, *BIS Working Paper 887, FinTech and BigTech Credit: A new database, September 2020*; data for the United States, the United Kingdom, the European Union, China, Australia, and New Zealand.

> We have had for almost five years now an open platform in investments for instance: we sell investments from third partners for most of our clients, we even sell time deposits from competing banks, funds from many different managers . . . We have an open platform in insurance . . . this is an important choice that we have to make, this choice of focusing on distribution. It requires lifting your skills in dealing with third parties, associating, acquiring, making co-operation agreements.[17]

The issues raised with BigTech firms and competition extend beyond Open Banking, with implications for antitrust law, consumer protection, and pricing transparency, and the nature of platform operations. But these issues will play an important part of the context in which Open Banking will operate over the next decade.

4. Data Asymmetries

With these shifting market and competition dynamics in mind, it is therefore a concern that while open banking seeks to expand competition, structural asymmetries in personal data frameworks could in fact run counter to this objective. Significantly, most mandatory Open Banking regimes have created an asymmetry between the entities that are obliged to make their customers' data shareable, and those entities that can receive that data. For instance, the UK Open Banking Standard and the European Union's PSD2 make payments-related information accessible to nonbank players. This payments-related data forms part of the core data that banks maintain about their customers. However, nonbank players do not have similar requirements to share their own core

---

[17] Candido Bracher, "Fireside Chat: Digitalization in Emerging Markets," *IIF Digital Interchange* (Sept. 14, 2020). https://www.youtube.com/watch?list=PLJDiecAPqXi3fKoF-u3IxKOa2zt_BLL44&v=KRd7O3YN H7A&feature=emb_logo.

customer data (which is usually not payments-related data) with other parties, including banks.[18] This asymmetry in data-sharing means that regulations intended to facilitate the entrance of new players and promote competition and end-user choice in the payments market has created a competitive advantage for nonbanks and a disadvantage for banks and other financial services firms vis-à-vis players from other industries.[19]

Information asymmetry is a particularly important concern given that data has emerged as the new vital asset in the digital economy, underpinning product development, risk analysis, and marketing. Products and services are based on data like never before, and new technologies have exponentially increased the capabilities to store, process, and transfer data on the behavior and characteristics of consumers. The fact that many digital services are offered to consumers at "zero-price" (i.e., in exchange for the information generated while using them) demonstrates the monetized value of data in the digital economy.[20]

As Georgetown University Law Center's Professor Chris Brummer observed, "One of the central paradoxes of digital finance is that in order to succeed, businesses will need to both (a) achieve economies of scale and (b) create customizable solutions for increasingly demanding customers."[21] The ability to rapidly upscale with vast quantities of consumer data, coupled with sophisticated analytical capacities, is central for strategies to optimize across Brummer's named constraints.

The ability to bring together multiple, distinct types of data about a customer can be extremely advantageous in modeling an individual risk profile for that customer. For instance, analysis by Tobias Berg, Valentin Burg, Ana Gombovic, and Manju Puri assessed the accuracy of credit scoring constructed under three approaches:

1. traditional credit bureau approaches;
2. customer's digital footprint approaches (e.g., their device type, operating system, time of day for accessing, channel used, email address, tendency to make spelling mistakes); or
3. a combination of both types of approaches.[22]

Berg et al. found that using either the credit bureau or the digital footprint approach in isolation gave fairly similar levels of accuracy. With models' discriminatory power measured by the Receiver Operating Characteristics curve (ROC-curve) and the Area Under Curve (AUC) on their sample data sets, the two approaches when applied independently generated AUC scores of 68.3 percent and 69.6 percent, respectively. However, where these data sets were combined, a substantially more accurate result was achieved, with an AUC of 73.6 percent, as shown in Figure 14.2.[23]

---

[18] To access payments data under PSD2, nonbank players are required to be registered as "account information service providers" and comply with some basic governance, internal control, financial, and security requirements, as well as having professional indemnity insurance or a comparable guarantee.

[19] IIF, *Reciprocity in Customer Data Sharing Frameworks* (July 30, 2018). https://www.iif.com/portals/0/Files/private/32370132_reciprocity_in_customer_data_sharing_frameworks_20170730.pdf.

[20] *Id.*

[21] Chris Brummer, Twitter, July 29, 2020.

[22] Tobias Berg et al., "On the Rise of the FinTechs—Credit Scoring Using Digital Footprints," *FDIC Working Paper Series* (Sept. 2018). https://www.fdic.gov/bank/analytical/cfr/2018/wp2018/cfr-wp2018-04.pdf.

[23] *Id.*

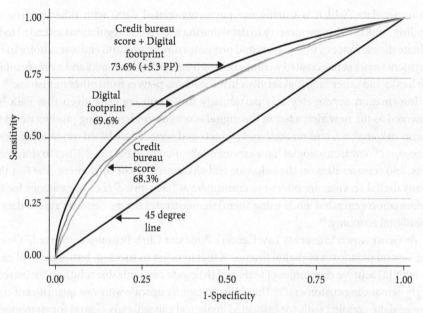

Figure 14.2 Model Accuracy Assessments Across Approaches
Source: Berg et al. Analysis by Berg et al. showing ROC-curves that are estimated using a logit regression of the default dummy on the credit bureau score, the digital footprint, and the combination of both credit bureau score and digital footprint. The sample period is from October 2015 to December 2016, only including customers with credit bureau scores.
Id.

Intuitively, these results should not be surprising: the more you know about a customer, the better that you (or more specifically, your sophisticated analytics) can project either their risk profile or which products and services they may be more amenable to. Relating data access back to an asymmetric Open Banking environment, the advantage is significant as one group of firms enjoys a unique opportunity to pursue building a consolidated, holistic view of the customer while the other group of firms cannot.

A BigTech firm is already armed with considerable data points about a consumer—for instance, their internet search history; their friend networks; their online buying, reading, and viewing patterns. By encouraging a consumer to instruct their bank to also pass their financial data via Open Banking, the BigTechs have an enormous opportunity to bring those data points together and achieve the uplift in customer insights and risk scoring, per the analysis of Berg et al. The unidirectional data-sharing structure of Open Banking (as opposed to a broader "Open Data" structure) denies a bank the opportunity to emulate this, such as by encouraging a transfer of the customer's other digital lifestyle data for customizing financial services and products. While it is arguable as to whether some banks would necessarily have the analytical capabilities in place to meaningfully act on data from a tech firm, an asymmetric regime does not allow them the opportunity to begin with, forcing a legislated outcome rather than a matter of investment strategies and market forces.

This may also ultimately represent a limitation on consumer choice where their data is aggregated, protected, and used. The Bank of England's Future of Finance report highlighted that 86 percent of consumers most trusted their bank to protect their personal data, in preference to the likes of consumer technology companies, payments providers, and social media firms.[24] It seems somewhat counterintuitive to enact a regime that favors certain entities to emerge as the likely centralized hubs for consumers' data, over firms that consumers already trust with their money.

5. COVID-19 Amplification

The COVID-19 pandemic makes competition issues with BigTechs not only more important but even more urgent. Amid the dramatic acceleration in digitalization trends through the economy, BigTech firms are increasingly embedded in our lives, and more important than ever in our economy.

Where other sectors of the economy are struggling, in particular smaller businesses, BigTech firms have continued to generate strong revenues, adding to their already enormous cash reserves. In addition, they are also playing important roles in supporting governments with health solutions. Where economists discuss a K-shaped trajectory to show divergent outcomes for different groups through and beyond the pandemic, this is sometimes represented across axes of the wealthy versus the poor, large companies versus small, diversified versus specialized, or digital versus physical sites.[25] The common element across each of those dimensions is that the BigTech firms are favorably placed to succeed and further grow their market power.

Perhaps the most important trend is consumers' increasing reliance on e-commerce channels. This is reshaping consumer preferences dramatically and urgently, with significant implications for the potential rebundling onto platforms of services from across sectors. In the United States, quarterly e-commerce retail sales took two decades to reach $160 billion in Q1 of 2020, but then immediately skyrocketed to $212 billion in Q2.[26] For example, Amazon has seized this moment. Its e-commerce business was the primary beneficiary of both Amazon's $30 billion capital expenditure and addition of 400,000 workers (more than a 50 percent workforce increase) in the first three quarters of 2020.[27]

This trend is not without precedent. The dramatic growth in e-commerce resembles the emergence of Alibaba and JD.com at the time of the 2002–2004 SARS crisis, as millions of Chinese consumers switched from in-person to online shopping experiences, and small businesses moved to sell on such market platforms.[28]

Concurrently, the landscape for smaller and newer fintechs has also changed during the pandemic. Some of those would-be challenger firms have found renewed struggles for funding, and several early-stage tech firms have stalled. These challenges present

---

[24] Bank of England, *Future of Finance* Report, June 2019.

[25] Melissa Repho and Lauren Thomas, "6 Ways the Coronavirus Pandemic Has Forever Altered the Retail Landscape," *CNBC* (September 29, 2020). https://www.cnbc.com/2020/09/29/how-coronavirus-pandemic-forever-altered-retail.html.

[26] FRED, St. Louis Federal Reserve. https://fred.stlouisfed.org/series/ECOMPCTSA.

[27] Christopher Mims, "Four Reasons the Stay-at-Home Economy Is Here to Stay," *Wall Street Journal* (Nov. 21, 2021). https://www.wsj.com/articles/four-reasons-the-stay-at-home-economy-is-here-to-stay-1160 5934806.

[28] Duncan Clark, *Alibaba: The House That Jack Ma Built*, Ecco, New York, 2016.

new implications for competition and market power, the distribution of talent across the tech sector, and the nature of partnerships between financial institutions and tech firms. Where the risk that asymmetrical data flows could have a distortive effect on competition may have seemed speculative in the pre-COVID environment, this sudden shift in dynamics has brought this anticompetitive possibility closer to reality.

6. The Future: From Open Banking to Open Data

To ensure that consumers can benefit from both (1) having direct control over their data and (2) an undistorted marketplace, we ultimately need to move beyond the sector-specific notion of "Open Banking" and toward a broader economy-wide framework for "Open Data." As well as modernizing our regulatory constructs for the reality of blurred industry boundaries, Open Data would unambiguously place the customer and their data at the center of a more consumer-empowered and equitable economy.

Australia, Brazil, and Singapore have already signposted moves in this direction. (See Chapters 10 and 6 for more about the Australian and Singapore approaches.) In addition, among Southeast Asian bankers, a common refrain is that "Open Banking is not about banking; it's all about data."

The Australian Consumer Data Right (CDR) initiative provides for the emergence of a broader data ecosystem in which the consumer can potentially control their data and direct its transfer between firms across different business sectors. For instance, the framers of the CDR noted the potential consumer benefits of exchanging data between their bank and telecommunications provider, to enable product development, greater choice, and convenience. (Jamie Leach and Julie McKay describe the Australian approach more fully in Chapter 10.) The Australian government's report on Open Banking,[29] which gave rise to the CDR, explicitly highlighted the risk of cross-sectoral inconsistencies between banks and tech firms, noting:

> It would seem unfair if banks were required to provide their customers' data to data recipients such as FinTechs or non-bank credit providers, but those data recipients were not required to reciprocate in any way, merely because they were not banks and therefore did not hold "banking" data. An Open Banking system in which all eligible entities participate fully—both as data holders and data recipients—is likely to be more vibrant and dynamic than one in which non-ADI participants are solely receivers of data and ADIs are largely only transmitters of data.[30]

The Australian government report consequently recommended if an entity that does not primarily operate in the banking sector (such as a tech firm) wishes to participate in Open Banking as a data recipient, then it should be required to also provide equivalent data sets (with the Australian Competition and Consumer Commission to assess what

---

[29] Australian Government, "Open Banking: Customers, Choice, Convenience, Confidence" ("The Farrell Report") (Dec. 2017). https://treasury.gov.au/sites/default/files/2019-03/Review-into-Open-Banking-_For-web-1.pdf.

[30] The term "ADI" refers to authorised deposit-taking institutions, a term commonly used in Australian financial regulation, and inclusive of banks, building societies, and credit unions.

constitutes "equivalent data").[31] While this requirement for reciprocal data-sharing was not included in the first stage of CDR implementation, it remains a likely feature of the eventual end game. Meanwhile, in Brazil, the central bank chose to establish requirements that all Open Banking participants are subject to reciprocal data-sharing obligations—with the potential expansion beyond banking to insurance and pensions products having been earmarked.[32]

Singapore's new Personal Data Protection Act also provides for a cross-sectoral Data Portability Obligation. This Obligation requires all organizations (without sectoral boundaries or limitations) to transmit raw personal data to another organization in a commonly used machine-readable format at the direction of the individual, although it exempts data that a firm has derived in the course of its business in order to protect commercial intellectual property.[33] As Zee Kin Yeong and David Roi Hardoon describe in Chapter 6, the Singapore initiative specifically seeks to support innovation and unlock economic gains by facilitating the ability to combine data from different sources, across industry "silos."[34] Indeed, the Singapore initiative notes that the economic benefits can only be realized if data portability is bringing together data sourced by different organizations is sufficiently different. With a similar view toward a broader data ecosystem as articulated by Australia, Singapore identifies the potential benefits as spanning not only certain financial services applications like enhanced risk assessment but also in the healthcare sector, transportation, and infrastructure planning.

As described in Chapter 2, the principle of consumer-led data portability has gained some recognition within the European Union's General Data Protection Regulation and the California Consumer Privacy Act. While these do not yet promote portability for the depth of data that might be considered equivalent to the scale of Open Banking, these laws hopefully can represent a legislative path for the future development of a sector-neutral data ecosystem.

Impetus may also come from regulatory and legislative developments in other sectors, including moves to provide for greater consumer control of other types of data, such as vehicle telematics that monitor vehicles using GPS and onboard diagnostics. During a recent election in the United States, Massachusetts state voters overwhelmingly passed a referendum requiring manufacturers of vehicles with telematics systems to equip them with a standardized open data platform that would enable vehicle owners and independent repairers to access and retrieve mechanical data and run diagnostics via mobile apps.[35]

---

[31] Australian government report; see Recommendation 3.9: "Reciprocal obligations in Open Banking."

[32] Ariadne Plaitakis and Stefan Staschen, "Open Banking: How to Design for Inclusion," Consultative Group to Assist the Poor (CGAP) Working Paper (Oct. 2020). https://www.cgap.org/sites/default/files/publications/2020_10_Working_Paper_Open_Banking.pdf.

[33] Ministry of Communications and Information (Singapore), "Closing Note to the Public Consultation on Draft Personal Data Protection (Amendment) Bill including Related Amendments to the Spam Control Act" (Oct. 5, 2020). https://www.mci.gov.sg/public-consultations/public-consultation-items/closing-note-to-pc-on-draft-pdp-(amendment)-bill-including-related-amendments-to-spam-control-act.

[34] Personal Data Protection Commission (Singapore), "Discussion Paper on Data Portability" (Feb. 25, 2019). https://www.pdpc.gov.sg/-/media/Files/PDPC/PDF-Files/Resource-for-Organisation/Data-Portability/PDPC-CCCS-Data-Portability-Discussion-Paper---250219.pdf?la=en.

[35] Massachusetts Question 1: The "Right to Repair" Law: Vehicle Data Access Requirement Initiative passed on November 3, 2020, with 74.9% support.

This Massachusetts law affirms consumers' ownership of the data, with rights to portability akin to API-enabled open banking. With an eye beyond the scope of vehicle telematics, SecuRepairs Founder Paul Roberts celebrated the referendum victory with the observation:

> We hope to carry the momentum . . . into the larger battle for a digital right to repair that protects not just cars, but smart phones, laptops, smart home appliances and array of other Internet-connected, software-driven stuff.[36]

Another example would be the United Kingdom, where Open Banking was pioneered (albeit in a very sector-specific form). The British energy retail industry is now also moving to adopt a framework for sharing customer data.[37]

These are important initiatives that will help the eventual realization of an open competitive environment that supports consumer control and innovation, although the journey toward that will be likely still uneven. For instance, where Australia's CDR points toward Open Data, it does so with a gradual implementation, phased across sectors. After starting with the banking sector, the CDR will then extend to include electricity retailers, then telecommunications providers, and eventually to other commercial sectors, which could include tech firms. While this could reinforce the risk of some sector-specific anomalies and distortions in the short term, it reflects a realistic approach to implementation.

Similarly, there are moves afoot in Europe to expand the scope of Open Banking across other parts of financial services, championed by Commission Executive Vice President Valdis Dombrovskis, who observed that "that there is merit in thinking about extending the approach we took in the Payment Services Directive, or PSD2, to other sectors. From open banking to open finance."[38] The UK Financial Conduct Authority is also looking beyond Open Banking's focus on payments data with its Open Finance proposal mapping out an expanded scope that could include insurance, mortgages, investments, and pensions.[39]

The expansion of Open Banking, which is generally limited to the payments sector, toward "Open Finance," which crosses into the investment and insurance sectors, is directionally helpful and points to the benefits of ensuring consumer control and security over their personally generated data across the financial service sectors. However, Open Finance would be still insufficient, particularly where tech firms can rebundle services from a broader array of commercial sectors. BigTech firms would be still better placed to exploit the opportunities presented by a digital economy beyond financial service sectors.

---

[36] SecuRepairs, "SecuRepairs Celebrates Huge Win for Right To Repair in Massachusetts" (Nov. 4, 2020). https://securepairs.org/securepairs-celebrates-huge-win-for-right-to-repair-in-massachusetts/.

[37] Liming Zhu, IIF, FRT Podcast, "Episode 77: Open Banking and Beyond" (Oct. 1, 2020). https://www.iif.com/Publications/ID/4112/FRT-Episode-77-Open-Banking-and-Beyond-with-Liming-Zhu-CSIRO-Research-Director.

[38] Valdis Dombrovskis, speech at Afore 4th FinTech and Regulation Conference (Mar. 3, 2020). https://ec.europa.eu/commission/commissioners/2019-2024/dombrovskis/announcements/speech-executive-vice-president-valdis-dombrovskis-afore-4th-fintech-and-regulation-conference_en.

[39] Financial Conduct Authority (UK), "Call for Input: Open Finance" (Dec. 2019). https://www.fca.org.uk/publication/call-for-input/call-for-input-open-finance.pdf.

Open Data is an important aspiration. While the journey may involve several incremental steps, it is where we ultimately need to go. The opportunities for customer empowerment need to be not only secured within the financial sector through a sustainably competitive marketplace, but customers should similarly benefit from commensurate access to transactional data in their activities in other sectors, including the likes of digital commerce, media, social networks, and telecommunications. We cannot view banking nor data in a vacuum.

The urgency underlined by the pandemic means that we need to start that journey sooner. Doubtlessly, there are challenges with the complexity of legislative and regulatory structures. As in most jurisdictions, an Open Data framework will invariably require the collaboration of the various sectoral regulators, as well as privacy and competition commissioners, to help promote design features that will support competition on a more sustained basis. It may be that banking (both as an industry and as a regulatory community) is the best prepared to be able to champion this cause for the wider economy. Similarly, as discussed in Chapter 2, a data rights framework for open data could be modeled after a data rights framework for customer financial data.

7. Concluding Thoughts: Open Data and an Open Approach to Identity

One key application of open data transfer with profound opportunity is in digital identity, which is discussed in greater detail by Greg Kidd in Chapter 12. Digital identity has emerged as a foundational building block for the post-COVID digital economy, particularly as many small businesses try to rapidly reinvent themselves as e-commerce businesses in the wake of the pandemic—and thus, often need to perform identity verification in a remote context. The exchange of identity data through secure APIs, when instructed by the customer, can have an important facilitative role.

As one example, the Open Digital Trust initiative is a collaboration of the financial industry via the Institute of International Finance and the OpenID Foundation. This is an interoperable and open-source initiative whereby the consumer could instruct a trusted verifier, such as their bank or telecommunications provider, to inform a merchant that the customer meets a particular criterion, such as age or residency, via a standardized API format. The merchant would not need to receive (or store) raw data points that might be sensitive but would instead receive verification of the requested criteria.

This presents a significant opportunity for banks and insurers to leverage and monetize their capabilities in protecting customer data and verifying identities. There is also further potential in helping to combat financial crime. Similarly, the Consultative Group to Assist the Poor has identified where the secure transfer of customer transactional data may assist in supporting customer due diligence and know your customer requirements in emerging markets.[40]

The leveraging of the Open Banking concept into enabling digital identity is an example of taking open data to its full potential. Data-sharing needs to evolve, and we

---

[40] Plaitakis and Staschen, *supra* note 35.

need to look beyond the sectoral boundaries. But the notion of consumer-directed exchange within a secure Open Data ecosystem could help to solve broader challenges across the economy.

Ultimately, as Greg Kidd discusses in Chapter 12, an open digital identity framework may be the necessary key to unlocking access to an increasingly platform-centric economy. Interfacing with a platformized world, the ability for consumers to control and transfer their identity credentials may be the powerful enabler both for the end consumer and for businesses wanting to participate in the economy pursuing diverse business models. Where Open Banking needs to evolve with the times and to transition toward an Open Data ecosystem, providing the forerunner to an open digital identity may prove to be Open Banking's most enduring legacy.

Index

For the benefit of digital users, indexed terms that span two pages (e.g., 52–53) may, on occasion, appear on only one of those pages.

Tables, figures, and boxes are indicated by *t*, *f*, and *b* following the page number.